POSTSOCIALIST PATHWAYS

Can property regimes be successfully transformed while citizenship rights are simultaneously extended to the propertyless? This is the postsocialist challenge analyzed in this comparative study of the new democracies of a distinctively East European capitalism. Tracing the diverse pathways from the collapse of communism, a leading American economic sociologist and a pioneering Hungarian political scientist examine the innovative character, born of necessity, of postsocialist institutions in which actors are recombining economic assets and redefining political resources. Under conditions of extraordinary uncertainty, networks of enterprises become the units of economic restructuring, blurring the boundaries of public and private and yielding distinctive patterns of interorganizational ownership. In contrast to recent calls to liberate the market or to liberate the state, this sustained comparative analysis demonstrates the benefits of deliberative institutions that are alternatives to markets and hierarchies. By extending accountability, actors bound through associative ties make agreements that extend the authority to carry out reforms.

CAMBRIDGE STUDIES IN·COMPARATIVE POLITICS

General Editor
PETER LANGE   Duke University

Associate Editors
ROBERT H. BATES   Harvard University
ELLEN COMISSO   University of California, San Diego
PETER HALL   Harvard University
JOEL MIGDAL   University of Washington
HELEN MILNER   Columbia University
RONALD ROGOWSKI   University of California, Los Angeles
SIDNEY TARROW   Cornell University

OTHER BOOKS IN THE SERIES

Catherine Boone, *Merchant Capital and the Roots of State Power in Senegal, 1930–1985*
Michael Bratton and Nicolas van de Walle, *Democratic Experiments in Africa: Regime Transitions in Comparative Perspective*
Donatella della Porta, *Social Movements, Political Violence, and the State*
Roberto Franzosi, *The Puzzle of Strikes: Class and State Strategies in Postwar Italy*
Geoffrey Garrett, *Partisan Politics in the Global Economy*
Miriam Golden, *Heroic Defeats: The Politics of Job Loss*
Frances Hagopian, *Traditional Politics and Regime Change in Brazil*
J. Rogers Hollingsworth and Robert Boyér, *Contemporary Capitalism: The Embeddedness of Institutions*
Ellen Immergut, *Health Politics: Interests and Institutions in Western Europe*
Thomas Janoski and Alexander M. Hicks, eds., *The Comparative Political Economy of the Welfare State*
Robert O. Keohane and Helen B. Milner, eds., *Internationalization and Domestic Politics*
David Knoke, Franz Urban Pappi, Jeffrey Broadbent, and Yutaka Tsujinaka, eds., *Comparing Policy Networks*
Allan Kornberg and Harold D. Clarke, *Citizens and Community: Political Support in a Representative Democracy*
David D. Laitin, *Language Repertories and State Construction in Africa*
Mark Irving Lichbach and Alan S. Zuckerman, eds., *Comparative Politics: Rationality, Culture, and Structure*
Doug McAdam, John McCarthy, and Mayer Zald, eds., *Comparative Perspectives on Social Movements*
Scott Mainwaring and Matthew Soberg Shugart, *Presidentialism and Democracy in Latin America*
Joel S. Migdal, Atul Kohli, and Vivienne Shue, eds., *State Power and Social Forces: Domination and Transformation in the Third World*
Paul Pierson, *Dismantling the Welfare State?: Reagan, Thatcher, and the Politics of Retrenchment*
Marino Regini, *Uncertain Boundaries: The Social and Political Construction of European Economies*
Yossi Shain and Juan Linz, *Interim Governments and Democratic Transitions*
Theda Skocpol, *Social Revolutions in the Modern World*
Sven Steinmo, Kathleen Thelen, and Frank Longstreth, eds., *Structuring Politics: Historical Institutionalism in Comparative Analysis*
Sidney Tarrow, *Power in Movement: Social Protest, Reform, and Revolution*
Ashutosh Varshney, *Democracy, Development, and the Countryside*

POSTSOCIALIST PATHWAYS

Transforming Politics
and Property
in East Central Europe

DAVID STARK
Columbia University

LÁSZLÓ BRUSZT
Central European University

PUBLISHED BY THE PRESS SYNDICATE OF THE UNIVERSITY OF CAMBRIDGE
The Pitt Building, Trumpington Street, Cambridge, United Kingdom

CAMBRIDGE UNIVERSITY PRESS
The Edinburgh Building, Cambridge CB2 2RU, UK   http: //www.cup.cam.ac.uk
40 West 20th Street, New York, NY 10011-4211, USA   http: //www.cup.org
10 Stamford Road, Oakleigh, Melbourne 3166, Australia

First published 1998
Reprinted 1999

Typeset in Garamond #3

A catalogue record for this book is available from the British Library

Stark, David Charles
Postsocialist pathways: transforming politics and property in
East Central Europe / David Stark, László Bruszt.
p.   cm. – (Cambridge studies in comparative politics)
Includes bibliographical references (p.) and index.
1. Privatization – Europe, Central. 2. Right of property – Europe,
Central. 3. Post-communism – Europe, Central. 4. Europe, Central –
Economic conditions. 5. Europe, Central – Politics and
government – 1989– . I. Bruszt, László. II. Title. III. Series
HD4140.7.S73   1998   97–21299
338.943 – dc21   CIP

ISBN 0 521 58035 8 hardback
ISBN 0 521 58974 6 paperback

Transferred to digital printing 2001

For our children

Agnes and Dorottya
Alexandra and Benjamin

CONTENTS

PREFACE AND ACKNOWLEDGMENTS

In this book we examine the innovative character, born of necessity, of postsocialist institutions in East Central Europe, where actors are recombining economic assets and redefining political resources. The innovative character of this book is no less recombinatory for it rests on a long-term collaboration, born in the mid-1980s, well before the collapse of communism, through which we, an American economic sociologist and a Hungarian political scientist, mutually redefined our research agendas and our categories of analysis.

In our survey of the political and economic landscapes of contemporary Eastern Europe, we came to see forms of economic coordination that were alternatives to markets and hierarchies. In these *deliberative associations,* actors bound through associative ties make binding agreements. Our book is no less deliberative, for we are bound in networks of accountability that have constrained us from making precipitous judgments and helped shape a more coherent argument. Our associative ties have provided these enabling constraints. We are indebted first to the collegial networks in which we were embedded at our home institutions, Cornell University and the Central European University in Budapest. Ron Breiger, Béla Greskovits, Peter Katzenstein, Victor Nee, Jonas Pontusson, and Sidney Tarrow have offered insightful comments on various chapters and were stimulating interlocutors throughout the project.

We have also been bound in broader networks of extended accountability, as we have benefited from the criticisms and suggestions by discussants at various conferences and workshops where we presented earlier drafts of our chapters. Our thanks go especially to Ivan Berend, Grzegorz Ekiert, Gary

Gereffi, Gernot Grabher, János Mátyás Kovács, Jan Kubik, Tony Levitas, Claus Offe, Ákos Róna-Tas, Andrzej Rychard, Philippe Schmitter, and Ivan Szelenyi. Because we can always count on her as our most persistent critic, we have inflicted more work-in-progress on Ellen Comisso than she might want to remember. Ellen has doubtless read every paragraph in this book more than once and, thanks to her, a good number were deleted. We are grateful for her consistent intellectual support and friendly encouragement.

For their comments and suggestions on drafts of various chapters, we thank Luc Boltanski, Rogers Brubaker, Janusz Dabrowski, Larry Diamond, Ilona Erös, Michal Federowicz, János Kornai, János Köllö, Peter Gedeon, Gerald McDermott, Sophie Muetzel, Peter Murrell, Guillermo O'Donnell, Peter Rutland, Arlene Saxonhouse, Mark Selden, Jan Szomburg, Marton Tardos, and Éva Voszka. We are especially grateful to Gernot Grabher and Wolfgang Seibel for their generous suggestions in revising several of the chapters. Errors of interpretation, of course, remain our responsibility alone. Despite close friendship, Geoff Fougere always managed to find the right distance from any particular formulation and, despite physical distance, always managed to stay one step ahead of the argument.

We also have a long-standing debt to János Lukács and László Neumann, collaborators in field work with David Stark. Their acute observations about the workings of Hungarian enterprises and their deep understanding of post-socialist politics inform every chapter of this book. István Gábor has been a constant guide throughout every stage of this project. Those insights that were not born in discussions across his kitchen table were subsequently refined and reconceptualized there. Monique Djokic pointed to new links, sometimes hidden and often not well connected, in the argument. Insightful criticisms, helpful suggestions, consistent encouragement – these fail to capture the unique association, for Monique has been our strongest intellectual ally.

This project would not have been possible without the generous support of numerous institutions and granting agencies. Our research has been supported by grants from the National Science Foundation and the National Council for Soviet and East European Research. Over the course of our research and writing, Stark received two fellowships from the Joint Committee on Eastern Europe of the American Council of Learned Societies/Social Science Research Council. The entire field of East European studies is indebted to Jason Parker of the ACLS, and for his continued support of our project we are especially grateful.

Several institutions provided release time from day-to-day academic obligations and invited us to join other scholars working on related topics. László Bruszt participated in the Democratization Seminar during a year's leave at the Wissenschaftskolleg-Berlin and is grateful for the warm wel-

come and intellectual stimulation from the community of Latin American-
ists at the Helen Kellogg Institute for International Studies at the University
of Notre Dame. Our special appreciation to Guillermo O'Donnell, Director
of the Kellogg Institute, as a source of intellectual inspiration and personal
encouragement to us both. David Stark is grateful for fellowships and leaves
at Cornell University's Society for the Humanities, the École des Hautes
Études en Sciences Sociales in Paris, and the Institute for Advanced Study/
Collegium Budapest. As a model of intellectual integrity, János Kornai,
Permanent Fellow at the Collegium, has given us confidence to proceed in
this project by appreciating the work even when he disagrees with parts of
the argument. Much of the writing for this book was completed – despite
efforts to the contrary by Bob Scott and the volleyball contingent – while
Stark was a Fellow at the Center for Advanced Study in the Behavioral
Science in Palo Alto, with financial support provided by the National Science
Foundation Grant No. SES-9022192 and the U.S. Department of State Title
VIII Funds Grant No. 1006-304101. The calm presence of Neil Smelser
fosters, at the Center, the peaceful tenor and lively intellectual comaraderie
in which it has been a joy to work.

We are grateful to Szabolcs Kemény and Jonathan Uphoff for exemplary
assistance in research and to Mary Ahl, Leslie Lindzey, and Debra Smith for
their friendly professionalism in the preparation of the manuscript.

Our book on *Postsocialist Pathways* has had its own pathway. Several of
its chapters appeared earlier in area studies publications. We considered
extensive revisions of these chapters in light of subsequent developments in
our East Central European cases. But we decided to keep these studies largely
intact – primarily because their tense and form capture the possibilities and
uncertainties facing East European societies and policy makers during the
early period of postsocialism. Readers can thus trace our own analytic pathways at the same time that they follow the policy pathways to find out what
happened in later chapters.

We are grateful to the following university presses for kind permission
to reprint articles or chapter, in whole or in part:

To Cornell University Press, for our chapter from *Eastern Europe in Revolution*, edited by Ivo Banac, 1992, pp. 13–55.
To the University of California Press for articles by David Stark in *East
European Politics and Societies*, 1990, 4(3):251–392 and 1992, 6(1):
17–53.
To the University of Chicago for several pages and figures from an article
by Stark in *The American Journal of Sociology*, 1996, 101(4):993–
1027. © 1996 by the University of Chicago. All rights reserved.

INTRODUCTION

SIMULTANEITY

Can the transformation of property regimes and the extension of citizenship rights be achieved simultaneously? This is the postsocialist challenge. Can the governments of postsocialist Eastern Europe successfully pursue economic reform when the citizens who bear its costs acquire the means to replace political incumbents and choose among competing political programs? This is the postsocialist experiment. The concurrent transformation of property and politics in postcommunist societies is occurring, moreover, in the context of a contracting world economy, thereby dramatically increasing the social burdens caused by economic restructuring. The simultaneous emergence of newly propertied classes and newly enfranchised subordinate groups poses the central postsocialist problem of how to restructure economies when those who perceive their interests to be threatened by economic change have the capacity to block the implementation and consolidation of reforms.

The twinned expansion of property rights and citizenship rights requires a twinned scholarship. This volume presents the results of our collaborative efforts, as an American economic sociologist and a Hungarian political scientist, to study the dual transformations of the polities and economies of Eastern Europe, not simply as parallel but also as interacting processes.

The more systematically we examined the ways in which the various East Central European societies are struggling with the dilemmas posed by the simultaneous attempts to transform politics and property, the more we

1

became aware of the rich organizational innovations that are taking place
in postsocialism. Told by many that their best strategy was to imitate the
tried and proven institutions of Western Europe and North America, the
political and economic actors of postsocialism faced distinctive challenges
that made it impossible simply to imitate – even where their initial self-
conceptions were not as innovators. "Instant," "Xerox," or "copycat" capitalism was not a possibility, if for no other reason than that the institutions
for transforming property regimes could not be identical to those of already
established orders. Told by some that their best strategy was to choose
between democratization and marketization – that they could do one or the
other but not both – the politicians and publics of East Central Europe
rejected the idea that the legacies of state socialism condemn them either
to authoritarianism or to economic backwardness, if not both. Instead, in a
little more than the half-decade after the fall of the Berlin Wall, each of the
East Central European societies has solidified its democratic institutions and
achieved economic growth.

Postsocialist societies can be seen as an extraordinary laboratory to test
existing social theories. This book does not formulate such a test – not
because the changes examined are not extraordinary but because momentous
changes are not likely to leave existing theories intact for simple testing.
The efforts of this book are less grandiose than elaborating a new theory of
social change and more ambitious than testing old ones. Its task is to craft
analytic concepts capable of registering and translating the specific insights
and patterned learning being generated in this social experiment.

developing concepts as key task of social science

DIVERSITY

The momentous political, social, and economic changes that have swept
through the once-Communist world have provoked some observers to announce the "end of history." The demise of the counter social paradigm,
they argue, completes a centuries-long project of modernization and marks
a new era of unchallenged dominance of a single logic of social organization.
Within this frame of historical homogenization of global sweep, social
change in the postsocialist world is best represented as transition, and the
major research questions concern the pace and timing of privatization, marketization, and democratization. Comparative questions are matters of degree: To what extent do the political and economic institutions of Eastern
Europe and the former Soviet Union conform to or depart from those of
advanced liberal democracies?

Comparisons East and West, of course, were not always so constructed.

For decades, capitalism was defined vis-à-vis socialism and vice versa. Their systematic comparison enriched our understanding of both, but the "method of mirrored opposition" is no longer as fruitful.[1] We shall not grasp the postsocialist world through the old dualisms of private/public, market/hierarchy, or capitalism/socialism, regardless of how creatively we search to find complex mixtures in particular cultural settings. The demise of socialism challenges that analytically forced choice, and it offers an opportunity for enriching comparative institutional analysis. When we stop defining capitalism in terms of socialism, we see that, in our epoch, capitalism as a construct is analytically interesting only in the plural: *Capitalisms* must be compared vis-à-vis each other.[2]

Our contribution to the developing field of comparative capitalisms is to describe and account for the emergence of a distinctively East European capitalism. To understand that specificity is not to highlight what is particular and what is general in the East European variant. Rather than search for the essence of capitalism, of which postsocialism is some particular form, we would do better to start with comparisons to other recent cases where societies have attempted economic and political reforms.[3] Several East Asian societies, for example, have embarked on the course of democratization but, unlike Eastern Europe, only after economic reforms had already opened their economies to world markets in a period of an expanding global economy.[4] In Latin America, economic liberalization and political democratization were undertaken at the same time but, unlike Eastern Europe, economic reforms did not involve a fundamental transformation of property regimes. Even where, as in Brazil and Mexico, economic liberalization led to privatization of state enterprises, these measures took place in settings where the legal, social, and economic institutions of capitalism were well entrenched and social structures were shaped by the dominance of private property.[5] Despite sharing with Eastern Europe many of the fundamental institutions of state socialism as the starting point, the Chinese experience is, along the two dimensions of property and politics, the polar opposite of postsocialist Eastern Europe, for China has not democratized, nor has it begun the privatization of large public enterprises.[6] Similarly to Eastern Europe, the societies of the former Soviet Union are attempting to transform both political and property regimes – but with the fundamental difference that these efforts are accompanied by yet another transformation, as these societies must simultaneously cope with the political (domestic and international) problems of creating new states out of the breakup of the imperial structures of the Soviet Union.[7]

These preliminary contrasts foreground the specificity of the simultaneous transformations of politics and property in Eastern Europe and suggest the potential fruitfulness of more systematic comparisons across regions. But *need concepts before + description before can really compare*

if a full appreciation of the distinctive character of an East European capitalism can be achieved only through comparison to other pertinent cases,
comparativists studying postsocialist Eastern Europe face a dilemma: How
are we to make that comparison without already understanding the major
contours of the various East Central European cases themselves?

Premature comparisons can be more misleading than instructive. To
attempt decisive comparisons of the Latin American or East Asian cases
with the East European type would falsely assume that scholarship on postsocialist Eastern Europe has already produced a corpus of work yielding
sufficient material for comparison. Thus, we focus here on the Eastern European cases themselves, but our investigation is not conducted in isolation
from the broader comparative literature. We engage comparativists in other
area specialties not only because we reject the idea that East European scholarship can pull itself up by its own bootstraps,[8] but also because the epochal
transformations of the postsocialist world pose new questions and generate
new concepts and categories that will be useful for understanding democratic and economic change elsewhere in the world. As the reader will see,
throughout this book we unabashedly borrow from and (equally unapolo-
getically) modify analytic tools of comparativists studying Latin America,
East Asia, Western Europe, Russia, and China.

As we focus on Eastern Europe, we adopt a comparative method to
produce middle-range concepts capable of describing the salient differences
among the East Central European cases. It is for the purpose of generating
comparative concepts to identify a distinctively East European variant of
capitalism, therefore, that we undertake the task of explaining variation
within Eastern Europe.[9]

Thus, in the following chapters, we adopt a comparative method to
highlight similarities and differences in the postsocialist pathways of the
East Central European societies, charting the diverse paths of extrication
from state socialism, mapping distinctive strategies of privatization, examining national differences in the network patterns of interorganizational
ownership in the economic field, and exploring how different institutional
configurations in the political field promote or impede policy coherence and
authority to pursue sustainable economic reforms.

IMITATION, INVOLUTION, OR INNOVATION?

For many analysts of postsocialism, the task of explaining variation among
the East European cases ranks low in their analytic priorities. This holds

especially for neoliberals who portray economic transformation as a project of social imitation. From that perspective, the road to an advanced capitalist economy is the same road, regardless of the starting point, whether that be from São Paulo, Singapore, or Slovenia.[10] This *transition as imitation* problematic approaches the postsocialist economies from the standpoint of a future that has already been designated. As the science of the not yet, designer capitalism studies postsocialism in terms of what it will or must become, not simply gazing into the crystal ball of the future but also examining the present through that distorting lens. By contrast, our examination of the postsocialist societies through a comparative lens seeks to understand the ongoing conflicts and alliances that are shaping the multiple possible futures present in contemporary East Central Europe.

If some hold that the postsocialist present is determined by its future (i.e., intelligible only in terms of a predesignated future), others argue that its present is condemned by its past. Whereas neoliberalism sees blueprints for the imitation of market institutions as the road to progress, the contrary view perceives the weight of the socialist past as so heavy that attempts at marketization and democratization become the path to retrogression. One advocate of this view, Michael Burawoy, for example, identifies the postsocialist epoch as a period not of imitation but of "involution." "Within Russia and [to] a lesser extent Eastern Europe," Burawoy argues, combined and uneven development "work through a common overall pattern of industrial involution, that is to say an economic regression that is not merely preparatory for a future resurgence but is chronic and persistent. Involution is the antithesis of evolution and . . . leads to systemic underdevelopment."[11] In short, postsocialism is less an imitation of the West than a pathetic self-parody: "Our case study suggests that, with the withering away of the party-state, the Soviet economy, far from collapsing or transforming itself, has assumed an exaggerated version of its former self."[12]

As the phrases *combined and uneven development* and *systemic underdevelopment* suggest, the notion of postsocialist involution bears strong affinities with the dependency theory of the 1970s. Like the *dependistas*, Burawoy looks favorably on the autarchic isolation from world markets that characterized state socialism. But the revitalization of dependency theory for the 1990s cannot retain the earlier suspicion of (if not outright hostility to) markets. For Burawoy, the failures of postsocialism reside less in the opening to world markets or the emergence of domestic markets per se than in the conditions under which they were introduced. Burawoy identifies two such starting conditions, and each can be traced to his understanding of the legacies of state socialism. He notes, first, that all market institutions have their national or regional specificity. In postsocialism, the specificity of markets is that "their effects are *governed by prior economic organization* based on monopoly, barter, and worker control."[13] Based on his research in the timber and mining industries, Burawoy indicates how the weight of these legacies of state socialism gives rise to the grossly distorted "markets" and mafialike developments that he sees in the present.

The second culprit explaining involutionary regression is the disintegration of the party state and the establishment of liberal democracy. Burawoy develops this argument through a sustained contrast of Russian foolishness in choosing democracy and Chinese wisdom in rejecting it. Whereas in Russia democracy has emasculated the strong state, in China authoritarian rule has kept central controls in place to guide and direct rapid accumulation: "Behind the mutual stimulus of production and exchange lies the Chinese party-state, behind the wanton destruction of Russian industry lies liberal democracy."[14] Contrasts between postsocialist, democratic Hungary and the regime that crushed its nascent democratic movement yield, for Burawoy, a similar conclusion: "Given that in Hungary guarded reform has led to poor performance, China's lesson is not so much one of gradualism but of the *necessity of the party state* to engineer the socialist transition to a market economy."[15]

Burawoy's prescriptions follow directly from the idea that the postsocialist present is condemned by its past. Democracy is inadequate to cope with the most important legacy of state socialism – a backward, underdeveloped, and often unruly society that must be tamed, managed, and directed by a party state capable of maintaining and (where necessary) imposing order.[16] To avoid involution in the transition from socialism to capitalism, the best solution is Market Leninism.

As our rhetoric already suggests, we see economic, political, and social change in postsocialist Eastern Europe as neither imitation nor involution. In contrast to the imitationists, who see in the collapse of communism an institutional void waiting to be filled with their recipes, therapies, and formulas, we look to the variation in how communism fell apart and how these partial ruins provide institutional building blocks for political, economic, and social reconstruction.[17] In contrast to the involutionists, who see in the Communist party-state a strong, authoritative agent capable of social engineering, we see the Communist party-state in its final stages as weak and ineffective. As we examine the particularities of how communism collapsed, we see that although the *party-state* disintegrated, the various paths of extrication from socialism in Eastern Europe did not dismantle state institutions so much as re-form them. Democratic institutions did not weaken states, they strengthened them, making them able to carry out the difficult tasks of economic stabilization and later economic transformation that its communist predecessors were incapable of pursuing. And as we shall see, the more state executives have been constrained by democratic institutions and the more they have been held accountable by deliberative institutions, the more coherent have been their policy courses and the more effective has been their authority to carry out reforms.

In contrast to the imitationists, who see in the present only the absent features of an ideal future, we are interested in what the present holds for the future. In contrast to the involutionists, who see in the present the dead weight of the past, we see that the past can provide institutional resources for change in the present. In contrast to the transition problematic that is common to both, we see social change not as transition from one order to another but as transformation – rearrangements, reconfigurations, and recombinations that yield new interweavings of the multiple social logics that are a modern society.[18] In struggling to cope with the extraordinary uncertainties of a transforming economy, actors discover and reorganize resources. Defying the forced dichotomy of market versus hierarchy, they create new property forms that blur the boundaries of public and private, blur the organizational boundaries of firms, and blur the boundaries of the legitimating principles through which they claim stewardship of economic resources.

Some of these recombinatory organizational innovations will fail. Others, perhaps even those that appear most monstrous from the standpoint of conventional organizational theory, might thrive.[19] Some will prove to be backward-looking strategies conserving the status quo. But we should not be too quick or too confident in our a priori ability to distinguish strategies of survival from strategies of innovation – for, as we shall see, some of the interorganizational property forms that buffer networks of firms from selection pressures, in fact, provide the organizational slack preserving assets in the short run for innovative restructuring in the next round. In short, survival can be the basis of innovation and risk spreading the basis for risk taking. We shall also see that where public policy ignores these network properties and operates only in the categories of state and market, there risk spreading can turn to risk shedding.

Thus, in contrast to the involutionists' theory of past dependency, we analyze processes of path dependency as we explore how strategic choices, often highly contingent, shape further policy courses.[20] It is by charting these paths that we can trace innovations – for it is precisely in reworking the institutional materials at hand that actors innovate. In our view, institutions do not simply constrain; they also enable. It is through a political and an economic bricolage that new institutions and new practices emerge.[21] Our task is to illuminate the ongoing activity, grounded in an organiza-

tional reflexivity and a social pragmatics, whereby actors redefine and recombine resources. This volume documents and analyzes these recombinant
strategies.

EXTRICATION, TRANSFORMATION, DELIBERATIVE ASSOCIATION

Our analysis proceeds in three parts. In Part I, we examine the distinctive
paths of extrication from state socialism. Part II addresses transformations
of property and politics during the formative period of institution building
in the first two years following the regime changes of 1989. In Part III, we
focus on the new institutions of deliberative association that are emerging
in postsocialist East Central Europe.

We begin in Chapter 1 by examining the turning point of 1989 in
Eastern Europe. Against the popular misconception that strong states can
be toppled only by mobilized societies, we argue that a scenario of weak
states confronting weak civil societies more closely approximates the events
now known as *1989*. But that latter conception can be misleading as well,
especially if it leads to static measurements of the relative strengths of hard-
liners and reformers (inside the regime) and of moderates and radicals (in
the opposition). In the alternative, interactionist perspective[22] that we propose, illustrated through a detailed analysis of the Hungarian case, the political identities of the major social actors change as they react to and interact
with the competing strategies in the political field. Similarly, we challenge
domino effect explanations by emphasizing the complex interactions among
the East European cases. As we shall see, contagion or diffusion models fail
to capture how not only citizens but also the old Communist elite learned
by observing the processes and outcomes of the interactions of rulers and
opposition in other countries. Thus, whereas the conventional view examines
differences among the East European cases primarily as differences in the
speed and timing of the collapse of the old regimes, we argue that the
experiences of these national cases differed not simply in degree but also in
kind. This chapter establishes these differing paths of extrication from state
socialism – compromise in Poland, capitulation in Czechoslovakia, colonization in the German Democratic Republic (GDR), unfettered electoral
competition in Hungary, and restricted electoral competition in Bulgaria
and Romania – as a frame for understanding subsequent political and economic developments.

Part II opens with an analysis of the initial debates over privatization
in the period during and immediately following the regime changes. The

empirical materials for Chapter 2 are drawn from Hungary, but the terms structuring comparable debates in other countries were the same across the region: foreign versus domestic ownership, state-directed versus spontaneous privatization, institutional versus individual owners, and concentrated versus dispersed ownership. In this chapter, we adopt an unconventional exposition taking the form of a stylized and extended dialogue between contending positions in the actual debate. By presenting persuasive arguments for the various positions back and forth across several rounds along each dimension, we hope the reader will gain a sense of the liveliness and complexity of the debate and will grasp the dilemmas facing policy makers.

Chapter 3 charts the resulting policy choices through a comparative analysis of privatization strategies in Hungary, Poland, the Czech Republic, and the former GDR. The cases are contrasted by locating the respective strategies within a typology constructed along three dimensions reflecting the central questions that must be addressed by any program of privatization: (1) How are the state's assets evaluated? (2) Who can acquire these assets? and (3) With what resources are ownership rights acquired? After analyzing each of the four cases in detail, we trace the differences in privatization strategies across the cases to the distinctive paths of extrication from state socialism identified in Chapter 1.

Part III opens with a critical assessment of the dominant positions in the current debate on economic restructuring. When asked how to restructure the postsocialist economies, neoliberals respond that the best way is to use the free market. An emerging neostatist position (drawing lessons for Eastern Europe from a particular interpretation of East Asian economies) responds that the proper course is to use a strong state. The problem, however, is that the societies of Eastern Europe lack both developed markets and strong states. With what institutional resources might they begin? Our analysis in Chapter 4 suggests that strengthening markets and strengthening states requires recognizing and facilitating institutions of coordination that are neither market nor hierarchy. Building on the pioneering work of Peter Evans[23] (on East Asia and Latin America) and Charles Sabel[24] (on Western Europe), we identify the associative (network) properties and the deliberative (discursive) properties of such institutions. That discussion leads us to challenge the widely held assumption that the operative unit of restructuring is the isolated firm. Instead, we pose the dual questions of how networks of firms might be the units to be restructured and how responsibility for carrying out this restructuring might devolve to network institutions of deliberative association.

These questions are addressed concretely in Chapters 5 and 6 as we analyze the emergence of forms of deliberative association in the economic and political fields, respectively, through systematic comparisons of the Hungarian, Czech, and East German cases. Chapter 5 focuses on the problems of economic interdependence across enterprises as we ask, for each of our cases, whether and how government economic policies recognize the network properties of assets and liabilities. In Germany, we shall see how the Treuhandandstalt learned to cope with a situation in which policies associated with political unification had quickly turned a bundle of enterprise assets into a bundle of liabilities. Yet, because this organizational learning was not augmented by integrated social networks in the economy itself, the efforts of the Treuhand failed to systematically exploit network synergies in economic restructuring. In Hungary, the rich legacy of ties across enterprises in the state socialist period has resulted in dense, extensive, and complex networks of interenterprise ownership to mitigate uncertainty in the postsocialist epoch. Yet official government policy continues to privatize on a purely case-by-case basis. Ignoring the interdependencies among enterprises, it passed a set of legislative measures leading to a wave of bankruptcies and severe financial crises. Having created an unintended market shock, the government then reversed course, bailing out the banks and saving firms in a manner reminiscent of the paternalist state of its socialist predecessor. By contrast, in the Czech case, despite the neoliberal rhetoric of its finance minister and later prime minister, Vaclav Klaus, government policy recognized the network properties of liabilities and assets yielding active antibankruptcy measures, on the one hand, and novel forms of interorganizational ownership, on the other. Our analysis of the different patterns of network ties – with tight coupling in direct enterprise-to-enterprise ties in the Hungarian case and tight coupling at the meso level among banks and investment funds in the Czech case – suggests important differences in the characteristic features of Hungarian and Czech metacorporate groupings and invites comparisons to business groups in East Asian economies such as those of Taiwan and South Korea.[25]

To explain why economic interdependencies are recognized in some cases while ignored in others and to account for the consequent differences in policy coherence among the cases, we turn in Chapter 6 to institutional features of the political field. In contrast to the conventional wisdom that unconstrained executive authority is more likely to yield coherent reform policies, we argue that state capacity to formulate and implement coherent reform programs can be increased by limitations on the unilateral prerogatives of executive authority. We base that argument on a sustained case comparison of constitutional, institutional, and conjunctural constraints on executive authority in Hungary, Germany, and the Czech Republic. We shall see that whereas in the Czech Republic limitations on executive authority produced more moderated, sustainable reforms, in Hungary concentrated authority gave policy makers free rein to lurch from one extreme policy current to another, each provoking new rounds of crisis. Germany is an intermediate case in which the relatively extreme policy current of the period immediately following unification was moderated after federal and corporatist institutions took root in the new *Länder* of Eastern Germany.

In contrast to the widely held assumption that authority and accountability involve a trade-off, we argue in Chapter 7 that deliberative institutions of extended accountability, through which executives are held accountable by other state institutions and held in check by organized societal actors, actually extend authority to carry out sustainable reforms.[26] By extending accountability horizontally, in time and in scope, the embeddedness of the decision-making center in networks of autonomous political institutions extends the time horizons of policy makers and of the public. Success in transformative politics entails a programmatic pragmatism in which the reform politician is doubly bound: bound by the chains of association in the accounts of an encompassing political program and bound by beneficial institutional constraints[27] that exert a pragmatic influence on that political vision. Whereas neoliberals advocate the liberation of the market and neostatists call for the liberation of the state, our analysis suggests strategies of de-liberation. To mitigate the possibility that short-term adaptation will undermine long-term adaptability, successful reforms require binding agreements at multiple sites throughout the polity and the economy.

PART I

EXTRICATION

REMAKING THE POLITICAL FIELD: STRATEGIC INTERACTIONS AND CONTINGENT CHOICES

AN INTERACTIONIST MODEL FOR THE STUDY OF EXTRICATION

The cataclysmic dissolution of the Communist regimes and the clamorous awakening of the East European peoples in 1989 prompted observers to overestimate the strength of organized democratic forces in these events. The stunning electoral victory of Poland's Solidarity in June, the public drama of Imre Nagy's reburial in Budapest that same month, the street demonstrations in Leipzig in October, and the massive assemblies in Prague in November were all signs of popular strivings for democracy. But many observers mistook the enthusiastic expression of these aspirations as evidence of far-reaching democratic organization and misinterpreted the first stage of transition as being the already-achieved triumph of citizenship and civic values.

This overestimation of the strength of democratic forces in 1989 was a direct consequence of an overestimation, by many observers, of the strength of Communist party-states in the previous epoch. If only months earlier the "totalitarian" regimes of the region were cast as powerful, stable, and immutable, their sudden demise could be explained only by equally powerful forces organized for democracy. Behind the metaphors of volcanic eruptions of democracy and popular revolutions sweeping aside powerful tyrants was the idea that strong states could be toppled only by strong societies.

The contrary view contains its own share of misunderstandings but is probably closer to reality: Rather than strong states confronting strong societies, the more typical cases in Eastern Europe in 1989 were those in which weak states faced weak societies. Instead of powerful party-states, this view sees cumbersome but weak bureaucracies, ineffective in achieving the goals of economic growth and social integration, headed by demoralized leaders whose belief in their own ideologies had withered apace with the exhaustion of their political and economic programs.[1] From such a perspective, it is no longer necessary to invoke a "democratically organized society" as the agent that "overthrows" the old order. Of course, the citizenry of Eastern Europe did act in 1989. But, with the exception of Poland, these were extraordinarily weak civil societies without organizations strongly rooted in their citizenry, without leaders experienced in national politics, without elaborated economic and social programs, and without deeply engrained traditions of democratic habits and practices.

This "weak states/weak societies" approach might, in turn, be modified: Maintaining some notion of the party-states of Eastern Europe as weak (with limited sovereignty and only a feeble capacity to achieve stated goals), it would shift from a dichotomous view of civil societies as either strong or weak to assess the level of development of civil society as a continuous variable.[2] A rough ranking of the societies of Eastern Europe along such a dimension would yield the following (from high to low): Poland, Hungary, the GDR, Czechoslovakia, Bulgaria, Romania, and Albania. Such a preliminary exercise suggests interesting hypotheses given that this rank order correlates directly with the ordering of transitional events and inversely with a ranking of the speed of the first stage of transition in the countries in the region.

Despite the observation that the relative strength of civil society seems a good predictor of the timing and sequencing of upheavals in Eastern Europe in 1989, we would argue that the preoccupation with the strength/weakness of civil society (however reformulated) remains misplaced. In the first place, the degree of organization of civil society should be analyzed not simply relative to that of other cases but, more important, in relation to the forces obstructing (or promoting) change inside the ruling elite. We argue that these relations can be only partially captured by objective and static measurements of the relative strengths of hard-liners and reformers (inside the regime) and of moderates and radicals (in the opposition). The critical measure of these capacities is not the analyst's but the actors', and the interactionist framework we propose directs attention to their *perceptions* of the strategies of their opponents. Moreover, as we shall see, these capacities, perceptions, and strategies are fluid rather than fixed. In fact, as our case illustrates, the political organizational identities of the major social actors change as they react to and interact with other competing strategies in the political field.[3]

In the same way that we shift the focus of analysis from relative strengths to strategic interactions within the particular national cases, we also shift attention from preoccupation with relative timing to interactive effects among the cases in the East European transitions. That is, the relationship among the various countries is not simply that some cases come earlier or later but also that experiences in earlier cases have demonstrable effects on patterns of change in later cases.[4] But this learning process is actually obscured and distorted by diffusion or contagion models that present the experiences of the stronger (bolder) civil societies as charting the course to be emulated by citizens in countries where civil society was far weaker.[5] As we shall see, not only citizens within the society but also actors within the old elite learned by observing the processes and outcomes of the interactions of rulers and opposition in other countries.

Attention to the ranking of the strengths of civil societies and the sequence and speed of transitions across the East European countries is further misleading because it perpetuates the widely held misconception that there exists some singular yardstick against which we could measure the particular cases as differing in degree, whether that be the intensity, speed, or level of development of the assertion of democratic impulses.[6] In our view, however, these cases differ not simply in degree but in kind. The year 1989 saw a plurality of transitions with diverse paths to different types of political institutions.[7]

During the course of 1989, regime leaders throughout Eastern Europe faced various forms of organized confrontation from society. The particular interactions of rulers and opposition, however, yielded different paths of extrication from state socialism: In some countries regime leaders capitulated; in others they attempted to maintain some hold on power through compromise or through electoral competition.[8] Figure 1 depicts a typology of these alternative paths. China is included in the typology as that case where state socialist leaders used massive force in 1989 to crush the democratic opposition. Because of their very different geopolitical circumstances, regime leaders across Eastern Europe were unable or unwilling to bear the costs of the decisive use of force.[9] The limited use of force against some demonstrations in the GDR and Czechoslovakia, in fact, proves the rule: In the final moment of the crises of escalating public demonstrations, lacking either the ability or the resolve to use decisive force, these East European rulers capitulated and their regimes collapsed.

In the other cases, key segments of the Communist leadership did not capitulate. Instead, they negotiated compromise agreements containing provisions for institutional guarantees for some aspects of their power or entered into direct electoral competition without such guarantees. In Poland, Com-

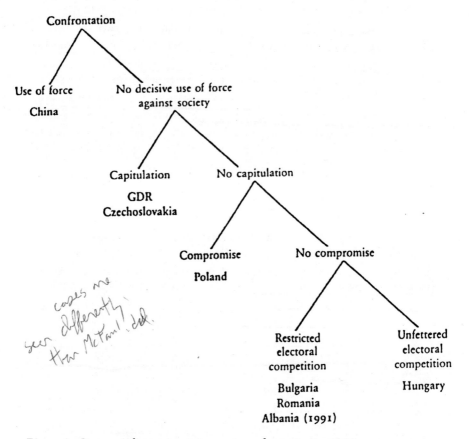

Figure 1. State socialist regime responses to confrontation in 1989.

munist reformers struck an agreement that guaranteed their continued control over critical institutions not exposed to the uncertainties of electoral
competition. In Hungary, Bulgaria, and Romania, by contrast, segments of
the old elite attempted to use electoral competition as the very means to
stay in power. Bulgarian and Romanian elites (and later, also the Albanian
one) managed to do so successfully (if only temporarily) by renaming their
parties, holding early elections, and maintaining tight control over key institutions that severely constrained their weak electoral rivals.[10] Hungary
followed a different path, and it had different outcomes. There the interacting strategies of the opposition and the ruling elite led to unfettered
competition.

The different paths (capitulation, compromise, competition, and so on)
of extrication from monocratic state socialism in Eastern Europe, moreover,
have yielded different transitional institutions in the new policies of the

region. That is, the strategic interactions of rulers and opposition (as well as patterns of conflict and alliance among competing opposition forces) have created different political institutions and rules of the game across these cases. The rapid reconfiguration of the political field as a field of party politics in the Hungarian case of unfettered electoral competition, for example, differs dramatically from the Polish and Czechoslovak cases, where political parties emerged more slowly and were initially based on social movements. Similarly, Hungary's parliamentary system contrasts markedly with Poland's presidential system. In short, the diverse (and possibly divergent) transitions in Eastern Europe are producing different kinds of political fields, with considerable variation in the relationships within the political elite and between them and their respective societies.

These important differences in political institutions, we argue, are not simply a by-product of differences in the relative strengths and weaknesses between power holders and oppositions in the respective countries. Instead, these differences can best be understood by focusing on the different dynamics of interactions between rulers and opposition (including their perceptions of the strengths, weaknesses, and strategies of their opponents), their changing perceptions of their geopolitical situations, and their learning from elites and opposition groups elsewhere in Eastern Europe.

Our task in this chapter is to analyze these interactive processes in the Hungarian case with the aim of understanding the specificity of its pathway of extrication through unfettered electoral competition. To encourage the reader to draw out comparative insights throughout our explication, we do not adopt the conventional formula of concluding with implications of the Hungarian case but instead open by highlighting some of the comparative issues that motivate our analysis. Stated differently, understanding the specificity of the Hungarian case requires some comparative reference points. All too briefly: In Poland and Hungary, leaders of weak party-states at the outset of the transition period attempted to increase their capacity for economic change by reforming but not entirely dismantling the political institutions of the old regime. In both cases, reform Communists eventually entered into agreements that resulted in the negotiated demise of Communist rule. But despite their similarities as negotiated extrications, the Polish and Hungarian cases differ dramatically in the institutional features of their reorganized political fields. Our task will be to explain how the perceived weakness of the Hungarian opposition (in its interaction with hard-liners and reformers in the ruling circle) led to the creation of an uncompromised parliamentary system there — in contrast to the Polish case, where the perceived strength of the opposition yielded a compromised institutional arrangement marrying aspects of liberal democracy and one-party rule to produce a malformed parliamentarism as its offspring. In Hungary, reform Communists facing an opposition not only much weaker than Solidarity, but also with a different organizational identity and a different institutional configuration, perceived an opportunity to stabilize their power through direct electoral competition without guarantees.

We should not conclude from this observation, however, that the conventional wisdom is correct in seeing Hungary as a case where regime change was initiated from above. Quite the contrary: Hungarian reform Communists were spurred to action only when confronted by the organized opposition — whose earlier strategy of compromise was replaced by a strategy of mobilization and uncompromised confrontation in response to a direct challenge from party hard-liners. It was the opposition's strategy of mobilization and confrontation (provoked by threats to its organizational survival), portending larger-scale popular upheaval, that catalyzed the polarization of forces within the regime and precipitated the reformers' ascendance within it. Yet it was also the anticipated electoral weakness of these same oppositional forces that allowed reform Communists in Hungary to change the party's course from the politics of confrontation to the politics of uncompromised free competition.

but why would they choose this outcome?

THE PROMISE OF COMPROMISE

In the summer of 1988, Hungary appeared to be the country in Eastern Europe most likely to embark on political reforms of a compromised character that would have institutionalized some form of power sharing without questioning many of the basic prerogatives of the Communist Party in the political system.[11] Hungary's organized opposition was vocal, visible, and a force to be reckoned with but was, nonetheless, far too weak to challenge the power of the party-state directly. Under these conditions, it seemed a willing and able candidate for a junior role in a reformed political system. The reform wing of the Communist Party, moreover, was certainly eager to engineer such a move. And although the reform Communists had not yet consolidated a hegemonic position within the party, compromise was unquestionably on the agenda in a country where even party hard-liners based their legitimacy on the claim not simply to be reformers but to be the leaders on the path of change in socialist Eastern Europe. From all sides one could hear of the search for a compromise solution to the questions of political power in order to "unite all forces" to solve the nation's momentous problems. Talk of some forms of "institutionalized power sharing" was everywhere in the air.

This promise of compromise issued not from some surge of fresh optimism following the ouster in May 1988 of János Kádár and his retinue from the pinnacle of the Hungarian Socialist Workers' Party (Magyar Szocialista Munkáspárt–MSzMP) but from a growing sense of foreboding crisis.[12] Hard-liners, party reformers, and independents (who, it should be emphasized, had not yet coalesced into an "opposition") shared a basic perception of the situation:

- Left unchecked, the widening scope and quickening pace of Hungary's downward spiral into economic, social, and political crisis could lead to chaotic threats to the social order.
- Reducing this threat called for large-scale economic changes of a qualitative character far beyond earlier efforts to reform the economy.
- The economic measures required to remedy the situation would unavoidably impose additional burdens on society and possibly further erode public confidence.
- Economic changes must thus be accompanied by some changes in the nation's political institutions.

The major political actors differed, of course, in the scope and type of political changes proposed, as well as in the rationale for them. To increase the role of the market in the economy and reduce tensions in society, the conservatives positioned around Károly Grósz (the party's new first secretary) advocated weakening the direct role of the party apparatus, giving a freer (but not unconstrained) hand to the press, and strengthening the position of interest groups (such as the trade unions, agricultural associations, and other similar satellite organizations). Unlike Kádár, who had remarked with bravado that "what Gorbachev is trying to do now, we already accomplished decades before," Grósz saw that Hungary was actually lagging behind the Soviet Union in the field of political reforms. He was acutely aware that by losing its image as being ahead of the pack Hungary was losing millions of dollars and deutsche marks in aid and credits during a period when its hard-currency foreign debt had doubled in only two years.

Placing greater emphasis on the importance of popular support to transform the economy, reform Communists in the circle around Imre Pozsgay stressed a liberalization of civil society that would allow greater scope for organizations that were genuinely autonomous from the party-state.[13] So great was their emphasis on dialogue ("a partner is needed") that they appeared at times to envy their Polish counterparts, who faced, in the still illegal Solidarity, not only a strong antagonist but also a potential interloc-utor. For their part, the leaders of Hungary's fledgling opposition move-ments (or *alternative organizations*, as they were so labeled at the time) were vocal advocates of measures that would institutionalize their participation in affairs of state.[14]

These arguments for institutionalized power sharing represented an im-portant development in the evolution of the rhetoric of the Hungarian op-position. During its infancy earlier in the decade, its simple plea to the party-state to *Respect human rights* had become the call to *Constrain yourself* as it called on the authorities to separate the state and society, to restrict state activities to those prescribed by law, to allow some scope for societal self-organization, and to provide equal rights for small-scale private prop-erty. By 1987, with increasing frequency and volume, Hungarian critical intellectuals did not encourage the authorities simply to exercise self-restraint but voiced a qualitatively new challenge to the party-state: *Allow yourself to be constrained.* Rather than imploring the state to draw the bound-aries beyond which it would not interfere with society, they now called on the state to allow society a voice in drawing those boundaries. The next step was to advocate that representatives of civil society outside of the party participate in decision making inside state institutions. Rather than asking the state to limit itself, it now called on the state to *Share power.* Such joint decision making would not be based on relations of parity; the meaning of power sharing was far from sharing power equally. In 1988 and as late as early 1989, the rhetoric of compromise from the Hungarian opposition was: *Your prerogative to have special discretionary rights will not be questioned, but our right to a voice should be institutionalized inside the state.*

Compromise, moreover, was on the political agenda not only in prin-ciple but also in detailed blueprints for institutional change. Budapest was full of compromise proposals circulating in networks of communication that crisscrossed the boundaries of opposition and officialdom.[15] Typical of these was the "Social Contract," written in 1987 by the editors of *Beszélő*, the most influential samizdat, or underground, journal of the democratic opposi-tion.[16] The institutional changes outlined in the "Social Contract" resem-bled the transition from unenlightened despotism to a constitutional monarchy in which the party's Central Committee would be the reigning but constitutionally constrained monarchy, with a two-chamber parliament giving special rights to the upper house (which, like the British House of Lords, would not be elected but *selected* from above) and allowing for the creation of a lower House of Commons with members chosen in competitive elections.

Focusing on such concrete proposals provides insights into the very precise and specific ways in which a variety of political actors were attempting to design institutions for political power sharing. To grasp the fundamental motivations underlying this intense preoccupation with resolving the crisis, however, we must understand how the search for compromise solutions in 1988 was everywhere underscored by the legacy of 1956. Although suppressed publicly, memories of the lost revolution of 1956 were never forgotten across the decades, and signs of crisis were the surest stimulant for recalling this haunting past. For the Communist elite, the ghosts of 1956 were the memories of the fury that can be unleashed when society has been pushed beyond its limits. It was above all the *fear of society* that so deeply embued the Communist leadership with the instinct to do everything to avoid another 1956. As the economic and political crisis deepened throughout 1988, the references to 1956 in party leaders' speeches increased. In mid-November, for example, party ideologist János Berecz (certainly no liberal reformer) drew out the "lessons of 1956." Noting the growing "deterioration in the country's situation" and pointing to the mounting "crisis in confidence and pressure from the increasing social dissatisfaction," Berecz asked: "Will revolutionary restructuring [of political institutions] or will chaos provide an answer to the great historical questions of Hungarian development? We cannot avoid this question when we analyze the tragic experiences of Hungary's recent past. This dilemma emerged between 1953 and 1956 too, . . . and the fact that forces in the party and society which demanded renewal failed to meet in solving the conflict should serve as a lesson that is valid to this very day. The result: Hungarian blood flowed on each side." To halt the deterioration of political crisis into chaos, Berecz concluded, "Our nation's interests require us to find today the points of a national consensus which could represent the framework and substance of a compromise. . . . The party is unable to implement the political renewal on its own. There is no such force in the society that could carry out this task on its own. Thus, the need for collaboration and cooperation is an elementary consequence."[17]

If it was the fear of society – the fear of the transformation of the economic crisis into social and political crisis similar to that of 1956 – that pushed the leaders of the regime to seek a compromise with the organized forces of society, it was the lesson of the Russian intervention in 1956 that made the leaders of the newly emerging social and political groups hesitant to question the legitimacy of the regime and to seek instead a compromise with its leaders. Mikhail Gorbachev did not automatically alter those calculations, for the limits of his toleration were neither clearly articulated nor yet tested in this period.[18] Moreover, until the showdown with Egor Ligachev in October 1988, his political survival was itself in question.[19] As late as 1987 the authors of the "Social Contract" concluded: "One cannot count on the Soviet bloc's disintegration within the foreseeable future. And there is no real chance of one or another of the satellite countries breaking away, either. But there is an opportunity for the satellites to increase their relative independence from the Soviet Union." Because Gorbachev's stability was far from certain, they argued, "The more we are able to get the Soviet leadership to accept today, the more we will be able to defend later during a possible backlash."[20] Given these perceptions, some measure of cooperation and considerable willingness to compromise, if not to form an outright coalition, seemed the wiser course.

Thus, with little exaggeration, we can say that the end of 1988 still marked a period of the "long fifties" in Hungarian history. The legacy of 1956 and the contradictions of Kádárist policies from 1957 on were still everywhere in evidence. Throughout the 1980s, nearly every major party program had begun with some variant of the formula: *We must make big changes in the economy to prevent the explosion of society. Society has reached the limits of its tolerance.* But execution of the policy changes prescribed in each of these programs was blocked in part by the fear of a popular response to the growing burdens that would be the inevitable outcome of the policies.[21] By 1988 the economy was as bankrupt and exhausted as the theory of reform economics. It was no surprise to Hungarians that state socialism was an economy of shortage, but now there was also inflation and talk of unemployment. Stabilization and economic transformation would exact additional sacrifices from a society already short on patience. How could popular support for such changes be secured?

The situation was thus very similar to that in Poland. In both cases, leading opposition figures were ready to accept a compromise solution on the condition that it limit the powers of the party-state and legalize and institutionalize the right of society to have its own autonomous representative organizations. In both countries, moreover, leading figures inside the Communist Party were talking about dialogue, cooperation, and the need for institutional changes to facilitate society's support for economic changes. The difference in Hungary was that, precisely at the time that compromise seemed most likely, the reformers were still too weak to speak in the name of the regime and the opposition was much too weak to speak in the name of society. Although there was a perceived need, a justification, the political will, and concrete institutional programs for compromise, the two major political actors who most favored compromise in 1988 did not have sufficient political power to bring it about. But, as we shall see in the following sections, the closer reformers and the democratic opposition came to establishing the conditions for negotiating a compromise, the more it became apparent that a compromise solution was an illusive and perhaps self-defeating strategy. In the end, both reform Communists and democratic opposition shifted from a strategy of institutional compromise to one of unfettered electoral competition. But they did not arrive at that solution directly. The perceived weakness of the opposition made it an inviting target for the party's hard-liners, who favored institutional changes only as long as they controlled all the terms. It was the hard-liners' strategy of confrontation and the opposition's confrontational response that ironically strengthened the hand of the reformers and finally brought Communists and democrats to the negotiating table. Thus, in the course of only ten months, Hungary moved from the politics of impending compromise, to the politics of escalating confrontation, to the politics of electoral competition.

Calls into question McFaul's static picture

THE POLITICS OF CONFRONTATION

THE STRATEGY OF THE HARD-LINERS

If Imre Pozsgay and his fellow reform Communists saw in the political crisis a pressing need to enlist the participation of the representatives of the organized political opposition, the conservatives who still controlled the party had their own ideas about the course to bring about "national consensus and cooperation." Basic to their strategy (in our view, definitional of hard-liners from late 1988 to mid-1989) was the notion that *a multiparty system could be created by the party itself* through political institutions that allowed for "consultation with society." The remedy for social crisis was limited liberalization within society, not democratization of the state. The desired result of these changes would leave virtually every fundamental political institution of the old order intact. The cornerstone of that strategy was confrontation through a variety of means, frequently combining frontal attacks and attempts at institutional incorporation in the time-honored practice of divide and conquer.

The hard-liners first considered the option of attempting to eliminate the nascent independent organizations. The tactical maneuver of attempting to criminalize the opposition was brief (coinciding for the most part with the apparent resurgence of a hard-line faction in Moscow in October 1988) and half-hearted.[22] Cracking down on dissidents, however inviting to the hard-liners, would have sullied the "nice guy" image they had worked so hard to construct. To conform to the new rule-of-law line coming from Moscow and to keep their hands clean for International Monetary Fund

(IMF) handouts, the Hungarian regime would have to tolerate the opposition and constrain it through legal means alone.[23]

If the autonomous political organizations could not be eliminated, the next step was to try to neutralize them. For the party hard-liners, the closing months of 1988 and the opening months of 1989 were a period of defensive liberalization:[24] "If some new political institutions are inevitable, then let us shape them as much as possible after our own image" seemed to be their thinking. First, they attempted to push through the parliament a new law on association that would give the party-state unlimited control over the formation of independent organizations. When the earlier ritualized practice of submitting the proposed legislation to "social debate" backfired, the hard-liners retreated and then, in an attempted outflanking maneuver, even accepted the principle of a multiparty system, pledging the party's commitment to its prompt realization at the February 1989 meeting of the Central Committee.[25]

Unsuccessful in their attempts to reshape the opposition in their own likeness and constrained by geopolitical circumstances to operate by strictly legal means, the hard-liners then became determined to ensnare the opposition precisely on the terrain of legality. They accepted a multiparty system but then proposed that the parliament (where 75% of the representatives were party members) adopt a new constitution allowing only for the existence of political organizations that accepted socialism. The task of protecting the societal goal of developing socialism enshrined in the constitution, moreover, would fall to a special constitutional court whose members would be appointed for life by the Hungarian Socialist Workers' Party. This court would rule on the constitutionality of legislation passed by a newly elected parliament and would have the responsibility for the registration, or nonregistration, of political organizations.

At the same time that it tried to weaken and marginalize the opposition, the hard-line faction tried to incorporate, coordinate, coopt, and corrupt it. Whereas some autonomous organizations were referred to as *ellenzék* (opposition), others were called *ellenség* (enemies). The latter received only opprobrium; the former might be promised resources in highly selective bargaining on a one-by-one basis: "So, your party would like to get back its former headquarters from the pre-1948 period" or "We hear that your organization is still in need of a telephone line."

More important than trying to pick off the various independent organizations through backroom deals, however, was another divide-and-conquer tactic: attempting to separate public negotiations. By February 1989, with the MSzMP committed to a multiparty system and with Po-

lish Communists already engaged in their Round Table negotiations
with Solidarity, it became obvious to all political actors that some kind
of national forum must be convened to discuss the creation of new political institutions. To this end, the leaders of the Communist Party
initiated a series of separate bilateral negotiations with various organizations, including some of the independent organizations that were beginning to call themselves political parties. Although this tactic failed to
split the opposition, the hard-liners still hoped to conquer even if they
failed to divide. At the end of March, the party's Central Committee issued a call to all the major social organizations (including its satellite
organizations, such as the National Council of Trade Unions) and virtually all the major opposition organizations for the creation of a national Round Table to be convened on April 8.

The hard-liners' conception of a national Round Table of "harmoniza-
tion and reconciliation" was to downgrade independent organizations to the
level of satellite organizations – organizations representing only partial social interests. According to the ruling party's claim that it was the ultimate
guardian of social order and national sovereignty during this difficult transition, its self-identified historic role was to act as the big broker. This
emphasis on negotiation was thus a new development in the party's claim
to represent society; yet it was but merely a step to a higher stage of paternalism.[26] It was now no longer as the monopoly holder of Truth but rather
as the *prime negotiator* that the party claimed to represent general societal
interests. In assuming this posture, the hard-liners did not perceive themselves as a party to a two-sided negotiation between the representatives of
power and the representatives of civil society. Instead, in their conception
of a Hungarian Round Table, the party as prime negotiator would resemble
a teacher sitting before a class of unruly students or an arbiter before squab-
bling disputants in a small-claims court.

But the opposition refused to accept such a paternalistic framing of
the negotiations and issued a united refusal to attend the April 8 meeting. Formal negotiations between the Hungarian Socialist Workers' Party
and an umbrella federation of the democratic opposition would begin
only on June 13. In the interim, the reformers around Imre Pozsgay had
gained the support of intraregime forces to confront the hard-liners with
a new conception of the party's future. In challenging the party's old, paternalistic representational claims, they established a framework for the
Hungarian Round Table negotiations more closely approximating the
civic principles of electoral competition in liberal democracies. To understand the ascendancy of the reform Communists, we must analyze the

strategy of the democratic opposition in its interaction with the hard-
liners' strategy of confrontation.

THE STRATEGY OF THE OPPOSITION

At the end of 1988, the independent organizations of Hungary's civil society
were neither large nor cohesive nor fundamentally committed to challenging
the legitimacy of the Communist regime. In fact, that the term *opposition*
could be used as a collective noun to refer to such a set of weak, diverse,
and fragmented organizations would have occurred to almost no one active
on the Hungarian political scene. As we shall see, the party hard-liners'
strategy of confrontation acted as the catalyst to change that self-conception.

In late 1988 the two largest autonomous political organizations, the
Hungarian Democratic Forum (Magyar Demokrata Fórum–MDF) and the
Alliance of Free Democrats (Szabad Demokraták Szövetsége–SzDSz), had
memberships of just under 10,000 and 1,500, respectively.[27] With no institutionalized means to coordinate (or even communicate about) the activities of the proliferating alternative political organizations, the MDF and
the SzDSz each offered to be the umbrella under which other movements
and independent-minded citizens could stand, as the two organizations
competed for the right to speak in the name of society.[28] More urban, liberal,
and secular, the Alliance of Free Democrats (together with the Federation
of Young Democrats–FIDESZ) was earlier inclined to take a more radically
challenging posture vis-à-vis the regime. The populist writers of the MDF,
on the other hand, were more likely to give expression to the national issues
and Christian traditions of Hungary's rural society, and its politicians were
initially more cautious about directly confronting the authorities. The MDF
leaders asserted repeatedly that they were neither an opposition nor aligned
with power. In this moderate posture they were typical of the fledgling
Hungarian opposition (labeled *alternatives*) before 1989.

The opposition's willingness and ability to challenge the legitimacy of
the regime can be gauged by examining a series of public demonstrations
from June 16, 1988, to June 16, 1989. On the latter date, a quarter of a
million Hungarians assembled in Budapest's Heroes Square to honor and
rebury the former prime minister, Imre Nagy, and other heroes of the 1956
revolution on the anniversary of their execution. For the same commemo-
ration only one year earlier, in 1988, police easily dispersed a crowd of only
several hundred people when virtually all independent organizations chose
to stay away from a demonstration whose premise directly challenged the
legitimacy of the regime.

The beginning steps toward a more radical approach were taken in

September 1988 when a group of environmentalists organized a demonstration before parliament that succeeded in gaining the endorsement of the major independent organizations in a protest against the construction of a dam on the Danube. The demonstration was the first major public questioning of the legitimacy of parliament, whose members had been chosen in elections that were competitive in name only. "Democracy or Dam!" the protestors declared. And when the parliamentary representatives (including all the leaders of the party's reform wing) bowed to the intimidation of the hard-liners and voted to continue construction, some of the alternative groups organized successful public campaigns for the recall of several representatives.

If the environmentalists' demonstration illustrated the potential gains of more active mobilization, the hard-liners' threats provoked recognition of the potential costs of failing to do so. That is, it was the hard-liners' escalating confrontational policies that determined the urgency and the timing of the opposition's shift to popular mobilization. By late 1988 and early 1989 the alternatives faced a conservative party leadership that was vilifying them in public, drafting piece after piece of legislation to exclude some organizations or tie the hands of those it legalized, and launching constitutional initiatives that promised to block any surviving autonomous organization from serious participation in political power. The alternatives could retreat, or they could change to a strategy of confrontation, popular mobilization, and efforts to undermine the legitimacy of the official political institutions. By the spring of 1989, most of them chose the latter course. And in mid-March the major independent organizations formed a loose umbrella federation to coordinate their activities.

Although it is clear how the hard-liners' assault could make it an issue of organizational survival for the alternatives to demonstrate their popular support, it is less obvious how that attack helped to bring about considerable cohesion among disparate oppositional groups. The fact that no single party or movement was strong enough to challenge the party on its own might be seen as a factor driving the alternatives toward mutual cooperation as an opposition. That is, perhaps it was the very fragility of the individual opposition organizations that provided the basis for their unity. But as any good game theorist or historian knows, the potential benefits of cooperation posited in the abstract are not sufficient to explain why some projects of collective action cohere and others dissipate. The problem is even more acute in this case, where the party was promising resources to organizations that would defect from or never join an oppositional coalition.

The emergence of an oppositional umbrella federation becomes understandable when we consider the following: Forced to conform to the formalities of *glasnost* and to the party's own rules of "social debate," the various public forums that accompanied the hard-liners' policies of defensive liberalization increasingly provided the occasions for opposition figures to assemble. Every draft of each new piece of legislation (the new law on strikes, the law on association, the proposed constitutional changes, and so on) – however restrictive in intent and however short the time given for public reaction – yielded another opportunity for the experts and organizers of the opposition movements to meet.

More important, at these meetings and then increasingly while working to prepare joint position papers, the opposition leaders punctuated their words in early 1989 with references to 1948: Now declaring their groups to be opposition political parties, the leaders of the independents were led to reflect on the disappearance of opposition parties during the postwar period, when the Communists succeeded in the same divide-and-conquer tactics that their counterparts were using in the present. The alternatives' leaders reminded themselves and each other that although some opposition parties had been eliminated quickly, whereas others lasted for a short time in coalition with the Communists, none survived. If they were not to repeat past mistakes, the nascent opposition groups would need to find some institutional means to coordinate their efforts. Whether the analyst uses the language of iterative games or of collective memories, Hungary's young opposition parties had learned important lessons from a previous confrontation. Thus, increasingly during the early months of 1989, public statements responding to this or that party initiative were circulated for endorsement by numerous independent organizations. In some cases, the list of signatory organizations was longer than the text, in which the independents collectively confronted the party with a blunt and dismissive challenge.

If the memories of 1948 provided the negative lesson, then the anniversary of the Revolution of 1848, celebrated on March 15, provided the occasion to manifest the opposition's shift in identity and strategy. Communist Party authorities, of course, hoped to fit the anniversary into their plan of marginalizing the opposition by incorporating it. Under the auspices of the Patriotic Front, they issued an invitation to most of the autonomous organizations to participate together in commemorating the Revolution of 1848. In the authorities' appeal, the national holiday could become a celebration of national unity in which everyone wanting "democracy" and a "multiparty system" could march together under the party's slogans for "renewal."

But in the streets of Budapest on March 15, 1989, not one but two commemorations were held. Twenty-four alternative organizations refused the party's invitation. Instead, they organized their own demonstration, which was attended by more than 100,000 participants and overshadowed the official ceremonies. That demonstration was the public signal that the alternatives could also engage in the politics of confrontation. In terms most concrete ("Are you going to *their* demonstration or to *ours?*"), it began the process of redrawing the boundaries of the political space along dichotomous lines between officialdom and the opposition. It was the act of standing with power or with those challenging power that created an opposition. The March 15 demonstration was the performative action that made possible the mutual self-recognition of an oppositional identity transcending the boundaries of the various participating organizations. Eight days later, on March 23, in the building of the law faculty under the auspices of the Association of Independent Lawyers, representatives of eight independent organizations met to formalize this new identity by establishing a mechanism for coordinating their activities. Acknowledging their commitment to resolving differences in a framework of equality, they called their umbrella federation a *Round Table.* Confirming their newly formed collective identity, they specified it as the *Opposition Round Table* (Ellenzéki Kerekasztal, or EKA). The stated purpose of the metaorganization was to create the basis for a common stance vis-à-vis the MSzMP, the "power holders."

The formation of this Opposition Round Table fundamentally altered the map of Hungarian politics. Its consequence was to unite and radicalize the opposition and eventually to polarize the political camps. At the beginning of 1989, even the more radical groups in the democratic opposition such as the SzDSz still made distinctions between reformers and hard-liners and discussed the possibility of alliance with the party's reformers. Their perceptions and depictions of the political landscape had changed dramatically by the time the EKA was founded only months later. In the lengthy debates and discussions that marked the first meetings of the new umbrella federation, the representatives of all the organizations of the EKA opposition (ranging from radicals to moderates to those who had only recently resigned their membership in the party's organizations) came to agree that there were only two political camps in Hungary: those who represented the monopolistic power *together with* those who wanted to compromise with them and, in contrast, those who wanted to reestablish popular sovereignty. Against the party's paternalistic representational claims, the EKA representatives argued, first among themselves and later to the public, for an alternative legitimating claim based on purely civic principles: *The political and economic crisis cannot be solved by any kind of power sharing. The solution to the crisis is not for power to be shared with society but for power to be legitimated by genuinely free, fully contested elections. Anyone who disagrees with this principle and anyone who is willing to compromise this principle is with "them."*[29] On the new political map being drawn by EKA there was no intermediate space, as there had been only months earlier, between paternalistic power and democracy. Those who continued to speak about the need to *reform* the system and who claimed that they were using their power to empower society for the future, the opposition argued, were but the Siren voice of monopoly power, which only obstructed *transforming* the system to one in which power resided in the citizenry. To the party's strategy of attempting to delegitimate, marginalize, and divide the opposition, the opposition now answered with its own strategy of delegitimating, marginalizing, and dividing the holders of power.

Although the opposition figures were committed to the escalation of confrontation as the only means to create a situation whereby they could negotiate with the representatives of the regime on terms that recognized them as major political actors, few believed that these goals could be achieved in a short time. Their plans for further demonstrations as tests of strength looked to dates already marked on the calendar: May 1 (Labor Day), June 16 (the anniversary of the execution of Imre Nagy), and October 23 (the anniversary of the revolution of 1956). They could use these opportunities to challenge the regime's legitimacy and expose its "naked power." Their reading of the changed geopolitical situation suggested not only that they could now move on to territory that was once unimaginable, but also that they must do so while Gorbachev was still able to hold off his hard-line rivals.[30]

FROM CONFRONTATION TO NEGOTIATION

The same perceptions that emboldened the opposition worried the power holders in offices high and low. With the use of force ruled out as an option, with a more liberal law on association ensuring that opposition groups would not be eliminated, and with the hard-liners' policy of attempting to freeze out the opposition not only sputtering but backfiring, office holders at the local level and members at the party's base were the first to voice concern.[31] Hungarian television had broadcast the parallel and competing March 15 demonstrations into every home. Local party officials could see which demonstration was larger, and it was easy to calculate which side's numbers would grow in future demonstrations. To those sensitive to shifts in the political winds, moreover, the opposition's refusal to attend the government-orchestrated Round Table of April 8 signaled the futility of the hard-liners' hope of dividing the opposition.

As the first to feel politically vulnerable, local officials and party activists were among the first to respond to the newly drawn boundary lines. Local apparatchiks had early seen the impossibility and absurdity of the orders coming from above to marginalize, coopt, corrupt, or divide and conquer the independents. From their vantage point, the strategy of confrontation would not work when combined with deteriorating economic conditions and liberalized regulations allowing for genuinely autonomous political organizations. By late March and early April, they were sending the message upward that *instead of trying to eliminate the opposition, we should be competing with them to offer better alternatives.*

Party members who were not officials were even more fearful that a cataclysmic rupture of the social order might threaten their personal safety or destroy their careers. Afraid that the party's leadership was headed toward disaster, they began to take the organization into their own hands. *Reform Circles* within the party's local branches had already begun to emerge at the end of 1988; by April they were sprouting up everywhere and taking the local party organizations as their targets. In one provincial city after another, reformist Communists ousted conservative leaders. From one county to the next, they battled successfully to hold party conferences to remove the staunchest supporters of Károly Grósz in the Central Committee. Slowly, almost imperceptibly at first, but then more rapidly and visibly, the Reform Circles were encircling the party leadership. Their chorus: *The hard-liners' policy has become a damaging liability. We cannot let ourselves be trapped with "them."* By late April, some Reform Circles were not only calling for unconditional acceptance of the EKA's preconditions for negotiations but were also threatening to split the MSzMP and create a new socialist party that would join the EKA opposition. The party was disintegrating at its base.

Defections from the conservative policy line were not limited, however, to local party organizations. Throughout the spring, an increasing number of parliamentary representatives declared their independence from party discipline. Together with the growing visibility and unpredictability of the "Independent Faction," this demarcation of a boundary inside parliament made things increasingly uncomfortable for "them." Each day, more and more high-ranking party officials and government bureaucrats were discovering that in their hearts they had always been reformers, and the press (now unleashed and hungry) was scarcely able to conceal its derision as it described yet another regime figure's conversion on the road to Damascus. So it was that on April 25, Prime Minister Miklós Németh (an appointee and protegé of Károly Grósz) took the unprecedented step of calling an evening television news program to repudiate a speech of Grósz and distance himself from the party hierarchy.[32] The *government* was clearly separating itself from the *party*.

May 1, the last glorious celebration of the highest (and only remaining) party holiday, marked the next stage in the polarization of the political field. With enough sense to avoid the traditional viewing stand located at the site where Stalin's gargantuan statue was torn down in 1956, the Communists had convened their May Day rally in the city's central park, where the party boss, Grósz, addressed the celebrants. But following the successful formula of March 15, the opposition also held a rally, this time organized by the League of Independent Trade Unions. Estimates vary, but the only question was whether the opposition's crowd of 60,000 to 100,000 was 10 times or only 6 times larger than the audience that came to hear Károly Grósz. With both rallies adjourning to separate public forums, the League used this opportunity to orchestrate the first public appearance of the EKA representatives as a collectivity. Both forums were televised in question-and-answer formats; the Independent Unionists' contacts among television reporters, producers, and technicians yielded proportional coverage, perhaps as important as the content: 50 minutes for the ruling party, 50 minutes for the united opposition.

The growing defections from the ruling bloc accelerated exponentially throughout the month of May. Their timing was caused less by the events of the past than by those of the future. After the May Day celebrations, all the political actors began to orient toward the next public demonstration of political identity and strength in which they would be forced to take a position. The next date circled on the calendar was June 16, the anniversary of the execution of Imre Nagy, hero of 1956. Under the pressure of public opinion, both domestic and international, the Grósz regime had been forced to accept the reburial of Nagy and his close associates.[33] Everyone in a leadership position had known for weeks that it was impossible to avoid granting permission for a public ceremony to honor the fallen heroes of the failed revolution of 1956. It was not difficult for them to imagine the possibilities for a dramatic declaration, demarcation, and enactment of the boundaries between "them" and "us." *Regardless of your cosmetic surgery and the new labels you now use for yourselves*, the opposition stated in effect, *you are still those who came to power with the Soviet tanks. You represent the interests of the empire, and even now, when the Russians give us a chance to loosen the chains, you are still trying to salvage your power with reformist tricks.* With each day, the time bomb ticked louder, threatening an explosive release of the ghosts of 1956.

Thus, whereas the hard-liners' strategy of attempting to divide the opposition had the effect of pushing the independent organizations together, the opposition's strategy of attempting to portray hard-liners and reformers as conjoined had the effect of forcing an open division within the ruling bloc. For the party's reform Communist leaders it was now a race against time. They had forty days to show that instead of a well-meaning but subordinated junior faction they were in a position to exert the decisive, if not entirely uncontested, leadership of the government and the party. Hundreds of thousands were likely to be in Heroes Square on June 16, and a national audience would watch the funeral on television. Would they see a line drawn between society and power, between democracy and paternalism, between popular sovereignty and illegitimate rule? Or would they see ambiguity and blurred boundaries – government officials in the nation's colors mourning heroes slain by foreign aggressors and Communists advocating popular sovereignty?

To reduce the dangerous dichotomy and inject even the slightest ambiguity into the public drama, the reformers would have to do more than remind reporters that Imre Nagy, too, had been a Communist or that the party's official commission had recently concluded that 1956 was neither revolution nor counterrevolution but a "popular uprising."[34] They would have to demonstrate that they had the strength to transform the party's policy of regarding the opposition as enemies into one of regarding them as equally legitimate aspirants to government office, and they would have to bind themselves publicly to a course of negotiating the institutions of electoral democracy. To do so they would have to dethrone, or at least neutralize, the reigning conservatives and navigate a complex series of intense prenegotiations to bring the opposition's mobilization for June 16 into a less explosive frame. The anticipation of the event produced effects preceding its occurrence.

A quarter of a million Hungarians filled Heroes Square on June 16, 1989. They and the national television audience heard the morning's reading of the names of fallen martyrs and the afternoon's speeches honoring the executed prime minister and denouncing the still-occupying foreign army. But they also saw three politicians bear wreaths and stand silently beside the coffins: Imre Pozsgay, minister of state and representative of the government; Miklós Németh, prime minister; and Mátyás Szürös, president of the parliament.[35]

For the millions who watched the eight-hour television broadcast, June 16 did not prove to be an unambiguous demarcation of "us" and "them." The division between the representatives of naked power and those of popular sovereignty did not emerge. Although they were the last to be cognizant of the danger, by the end of May even the hard-liners saw the need to defuse the situation. So as not to be the last in the castle, they moved with uncharacteristic speed and solicitousness to reach agreement with the united opposition for direct and almost unconditional negotiations. On June 10 – six days after the electoral debacle of the Polish Communists and six days before the reburial of Imre Nagy — representatives of the MSzMP and the EKA signed an agreement to enter into negotiations to construct the new political institutions of liberal democracy. The Trilateral Negotiations at which the new rules of the political game were written opened on June 13 in the parliament building. The opening speech on the part of the EKA was delivered by Imre Konya, who had chaired the first organizational meeting of the opposition umbrella only months earlier. Speaking for the Communist Party was Károly Grósz, the architect of the party's confrontational strategy. At a Central Committee meeting 10 days later, Grósz was officially placed under the tutelage of the party's three leading reformers, who were assigned the task of heading the party's delegation at the negotiations.

THE POLITICS OF COMPETITION

ACCEPTING UNCERTAINTY

In the summer of 1988, we recall, Hungary had seemed a likely candidate for an institutionalized power sharing: Leading figures inside and outside the regime could point to concrete proposals for a compromise solution to the generally perceived crisis. But reform Communists at that time were still too weak to grant concessions in the name of the regime, and the promising path to compromise was blocked by conservatives, who controlled party policy. By the early summer of 1989, these obstacles to compromise had been removed: The opposition had emerged strengthened by its confrontation with the party's hard-liners, and reform Communists had become the hegemonic (although far from exclusive) force within the regime.[36] The road to compromise now seemed clear. Moreover, it was already well charted by their Polish counterparts, whose own Round Table negotiations had resulted in comprehensive agreements in April.

But the same processes that eliminated the old obstacles to compromise produced new political identities, new goals, and new perceptions of opportunity structures that removed compromised power sharing from the political agenda in mid-1989. The closer reform Communists and opposition groups came to realizing the conditions under which they could negotiate a compromise agreement guaranteeing the ruling party control of designated institutions, the more they came to see compromise as self-defeating.

From the viewpoint of the united opposition, agreeing to a compromise solution would have undermined their own basis of legitimacy. During the months of confrontation with the old regime, the opposition had developed a coherent rhetoric that had come to serve as the basis of their own self-understanding and of their self-presentation to society. The basic principle that unified otherwise divergent organizations within the EKA and the basic principle that orchestrated its appeal to the public during the spring of 1989 were the same: *There is no legitimate power in Hungary today; until legitimate authority is created through fully contested free elections, no organization – including those in the opposition – has the right to decide the nation's future political and economic institutions.* Unless it wished to undercut its own legitimacy, the opposition could not bargain about power sharing and institutional guarantees, but could only negotiate about the creation of the institutions and rules of the game for free elections.

Of course, the opposition might have argued to itself and to the public that the balance of forces (domestic and international) was such that it had no other choice but to concede institutional guarantees as the only way to begin the process of democratization. In such a view, Hungarian society, as in Poland only months earlier, would be forced to accept a two-step transition to democracy (compromise guarantees followed eventually by genuinely free elections). But even if the opposition had been willing to retreat from its first principles and mitigate the threat to its legitimacy by such arguments of realpolitik, both the Hungarian opposition and the reformers recognized an even more compelling argument against compromise. Imagine, went their argument, that the organized opposition is willing to ignore the illegitimacy of the regime, even temporarily, and agree to a deal. Some might think this will give the regime time to solve its legitimation crisis, but it will only deepen that crisis. Institutional guarantees will only institutionalize the competing legitimating principles. They will make it dramatically obvious to the whole society that some offices are held on civic principles and others are derived from paternalistic principles – some from elections and some from deals.

Moreover, they wondered, even if the opposition, from expediency, accepts the conditions of such guarantees, who can guarantee that *society* will accept them? Can the representatives of the organized opposition guarantee that society will not be outraged by a compromise? The independent organizations are strong enough to bring the representatives of the regime to the negotiating table, but they are not strong enough to ensure that society will comply. If compromise provokes an even greater crisis of legitimacy, that crisis will be "yours *and* ours," and when it sweeps the regime away, it will carry along anyone who made a deal with it.

The Hungarian situation at the outset of negotiations in the summer of 1989 thus contrasts markedly with the Polish Round Table launched in February of the same year. The basic premise of the Polish negotiations, shared by all sides, Wojciech Jaruzelski no less than Lech Walesa, was that

Solidarity represented society and spoke in its name. However curious it might sound, although Solidarity's *legality* was one of the subjects for negotiations, its *legitimacy* to speak for society during the negotiations and its credibility to speak to society after the negotiations in enforcing the conditions of the agreement were never in question. That is, in Poland the ruling party had to contend with an opposition that had already established its *claim* to represent society but that sought to reestablish its legal *right* to do so. Because of the perceived strength of the opposition's claims, both the ruling party and Solidarity agreed to compromised political institutions. The government could not risk freely contested elections, and Solidarity did not wish to participate in any. For the ruling party, the price of sharing political power was the recognition of a legal trade union movement; for Solidarity, the price of legal recognition was the obligation to participate in less than free elections.[37]

In Hungary, by contrast, it was the very weakness of the opposition groups that forced them to be uncompromising. With their organizational membership still numbering only in the thousands and with their strength in society still untested, they could neither make an undisputed claim to speak in the name of society nor anticipate the capacity to call on society to agree to a compromise.[38] For these reasons, the united Hungarian opposition went into negotiations insisting that the goal of any agreement was the establishment of free, open, fully contested, uncompromised elections.

It was not this insistent strategy alone, however, but its interaction with the perceptions and strategies of the reform Communists that brought Hungarian negotiations to an outcome of unfettered elections. As they surveyed the confrontational politics of the spring of 1989, Pozsgay and other leading reform Communists granted that the opposition had demonstrated that it could draw crowds challenging the regime; the question now, however, was whether it could attract voters for its program and personalities. The reform Communists' conclusions were not discouraging. Their potential electoral opponents were young parties with few activists, meager organizational resources, no charismatic leaders, and only shallow roots in the society. If they could seize the high ground as champions of democracy, the reform Communists calculated that with their hands no longer tied by the Brezhnev Doctrine they could use their superior resources, organization, and nationally recognized candidates to defeat the opposition in a straightforward electoral contest with no strings attached.

If the basic perception of the electoral weakness of the opposition led reform Communists to conclude that there was no need for compromised institutional guarantees, the Polish election of June 4 was a warning sign of the dangers of compromise. With numerous parliamentary seats assured to them by the Roundtable agreements, Polish Communists had proceeded, to the surprise and consternation of the leaders of Solidarity, to lose virtually every contested seat in the election. For the Hungarian reform Communists about to embark on their own talks of national conciliation, the lesson from Poland was not that they should secure even more guarantees but that guarantees can explode when society decides to reject the agreements. Given their electoral expectations, it seemed better to risk the uncertainty of free elections than to negotiate certainties that risked spoiling the chance to make a bid for legitimacy.

At the same time that the Polish elections signaled calamities to be avoided, to the Hungarian reform Communists the election seemed to be an opportunity for the taking. By holding a fully contested election without guarantees, Hungarian reform Communists could reclaim the position, temporarily usurped in their view by Polish Communists under Jaruzelski, as the front runners among the state socialist reformers. By winning such an election, moreover, they could achieve an historic precedent as the first Communists in the world to base their power on popular elections. The stakes were high, but the Hungarian reformers were confident that they could secure agreements for an early election and take advantage of a relatively weak opposition to win at least a plurality of the votes in a free election.

The reform Communists' basic perceptions of the opportunities, incentives, and advantages of shifting from a strategy of confrontation to one of competition were bolstered by the results of the first surveys of public opinion on party preferences published in May 1989.[39] According to these early surveys, if elections were held immediately, the Communists would win a decisive plurality of the votes, as 36% of the respondents indicated their intention to vote for the Hungarian Socialist Workers' Party. This was lower than the most self-confident leaders of the MSzMP had expected but was still three times higher than the percentage of respondents choosing the next highest party (the Social Democratic Party).[40] The surveys also indicated that the opposition parties would be hard pressed to field candidates for national office. A majority of the respondents did not recognize the names of the opposition's leaders, whereas Pozsgay, Németh, and others were not only widely recognized but also growing in popularity. In general, the surveys suggested that Hungarians in 1989 were deeply distrustful of all political institutions and organizations. And although the level of distrust of the MSzMP was so great as to frighten some of the more hesitant regime leaders, the level of support for and trust in the opposition was not much higher.[41]

The reform Communists, of course, could not be certain that they would triumph in the strategy of competition. But their perception of the weakness of the opposition and their assessment of their own electoral prospects gave them enough confidence to accept that uncertainty. Thus, they took the decisive step of accepting the principle of "certain institutions of uncertain outcomes" that is at the core of liberal democracy.[42]

NEGOTIATING UNCERTAINTY

By late May 1989 the question was thus how to create the institutions for generating uncertain outcomes. What should be the new procedures for elections and the new rules of the game for a competitive party system? All sides could agree to negotiations in principle, but they disagreed considerably about the scope and character of such talks. To get to the table, they had to resolve the basic questions of the range of issues that should be addressed and who should participate in the formal negotiations. Central to these questions about framing the negotiations were the competing legitimating principles of the various sides to the negotiations.

In the prenegotiating stage, the nine organizations of the EKA opposition sought to frame the talks as two-sided negotiations between the representatives of power and the representatives of society. Their self-representation based on civic principles dictated that the only issues for negotiation should be those directly related to establishing free elections (e.g., party registration, access to the media, and neutralization of the state's repressive apparatus).

Party conservatives, on the other hand, still insisted on framing the negotiations in terms congruent with their paternalistic representational claims. That principle dictated involving the greatest number of organizations to discuss the greatest range of issues, including such distributive issues as housing, labor market problems, social security, wage indexation, and the like. From the paternalistic vantage point, an immature society would be less interested in the details of legal paragraphs on the negotiating table than in what was available to eat at the kitchen table. Hence, for the party's conservatives, the legitimacy of the negotiations should rest on the demonstration that "we care about your problems."

By focusing the negotiations on competitive elections, the reform Communists around Pozsgay dramatically dissociated themselves from the paternalistic themes that had permeated the party's entire postwar history. In the Stalinist period, of course, paternalism based on the party's claim to superior knowledge of long-term interests superseding shortsighted, narrow preferences had been expressed as *We know your interests and take your future into our hands.* Under Kádár, paternalism had taken the form of *We take your interests into account.* Kádárist paternalism shifted the temporal focus from the future to the present, and the party thus claimed to represent society as servants who cared about present preferences. Pozsgay's new formula, by contrast, was genuinely postpaternalistic. *We give you back the future as we lead you to democracy* was his apparent message. This postpaternalistic principle dictated strict adherence to the appearance of democratic propriety, especially to formulas rendering the participants equivalent – insofar as they could be made consistent with the latent image that among the equal participants there was an older brother with maturity and experience who could be called on in the most difficult times to lead the younger siblings through the dense forest of extrication from authoritarianism.

The Hungarian Round Table negotiations that opened on June 13, 1989, were ambiguously framed: Civic principles dominated, but they coexisted with elements of late paternalism, reflecting the persistent but by now minor role of the hard-liners on the political stage. On the basis of the configuration of issues on the agenda, it seemed that the various parties had arrived at a formal, almost equitable, compromise between the civic and paternalistic frameworks: The detailed negotiations of the Round Table would be conducted in 12 subcommittees, 6 on political questions (constitutional changes, elections procedures, and so on) and 6 on economic questions (property reform, budgetary reform, and the like). But this apparent compromise was more a façade than the real structure of the negotiations, for the EKA umbrella had succeeded in excluding such immediate issues as wage indexation (in marked contrast to the Polish Round Table) from negotiations. Moreover, as negotiations proceeded throughout the summer, the work of the economic subcommittees receded almost entirely from view, and in the end, no agreements were reached on any economic issues.[43]

The patterns of exclusion and inclusion of participants in the negotiations yielded an apparently even more complex framework of coexisting principles. The negotiations that opened on June 13 were tripartite talks, involving representatives of the MSzMP, the EKA, and the satellite organizations of the party. As with the range of negotiable issues, the inclusion of these last-mentioned "social organizations" was more a face-saving gesture for the party conservatives than a substantive compromise of civic principles. The prenegotiation agreement reached between the MSzMP and the EKA specifically relegated the "third side" to a minor role by stipulating that any agreements reached by the first two sides could not be blocked by the third. From the opening plenary session, these were in fact bilateral negotiations, and when the most important representatives of the third side (the official trade unions) walked out of the talks later in the summer, their absence went virtually unnoticed.

More important than this readjustment of the sides of the negotiating table was the reconfiguration of the identities of the actors and a shift in the self-legitimations of the negotiations. In a fundamental sense, the real negotiations in the Hungarian setting could begin only when both sides suspended their claim to represent society. But whom, then, did they represent? As the negotiations proceeded, the answer became clearer: They represented the would-be parties of an anticipated competitive polity. As they negotiated the institutionalization of uncertainty, they were making the new rules of the political game and defining it as *party* politics.[44] This was a tremendous work of reconfiguration – not simply of remaking explicit rules and legal codes but also of establishing codes of personal conduct with each other and of trying out new vocabularies, rhetorics, gestures, and clothing as party functionaries and dissenting academics became politicians. For this they had an entire summer, largely behind closed doors, away from the glare of publicity.[45] The new rules of the game would be hammered out among those with the highest and most immediate stakes in the new political institutions – the potential winners and losers in electoral contests. The Hungarian Round Table negotiations were, above all, the occasion for the making of a new political class.

HEDGING UNCERTAINTY

With the basic triumph of civil principles on the near horizon and with their identities as electoral parties mutually confirmed during each day of the talks, the negotiators now began hammering out the specifics of the new rules of the game. There could be any number of institutional arrangements compatible with liberal democracy (a stronger or weaker presidency, direct constituency representation versus party lists, minimum percentages for parties to be seated in parliament, and so on). But each of these would have a differential impact on the actual political success of the various parties.[46] In principle, the opposition parties could participate in designing new political institutions from behind John Rawls's *veil of ignorance* in which none of the actors could know his assets in advance.[47] But as the chances for successful negotiations improved, each organization lifted that veil to scrutinize its potential electoral resources and began to negotiate accordingly. From arguing about principles the parties turned to calculating the relationship between their interests and particular institutional outcomes. Although these political parties accepted the basic institutionalization of uncertainty, each sought the best array of institutions and rules that would provide it with some hedge against uncertainty.

Such calculations intensified when, several months into the negotiations, the new party leaders could read the results of actual elections for four parliamentary seats recently opened by the recall campaigns. The reform Communists lost every race. This crack in their electoral self-confidence led them to push even harder in the negotiations for the institution of a strong presidency and for scheduling early elections for the position. Perhaps they might not win a plurality in parliament, but with their candidate, Imre Pozsgay, as the only nationally recognized figure in the race they were sure to gain the presidency.

The defeat of the Communist candidates in the summer elections, however, was not a flood that raised the entire EKA ship: One party, the Hungarian Democratic Forum, had won all four of the contested seats. The Forum's negotiators now pressed to wrap up the Round Table talks. As the Forum was the clear front runner, they were for striking an agreement and getting on with elections, tactics that coincided with the hopes of the reform Communists. The smaller EKA parties meanwhile pressed for relatively strong rights for minority parties in the parliament lest they be squeezed out by the MDF, the MSzMP, or the two in coalition. The resulting package, concluded expeditiously, would have established an eclectic set of political institutions consisting of, on the one hand, a strong parliament with the provision that almost all important legislation would require a two-thirds vote (thus strengthening the voice of minority parties) and, on the other hand, a presidency to be directly elected by popular vote before the parliamentary elections but without especially strong institutional authority. The agreement was signed on September 18, 1989, and presidential elections were scheduled for late November.

But one group of opposition parties examined the package and concluded that the timing and terms of this particular institutionalization of uncertainty would almost certainly lead to their marginalization. While claiming that the parties to the negotiations had no authority to create a new state institution (the presidency), the Association for Free Democrats, from vital self-interest, refused to sign the agreement and launched a national referendum challenging the presidential component of the Round Table package. They were joined in this challenge by the Federation of Young Democrats.[48] Little known to the electorate at the time, the two liberal parties calculated that their best hope of gaining attention from the public was a frontal assault on the Communists and those who had made a deal with them. That accommodation, of course, had not compromised civic principles. If the reform Communists were likely to win the presidency, that expectation was situational and not an institutional guarantee. But the arrangement, the SzDSz and FIDESZ hoped, might be portrayed as a deal. And it could be especially damaging politically if it could be tied in a referendum to three other problems represented as attempts by the Communists to "salvage their power": When they created the presidency, the Round Table signators had failed to exclude the Communist Party from the workplace, to abolish the party's armed workers' guard, and to provide a process for public accounting of the party's considerable assets.[49]

In sponsoring the referendum, the SzDSz and FIDESZ hoped to increase their recognition and the size of their constituency. Portraying themselves as the authentic anticommunists was the ideal move because it would indirectly question the credentials of the MDF on exactly that score. The more they turned up the volume of anticommunism, the more uncomfortable became the MDF. As signators of the Round Table agreement they could hardly reject the presidential clause in that document. But the temporary coincidence of interests with the reform Communists was now becoming a liability. And so they asked their potential voters to stay away from the polls in the November referendum. The SzDSz countered with an effective slogan: "Who stays home votes for the past." The referendum carried by the narrowest of margins.

The reform Communists lost much more, however, than the referendum. They also lost precious time. Had they not insisted on the presidency and moved, instead, to early parliamentary elections soon after the conclusion of the Round Table talks, they might have taken full advantage of the weakness of their electoral rivals, secured a place at least as the second largest party, and perhaps entered a coalition government. Instead, they entered a long winter of campaigning in which their opponents thrived week by week. In losing the referendum, they also lost the ability to use the institutional leverage of a popularly elected president during the course of the parliamentary campaign. Nonetheless, they tried to use some of the advantages of being the governing party (control of television, for example) until the March elections. But with the public alerted by the referendum to any attempts at power salvaging, these clumsy moves only sullied their other efforts to demonstrate a commitment to civic values – a key component of their strategy of uncompromised competition once they had abandoned the tactic of institutional guarantees. Finally, the referendum cost the reform Communists the ability to set the tone of the parliamentary election. Instead of emerging from the Round Table talks as the party that had successfully navigated the nation to the shores of democracy and was now prepared to lead it into the future, the reformers were forced into a defensive posture as the opposition parties competed among themselves for the title of the most authentic anticommunist. Just at the moment when they hoped to be rewarded by the citizens for giving them back the future, the reform Communists were confronted at every turn with their own awkward past.

Once hopeful of being the first Communists to win a popular election, the renamed Hungarian Socialist Party emerged from the March and April 1990 elections with only 8% of the parliamentary seats. The victorious Hungarian Democratic Forum, with 43% of the seats in parliament, formed a governing coalition with the Independent Smallholders (11%) and the Christian Democrats (5%). Within less than nine months the Association for Free Democrats had gone from less than 7% in opinion polls to the second largest party in parliament. With 24% of the seats, it emerged as a strong opposition party.

But the electoral results tell only one part of the story of the outcomes of the negotiated politics of competition. The institutional outcomes are perhaps even more important. Unlike countries with strong presidencies that have hijacked transitions from authoritarianism elsewhere in the world, Hungary now has a governmental structure with a weak presidency (elected by the parliament) and a strong parliament.[50] Observers have marveled at the relative ease with which the government and the opposition settle their differences and the speed with which parliamentary committees began extraordinarily smooth functioning. With only a few exceptions, this is a political elite with a high degree of agreement about the formal and informal rules of the game. Hungary's political institutions would appear to be a political science textbook recipe for democratic governance. But this neat structure of political institutions and the new political elite occupying it carry liabilities as they undertake the transformation of Hungary's inherited economic system to solve the fundamental problems that provoked the democratic transition.

COMPARATIVE PERSPECTIVES

In 1990, the citizens of Poland discovered that compromises had strewn the road of their transition with enormous and difficult obstacles. Although a noncommunist government was in office, the presidency was still occupied by the martial-law general, and parliamentary seats were still being occupied by representatives with dubious legitimacy. Even after Walesa's election, the major constitutional issues remained unresolved and the final character of many of its political institutions were still undetermined. In Poland an initially undifferentiated social movement had come to power, and its breakup into a competitive party system would not be without friction. Yet despite difficulties that seemed to hinder the rapid consolidation of liberal parliamentary democracy, the events of the first year of the transition were far from discouraging from the viewpoint of regime transformation. Although Solidarity had been greatly reduced from its base in 1981, its leaders still enjoyed the trust of millions of members, who accepted its goals through deliberation and identification with those leaders. Deeply rooted in the society, these organizational ties were able to mobilize popular support for an ambitious economic program of stabilization, marketization, and privatization – at least in its first crucial period.[51]

In Hungary, by contrast, the transformation of political structures was so rapid and comprehensive that its party system seemed to whir like a finely calibrated, well-oiled machine. These parties had developed in a hothouse atmosphere where the transition from social movements to political parties could be measured in months rather than years. If for a decade or more some of their leaders had been courageously calling on the state to change its ways, the period in which they addressed society and mobilized it for a confrontation with the state was very brief; and the week marking the crescendo of this mobilization on June 16, 1989, was the same week that it began rapidly to subside. The summer of 1989 was not a season of organizing society but of negotiating with other political parties, and the fall and winter were devoted to electoral campaigning. Given the one-step, uncompromised jump start into electoral competition, the preoccupation with party politics, albeit necessary, was not conducive to sinking deep roots into the society. Moreover, the rapid and successful emergence of political parties was achieved at the expense of other organizations representing society. Despite their short life and their shallow roots, the political parties have been remarkably successful in filling the entire political space. But the almost totalizing supremacy of party politics found the society unorganized and still lacking intermediary forms of political organization such as trade unions, corporatist institutions, and broad social movements. As a result of this abrupt transition to entrenched parliamentarism, no organized extraparliamentary forces could challenge the dominance of the parties. But the absence of other representative institutions meant that the Hungarian elite would embark on a course of economic transformation without trusted intermediaries and partners for dialogue.

One might think that the absence of a strong, politically organized civil society would make it easier for a new elite to reorganize the economy. Strong trade unions, for example, might pose serious obstacles to marketization. But the Polish case demonstrates that vital trade unions not only mobilize but also demobilize. In their first year in office, the new democratic leadership in Poland was able to call upon society to make the sacrifices that accompanied economic stabilization. By comparison with the Poles' ambitious schemes, Hungarian economic policy in the first year of liberal democracy was characterized by extreme cautiousness – for in the absence of organizational ties to the society, it had neither the means to know the limits of the society's tolerance nor the channels to persuade it to make those sacrifices. Thus, the relative weakness of the organized forces of civil society that made it possible for Hungary to travel the path of uncompromised competition meant that Hungary faced a deficit of institutional resources to mediate between state and society that might secure social support to remedy the economic crisis that had provoked the installation of liberal democracy.

But whereas Hungary's civil society looked weak in comparison to Poland's, it had a healthy, dynamic, thriving public sphere compared with its counterparts in Bulgaria, Romania, and Albania. In those countries, elites within the old ruling order took advantage of the extreme feebleness of the opposition to schedule early elections, control the registration of their electoral rivals, and limit their access to the media. They were elected to office by extraordinary majorities. In this they learned from their Hungarian counterparts that it was not necessary to seek institutional guarantees but that renamed Communists might attempt to stay in office via competitive elections. The difference was that state socialist elites in the later cases moved with much greater speed and confidence and showed a clearer sense of knowing exactly which institutions they needed to control in order to succeed.

The preceding description parallels the conventional wisdom about how the citizens in the later revolutions of 1989 differed from those in the earlier ones. The East German people moved with greater speed than the Hungarians, the Czechs were more confident and directed than the Germans, and so on – so goes the domino theory of mass mobilization. There can be no doubt that the citizens of Eastern Europe learned from the series of dramatic events of 1989. But the flaw of *contagion theories* is that they ignore the possibility, suggested in our comparison of Hungary, Albania, Bulgaria, and Romania, that the elites also learned. The consequences of this learning are felt daily in Albania, Bulgaria, and Romania. By ignoring the ways in which elites could modify their strategies on the basis of earlier experiences, by examining only the citizens (and discussing elites only in terms of their being supported or ditched by Moscow), and by neglecting the complex interactions between forces inside and outside the regime, contagion theories can only register the time of collapse; they cannot account for important differences in outcomes.

Perhaps the most widely repeated statement about the events of 1989 has been some variant of Timothy Garton Ash's comment that they took ten years in Poland, ten months in Hungary, ten weeks in the GDR, ten days in Czechoslovakia, and ten hours in Romania.[52] The statement itself is irrefutable. But looking to the longer-term consequences of the upheavals of 1989, our examination of the Hungarian case and the comparative insights into the other East European cases suggests that the shorter the period of extrication from state socialism, the more protracted the subsequent period of economic transformation and democratic consolidation.

PART II

TRANSFORMATION

THE PRIVATIZATION DEBATE: FROM PLAN TO MARKET OR FROM PLAN TO CLAN?

The Round Table negotiations that opened in mid-June 1989 signaled the end of the monopoly rule of Hungary's Communist Party. In over three months of intensive negotiations, representatives of the ruling and major opposition parties hammered out the new rules of the political game covering the constitution, registration of political organizations, election procedures, the mass media, and the disposition of the coercive apparatus of the state. But although negotiations in six economic subcommittees (charged with property relations, antitrust regulations, budgetary matters, and the like) were held parallel to the political discussions, no decisive agreements were reached on the economic front. The problem was not that the committees were deadlocked, for in fact the experts representing the various sides of the negotiations shared a common framework that should have made consensus possible. The failure to rewrite the rules of the economic game rested more in the organizational composition of the negotiating partners. The political rules could be restructured because the key actors with an immediate stake in the newly redefined political field were all at the negotiating table. The rules of a new economic order, however, could not be rewritten because the key actors in the economy were decidedly absent.

As we saw in the preceding chapter, the actors at the Round Table were the would-be parties of an anticipated competitive polity. Rather than mutually denouncing disparate legitimating claims to represent society, they established the preconditions for progress in the Round Table negotiations that the organizations on both sides temporarily suspend the claim to speak in the name of society and that the personalities in the negotiations speak as representatives of political parties. It was in this capacity that they could reconstruct an electoral system in which society would have its chance to speak. The economic negotiations, by contrast, were paralyzed by this very framing of the Round Table structure in which the parties to the negotiation were exactly that – *parties*, not capital and labor, not peak associations, not corporate groupings, not employers' associations, not trade unions.[1] There could be no decisive, binding agreements about economic matters in the Round Table context because the negotiations did not include the key economic actors with the greatest stakes in the new rules restructuring the economy.

Thus, whereas the Round Table framework successfully negotiated the key issues of the transformation of politics, the fundamental questions of the transformation of property were left unresolved. Those questions were being debated not simply by the newly emerging political elite in the closed economic committees of the Round Table but also in multiple forums throughout the society. As a genuine public sphere opened in Hungary, one of its first and most passionately pursued topics was the problem of privatization. This chapter addresses that debate – within the terms posed by the actors themselves.

For nearly three decades, the conception of reform of the state socialist economies of East Central Europe was dominated by the search for the correct mix of plan and market within the state sector. By the mid-1980s, a new conception of reform had emerged in Hungary focusing on the small-scale private sector as economists debated the correct mix of public and private ownership across sectors of the economy. The year 1989 witnessed, in both Hungary and Poland, a fundamental break with these conceptions of reform: Rather than simply stimulating the expansion of the traditional private sector, policy makers began designing a variety of measures for the privatization of the public sector itself. Whereas previous debates had addressed questions of how to *reform* the economic mechanism of state socialism, the new efforts sought to *transform* the fundamental institutions and property relations of these societies.

This shift represented the speedy divorce of the Hungarian economics profession from the enchanting concept of *market socialism*. The lesson of the last 20 years of reform experiments in Hungary, its economists now concluded, was that the dominance of public – that is, state – ownership was fundamentally incompatible with market coordination.[2] And because there was no one in Hungary after 1989 who spoke with any credibility against market coordination, virtually every party and every economist argued favorably for privatization of state property as the necessary road to marketization.

But if there was widespread consensus among economists, politicians, and policy analysts about the necessity and desirability of privatization in principle, there was considerable disagreement about how best to carry out such a program. From early 1989 to May 1990, the privatization issue was fiercely debated in Hungary's scholarly literature, newspapers, business press, and popular media. This chapter seeks to clarify the main issues in that early debate.[3] Rather than summarizing the policy packages of different political parties or of particular economists, our aim is to distill the major analytic dimensions that structured and shaped that discursive field. We argue that the privatization debate can be analyzed along four independent dimensions:

- foreign versus domestic ownership;
- spontaneous privatization versus privatization controlled and directed by state agencies;
- institutional versus natural ownership; and
- concentrated versus dispersed ownership.

These four dimensions are not reducible to each other, that is, a position along one does not imply a particular position along another. Institutional ownership, for example, could be spontaneous or controlled, concentrated or dispersed.[4] A comprehensive delineation of the various permutations would thus yield a grid on which we could map the particular policy packages of various models of privatization. Our task here is not to locate competing actors (parties or persons) on such a map but to chart its principal axes and identify the major points of orientation.

To this end, the rhetoric of exposition in this chapter is dialogic. But this is not a dialogue between the analyst and the observed so much as between stylized interlocutors within the Hungarian debate itself.[5] That is, the logic of exposition in this chapter is to counterpose arguments along the various dimensions presenting, at one moment, the strongest case for a given position and, at the next, the strongest criticism from the countervailing position. The resulting dialogues between these stylized interlocutors constructed in the following sections read at times like heated conversations among actual participants, but it should be emphasized that our method here is not reportage or documentary. Instead, the positions are analytically constructed and the expository dialogue is a device to explore the central problems of privatization. By repeatedly taking alternative sides, we consider the merits of each position and thus portray the full perplexity of the dilemma and the rich complexity of the debate.

THE MAJOR DIMENSIONS OF THE PRIVATIZATION DEBATE

FOREIGN VERSUS DOMESTIC OWNERSHIP

As a small country with a relatively high percentage of its gross national product involved in foreign trade, Hungary has long been accustomed to strangers in its midst. But for the better part of the post-World War II period, foreign participation in channeling and directing resources came from the East in the form of trading agreements within the Council for Mutual Economic Assistance (CMEA/COMECON) that designated some part of the output of key industrial branches for ruble export. The détente of the late 1960s and early 1970s brought a different set of foreign participants as Hungarian authorities financed partial reforms – and later forestalled more radical reforms – with ever-increasing infusions of Western credits. The mounting hard currency debt triggered institutional arrangements for debt management: membership in the IMF and the World Bank. Yet, despite repeated campaigns of retrenchment to curb imports and stimulate exports, the balance of payments worsened and foreign debt roughly doubled during the 1980s. By the end of the decade, Hungary's $20 billion hard currency debt was one of the highest per capita foreign debts in the world. Whereas membership in international monetary institutions had signaled increased autonomy from Moscow at the outset, by the decade's close it marked increased dependence on Washington and Bonn.

It was in this context that the first shots in the privatization debate were fired – not by laissez-faire liberals of the opposition parties but by senior officials in the Ministries of Finance, Industry, and Commerce of the Communist government itself. On June 21, 1988, Károly Grósz remarked in a meeting to business leaders in San Francisco: "We would be very pleased if perhaps you would purchase some of our enterprises . . . even if they became 100 percent foreign owned." The new party secretary's comments echoed softly at first in Budapest, where economic researchers broached plans for debt – equity swaps in the Hungarian business press during the summer and early autumn of 1988.[6] But the real opening salvo came in a press conference on January 31, 1989, when the Minister of Industry mentioned a list of 51 Hungarian state enterprises marked for sale to foreign buyers. Within days, reporters were following the story of how Minister of Commerce Tamas Beck was traveling throughout Western Europe with this same list to look for buyers for enterprises constituting about one-quarter of Hungarian industrial production.[7] In the ensuing 18 months, hardly a handful of the firms on that list actually made it to the auction block, although in the same period numerous other Hungarian firms did find foreign buyers.

More important than the fate of those 51 enterprises (on a list that initial observers found highly arbitrary) was the debate on foreign ownership provoked by the awkward moves of the Grósz government.

Proponents of policies intended to yield a significant proportion of foreign ownership in a privatized Hungarian economy argued first that the hard currencies generated by the sale of state enterprises promised a sure means to begin reduction of the country's debilitating foreign debt. Such revenues could be used as immediate resources to avoid defaulting or rescheduling loan payments in the short run. More strategically, a sizable infusion of capital from the West was necessary to modernize Hungarian industry, for only then could it produce commodities at world market standards for hard currency exports to reduce the debt in the long run. Hypothetically, industrial modernization might be financed through more loans and more credits. But even if the favorable political climate inclined Western governments to support such measures, the available funds from commercial institutions (already worried about the size and composition of Hungary's debt) would not be sufficient for the enormous project of modernization (and, in any case, would come with strong strings attached).

Direct foreign investment, proponents argue, has the additional advantage of bringing benefits unobtainable through further loans and credits: Western firms bring new technologies, new products, access to advanced research and design, better marketing techniques, expanded access to Western markets, and modern managerial skills. Of course, Western managerial talent could (at least hypothetically) be employed by Hungarian firms with aggressive hiring practices, and new products and technologies could be acquired through licensing and leasing arrangements. But, proponents argue, such measures (attempted without significant payoffs in the recent past) are no substitute for the intense involvement in strategic decision making and day-to-day management that accompanies direct foreign investment. Technological and organizational modernization can best be achieved if Western firms have an equity stake in the profitability of their Hungarian properties. Finally, direct foreign investment has an additional effect: Over and above the immediate input of new managerial skills in foreign-owned firms and the consequent demonstration effects of this know-how to domestically owned firms, the market orientations of Western management (presumed to be cost-sensitive, competitive, and profit-oriented) will provide a much needed disciplining effect to reshape orientations in the period of transition to a real market economy.

Assuming for the moment that these benefits can be realized, why should Western firms find prospects in Hungarian acquisitions? Logically, the first and most obvious answer from proponents had to be that the selling price will be attractive. But (and now some of the criticisms) this raises the equally obvious question of how to determine the value of the assets to be sold. The typical answers from mainstream economists, that "the firm is worth whatever someone is willing to pay for it" or "let the market decide," are problematic where there is not yet a market – and where, in fact, the explicit motive for the sales is to *create a market*. Additional complications in determining worth arise from the fact that the accounting practices of Hungarian and Western firms differ. But even where these can be squared in technical terms, there remains the problem of which measure of worth to use. Should one look at the book value? If so, by calculating amortization or replacement costs? Alternatively, one might with considerable merit argue that a better measure of a firm's worth is its profitability, or its volume of sales, or projections of these under new management, and so on. The difficulty of determining a fair price leaves the agents who conclude these sales open to the charge of undervaluing the firm's assets and squandering the nation's resources. Such charges are especially likely when the agents and the general public are entirely unaccustomed to such transactions.[8]

Proponents of direct foreign ownership are not easily dissuaded by charges of undervaluation. Hungarian authorities can negotiate firmly, they maintain, because Western investors will be willing to pay a fair price for enterprises with real growth potential. Hungary's literate labor force, with training in science and mathematics relatively higher than in comparable developing countries, presents one of the major attractions, especially because it can be employed at wage levels lower than those in South Korea and Taiwan. For American and Japanese investors, moreover, as the GE–Tungsram deal and the Suzuki venture illustrate, Hungary provides a convenient platform for export to Western Europe. And because the domestic needs are so obvious and the benefits so promising, direct foreign investment should be actively courted with liberal tax holidays (five years when the foreign partner brings considerable new capitalization). In turn, critics with more nationalist pride than global perspective bridle at the comparison to developing countries. The more realistic among them question whether Hungarian-made products will enjoy favorable tariff access to West European markets and observe that officials at the World Bank have voiced concern that tax holiday incentives may be excessively generous under terms in which the lower limit of considerable new capitalization to qualify for the five-year holiday is set at only several hundred thousand dollars.

Whether the deals were fair or the incentives too liberal, Hungary was relatively successful in attracting new foreign investment. According to estimates of the Hungarian National Bank, in 1989 (under the Grósz regime and the later caretaker government of Miklós Németh), direct foreign investment in Hungary totaled approximately $300 million compared to a cumulative total of only $200 million in the previous decade. But we should emphasize that the yardstick here is past performance rather than absolute standards, as the volume was doubtless less than proponents desired and more than detractors feared. The most vocal opponents of direct foreign investment raised two fears above all others: Foreign ownership would lead to widespread unemployment and the surrender of national economic sovereignty. Defenders of foreign ownership conceded that layoffs were indeed the first step that could be anticipated with new management. But they maintained that although the proximate timing of unemployment might be determined by the change in property relations, its inevitability and eventual overall level would not be the product of new market forces so much as the grim legacy of the old state-socialist economy, which had wastefully kept workers in outdated, inefficient, and unprofitable enterprises. As for national economic sovereignty, the choice was not between state socialism, which had protected economic independence, and a new capitalist or hybrid economy, which would sacrifice it. The sacrifice of independence had already been made by the previous regime, and society was already paying the cost: Four-fifths of the country's hard-earned convertible currency profits were going annually to pay the interest on the accumulated debt. If it was not to slip into economic oblivion, Hungary must fully enter the world capitalist economy. But such an entry at this moment necessarily implied constraints; would they be imposed by foreign creditors or by foreign investors? Proponents of foreign ownership regarded the latter as preferable: Better to be constrained by foreigners with a direct ownership stake in the performance, efficiency, and profitability of Hungarian firms.

The most articulate critics of the first phase of privatization to foreign owners took these arguments into account but questioned whether the presumed benefits were actually forthcoming. First, the use of such revenues to reduce foreign debt and counter the state's budget deficit, for example, seemed dubious in the initial phase, when the proceeds of privatization were retained by the firm itself. Second, the supposed benefits of new management seemed equally elusive under circumstances in which the enterprise elite of the old order was using the measures of privatization to retain managerial positions in the restructured firms. Third, critics questioned whether the haphazard pattern of foreign sales reflected any coherent policy strategy. In particular, foreign ownership might be part of a strategy to curb the inordinate power of monopolistic firms in any number of industrial branches; yet there was little indication that sales were motivated by this intent or that they would have this effect. In general terms, because almost all participants in the debate agreed that some significant level of direct foreign ownership was desirable, disagreements centered on the timing, pace, patterns, and forms of privatization. It is to these issues that we turn.

SPONTANEOUS PRIVATIZATION VERSUS PRIVATIZATION CONTROLLED AND DIRECTED BY STATE AGENCIES

If the desperate search for convertible currency by the incumbent Communist government triggered the debate about direct foreign investment, the search for career stability by incumbent enterprise directors stimulated the debate over *spontaneous* versus *controlled* privatization. To understand the conditions in which enterprise directors began to move unilaterally, we must briefly describe how the political vacuum of mid-1989 was not a legal vacuum and how the negotiated transformation of political power was not a negotiated transformation of economic power.

If the virtual exclusion of any organizations other than political parties was one precondition (and the distinguishing feature) of the Hungarian Round Table negotiations, another was the agreement at the outset that the existing parliament, chosen (one hesitates to use the term *elected*) under entirely different circumstances, should pass no legislation that would prevent the subsequent, newly elected parliament from carrying out its mandate. The immediate objective of this preliminary agreement was to prevent the existing parliament from adopting any measures that might outflank or deflect the *political* agreements struck at the Round Table, but the restriction held in principle for *economic* questions as well. Thus, from the outset of the negotiations until the convening of the new legislature in May 1990, parliament was not simply passive but seemingly handcuffed. Nor could other branches of government act with any greater capacity: The Communist Party's claim to represent the interests of stability and national sovereignty was shattered when subsequent events throughout Eastern Europe in the autumn of 1989 demonstrated that this final "historic mission" had been relegated to history. The state-socialist economy, criticized for decades as too tightly controlled by the state, now found itself in a situation where the already fuzzy lines of control were spinning from ambiguity to near dissolution. In such circumstances, enterprise directors, as the most powerful agents in that economy, could act with unparalleled independence. Their most decisive actions were in the new arena of privatization.

These remarks should not imply that the Hungarian economy was out of control. The caretaker government of Miklós Németh succeeded in gaining some degree of legitimate authority by asserting increased independence from the flailing renamed Socialist Party, with heightened appeals for a technocratic managerial style. Nor do these remarks imply that enterprise directors acted illegally. It was not necessary for them to entice the existing parliament to pass new laws because the combination of two disparate and unrelated pieces of existing legislation gave them ample room for maneuver. These two laws formed the legal basis for spontaneous privatization.

The first piece of legislation, innocent in itself, was the 1984 Law on Enterprise Councils. This act had formally transferred some ownership functions from ministries to the newly created Enterprise Councils. Appropriately named, these bodies bore no resemblance to authentic Workers' Councils: With half of their membership appointed by management, they were thoroughly controlled by enterprise directors. No serious scholarly study of the Enterprise Councils indicated that this law had made any difference in the actual management of firms or in the overall operation of the economy. Indeed, it had not – until it was combined with the second piece of legislation, the Law on Business Associations, enacted January 1, 1989. This legislation included provisions for establishing joint stock companies and limited liability corporations. Unlike the later Law on Transformation of May 1989, the Law on Business Associations did not anticipate and made no provisions for the actual transformation of state enterprises into privately held corporations. But it contained one important clause that allowed state enterprises to found shareholding corporations and limited liability companies. This clause provided the critical legal vehicle for spontaneous privatization of state enterprises.

The basic steps in the process are as follows. First, the Enterprise Council, exercising its ownership function in the state enterprise, creates one or more of the new property forms. These new companies issue share capital and then proceed to exchange these shares for the assets (land, buildings, equipment, etc.) of the state enterprise. The state enterprise now holds shares, to be sure, but it has been stripped of its actual assets, which have become the property of its own creations – the new limited liability companies. In a further twist, the new companies next issue bonds (at fixed returns) that are purchased by the original state enterprise *with the shares* that the state enterprise had acquired in exchange for its assets. In the pure case, the state enterprise has become a virtual shell: It holds bonds, *but the assets and the shares* are now held by the newly established venture(s). These shares can then be sold to other Hungarian firms, to foreign corporations, or to private persons.

Such schemes obviously provide considerable opportunity for abuse, especially because the original owner, with the authority to decide on the terms of the various transactions just outlined, is the Enterprise Council. What's going on, critics charge, is that senior management – who report to no board of directors, or trustees, or stockholders, but only to the Enterprise Council, which is in their pocket – *are able to choose their own owners*. Sometimes they choose foreign owners on terms favorable to the buyer, permitting them to maintain their current positions or to gain controlling interests in a profitable venture carved out of the original state enterprise. The difficulty of evaluating the assets of the firm gives enterprise managers considerable room for maneuver in negotiating such contracts and provides some immunization against the charge of squandering resources. In other cases, they choose *themselves* as the new owners. Take the process just outlined. Add a new first step in which the Enterprise Council votes large bonuses for senior management. Include in the final step that directors use the bonuses to buy shares in the new corporations or limited liability firms. Moreover, in addition to enterprise management, the elite from the party-state apparatus are also taking advantage of the transformation process. In these *nomenklatura buyouts*, apparatchiks with no prior industrial experience or expertise in production or marketing are bailing out into quite profitable ventures. As Hungarian workers told us, "instead of *peristroikists* we find *parachutists* holding shares in our new units." Spontaneous privatization is thus a process whereby political capital is converted into economic capital.[9] Critics contend that it is a way for the old oligarchy – the apparatus and its managerial functionaries – to salvage its power.

Opponents of spontaneous privatization advocate the creation and strengthening of central agencies to manage and coordinate the transformation of state property. Pointing to abuses of decentralized ownership claims by Enterprise Councils on behalf of enterprise management, they argue for the recentralization of the ownership function in the disposition of property. If privatization is not brought under public control, they maintain, its consequences will be merely for private gain and not the public good. Thus, the search for a more rationally directed process of transformation reaches a curious conclusion: In order to denationalize property, it is first necessary to renationalize it.

Throughout the latter part of 1989, much of the public and professional debate about privatization centered on the organizational features of various proposals to establish an agency responsible for overseeing the transformation process. With the public incensed about the most well-publicized cases of pilfering of national resources, with courts refusing to register some of the most shady deals, and with the major opposition parties on record against uncontrolled privatization (although some more vigorously than others), the lame-duck parliament finally asserted itself and produced the Law for Defense of State Property in January 1990. This legislation outlined a set of high-sounding objectives, but the government still lacked an organizational instrument to put its policies into effect. Throughout this entire period, the office of the State Commissioner on Privatization issued guidelines and directives, but cases were decided on an ad hoc basis and, not uncommonly, reversed by some other body claiming jurisdiction. The maze of contradictory regulations meant that conforming to the relevant legal codes in a particular case was an uncertain process at best.

A State Property Agency was finally established in March 1990 with full responsibility for coordinating privatization. But the appointment of its permanent director, the composition of its staff, and the delineation of its real political mandate had to wait until the results of the run-off elections in early April and the formation of a new government. In general terms, the principal task of the agency is to exercise prepurchase rights over state enterprises to be organized into corporations. Before any sale, the agency must approve a transformation plan prepared by the enterprise, including the percentage of revenues (or value of land) that goes to local governments and the percentage of discounted shares issued to enterprise employees.

For our purposes here, the detailed features of the new property agency are less interesting than the general debate about the role of central authorities in coordinating and controlling the process of transformation. For their part, enterprise managers and some economists who are critical of centralized control argue that the new state agencies are just new bureaucratic organizations. Why should we assume that they will manage social property any better than the old ministries? At best, these agencies spring from budget hunger; at worst, as an organizational imperative, they would start to accumulate property. Speaking derisively of a "ministry of ownership," the critics contend that the old central authorities, faced with the prospects of empty ministries, have found in bodies like a national trust fund the means to salvage their power.

Proponents of centrally directed privatization respond that the new asset agency will be accountable to a new, democratically elected parliament. Its task will not be to accumulate property but to dispose of it. If spontaneous privatization is not slowed down, there will be no property left for the new state to transform in a rational manner.

The proponents of spontaneity: Slow down? The current pace is not fast enough. A rapid transition is urgent. If we have to wait for new institutional controls and for the new parliament to act this year, and then again the next year, and so on, it will be too late. *Radical pragmatists* within the camp of spontaneity assert: What if there is some squandering? It is a small price to pay for the transition to a more efficient system. Put it on the bill as one more, but the final, cost of 40 years of Communist misrule. What does it matter if the former managerial elite become the new owners? What matters is not the person but the role and the criteria for making decisions. Any real, profit-maximizing owner is better than no owner at all. And the sooner the economy's resources are managed according to such criteria, the sooner tax revenues, wages, and national wealth will increase.

Those favoring controlled privatization counter that squandering does matter. The revenues from privatization are a one-time event. This opportunity for reducing deficits and repaying debt will not be repeated, and so these revenues must be maximized. It is true that timing matters: Hasty measures to bring too many firms onto the auction block all at once will drive down selling prices.

Advocates of spontaneity accuse the proponents of central controls over the "maximizing" scenario of wanting to have their cake and eat it too. It is impossible simultaneously to maximize the selling prices of state enterprises, long-term efficiency, cost reduction, antimonopoly practices, access to foreign markets, maintenance of full employment, and so on. We can only optimize, and the most optimistic policy is the one that gets the economy moving quickly from publicly owned redistribution to privately owned market coordination. The centralizers are moralistic and shortsighted. In the name of national interests they focus on short-term revenues. And in so doing, they hinder the private initiatives that hold the only promise for long-term prosperity. Of course privatization will involve private gain – for if enterprise did not go into private hands there would be no transformation, and if privatization did not promise gain, then who would buy them? We must make a break with the old ideologies in which collective interests smothered private interests to the detriment of any rational economic interests. It is the pursuit of private gain that will bring public benefits. Proponents of these unnecessarily restrictive central controls should cut out the demagoguery and simply admit that they oppose privatization.

Advocates of centralized coordination respond emphatically that their opposition to spontaneous privatization is not opposition to private enrichment per se but outrage at such enrichment based on the private appropriation of public property through insider deals at less than a fair price. By giving insiders a distinct head start in the race for state assets, they contend, spontaneous privatization discriminates against entrepreneurs who are equally or perhaps even more worthy to manage these resources. When the rules of the game are written by those already in positions of economic power, they will privilege only a limited set of interests. Only by equalizing opportunity (or at least by eliminating the opportunities for insider dealing) can there be any assurance that the economy's resources will be managed by the most capable. State regulation in the process of transformation is not antithetical to the market but is necessary for the transition to it. Slower, more deliberate, and controlled privatization will improve the chances that the state's former assets will be managed by those who can prove their abilities in the newly emerging market institutions rather than by those who demonstrated that they could climb to the top in the old institutions of the state socialist economy. Such will be the more certain path to prosperity in the long run.[10] Thus, critics charge that it is the shortsighted perspective of the advocates of spontaneity that makes them oppose the principles of a liberal market.

With the passage of the Law for Defense of State Property and the establishment of the State Property Agency, it might seem that the dimension of spontaneous versus controlled privatization would be of only historical interest because the centralizers seem to have won the battle. But there remained numerous avenues for evading central controls. To take only one example, enterprises are obliged to file transformation plans with the new agency only when the value of the contract exceeds 30 million forints. The creation of a medium-sized to large limited liability company is usually safely under this minimum and therefore falls outside the agency's jurisdiction. Technically, an enterprise could sequentially form several (perhaps even a dozen) satellite companies without interference by the central authority. Such a maneuver would not only evade constraints from the top but would also avoid potential conflicts from the bottom: Workers in the newly created company are not protected by collective contracts negotiated by unions with the state enterprise, and the units are not governed by Enterprise Councils. Whereas Enterprise Councils were the marionettes of management in the earlier period (when no independent political or trade union organizations existed at the workplace), in the new political setting they might become a source of uncertainty for senior management.

The debate about spontaneous versus controlled privatization, moreover, still continues over the operational meaning of the term *control*. Control can refer to direct coordination, but it can also imply the much less directive processes of post hoc oversight and monitoring. In light of current public opinion, policy makers who advocate spontaneity will go on record as supporting "control" – in the hope that it will be of the latter variety. In the best of worlds, they could have their preferred strategy *and* the patina of legitimacy. Such an outcome is not unlikely if the directors and staff of the regulating agency are drawn from the ranks of the regulated (not uncommon in regulated industries in the West) or if the career trajectories of this same staff carry them up to the boards of directors of the companies whose transactions they currently approve (not uncommon in our own military–industrial complex). If so, privatization would be monitored, but the transformation process would be only slightly more controlled and slightly less rapid than in the first wave of privatization. The danger, as we shall see in the following section, is that the kind of economic system that may arise from such privatization would not only have the old oligarchy at its helm but may well have more in common with the old shortage, soft-budget, constrained economy than with dynamic market economies. That is, the fastest privatization might actually not be the road to a real functioning market but a costly detour.

INSTITUTIONAL VERSUS NATURAL OWNERS

Given the ratio of public assets to private savings (most estimates are that private domestic savings, even with credit, could buy only about 10% of current state assets), and given the weight of convertible currency foreign debt, rapid sales of state enterprises would tend to favor foreign buyouts. As for domestic ownership, rapid privatization would tend to yield patterns of *institutional ownership* of two broad types: (1) endowments of nonprofit institutions such as hospitals, educational institutions, and foundations and (2) intercorporate holdings in which banks, insurance companies, and industrial enterprises hold shares in other Hungarian corporations.

In the first type of institutional ownership, nonprofit institutions receive endowments in the form of shares issued by former state enterprises. That is, the Hungarian state would designate hospitals, foundations, educational institutions, organizations conducting medical or other basic research, and similar institutions as (substantial) holders of newly privatized firms. Proposals range from a master plan to achieve property transformation by means of endowments granted by the privatization agency to more gradual approaches in which enterprises would be encouraged (perhaps in cooperation with local and provincial governments) to include nonprofit institutions in the transformation plans they submit to the State Property Agency. In either case, nonprofit institutions that had formerly received virtually all of their revenues from the state budget would now look to the dividends from their shareholdings in Hungarian firms to finance part (or perhaps all) of their operations.

Endowing nonprofit institutions promises to accomplish the core objectives of privatization: It creates knowledgeable stockholders independent of enterprise management who have a direct interest in the long-term profitability of their holdings. To the extent that their revenues from the state budget are reduced in proportion to anticipated portfolio earnings, endowed institutions have a pressing stake in increasing the value of their shares. Unwilling and unable to tolerate poor performance, they will use their voting rights as shareholders to remove incompetent managers or sell those stocks for shares in firms with more promising returns on investment. Curiously, nonprofit institutions in the public welfare sector become the organizational means to secure profits from enterprises in the industrial sector. Institutional investment carries an additional advantage because the smaller number of investors, relative to millions of individual shareholders with employee stock ownership schemes or universal citizen grants (discussed in the next section), create a more manageable stock exchange during the turbulent transition period. Moreover, privatization through nonprofit endowments is a potential solution to the problems of legitimation discussed in the previous section. Endowments create economic actors with a private interest in profitability, but the recipients of those profits are institutions that provide public goods and services. By expanding the range of beneficiaries of privatization, endowments thus increase the political support for the overall process of transforming property relations.

In principle, endowments could encompass a very sizable proportion of the privatized assets in the Hungarian economy. But a number of serious objections are raised by opponents of institutional ownership that should be considered. First, where are the financial planners with experience in portfolio management? The greater the number of endowed institutions, the greater the need for persons with these skills. Second, where are the organizational routines – the complex incentive schemes that evolved over decades to deal with principal–agent problems in the relationship between endowed institutions and professional property managers? These professionals and these routines can, of course, be produced over time, but the problem is that they are needed now, in the transition period.

More important, public institutions (like state industrial enterprises) in redistributive socialism are accustomed to reading the bureaucratic signals of budgetary infighting rather than the market signals of the stock exchange. Transplanting institutional arrangements that work relatively smoothly in market economies may not be the means to achieve functioning market institutions during the transition.[11] In particular, a successful transition to endowments requires striking a delicate balance in weaning nonprofit institutions from the state budget: Too abrupt, and they will be forced to make high-risk investments in the hope of immediate returns; too slow, and they will remain tied to the purse strings of the state, paying too little attention to the performance of the shares in their portfolios. The current crisis of the Hungarian state budget inclines the seesaw in the former direction. Decision makers will find it hard to resist the opportunity to achieve two policy objectives with a single program – privatization and deficit reduction. As a consequence, the leaders of newly endowed nonprofit institutions are likely to find that their resources through the old budgetary lines have been cut much more drastically than the earnings from their new shareholdings can make up. This poses the probable danger that nonprofits will invest in risky stocks that promise short-term payoffs to cover the sudden reduction of revenues from the state budget. Moreover, even if they were to choose a more cautious investment strategy, the primitive state of the stock market and the lack of any track record of a corporation's shares make it all but impossible to identify blue-chip stocks with proven performance. This increases the likelihood (already high due to the paucity of professional skills and the pressure for short-term gains) that a considerable number of the endowed nonprofits will suffer serious losses on the stock market rather than enjoy a stable increase in their revenues. These institutions will revert to polished skills of budgetary pleading; and local, provincial, and national government officials will face the difficult choice of bailing them out or closing hospitals and educational institutions.

An equally likely scenario is that a given nonprofit institution, faced with choices in investing its endowment, will put it all into one (or only a few) corporations. Such an investment strategy would raise goose bumps on a seasoned portfolio manager, but the decision might not be irrational in the current Hungarian setting. Given the general lack of knowledge of the stock exchange and the necessarily poor information about corporate performance under the new economic conditions, it is entirely likely that a given hospital, for example, will invest in a prominent local firm where the hospital's board of directors are acquainted with enterprise management. (That the newly endowed hospital will choose its trustees from among local notables with some economic experience only increases the likelihood of this strategy.) At first glance, the choice of tying a major part of one's operating budget to the success or failure of a single venture appears extraordinarily risky. But if almost any investment at this point in time is objectively risky, why not venture with a known and proximate entity? If the enterprise is in danger of failing, then all the better that the trustees of the endowment can walk arm in arm with representatives of enterprise management and the enterprise union to threaten simultaneous plant closings and hospital closings in requesting subsidies from local or provincial politicians and state officials. Such are the basic ingredients for reproducing soft-budget constraints in the transition to a market economy.

The second type of institutional ownership – intercorporate ownership – is found when Hungarian firms (banks or insurance companies, for example) buy shares issued by other state enterprises in the process of transformation. Formulated earlier in the 1980s,[12] the initial concept of institutional ownership was that a relatively small number of banks (or other holding institutions), independent of the state and in competition with each other, would have a greater interest in the profitability of their holdings than the currently responsible ministries. As owners, they would have a real stake in imposing tougher performance criteria. Long popular in an influential circle of economists, the concept of institutional ownership has been realized only in the most recent period. Its rapid evolution has now undergone a twist – in the form of *institutional cross-ownership* as companies purchase or exchange shares with each other.[13] Your company issues shares, mine issues shares; we buy each other's, plus those of a third, and we appoint each other (along with representatives of the commercial bank that lends credit and owns shares) to the boards of directors of the newly transformed enterprises. The results, critics argue, is not the shift from plan to market but a shift from plan to clan.

Opposition to such institutional ownership is based on the following argument: The problem with the old system was not merely that it lacked owners and markets but also that its organizational structure of industrial concentration gave the huge enterprises monopoly positions. Institutional ownership will not change that organizational structure. If anything, cross-ownership and interlocking directorates will produce even more powerful megaorganizations. Banks that issue credit *and* own shares, moreover, will be all the more encouraged to assist these firms in lobbying for subsidies, favorable import licenses, and lenient regulations.

The problem with the old system, moreover, was not that it didn't have incentives or that it didn't involve risks, but that the objective incentives were all there *to take risks with other people's money*. Institutional ownership will not change that structure of incentives and risks: The impersonality of state ownership is simply replaced by ownership that is private in name only because it is equally impersonal. The solution to the problem of monopolistic power is to break up the large firms and sell the leaner pieces to genuine entrepreneurs. The problem of incentives and risks can be solved only when state property is in the hands of *natural owners* – individuals or partners who risk losing their personal property if the venture fails.[14]

On both counts, the preferred solution involves strengthening and expanding the existing private sector that had slowly emerged in the previous fifteen years in the shadow of the central plan. At present, advocates concede, production in typical units of this *second economy* is necessarily small in scale, and although some private entrepreneurs have adopted technology, the overwhelming majority have been so hampered by the absence of credit and by state-imposed limits on capital accumulation that their equipment and techniques are outdated. Nonetheless, by their proven inclination to take real risks and by their demonstrated ability to take advantage of every market opportunity, these energetic entrepreneurs are the best candidates for the more ambitious tasks of managing the economy's resources. To release this energy, the first state policy in the new era of transformation must be massive deregulation – the elimination of all administrative codes that artificially restrict the growth of this potentially dynamic and truly private sector.

Critics of such proposals, with a mixture of condescension and impatience, inquire: "This is all well and good for restaurants, car repair shops, and urban boutiques. But what about the large industrial enterprises?" Proponents of natural ownership respond without hesitation that their proposals definitely apply to manufacturing as well as services. Because they believe that transferring industrial assets to natural owners will be a lengthy process, their proposals contain a second plank to deal with large state enterprises that will remain for some time under public ownership: Corresponding to deregulation of the private sector, they advocate *reregulation* of the state sector. *Liberalization,* the relaxing of controls on public enterprises, continues to suffer from the illusion of market socialism that markets can be simulated either through state policies or through institutional ownership. Until real market coordination exists, liberalized measures that give enterprise management more room in setting prices and wages will only lead to "shortage-flation" – the worst combination of shortage (under soft-budget constraints) *and* inflation. Instead, under the stricter controls of reregulation, managers of state enterprises (who are still risking the citizens' money) will be made more accountable to the democratically elected government responsible for guiding the economy in the transition.

Deregulation and reregulation must furthermore be combined with additional measures to promote the transfer of economic resources to genuine entrepreneurs. With reference to the January 1989 Law on Business Associations, which prohibited administrative codes that discriminate against one or another form of property, advocates of natural ownership argue that policies regarding taxation, credit, and the sale of state assets should not be *property neutral*. That is, it is not enough for the state to be committed in principle to equal opportunity, for such abstractions only hide the underlying reality that the powerful stand in privileged positions. To promote a real private sector, private entrepreneurs must be treated preferentially: They should receive credit on more favorable terms, face lower taxation, and stand first in line for contracts to manage the smaller, disassembled parts of former state enterprises.

Puzzled advocates of institutional ownership inquire: Do we want the model for a new economy to be based on the capitalism of the nineteenth century? First, look at many West European economies and you will find a predominance of institutional ownership. It has not blocked their development. Second, of course we have interlocking directorates. How else can we create a stable set of intertwined financial and industrial institutions capable of surviving in a rapacious world economy? As for your pejorative label, *clans* were a feature of the old system in which the elite of the party apparatus and the economy worked hand in glove. It was planning and clanning that went together; our ties are based on business logic, not on the bonds of party loyalty. On second thought, perhaps the clanlike attribution is not so mistaken — provided that it refers not to some Southern European mafia but to the cohesive networks of trust, cross-ownership, and stable subcontracting that made possible the Japanese miracle. In the modern world economy, the strategic choice is not between clans *or* markets but of clans *for* markets.

Advocates of natural ownership respond: Your insights about institutional ownership in Western Europe are valid but inapplicable to the problems at hand. In the typical economy of Western Europe, a sizable proportion of the production comes from units with fewer than 100 employees, and the habits of calculation throughout the economy come from a deeply ingrained market logic. In Hungary, by contrast, 90% of the economy's assets are state owned, and habits and routines that have become second nature were shaped for four decades under the logic of soft-budget constraints. To transform that economy, it is not enough to select new institutions; new habits must be cultivated as well. Because these cannot be created from above, we must start from where they are already manifested — in the existing second economy, where habits of risking one's shirt, of thrift and industriousness, are commonplace.

You were right, they continue, to note that clans were a key feature of the old regime, but it is exactly the similarity in patterns of the old and new networks that we see as hindering market development. These clan networks, combined with deeply ingrained habits shaped by soft-budget constraints, cause us to fear that under conditions of institutional ownership, firms will continue to look to the state for subsidies, and that their inordinate size will give them the means to blackmail the new state in the foreseeably long period of economic difficulties to come. It is for this same reason that your Japanese analogy is inappropriate. Rapid institutional privatization might create a twentieth-century form all right, but one not prepared for the flexibility that will be required in the twenty-first century. Rather than emulating Japan (entirely improbable in any case, given the vast differences in wealth, technology, and position in the world economy), we would do better to look to Italy, where smaller-scale production responds flexibly to rapidly fluctuating markets. Slower privatization might yield leaner firms with real entrepreneurial, innovative character, more capable of such flexible adjustment.

The institutionalists: All this talk about "natural owners" is just so much romanticism about the petite bourgeoisie. You might see habits of thrift and industriousness in the existing second economy, but one could equally point to its habits of corruption, of tax evasion, and of extracting monopoly rents in totally artificial market conditions reproduced by the absurdities of state socialism. Propose deregulation if you like, but the habits of your pseudoentrepreneurs will incline them to erect new barriers to entry rather than fostering real competition. In any case, your nineteenth-century virtues might have been appropriate for that century but not for the leap to the advanced technological society of the computer age. We Hungarians live in the modern world. Our managers are sophisticated business professionals who travel in international circles. We can't afford to wait for the development of our own middle class, for there is no need to reproduce the road to capitalist development step by agonizingly slow step.

"But that is what we must do" respond the advocates of natural owners, and they continue: Those who talk about magnificent leaps into the future should think twice before accusing others of romanticism. We have heard the phrases *bold experiments* and *leaping over stages of history* before – during the late 1940s and 1950s from visionaries with no less confidence than your own. But see how our economy has suffered from those sweeping gestures! Society is not prepared to be the dutiful subject of another experimental leap. The failure of Leninism was that it posited abstract historic interests and tied them to a class. But because that class, the proletariat, did not yet exist in the countries of the East, the state had to create it while the party ruled in the name of those abstract interests. We should not repeat that mistake by positing an abstract interest in private ownership before a sizable propertied bourgeoisie really exists in our society. A propertied middle class is not some test-tube baby that can be artificially created. At best we can adopt policies that encourage healthy growth or, alternatively, as with your plans of pseudoprivatization, we can choose policies that will stunt it. But the road to a market economy will be traveled by a propertied middle class or it will not be traveled at all.

CONCENTRATED VERSUS DISPERSED OWNERSHIP

At first glance, this final dimension of the privatization debate appears simply derivative of the three dimensions discussed earlier. Although it is difficult to find any participants in the debate who advocate concentrated ownership per se, the predominance of foreign and/or certain patterns of institutional ownership would suggest more rather than less concentration in proprietary relations. Similarly, those who give high priority to a speedy transition are inclined to opt for more concentrated ownership under conditions where the private savings of the population are inadequate to purchase more than a small fraction of the assets of the large state enterprises. We shall see later in this section, however, that there is an alternative position·in the debate that holds that the greatest dispersion of ownership in the initial phase of privatization could actually be the most rapid means to achieve the goal of marketization. We shall also see that at least one variant of institutional ownership, employee stock ownership, is congruent with dispersed rather than concentrated shareholding.

Although the Law on Business Associations that took effect on January 1, 1989, did not explicitly justify concentrated ownership, it had the practical effect of promoting concentrated rather than dispersed wealth in the Hungarian economy. In the first place, the new legislation establishing joint stock companies set the minimum price of a share in such ventures at 1 million forints. This stipulation, of course, was compatible with predominantly institutional ownership and could be seen as dictated by ideological considerations at a time when the party-state was still uncomfortable with ownership by private persons. But although few individuals or families had the resources (whether as cash reserves or collateral) to make such investments, not all were excluded. The tendency to encourage private accumulation within a narrow stratum was accelerated, moreover, by a second administrative measure: Hungary's new personal income tax code allowed families to exempt part of their income from taxation when they participated in the new joint stock companies. To benefit from this particular investment tax credit, however, a family had to be able to afford the 1 million forint minimum *and* have a yearly income high enough to make the exemption meaningful. The combination of the two measures meant, in fact, that the estimated 6,000 families who qualified on both counts would be able to reinvest almost without cost, as the credit/exemption in one tax year would provide the means for the purchase of additional shares the next year, thus qualifying the family for further tax credits, and so on.[15] Because the language of tax loopholes confronted no linguistic barrier at the Hungarian frontier, the rich could get richer there, too.

The advocates of dispersed ownership are not opposed to investment credits and tax exemptions, but they argue that these are going to the wrong units. Rather than offering tax shelters to the domestic elite and luring foreign investors with promises of easily repatriated profits, this position proposes tax holidays and more liberal credit to those Hungarians who have already demonstrated a practical interest in private ventures – the sizable proportion of the population actively participating in the second economy.

In contrast to a development strategy based on the prosperity of the 2,000 or perhaps (more generously) 20,000 wealthiest families, this strategy links the prosperity of the economy to the viability of capital accumulation among some 2 million families who have already invested time and resources in small-scale, often part-time private production in agriculture, services, and industry. Ivan Szelenyi is among those who have argued that such a policy of dispersed ownership is not simply justified on moral grounds but makes good economic sense.[16] Emulation of the South Korean or Taiwanese model of mass production based on cheap labor would not only sacrifice national economic sovereignty but would actually ignore the opportunity to capitalize on those areas where the Hungarian economy has some potential for achieving a comparative advantage, namely, in labor-intensive products (especially, but not limited to, high-quality foodstuffs). This image of a *garden Hungary*, or Hungarian craft production, builds on the skills and ingenuity already displayed in Hungary's second economy. To be successful it would require, at the very least, that current second economy producers shift from their present part-time, income-maximizing orientation utilizing household labor to a full-time, capital-accumulating orientation employing wage labor. Szelenyi contends that his field observations and survey research among Hungary's rural entrepreneurs provide evidence that the energy, ambition, and capacity for such a shift do exist and could be realized provided that long-standing restrictions on small-scale production are lifted, credits liberalized, and taxes reduced. His fear is that policies in the latter part of 1989 and early 1990 were moving exactly opposite to the desired direction and that, if these continue, they will strangle the million geese that could lay small but nonetheless golden eggs.

As just outlined, a strategy for development based on the transformation of the existing second economy into a legitimate, dynamic, entrepreneurial private sector leaves aside the question of the transformation of the large state enterprises. Indeed, some might argue that positions similar to Szelenyi's are outside the boundaries of the privatization debate because their primary emphasis is not on the disposition of assets currently held by the state.[17] Such a criticism stands behind an alternative conception of dispersed ownership that aims to expand the beneficiaries of participation in private ownership *within the sphere of the large, formerly state enterprises* without necessarily expanding the circle of entrepreneurs outside it. In Hungary, as in Poland, the main organizational vehicle for widening such participation has been the proposal for employee share ownership.

Proponents of employee stock ownership programs (ESOPs)[18] argue that the obvious alternative to nomenklatura buyouts is employee buyouts: Workers' investments of skill and energy in their firms give them rightful claims to equity in these same companies, and they should be eligible to purchase such shares at discounted rates. Addressing the problem of limited savings among the general population, ESOP advocates propose that the government should encourage (and subsidize if necessary) lending institutions to provide financing for these employee buyouts at favorable interest rates with delayed repayment schedules. These loans would be repaid from future dividends, and soon enough, employee shareholders with a direct interest in the value of their holdings would come to see the connection between performance, profitability, and the economic viability of the firm in which they hold a stake. This interest in profitability would stimulate performance both directly at individual workplaces and indirectly through the institutions of shareholder councils in which employees would monitor managerial performance and promote a more efficient participatory organization of work. Proponents of ESOP schemes emphatically stress that employee buyouts should not be restricted to failing firms. They further argue that not all plants targeted for closing under industrial restructuring are economically unviable, and that the performance gains foreseeable under ESOP management might yet demonstrate that viability. Moreover, because employees would have a stake in long-term profitability, they would have an interest in converting facilities to new product lines in order to keep their jobs at the same enterprise, even if this meant that their production would then be in a different, but perhaps related, industrial branch. Thus, in addition to equity issues and the stimulation of performance, dispersed employee share ownership would reduce the currently anticipated high level of unemployment in the immediate transition period and provide a way for employees to retain their workplaces in the long run.

Detractors of the ESOP alternative are quick to suggest the free-rider problems inherent in the hypothesized connection between employee shareholding and worker performance. Why should any worker in a firm of several thousand employees believe that the value of his or her shares will increase because of his or her own improved performance? In fact, if that value might increase even if one slacks off, doesn't this encourage one to coast while hoping that others will work harder? ESOP advocates, in turn, point to the existence and even growth of employee shareholdings in large enterprises in Western economies, contending that improved performance will come from better work organization due to management's accountability to worker-owners rather than from the individual psychology of game theory. The detractors counter that organizational studies of ESOPs in the United States and elsewhere indicate that the relationship between employee ownership and enterprise performance is ambiguous at best,[19] that the recent growth of ESOPs may be as much attributable to managerial strategies to avoid hostile takeovers as to any profitability gains, and that there is no shortage of evidence from Japan or West Germany that better work organization and close cooperation between workers and managers are possible without employee ownership. For these and other reasons, economists such as János Kornai and Márton Tardos, while not dismissing employee ownership entirely, have limited their endorsement to smaller firms, especially in crafts (as in the famous Herend china factory), where human capital is dominant in the production process.

But the strongest criticisms of ESOPs in the Hungarian context are directed at those elements of employee shareholding that are perceived by economists to slow down the desired consequence of privatization, namely, marketization. Employee ownership, they argue, will limit the mobility of capital and retard the emergence of a real labor market. Further, it will delay industrial restructuring. Together with the enormous foreign debt (which employee buyouts will not reduce), the other catastrophic legacy of centralized mismanagement is the multitude of technologically obsolescent factories incapable of competing in domestic markets, much less meeting international standards. Is it in the national interest, or in anyone's interest, to continue to produce steel (or similar products) when it is vastly cheaper to purchase it abroad? The continued operation of aging plants and equipment will only place a further burden on an already sagging economy; delays in industrial restructuring today will only prolong and perhaps exacerbate the agony tomorrow.

ESOP advocates respond that such macroeconomic policy making ignores the human factor. The human material of the production process, workers, are not commodities that can be displaced from their communities and shunted from one worksite to another. With their roots in particular locales and their investments in particular firms, workers have a right to remain in their given workplaces – a right that should be defended. Employee ownership provides a means to do this. Industrial restructuring will proceed apace because workers who have an interest in the value of their shares will have every incentive to make rational choices about company changes.

The detractors counter that it is the well-intentioned illusions of employee shareholding that ignore the human factor. Workers will not have an interest in the value of their shares (a fraction of their total earnings) so much as in the value of their skills and compensation for their labor. Institutions that delay the creation of a free labor market will delay the time when workers can bargain to receive the market value of their labor. Institutions that delay restructuring will keep a significant segment of the labor force in jobs where the pay is low because productivity is low. As for the bitter pill of unemployment that necessarily accompanies plant closings, which is preferable: a certificate and a voice in a failing company that depends for survival on continued subsidies and more worker sacrifices, or a comprehensive program of job retraining that allows workers to add new skills to old ones in restructured enterprises with better prospects of economic viability?

At this point, the proponents of employee shareholding pull out their trump card. It is because we share the goal of marketization, they argue, that we advocate employee share ownership. For we too are thinking about the long term – not the viability of individual enterprises, but the political stability of the new economic system that results from the transformative process of privatization. Systemic stability will rest, in the long run, on the perceived legitimacy of the privatization process. Private property that is perceived by workers as illegitimately appropriated will not be secure. For four decades workers were told that they were the owners of Hungarian industry. It was demagoguery, to be sure. But what shall we tell them now? That they are to be excluded from the opportunity to purchase the property that they see as, in some sense, rightfully theirs? Stability requires legitimacy; legitimacy requires equitability; and equitability in this case requires equity – equity in their own enterprises.

The detractors: Yes, questions of equity and equal treatment are at the core of the ESOP problem. Under your proposals, all workers have the same right in principle to purchase discounted shares – but only in the firm in which they are currently employed. Is it equitable that one worker can apply for credit to purchase a worthless certificate in an inefficient, run-down plant while another (perhaps with the same skills and the same level of performance) can participate as a shareholder in a technologically sophisticated plant recently modernized under the old system of state subsidies drained from the enterprise of the first? Why should employment in a particular firm translate into equity in that firm? And what about employees in the remaining public sector working in hospitals, schools, and state administration? Where is their equal treatment? ESOP schemes will not solve the problems of the old system but perpetuate them – for they are not an alternative to nomenklatura buyouts but a complement and partner to them. In both cases, incumbency in a position serves as the basis for an ownership share. So we shall not be surprised if partial buyouts by enterprise directors and partial buyouts by employees work in tandem rather than in opposition. The further consequence will be to perpetuate the old system of favoritism and subsidies as the new block of managers and employee-shareholder-voters in particular firms will make it all the more difficult for government officials to ignore their special pleas in the inevitable times of business downturns.

These same issues of equity lie at the core of the position advocating the most dispersed ownership through the mechanism of *universal ownership grants*. According to proponents of such schemes,[20] the political revolutions that are sweeping aside the old regimes in Eastern Europe provide a unique historical opportunity to rebuild a social order based on principles of equality and justice. Because the collective wealth of the Hungarian economy is the product of the work of the entire society, this wealth should not be sold to the highest bidder or parceled out on the basis of current employment but distributed to everyone. The plans for such distribution differ in technical details, but the essential feature is that the government should privatize the assets of state enterprises by issuing certificates representing an abstract ownership right to all citizens. These certificates would not in the first instance be tied to particular firms (that is, citizen Kovács would not directly receive a share of MALEV Airlines, nor would citizen Szabó immediately receive title to a share of the former Lenin Steelworks). Instead, these certificates could be held as bonds (to be redeemed later ar some fixed or variable interest rate) or, more important, could be converted directly into ownership shares in particular firms, banks, or mutual funds. With each citizen free to convert his or her certificate into shares in the company that seems to have the most promise, the universal ownership arrangement would not only solve the problem of equality in equity but would also be the most rapid means to create a capital market governed by investor confidence.

Those skeptical of the universal grants schemes point first to the enormous technical difficulties of coordinating the conversion of certificates into ownership shares. The existing securities exchange in Budapest consists of several personal computers. And even if all the technological requirements of a central stock exchange were in place, where are the thousands of experienced brokers needed to handle the heavy volume of transactions involving millions of individual investors? Others note that the resolution of these difficulties would merely distribute the assets of the society without attracting the foreign capital that is needed to modernize the economy. Critics also charge that universal shareholding chases an illusive equality — for all citizens are not equally capable of making informed decisions to convert certificates into discrete investments. Leaving aside questions of unequal access to information, what about children or the aged? Who should be responsible for their holdings? Advocates respond that this is a minor detail that could be handled by depositing their certificates with professionally managed mutual funds or, in the case of children, issuing bonds that could be redeemed at the age of maturity. More significantly, won't the larger part of the citizenry, especially in times of enormous economic difficulties, immediately sell their shares for much needed income? Equality of shareholding and dispersion of ownership might last only a few months at best – and the flood of shares sold for meager but needed short-term benefit would so depress prices that those only relatively more wealthy at the outset could quickly gain ownership rights over most of the economy. In anticipation of such developments, some proponents of universal shareholding advocate special temporal conditions: A certain part or percentage of the shares of each citizen cannot be sold for income for some specified period, and so on. But critics quickly note that the citizens of the former state socialism will easily find unofficial means to sell shares, and that the discounted rate in such informal sales will mean that the neediest will receive even lower value for their initial (abstractly equal) certificates. Other proponents of the grants scheme allow that some concentration of ownership cannot be administratively curbed and should, in fact, be expected in the first phase of the transition to capital markets. They maintain, nonetheless, that the initial distribution of state assets will include a much wider segment of participants in market transactions, which encourages market development and will produce broader popular political support for privatization.

For some opponents, this political component is a vice rather than a virtue of universal shareholding. János Kornai, for example, argues that citizenship grants create "the impression that Daddy state has unexpectedly passed away and left us, his orphaned children, to distribute the patrimony equitably. But the state is alive and well."[21] On similar political grounds, others contend that even if we assume the most optimistic scenarios of universal shareholding, the dispersed ownership that would result might be congruent with oligarchic control of the economy rather than act as a check on it. If the organizational structure of large public enterprises remains unchanged and unchallenged by smaller (and genuinely entrepreneurial) ventures, diffuse formal ownership could make it all the easier for corporate insiders (directors and bankers) to control business strategy with an even smaller bloc of shares.

STEPPING OUTSIDE THE PRIVATIZATION DEBATE

Our analysis of the privatization debate has revealed an extraordinary range of informed judgments about the proper course of public policy in this field. Before turning in the following chapter to comparative questions about the actual policies adopted in Eastern Europe, it is useful to review the privatization debate not as a summary of the various policy positions taken, but with an eye to the factors that it neglects and the underlying assumptions that it makes. First among these is the core assumption, shared by virtually all Hungarian economic thinkers, that the inauguration of private property (whether foreign or domestic, spontaneous or controlled, institutional or individual, dispersed or concentrated) will be sufficient to achieve a far-reaching marketization of the economy. But that assumption might be re-stated as a question: If more than two decades of experimentation with economic reforms under state socialism demonstrated that markets are not possible without private ownership, does it follow that private ownership is sufficient to produce dynamic market competition?

This assumption is a first cousin to a second: Despite enormous diversity, each of the policy stances outlined earlier assumes that its prescribed course of property transformation will yield the undisputed dominance of private property. At first glance, the logic seems impeccable: Privatization will yield private property. Behind that logic lies an unstated equation: Property transformation equals privatization. Again, the assumption can be restated as a question: If a wide range of public policies invoke the creation of private property as their major objective, does the outcome follow directly from this intention? Under the peculiar circumstances of economic restructuring during postsocialism, does property transformation always equal privatization? Could it happen that property is transformed – but into forms not easily recognizable as the institutions of private property familiar to us in Western capitalism? Despite intentions, might privatization yield new forms of property – hybrid forms combining aspects of public and private property or novel forms departing as much from the traditionally statist forms of late socialism as from the conventionally private forms of its capitalist counterpart?

If the privatization debate can be reconsidered from the viewpoint of its core assumptions, it should also be reexamined for the social processes it neglects. In particular, its narrow focus on the institutional mechanisms of privatization ignores how powerful social groups can subvert institutions and neglects how social networks outside a narrowly economic analysis can provide resources to achieve economic goals. An alternative approach focuses on social groups and the characteristics of their networks of affiliation that impede or facilitate economic restructuring.

Economic transformation of the scope desired in contemporary Eastern Europe calls for a dramatic reallocation of existing economic resources – a transfer of resources from one institutional form where they appeared to be underutilized (or wastefully misutilized) to another that promises more efficient and effective utilization. Proponents of such change act with the hope that unhesitating commitment to restructuring will itself stimulate the inputs of some new resources necessary to put the new system in motion: new sources of credit and investment from abroad, new energies from individuals whose talents were not productively used under the earlier system, and a fresh reserve of goodwill and patience from the citizenry at large. But the underutilized resources that are at once the most sizable and the most uncertain (as to their future operation) are the informal networks of interaction that operated quite apart from officially sanctioned ties, whether in the interstices of bureaucracy or outside it altogether. Will the informal networks that got the job done despite institutional barriers in the earlier socialist system promote economic restructuring or will they inhibit it?

In Chapters 4 and 5, we directly address these questions of the transformative capacity of social networks and the characteristic forms of postsocialist property. But before doing so, we must examine the privatization policies actually adopted in the region. It is to that comparative problem that we turn.

3

PATH DEPENDENCE AND PRIVATIZATION STRATEGIES

CAPITALISM BY DESIGN?

Across the ruins of communism, a clear breeze blows from the West. Like the "fresh winds" that had been hailed from the East across the ruins of war more than four decades earlier, it promises prosperity through sacrifice. And like the old vision with its road maps to the promised land, this new vision comes with packaged formulas for applying economic science to the grand project of institutional reconstruction. In the postsocialist 1990s no less than in postwar 1948, devastation is seen as mandating boldness of action but also as presenting an opportunity: The collapse of the old order sets the imperative for ambitious experiments but also offers the occasion to build anew, this time with a fresh start to create capitalism by design.

As the juxtaposition of postwar Bolshevism and post–Cold War designer capitalism suggests, we are highly skeptical about analyses that approach the economic transition in East Central Europe as a problem to be solved by the rational design of economic institutions. Three sets of reasons inform this skepticism.

First, proposals for all-encompassing institutional change according to comprehensive blueprints suffer from an inadequate comparison of socialist and capitalist economic systems.[1] Misled by the obviously superior efficiency and performance of capitalist institutions, the makers of such proposals mistakenly draw the conclusion that these institutions can be replicated according to instructions, whereas the deeper and more pertinent comparative lesson is that the failure of socialism rested precisely in the attempt to organize all economic processes according to a grand design. The notion that the more rational institutions can be implemented by conscious design thus duplicates the rationalist fallacy evidenced during the introduction of socialism with, for example, the Leninist notion that property relations could be changed overnight by administrative decree. Moreover, the premise that efficient institutions can be drafted at the systemic level ignores, as Peter Murrell acutely observes, the actual operations of existing capitalisms.[2] The origins of capitalism in the West were not by blueprint, its development has not been directed by conscious design, and, as recent research in evolutionary economics and organizational ecology has demonstrated, its processes for selecting technologies and organizational forms are governed more by routine than by rational choice.[3]

The second reason to be skeptical about cookbook capitalism is that the systems designers and international advisory commissions who fly into the region, with little knowledge of its history, tend to approach the problem of economic change exclusively through the lenses of their own general models. Through such lenses, differences among the countries in the region are merely differences in degree (the timing and rapidity of collapse, the strength of elite commitment to reform, the speed of introducing new policies, etc.). As a consequence, their analyses of developments in the region are the simple measurements of the degree to which a particular strategy conforms to or departs from a given therapist's prescriptions. Contrary to such views, we are arguing that East Central Europe must be regarded as undergoing a *plurality of transitions* in a dual sense: Across the region, we are seeing a multiplicity of distinctive strategies; within any given country, we find not one transition but many occurring in different domains – political, economic, and social – and the temporality of these processes is often asynchronous and their articulation seldom harmonious.[4] Most important, because their models of economies are abstracted from the social institutions in which societies (and hence economies) are reproduced, analyses that begin with blueprints ignore the ways in which actual policy makers are shaped and constrained by the citizens of the newly emergent democracies of East Central Europe. Capitalism cannot be introduced by design in a region where the lessons of 40 years of experimentation by a rational hand have made the citizenry cautious about big experiments. A new social order cannot be created by dictation – at least not where citizens themselves want a voice in determining the new institutions. And these voices will be loudest where economic transformations are, as they must be in East Central Europe, painful and difficult. That is, attempts to reduce production costs and lower transaction costs can be successful only where society is willing to bear the *transformation costs*.

Because the actions of policy makers will be shaped by their perceptions of society's tolerance of these costs, instead of focusing exclusively on their recipes for change we would do better to analyze the resources at their disposal for securing support for burdensome measures. Such resources are not likely to be evenly distributed across the countries in the region. Even more important, these resources are not simply material, financial, or economic, but are above all political, as they entail the historically shaped patterns of mediation between state and society that differ qualitatively from country to country. In such a view, social change is not a process *either* directed from above *or* initiated from below but a result of interactions in which the designs of transformation are themselves transformed, shaped, and modified in response to and even in anticipation of the actions of subordinate social groups.[5] By attending to these interactions, our examination shifts from preoccupation with the "one best way" to scientifically manage the transition to a more comparative analytic strategy deliberately attuned to diverse institutional configurations differing across the countries not in degree but in kind.

The third reason for skepticism about analyses that begin with blueprints is that they often take the collapse of communism to indicate the existence of an institutional void. Indeed, this myth of starting from scratch explains some of the academic fascination with the region and the hasty proliferation of marching orders to create capitalism in 6 steps or 60. But the devastation and destruction wreaked by communism and the explosive rapidity of the demise of its party-states have not left an institutional vacuum. Our concern here is not with some lingering traces of socialist ideology or with the reconstructive surgery that gives new anatomies to the old nomenklatura but with the institutional legacies of the transitions themselves. To extend the metaphor of collapse: It is in the ruins that these societies will find the materials with which to build a new order; therefore, differences in how the pieces fell apart will have consequences for how political and economic institutions can be reconstructed in the current period.[6] In short, it is the differing paths of extrication from state socialism that shape the possibilities of transformation in the subsequent stage.

The following analysis thus takes as its point of departure a proposition that is implausible only on first acquaintance: The economic transformations currently attempted in East Central Europe will be marked by *path dependency*. This hypothesis is unlikely from the vantage of the drafting board where the designer sketches new institutions on a tabula rasa. Why should we expect continuities where departures are imperative? The strength of the concept of path dependence,[7] however, is precisely its analytic power in explaining outcomes where strategic actors are deliberately searching for departures from long-established routines and attempting to restructure the rules of the game. Actors who seek to move in new directions find that their choices are constrained by the existing set of institutional resources. Institutions limit the field of action, preclude some directions, and constrain certain courses. But institutions also favor the perception and selection of some strategies over others.[8] Actors who seek to introduce change require resources to overcome obstacles to change. This exploitation of existing institutionalized resources is a principal component of the paradox that even instances of transformation are marked by path dependence.

Such a view does not preclude the possibilities of changes that are far-reaching and dramatic. But it departs emphatically from those all too prevalent approaches that argue that economic development requires a rapid, radical, extensive (and even exhaustive) *replacement* of the current institutions, habits, and routines of the former centrally planned economies by an entirely new set of institutions and mentalities. Such wholesale replacement is rejected not from some illusions or nostalgia for socialism but from an appreciation of the evolutionary character of capitalism. And if the massive social engineering that would be required to effect it is undesirable, it is also unlikely. It is for these reasons that we argue that the structural innovations that will bring about dynamic transformations are more likely to entail complex *reconfigurations* of institutional elements rather than their immediate replacement.

From this perspective, we become more circumspect about such notions as *the transition to capitalism* or *the transition to a market economy* – alert to the possibility that behind such seemingly descriptive terms are teleological constructs in which concepts are driven by hypothesized end-states. Presentist history finds its counterpart here in futurist transitology. Thus, in place of *transition* (with the emphasis on destination) we analyze *transformations* (with the emphasis on actual processes) in which the introduction of new elements takes place most typically in combination with adaptations, rearrangements, permutations, and reconfigurations of already existing institutional forms.

This chapter examines these transformative processes through a comparative analysis of strategies of privatization in four East Central European economies – Hungary, Poland, the Czech Republic, and the former East German territories – during the first phase of transformation in the early years following extrication from state socialism.[9] The purpose of such a four-way comparison is not to construct some essentialist model of privatization against which the respective cases differ only in degree but to produce a comparative framework in which the specificity of each case will be revealed through its simultaneous mutual contrast with the other cases.[10] The comparative study of East European capitalisms is best launched not by taking its point of comparison in a general model of capitalism but by an analysis in which the specific content of the analytic categories is developed through a relational comparison of the East European cases themselves. The privatization programs of the region offer an opportunity to adopt such a methodological strategy. In the analysis that follows, we shall see that, despite broad and pervasive similarities in the systemic problems encountered, there are significant differences in the privatization programs that typify transformative processes across the four national cases. Seen from this vantage point, transformative processes taking place in contemporary East Central Europe resemble less architectural design than bricolage.

SPECIFYING THE DIMENSIONS OF THE EAST EUROPEAN VARIANT(S)

Privatization in this chapter refers to the process of *transferring ownership rights of productive assets* held by the state. Although in the contemporary East European context such transfer is conventionally seen as the principal means of *creating a private sector* in an economy dominated by a public sector, the two processes should not be confused or conflated. First, transferring ownership from state to private hands is unlikely to be sufficient to create a dynamic private market economy. Second, such a marketized private sector might be more effectively produced by measures to stimulate the startup of new ventures and expansion of existing units in the nascent private sector (formerly the second economy) than by transforming state assets into private assets. Nonetheless, each of the new governments in the region considers privatization (i.e., ownership transfer) the fundamental step toward the creation of a market economy. Our discussion here brackets the question of that causal relationship and focuses on the *variation* in privatization strategies across the cases. How do these new governments differ in their policies for transferring ownership of the assets of state enterprises? While acknowledging the similarities among the cases, we identify the distinctive privatization programs that typify each new government's strategy of privatization during its initial period in office.

For a typology to portray these differences, we propose three dimensions reflecting three central questions that must be addressed by any program of privatization: (1) How are the state's assets evaluated? (2) Who can acquire these assets? and (3) With what resources are ownership rights acquired? In the following section, we specify the categories of these dimensions for the East Central European variant(s) of privatization strategies.[11] We then look to the individual country cases to find programs exemplifying the various combinations of methods of asset evaluation, identities of participants, and resources for participation in privatization.

VALUATION OF ASSETS

The polarities of this dimension are straightfoward. At one pole, assets of the large public enterprises are evaluated by *administrative* means. At the extreme, we would find a single agency responsible, as part of the state bureaucracy, for every aspect of the privatization process. That bureaucratic agency would assess the economic viability of firms, selecting some for foreclosure and others for privatization, and would seek out buyers for those designated to be privatized. Although bureaucratic agents might solicit economic assessments of market performance when conducting these evaluations, actual decisions would be made on the basis of administrative measures rather than spontaneous market mechanisms. The other pole is already anticipated in our presentation of the first: Valuation would take place directly through *market* mechanisms. Here policy makers see markets not only as an outcome of privatization but also as a means of privatization. At the extreme, we would find spot market transactions in the form of public auctions. Auctioneers could, of course (as with the sale of farm implements), announce a figure at which bidding could begin, but the final selling price would be determined by the competitive bidding.

The two poles, however, do not entirely capture the complexity of this dimension, for in between are some mechanisms of price formation and valuation that can be conceptualized either as combinations of bureaucractic measures and market mechanisms or as alternatives to them. Examples of such hybrid or alternative mechanisms are *relational contracting* (in which state agencies contract the task of privatization to consulting firms based on their international reputation or in anticipation of long-term associations in which agency and firm would share information through channels not easily expressed in market terms) and *bargaining* (a loose term denoting patterns in which price setting is strongly influenced by network connections differing from purely market transactions or political considerations differing from purely administrative criteria).[12]

ACTORS TARGETED TO ACQUIRE ASSETS

In constructing a strategy of privatization, the new governments of these emergent democracies can present privatization as a process that will increase the wealth of the nation. Firms will be more accountable, more likely to economize on costs, and more oriented toward effective and efficient performance, they can argue, when property rights are exercised by private owners instead of state bureaucrats. But if privatization will increase the national income, it will also increase private wealth. Regardless of how they choose to portray private gain as contributing to the public good, governments that undertake privatization on a scale so potentially vast as that in contemporary East Central Europe (where over 85% of productive assets are state property) must address questions of distributive justice.[13]

We are thus interested in the question of whether these new governments attempt to forge an explicit link between the economic objectives of privatization and the new civic principles of the emergent democratic polities. Specifically, is *citizenship* (that most fundamental civic principle, with its attendant concept of the abstract equality of all citizens) invoked as a principle for distributing property rights? At issue is not whether individuals are favored over collectivities but whether individuals are explicitly targeted in their capacity *as citizens* to be recipients of property rights in the privatization of the assets of the large public enterprises.

Whereas some governments will utilize civic principles to target citizens as recipients of the state's former assets, others will utilize purely economic principles to target corporations. In the latter case, although private persons might participate in some programs of privatization (in agriculture, in the "small privatizations" of retail shops and restaurants, etc.), the fundamental strategy of the privatization of large state enterprises will be based on distributing property rights to incorporated units. In short, privatization strategies will differ according to whether the state specifically seeks to involve *civic persons (citizens)* as participants or, alternatively, eschews civic principles in favor of basing large-scale privatization on *legal-economic persons (corporations)*.

RESOURCES UTILIZED TO ACQUIRE OWNERSHIP RIGHTS

Privatization strategies can also vary according to the kinds of resources that are utilized (we might say converted) to acquire ownership rights. *Monetary* or financial resources are the obvious first category along this dimension. But in addition to being differentiated according to their financial holdings or monetary savings, actors in the transitional societies of East Central Europe differ according to the powers and capacities invested in their *positions*. In fact, the prohibition of private property in productive assets meant that the stratification systems of state socialist societies were organized more around differences in positions than differences in wealth. Thus, at the very moment when these economies embark on privatization, they must deal with a continuing legacy of the stratification system of state socialism: Society is not greatly differentiated according to wealth in a system where advantages accrued to positions. Thus, our third dimension contrasts privatization schemes and strategies that are organized primarily around the utilization of monetary (including credit or other financial) resources with those in which the participating agents capitalize on their *positional* resources. The concepts of *position* and *positional property*,[14] of course, carry connotations of office holding. We also start from that Weberian conception, but we will find it useful as well to extend the application of the concept from office holding to a broader set of organizational posts and locational positions. We should stress that our attention to positions should not be interpreted as a narrow preoccupation with the fate of those who held political positions in the old order and with whether and how they are converting their political capital into economic capital.[15] Our concern here is more with *economic job holding* than with *political office holding*. Some privatization strategies will be structured in such a way that the occupants of certain positions will be able to utilize that occupancy for advantage in acquiring property rights. *Managers*, for example, might be able to utilize positional resources to gain effective ownership rights. Similarly, privatization strategies that place importance on *employee* ownership plans are instances of inclusion/exclusion in which ownership rights are acquired through positional resources.

Our three dimensions are cross-classified in Figure 2 to yield a preliminary typology of privatization strategies in East Central Europe. The dimensions referring to **actors targeted to acquire assets** and **resources to acquire ownership rights** form a two-by-two table. The remaining dimension, referring to the **method of evaluating assets**, is represented by shading ("administrative" lightest and "markets" darkest, with "bargaining" in between). Also located in the figure are those strategies for privatizing large public enterprises that *most closely exemplify* four of the possible combinations of the categories along the three dimensions.

To avoid possible misunderstandings in interpreting this typology, we should state at the outset how we have delimited its object of study. First, the typology addresses questions of the privatization of *large public enterprises*. That is, we have not included here the multitude of schemes for privatizing retail trade, catering establishments, and agricultural cooperatives.[16] Second, our decision rule for placing country cases within the typology was to find cases that *exemplify* particular intersections of its dimensions. Our task here is to identify distinctive traits rather than to produce an exhaustive description of the full range of privatization programs in each country. Thus, the

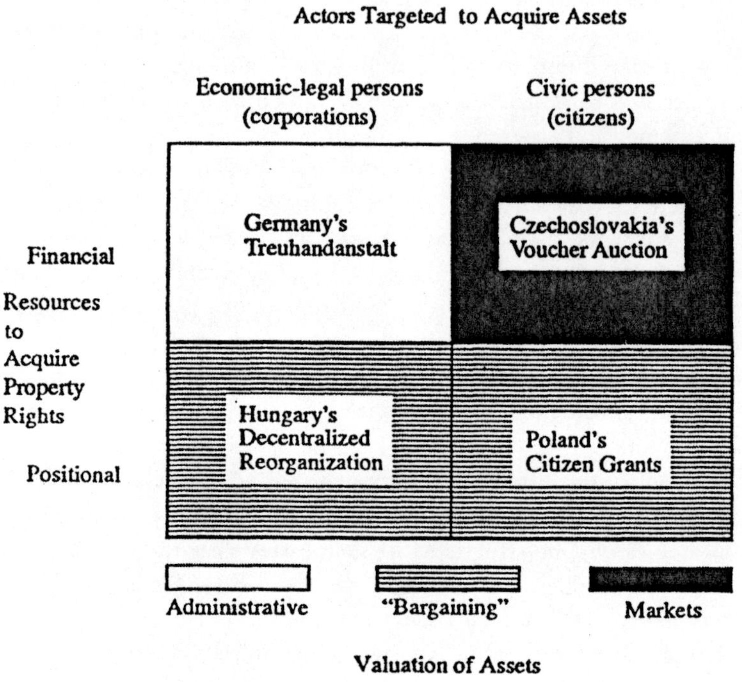

Actors Targeted to Acquire Assets

	Economic-legal persons (corporations)	Civic persons (citizens)
Financial	Germany's Treuhandanstalt	Czechoslovakia's Voucher Auction
Resources to Acquire Property Rights Positional	Hungary's Decentralized Reorganization	Poland's Citizen Grants

Administrative   "Bargaining"   Markets

Valuation of Assets

Figure 2. A typology of privatization strategies in East Central Europe.

location of a particular country case in a given cell of the typology is not meant to capture all aspects about its course of privatization.[17] Third, our typology focuses on the *strategies of policy makers* in approximately the first year of the newly elected governments.

DISTINCTIVE FEATURES OF THE COUNTRY CASES

GERMANY'S TREUHANDANSTALT

Our discussion of the typology of privatization strategies represented in Figure 2 begins with the position denoting the administrative evaluation of assets favoring corporate actors utilizing predominantly monetized resources. No privatization strategy better exemplifies this particular combination of elements than the institution of Germany's Treuhandanstalt. Charged with the task of performing triage on the wounded enterprises of the formerly East German economy, the Treuhandanstalt has singlehandedly carried out functions that are performed elsewhere in the region by diverse governmental units scattered across the Ministries of Industry, Planning, Finance, Labor, and Privatization. Following the monetary union of the two Germanys in July 1990 and their political unification on October 3, 1990, the Treuhandanstalt became the world's largest industrial holding, with a staff of 2,500 to privatize and monitor the operations of the former East German state enterprises employing more than 3 million wage earners.[18] By May 1991, the Trust had privatized 1,670 firms out of the approximately 7,000 that had been operating in the former East German lands, taking its largest strides in the branches of energy, food-stuffs, construction, trade, and tourism. Ninety percent of these properties were sold to West Germans (primarily corporations), 5% were purchased by foreign (i.e., non-German) investors, and 5% are now held by their former managers. In preparation for further privatizations, the Treuhandanstalt has also split up 316 *Kombinat* (megaconglomerates in the old socialist economy) into 8,500 smaller firms involving some 45,000 plants.[19]

This aggressive posture of attacking a problem by means of a strong bureaucratic agency with an almost unquestioned mandate to impose radical, sweeping, and rapid restructuring is thus the defining feature of the German privatization strategy. But if the German state has moved with far greater speed and determination than other Central European governments in the first stage of privatization, there are some indications that its greatest difficulties still lie ahead. The question remains, of course, whether these obstacles will be met with an even quicker pace and stronger administrative measures. But we should not rule out the possibility that the difficulties facing the Treuhandanstalt will retard its speed and lead to some modification of its methods.

The irony of the East German case has been that the very strength of the West German economy that was presumed to yield a smoother transition (relative to its East Central European neighbors) has proved in the initial stage to be also a source of problems. In particular, the dramatic surge in the demand for consumer goods in the newly incorporated lands was met in the first instance by expansion of output by West German firms. Thus, if it indeed might be the case that the "wealthy brother" will save the situation by buying firms in the long run, in the short run he began by selling goods to his desiring and poorer siblings. Uncompetitive on the world market, unable to sell goods on the West German market, and now uncompetitive on their own territory, the former East German enterprises saw their markets evaporate within weeks. With no orders and no work, millions of employees in these failing enterprises have been receiving scarcely disguised unemployment compensation in the form of short-time work in which they remain on the payroll, with little or nothing to do at their place of employment.[20]

For some intellectuals who attempt to shape German public opinion, the most attractive solution to this problem is massive migration. "Everyone who is willing to work hard can find a job here in our prosperous country" they can be heard to say. But even if western Germany could absorb a significant proportion of those seeking work, the consequences might prove not only catastrophic to the social fabric but also devastating to the local economies they leave behind. Massive migration, even on a scale far lower than some policy makers have in mind, could lead to a massive devaluation of the human capital of the economy of the former East German lands. Such devaluation would be triggered not simply by the aggregate loss of highly skilled *individuals* but also by the destruction of the *work teams* in which those skills had previously been utilized. Not as a direct outcome of foresight and planning but as an unintended consequence of the macroeconomic mismanagement of state socialism, the organization of work in the microsphere of the redistributive enterprise had evolved into a *forced autonomy* and a *distorted flexibility*.[21] At the level of the shop floor, work teams developed, indeed were forced to develop, patterns of adaptation to adjust quickly and flexibly to supply shortages and other irrationalities of central mismanagement. Such adaptations should not be idealized – they were constrained and distorted – but it remains the case that over time they evolved into work units in which the human capital of the teams was more than the sum of its parts. In such a case, the departure of two or three from a team of a dozen can cripple its functioning and shatter a small but potentially significant resource that might otherwise be a basis for reconstructing a failed economy. In short, migration stimulated by the close proximity to prosperity on the same national territory might alleviate unemployment, but it might also erode organizational capacities and retard the development of a dynamic economy in the former East German lands.

Unemployment and severe economic crisis will have important consequences for the further work of the Treuhandanstalt. As the situation inside the Eastern enterprises rapidly deteriorates, it will prove increasingly difficult to find buyers for them. Meanwhile, as unemployment explodes to unprecedented levels, pressures will mount to slow the pace of liquidation. Firms that can be neither sold nor shut down (and we can expect that they will number in the thousands) will remain under the bureaucratic authority of the Treuhandanstalt, and that state agencies will be forced to intervene directly in reorganizing these properties, using subsidies to keep them afloat in the meantime.[22] But we can further expect relentless pressures on the Trust to demonstrate that it remains committed to a determined course of privatization. After all, its mandate was for sweeping and rapid privatization. Federal politicians and other governmental officials will not look favorably on an agency that resorts to subsidizing instead of privatizing, and bureaucratic superiors will frown at subordinates in the agency whose quarterly record of completed privatizations falls below the norm. From the combination of these factors, we can expect that the Treuhandanstalt will increasingly look to the enterprise managers as a potential pool of new owners for the failed but salvagable smaller units that have already been (or soon will be) broken off from the large state enterprises. In this scenario, the evaluation of assets is likely to take place increasingly through bargaining between the agency and enterprises, with managers utilizing positional resources to exercise new and expanded property rights. These processes suggest a shift in the Treuhandanstalt's operations as restructuring becomes the critical task of the agency: To organize the market for potential buyers, the first task is to reorganize firms.[23] The *Kombinate* are too big to sell all of a piece; and the pieces that can be broken off and sold by themselves are too small to make a difference. Restructuring thus often entails the simultaneous disaggregation of several large enterprises and the strategic *recombination* of these newly available constitutive parts (from across different enterprises) to create new ventures.

THE CZECH VOUCHER-AUCTION PROGRAM

In strong contrast to the decidedly statist orientation of the German privatization strategy, the Czech strategy[24] is an exemplary case of evaluating assets directly by the market, involving participation on the basis of citizenship and utilizing monetary resources. In fact, this particular combination of categories along our three dimensions is represented in a single institutional innovation in the Czech strategy – the use of citizen vouchers in public auctions of shares of the large state enterprises.

The program that the Czech economic authorities have launched[25] involves the distribution of over 50% of the equity of more than 1,000 large public enterprises through a citizenship voucher scheme. Each Czech citizen over 18 years of age receives vouchers equal to 1,000 *investment points*. These investment points can be exchanged for shares in the enterprises designated for privatization through the voucher program. But if every citizen receives these vouchers as a matter of right, only those who pay a registration fee of 1,000 korunas (about half the average monthly earnings of industrial employees) will be able to use the vouchers in the public auctions. To indicate that the equity shares obtained through the voucher program are emphatically not a free gift from the state, to signal that there will be risk involved, and to filter out citizens with no serious interest in share ownership, Czech officials have designed a voucher scheme that combines citizenship participation and monetary resources.

As we shall see, the actual process of exchanging vouchers for shares is fairly complex (and Czech authorities undertook a major program to educate the public about its basic principles and its logistical intricacies). The first stage of the voucher-auction began May 18, 1992. For each wave of privatization the Ministry of Privatization designates the enterprises whose equity will be distributed through auction.[26] For each enterprise, the ministry posts an initial asking price for the shares of that particular firm. To understand the principles of the auction, it is important to note that this "price" is not expressed in monetary units but *in terms of investment points*. Basically, the state announces the number of investment points at which it is willing to exchange a share of a given enterprise. A single share of a blue-chip company, for example, might begin at an initial level of 200 investment points; a share of a firm with a less prominent record or less promising future prospects, on the other hand, might be posted at only 10 investment points. In the first round of the auction, then, one citizen might decide to place all of his 1,000 investment points on five shares of the blue-chip company; another could indicate her willingness to exchange all of her 1,000 points for 100 shares in the less promising venture; and a third could diversify his portfolio of investment points across firms with differing initial asking prices.

Equally important in understanding the principle of asset evaluation represented in the voucher-auction is that the auction is conceived as an iterative process occurring in multiple rounds. That is, although the economists in the Czech Ministry of Privatization must conduct a rough-and-ready evaluation of the performance of firms to set the initial price of shares in the first round of bidding, the final price in investment points in the simulated market of the voucher-auction (and, more important, the later price of shares bought and sold on an actual market) is determined by the supply of and demand for these shares. What Vaclav Klaus and his team in the Ministry of Finance seem to have in mind is a kind of *Walrasian auctioneer*.[27] The auctioneer (actually a computerized network) accepts offers to buy shares of a given enterprise at a certain asking price in investment points. Unlike a commodities exchange (or the typical auction we might know from an estate sale or a sale of objects of art), the bidder-citizens are not, strictly speaking, bidding up the price in a given round. At the end of the first round, the auctioneer identifies those shares for which demand exceeded supply, as well as those in which the reverse was the case. As the seller, the state can then accept offers from that round, or adjust prices upward or downward for the next round to be held two weeks later. The auction proceeds for three of four rounds, with the state accepting offers where the demand for shares of a particular enterprise is lower than their supply (the number of shares for each firm in the auction is fixed) and revising "prices" upward for those shares for which demand exceeds supply.

The major principle underlying the voucher-auction as a key feature of their overall privatization strategy is that the Czech leadership is committed to using a simulated market to rapidly achieve an actually functioning equity market in the shares of a significant proportion of the former state enterprises.[28] The question of whether investment points reflect the real value, or even a true *relative* value, of shares is beside the point; the purpose of the voucher-auction is to get shares into private hands, where they can be actually bought and sold.[29] According to the designers of the auction, it is in such a market (where speculators are not to be disparaged but encouraged)[30] that the real evaluation of assets will take place. It is for this reason, rather than primarily because of the registration fee, that we locate the Czech privatization strategy in that cell representing the intersection of market evaluation and monetary assets.

The Czech leadership appears prepared to accept relatively dispersed ownership in the initial stage of its privatization program in the hope that later transactions in the actual capital market will yield relatively rapid concentration of ownership in midlevel enterprises. Several design features (the combination of offering the shares of some firms at initial low asking "prices" and accepting offers where the supply of shares exceeds the demand) suggest that the Czechs hope that some enterprising individuals will quickly buy up these relatively cheap shares and gain controlling interest in these firms. Such a scenario would most likely be accompanied by continuing dispersed ownership in the most highly prized enterprises where the economic leadership presumably has more confidence in the enterprises' managerial talent and is therefore more willing to tolerate the managerial control that comes with highly diffused shareholding. These same features also suggest that the Czech leadership is aware of the likelihood of resistance to the voucher-auction on the part of managers of the enterprises designated for auction and is designing some features of the program in an attempt to neutralize or mitigate this resistance. At the bottom end, firms whose shares find no buyers might be more easily liquidated after a strong vote of "no confidence" by the citizen investors. At the top, economic officials can point to the likelihood of diffused shareholding in the blue-chip companies to persuade their managers (precisely the ones with the most bargaining power) that the auction is not against their interests and should not be resisted. For the broad range of enterprises in between, the Czech ministers can probably count on resistance from managers, but they seem to hope that relatively quick concentration of ownership will bring these firms under the control of the new owners.

POLAND'S UNIVERSAL CITIZEN GRANTS AND EMPLOYEE SHAREHOLDINGS

The story of Poland's privatization strategy begins in Gdansk, the birthplace of the first and, for a while, the largest independent trade union in Eastern Europe. But Solidarity and the most famous offspring of the Lenin Shipyards, who became the president of the Polish Republic, are only half of the story. For, not without historical irony yet not entirely by coincidence, Gdansk was also the birthplace of Polish neoliberalism. During the mid-1980s, while the intellectuals of Warsaw and Budapest debated in urban coffeehouses, a group of young private businessmen and young provincial intellectuals in Gdansk formed a Liberal Club and at its meetings began reading and discussing major theoretical statements on property rights. From the practical experiences of these entrepreneurs and their organic intellectuals arose the Liberal Congress, a small but extraordinarily influential party that has produced Jan Krzysztof Bielecki, the former prime minister, and a disproportionately large number of the cabinet ministers in the government formed after the election of President Lech Walesa.

Privatization in Poland, of course, did not begin under the leadership of Walesa's liberals but instead under Jaruzelski's Communists. During the power vaccuum of 1989, an untold number of apparatchiks landed comfortably as the new owners of promising units carved out of the former state enterprises. The Liberals thus came to office (first with Finance Minister Leszek Balcerowicz and later with Bielecki's larger retinue) in a period in which the scandals of such *nomenklatura capitalism* were aired in public circles narrow and wide. Property reform was, nonetheless, clearly on the agenda; and the first non-Communist government (under Prime Minister Tadeusz Mazowiecki) announced a program of clean privatization, with the promise of attracting foreign investors and a series of large public offerings based on the British model as its centerpiece. But foreign investors were slow and few (looking more to Hungary and, for different reasons, to eastern Germany), and the public offerings made only a little dent in the state-owned assets of the large socialist enterprises. In fact, the major achievement of the first year of the Ministry of Property Transformation (a few unrepresentative foreign buyouts aside) was privatization through liquidation – a dubious achievement, given the stated aims of the ministry, because the assets of 159 of these 160 so-called privatizations were leased to the managers and employees of the liquidated firms.[31]

After the election campaign in which he promised "acceleration," President Walesa turned to Janusz Lewandowski, the new Minister of Property Transformation from Gdansk, asking him to elaborate and concretize the sweeping program for mass privatization that Lewandowski had proposed years earlier together with his Gdansk compatriot, Jan Szomburg (currently director of the Research Center for Marketization and Property Reform).[32] The young transformers confronted two obstacles. First, from the other side of the Gdansk story, they faced the Workers' Councils reactivated after 1989, which saw property transformation as their opportunity to solidify employee ownership.[33] Second, they faced the enormous problem that domestic savings could cover only a fraction of the assets of the large state enterprises. On this subject Lewandowski had commented before accepting his new position that "privatization is when someone who doesn't know who the real owner is and doesn't know what it's really worth sells something to someone who doesn't have any money."[34]

The program of mass privatization calls for the property transformation of some 400 Polish enterprises in the first stage of its operation. Within the program is a major peace offering to the Workers' Councils: Employees in the privatized firms will receive gratis 10% of the shares of their companies. That is, lacking savings and credit, employees will be able to use their positions as job holders to gain an ownership stake in their enterprises.

At the center of the mass privatization program, however, stands a universal citizenship grant in the form of share vouchers issued to every Polish citizen. In marked contrast to the Czech program, no registration fee is required to participate. With this signal and with all of its rhetoric, the Polish government seems eager to send the message that this is emphatically a free gift from the state.

Unlike the Czech citizen, moreover, the Polish citizen will not exchange vouchers directly for shares in a privatized enterprise. Instead, the vouchers will be exchanged for shares in one or another *asset manager*, who will, in turn, exchange the vouchers for shares in the transformed enterprises that it chooses (or is assigned) to manage. Current proposals call for this role to be played by experienced foreign companies, perhaps as few as ten. These asset managers, large holdings of many of the largest firms, should not be confused with the managers of pension funds or mutual funds, to which they bear only superficial resemblance. According to the program's designers,[35] these asset managers will not influence firms indirectly by buying and selling shares on the market but instead will exercise authority through active and aggressive property management, directly involved in formulating the policies and business strategies of the firms under their ownership control. Thus, in place of the Czechs' fascination with Anglo-American practices, the Poles seem to be looking to models in Germany and Japan.[36]

Several other features of the Polish program of mass privatization complete the contrast to the Czech voucher schemes. According to Polish officials and experts, the situation in the immediately foreseeable future is not likely to be developed enough to establish an open-ended program in which citizens are free to withdraw shares and change asset managers. Presumably to avoid inflation, citizens will be initially limited to collecting dividends from the results of the voucher-asset manager program. That is, for a still undetermined period (but certainly lasting for several years), citizens cannot capitalize their shares by turning them in for their nominal value. The system is further closed-ended by prohibiting citizens from changing to a different asset manager. Because they will not be exposed to the discipline of disappointed shareholders who seek higher dividends elsewhere, the mass privatization program will include a complex incentive program for the executives of the limited number of asset-managing companies. The hope, meanwhile, is that the managers of the former state enterprises will now be under the firm discipline of the foreign asset managers. Obviously more concerned than the Czechs about the consequences of dispersed shareholding, the Poles are hoping to target citizens as owners while using the universal citizenship grant to achieve extraordinarily concentrated corporate control.

Thus, with its unrestricted access, the Polish voucher program is more inclusive than the Czech scheme. Yet its citizens' participation is almost entirely passive. What can the Polish citizens do with their shares? They cannot capitalize these shares, nor can they withdraw them from the current asset manager and deposit them with another. In exchange for their passivity, the citizens get a dividend, and that alone.

But why then have a voucher program at all? The answer lies in the goal of the Polish program: to give aggressive property management to foreign companies within the constraints of a politicized citizenry. No Polish politician or official could propose an outright giveaway of Polish firms to foreign asset managers. But, strictly speaking, this is not what they will do. In a legal and political sense, they will give the *ownership to the Polish citizenry* and the *stewardship of the citizen-owned assets* to presumably competent managers. The Polish voucher program will not be *popular capitalism* in the sense of creating millions of small, active investors with an interest in the ups and downs of the market. Instead, its designers hope to increase the chances that a capitalism with quite concentrated effective ownership can be made popular with the Polish citizenry.[37]

HUNGARY'S INSTITUTIONAL CROSS-OWNERSHIP

The fourth cell in our typology is exemplified by Hungary – characterized by the combination of bargained evaluation of assets, corporate owners, and positional resources. Although Hungary's centralized State Property Agency (SPA) has a strong legislative mandate (and a firmly established bureaucratic office) to directly supervise and control all aspects of the privatization process, asset evaluation in Hungary, unlike that in Germany, is not conducted through administrative means. And although the shares of Hungarian firms can be sold on an embryonic stock exchange, the evaluation of assets, unlike the auctions in the Czech and Slovak republics, is not performed primarily by market mechanisms. As a case that falls between the polarities of administrative and market evaluation, it is represented in Figure 2 as *bargaining*, yet this residual or negative definition fails to convey the more precise institutional character of asset evaluation performed by the Hungarian authorities. As we shall see, in the spontaneous and controlled transformation of property rights that is occurring through decentralized processes initiated by the large public enterprises, bargaining is indeed the prevalent modality. But within the SPA itself, and especially for the very largest firms designated by that agency to be sold to foreign investors in hard currency transactions to reduce the state deficit, the mechanism of asset evaluation can be more accurately characterized as *relational contracting*.

Within months after taking office in the spring of 1990, Hungary's coalition government (under Prime Minister József Antall of the leading party, the Hungarian Democratic Forum) responded to the criticisms of the opposition parties by adopting the opposition's call for the "privatization of privatization." The central feature of this measure was a dramatic increase in the role of international investment banks and leading consulting firms in the privatization of the large state enterprises. When it nominated a list of twenty enterprises to be sold in the first round of privatization, the SPA also announced an open invitation to investment banks and consulting firms to place proposals with the agency indicating, in general terms, how they would evaluate assets, arrange credit, and find a buyer for a given enterprise. That is, the agency put up for tender the right to manage the restructuring of a particular company. The investment and consulting firms that won this competition would be compensated with a percentage of the final selling price. In an important sense, the SPA was not directly selling enterprises but instead selling the right to lead and manage their privatization.

Dozens of consulting firms and investment banks responded to these tenders; whole rooms in the SPA were filled with shoulder-high stacks of proposals. Several of the most internationally prominent firms (Solomon Brothers, Goldman Sachs, Barclays, Price Waterhouse, Coopers and Lybrand, and others) had submitted prospectuses for eight or more of the tenders. Each thought that, if selected on its merits, the firm would be leading several of the reorganizations. But when the SPA announced its decisions only three weeks later, it became obvious that its assignment of the tenders was based less on careful reading of the proposals than on the aim of maximizing the number of cooperating partners in the first round: The 20 enterprises slated for privatization were distributed among 20 different leading banks and consulting firms.

These organizations are forming the core of a relatively stable set of participants involved in an ongoing relationship with the agency. In assigning tenders (and even in selecting enterprises to be restructured) in subsequent privatizations, the SPA is working closely with the international partners with which it has had positive experiences in the first round. Invitations are not entirely open; in some cases, the agency approaches only a few international firms, sounding them out about plans for this or that enterprise. We should not rule out the possibility that effective decisions are being made before the announcement of competitive bidding for the right to manage a particular restructuring. When making contracts in these cases, both sides are calculating not simply in terms of the immediate contract at issue but in terms of past performance and in anticipation of future exchanges. Our purpose here is not to denounce a too cozy relationship between the SPA and the communities of international banking and consulting. On the contrary, these practices have an economic rationale: Relational contracting provides a mechanism by which both parties can gain more information than through more restricted market transactions. On the side of the SPA, such relational contracting lowers transaction costs (e.g., the administrative costs of handling an overabundance of bids or the costs, in time and resources, of working with too many partners) and can yield more extensive and better information (about capital markets, international investors, the marketing and production strategies of foreign companies, etc.) than might be obtained when contracts are made through open competition on a strictly case-by-case basis.[38]

We would seriously fail to understand the process of privatization in Hungary, however, if we focused our attention too narrowly on the SPA — for although this agency has the legal authority to supervise privatization, the predominant processes restructuring the ownership rights of the large public enterprises are not initiated there. Instead, the prevalent form of transformation in Hungary should be characterized as the *decentralized reorganization of property*. Simplifying a more complicated web of transactions and a wider network of connections, the basic course of such reorganization can be outlined as follows: Under the pressure of enormous debt, declining sales, and threats of bankruptcy, or (in the cases of more prosperous enterprises) to forestall takeovers or to attempt to increase autonomy from state ministries, directors of many large public enterprises are taking advantage of several important pieces of legislation that allow state enterprises to establish joint stock companies (*részvénytársaságok* or RTs) and limited liability companies (*korlátolt felelösségü társaságok* or KFTs). To be clear, typically in such reorganizations the state enterprise is not itself transformed into a joint stock enterprise;[39] rather, the managers of the enterprise break up the organization (along divisional, factory, departmental, or even workshop lines) into numerous corporations. As newly incorporated entities with legal identities, these new units are nominally independent – registered separately, with their own boards of directors and separate balance sheets. The more interesting question is, of course, who owns the shares of these new units? An examination of the computerized records of the Budapest Court of Registry [40] indicates that the controlling shares (in overwhelming proportions) of the corporate satellites launched around the large public enterprises are held by the state enterprises themselves. For this reason, we prefer to use the term *VKFT* or, *enterprise limited liability company* (in Hungarian, *a vállati-KFT*) to denote their semiautonomous organizational status.[41]

Property shares in these satellite organizations are not limited, however, to the founding enterprise. The typical cases involve patterns of more mixed ownership. Top and midlevel managers, professionals and other staff, and (rarely) highly skilled workers can be found on the lists of founding partners. But their shares are not large and should not be taken as evidence of managerial buyouts. More important than private persons is the participation in share ownership in a given corporate unit by *other* joint stock companies and limited liability companies – sometimes by other VKFTs in a similar orbit around the same enterprise, more frequently by joint stock companies or VKFTs spinning around some other enterprise with lines of purchase or supply to the corporate unit.[42] Most important among the outside owners are banks. In many cases, the establishment of VKFTs and other corporate forms was triggered by enterprise debt, and in the reorganization the creditors, whether commercial banks (whose shares as joint stock companies are still predominantly state-owned) or other credit institutions (also state-owned), exchange debt for equity.

What then is the fastest-growing new ownership form in the Hungarian economy?[43] The terminology is cumbersome but it reflects the complex, institutionally intertwined character of property transformation in Hungary: a limited liability company owned by other limited liability companies owned by joint stock companies, banks, and large public enterprises owned by the state.

Has the decentralized reorganization of property rights taken place beyond the control and outside the purview of the governmental agents responsible for privatization? Consistent with its campaign rhetoric in the parliamentary elections, on taking office in May 1990 the new Hungarian government adopted a deliberate strategy that promised to slow down privatization and to provide for its centralized management.[44] But within months, the SPA seemed to have realized that it had neither the capacity nor the ability to directly oversee the privatization of thousands of state enterprises. Toleration (bordering on encouragement) of decentralized reorganization appears to be its posture. This statement should not imply that the SPA is unaware of the particular character of these reorganizations. Each corporate spinoff of the kind described earlier involving assets valued at more than 30 million forints (approximately $400,000) or a series of such spinoffs that represents in the aggregate more than 50% of the assets of the state enterprise must be approved by the agency. Although not virtually automatic, the approval rate of such proposals is extraordinarily high. This high rate of approval suggests that negotiations with the SPA precede the submission of a proposal for reorganization. Moreover, case studies and summary reports of corporate reorganizations indicate that the dominant modality of asset evaluation in these cases is unquestionably bargaining.[45] Whether at the level between the state enterprise and its affiliated corporations or between the enterprise and the state agency, actors exploit every available means of bargaining power.

In which direction will corporate reorganization evolve? At this stage, several possible alternatives can be clearly stated. In the first scenario, the current ambiguities in the distribution of property rights will be clarified in favor of the managers of these enterprises. That is, decentralized reorganization will lead to a further *concentration of managerial control*. In the second scenario, decentralized reorganization sets the stage for a later round of *genuine privatization*. That is, although senior management might have broken up enterprises with the aim of protecting the firms from inevitable bankruptcy or increasing their autonomy from state authorities, the establishment of even semi-independent corporate forms might create inviting opportunities for a takeover by foreign firms or indigenous private entrepreneurs with limited means to acquire properties when they were more closely bound within the large state enterprises.[46] In the third scenario, decentralized reorganization is but the first phase of a *reconsolidation of state ownership*.[47] This outcome might be only seemingly paradoxical. State elites may be willing to tolerate corporate reorganization (even on a wide scale and together with some genuine privatization of the smaller units[48]) provided that the controlling shares remain in institutions over which the state can continue to exercise control.

Whatever the outcome, the predominant form of the transformation of property relations in Hungary is the outcome of bargaining about asset evaluation and takes the form of institutional cross-ownership in which enterprise managers use their resources as office holders to extend their effective exercise of property rights. For these reasons, Hungary exemplifies that cell in our typology representing the intersection of bargaining, corporate owners, and positional resources.

PATHS OF EXTRICATION AND PATTERNS OF TRANSFORMATION

How can we explain these differences across our country cases? In our view, an explanation of these distinctive strategies of privatization must begin by taking into account their distinctive paths of extrication from state socialism – *reunification* in Germany, *capitulation* in Czechoslovakia, *compromise* in Poland, and *electoral competition* in Hungary. These diverse paths of extrication, and the preceding differences in social structure and political organization that brought them about, have had the consequence that the current political institutions and forms of interest intermediation between state and society differ significantly across our four cases. The collapse of communism in East Germany resulted in the colonization of its new political institutions during incorporation into the powerful state of the German Federal Republic. The capitulation of Communist authorities in Czechoslovakia after harsh decades of suppressing almost all institutions of civil society resulted in the rapid restructuring of its political institutions, with relatively few remnants remaining from the earlier period.[49] Communism did not collapse in Hungary and Poland; its demise was negotiated in both countries. Faced with a powerful, indeed mono-organizational, opposition with deep roots in society, Poland's Communists attempted a compromise solution. And the legacies of this path of extrication, with its institutional guarantees for Jaruzelski and company, remained in a compromised parliament and a strong presidency together with a nationwide, though weakening, workers' movement. Hungary's reform Communists, by contrast, attempted to salvage some of their power by entering into direct electoral competition with a seemingly weak political opposition. That political opposition, of course, won electoral victories and came into government, but the legacy of Hungary's peculiar path remained. In the first two years following its Round Table negotiations, Hungary saw the rapid flourishing of political parties without roots in society, the further fragmentation of its weak labor movement, and the emergence of its enterprise managers (as the best-organized social group during the previous decade) as the most powerful social actors in the society.

Thus, it is the relationship between *different types of democracy* and *different types of capitalism*, rather than the abstractions of democracy and capitalism, that explains the differences in contemporary Eastern Europe.[50] The diverse paths of extrication from state socialism yield distinctive patterns across a triangle formed by the state, the market, and the society.

With their political incorporation into the German Federal Republic, the citizens of the former East German territories found their futures charted by a political leadership with a strong commitment to thorough marketization. But together with an abiding confidence in the market, this political leadership has profound *confidence in the state*. This trust, moreover, is accompanied by a deep and almost indiscriminate *distrust of East German society*. Forty years of communism, according to the German leadership, have produced a terrible human tragedy – the personality structures, habits, dispositions, expectations, and mentalities of the citizens of the new lands make them unfit and incapable of managing their affairs. It is not their fault, but they are no longer trustworthy. They must be remolded and reeducated, not simply in industrial skills but with new mentalities. Those too old or too thoroughly spoiled by old habits and inclinations must be prevented from obstructing the new course; in the yet undamaged youth of the eastern lands lies good fortune.[51] It follows that the German leadership will use the state to transform the economy and reconstruct the society.

The Czech leaders, like their German counterparts, have profound confidence in the market. Unlike the Germans, they lack a strong state; yet unlike the Poles, they are not faced with deeply rooted institutions in civil society that might negate their leadership. From this it follows that the Czech political leadership is attempting to *use the market to transform the economy*. So deep is their confidence in the market that they will use it to privatize the economy. Citizen vouchers in the Czech Republic are not an ideological method to win support through some extraeconomic means; instead, they are the institutional vehicle to achieve the economic goals that will provide the basis for short- and longer-term social support. It would be entirely misleading, therefore, to interpret the Czech leadership's use of a civic principle as an indication of their deep and abiding commitment to equality. Auctioning the assets of the large public enterprises is likely to give rise to a relatively rapid differentiation of wealth because some individuals are acquiring properties at truly bargain basement prices.

Hungary, by contrast, is in many ways the opposite of the Czech Republic. There we find a state elite that is profoundly ambivalent about the market, so much so that we can say that it *distrusts the market*. But at the same time, this is a state elite that is highly *uncertain about society's trust* in its leadership. Its postsocialist governments are popularly elected, but this legitimacy does not convey confidence that the burdens that will necessarily accompany marketization will be accepted by the population. Lacking intermediary institutions (such as strong, cohesive trade unions) with which it can publicly negotiate, that elite has very few means to know the limits of society's tolerance. Thus, it avoids taking decisive steps in fear of society's reaction. And all the while, it engages in a cyclical process of here tightening, there loosening the reins on the galloping enterprise managers.

If the German state leadership trusts the state to remake the society, the Czechs trust the market to remake the economy, and the current Hungarian leadership distrusts the market while being distrusted by the society, Poland is that case where *to keep the trust of society the state must win society's faith in the market*. Like the Czech voucher program, the Polish citizenship vouchers are intended to perform the economic function of promoting privatization where domestic savings are too little to cover the value of the assets. But unlike the Czech program, the Polish strategy of appealing to the civic principle is not simply auxiliary to, or instrumental for, an economic logic. Whereas in the Czech Republic the voucher system is a means of *achieving a market that is seen as self-legitimating*, in Poland the citizen voucher system is a *means of legitimating the market*.

A MARKET ECONOMY OR MODERN CAPITALISM?

As we noted at the outset of our discussion of privatization strategies, these programs will inevitably be modified as the work of the transformers is transformed by the societies of East Central Europe. The resulting process will resemble bricolage (innovative adaptations that combine seemingly discrepant elements) more than architectural design. We should not be surprised, however, if the blueprints of foreign experts continue to figure in the transformative process. Although the grand designs of cookbook capitalism will not be utilized faithfully as guidelines for action, they will nonetheless be useful resources. This hypothesis stems from a view of contemporary East Central European politicians and policy makers as located between their populations, who must bear the transformation costs, and international agencies and foreign governments, which are the potential providers of capital, aid, and access to Western markets.

Master blueprints are not substitutes for stabilization measures, but which East European finance minister would dare enter into negotiations with international lending institutions (the World Bank, the IMF, the European Bank for Reconstruction and Development, etc.) without one? With the diffusion of grand models from one economy to the next[52] we should expect, however, that formulas for external legitimation will be decoupled from actual practices.[53] At the same time, we should note the possibility that politicians might present their own policy preferences as mandated by international agencies. ("The IMF made me do it.") The question of who is legitimating what and by which means is, thus, much more complicated than a matter of powerful international agencies dictating to East European politicians who have no choice but to comply.

Skeptics will question whether bricolage is a viable alternative to comprehensive institutional design. But our appreciation of the evolutionary character of capitalism and our understanding of the lessons of state socialism incline us to the bricoleurs instead of the system designers. The pertinent lesson of decades of state socialism is that large-scale social engineering might so badly tear the social fabric that its damage will take decades to repair and that a totalizing institutional uncertainty will preclude the longer-term calculations so central to the efficient functioning of economic institutions. That is, the greater the scope of an experiment, the greater the risk of catastrophe.[54] Our intention here is not to denigrate institutional design. Institutional designs can be for the better, especially if their purpose is to solve particular problems of governance and coordination for specific sectors or localities (rather than to provide global solutions to the problems of an entire economy). In place of grand experiments, we should hope for more, not fewer "designs" – partial solutions to limited problems in which transformation becomes a process undertaken by a multiplicity of dispersed agents at many institutional sites. Well-functioning markets are more likely to come from trials and errors that can be corrected, and new opportunities are more likely to be perceived and exploited when transformative processes are decentralized than by grand experiments that are centrally imposed on society.

This view raises the question of whether the most far-reaching marketization of all aspects of economic life should be the policy goal in contemporary East Central Europe. Advocates of such a goal suffer from two analytic shortcomings: (1) they mistake one possible means as the end itself and (2) they operate in a theoretical universe in which the dichotomies of the state or market exhaust the range of viable coordinating mechanisms in modern economies. But (to take the first point) surely the goal of marketization has been, among other ends, to modernize the production processes and improve the international competitiveness of these damaged economies. Yet (moving to the second point), as various currents of thinking in political economy recently indicate, there are sectors in which the most competitive forms of economic coordination are *neither market nor statist*, but new forms whose alternative operations we are only beginning to understand and identify (with preliminary labels such as *networks, alliances, interfirm agreements*, and the like).[55] An exclusive policy of all-encompassing marketization across all sectors would therefore pose a new obstacle and not a means to international competitiveness.

Such a tragedy is likely so long as the policy debate in the transition from state socialism is dominated by those who mistake the triumph of capitalism for the triumph of the market and look only to the *market revolutions* of Reagan and Thatcher, when the real victories involved the industrial reorganizations in Germany and Japan that were neither market nor hierarchical. But modern capitalist economies should not be reduced to only one of their parts: Markets are but one of multiple coexisting coordinating mechanisms in modern capitalism.[56] Transformative schemes that rely on an exclusive coordinating mechanism do not so much emulate existing capitalism as echo the implementation of state socialism and, like it, carry the danger of sacrificing the dynamic efficiency and flexibility that depend on diversity of organizational forms.[57]

PART III

DELIBERATIVE ASSOCIATION

4

MARKETS, STATES, AND DELIBERATIVE ASSOCIATIONS

EAST MEETS EAST

Liberalism has not abandoned its plans for the liberation of the economies of the once-socialist world, but the thrill is gone. Although only the most naive had promised quick fixes back in 1989 and 1990, no one foresaw that declines in production would be deeper or last longer than during the Great Depression of the interwar years. Although economic recovery started in some of the East Central European countries as early as 1994, the heady heydays are gone, with electorates fatigued by years of reform. New governments in Poland and Hungary promise to keep their ships on the liberal course – but with socialist colors on the mainsails. Elsewhere in the region, the liberal enthusiasm ended almost before it started. If you were marking off the days on Alexander Shatalin's program to create a mature market economy for Russia in "500 days," you could have stopped before you had to sharpen your pencil. Yegor Gaidar's program of shock therapy went up with the smoke billowing from the burning parliament building, and Jeffrey Sachs surrendered hope that his advice would be heeded by the Russian government. The market shock, he argued, was halted before the therapy could take effect and will remain unfinished business so long as the political climate and the will of the Russian leadership fail to match the ambitions of his policy prescriptions.[1]

Although the neoliberals are packing their bags, the postsocialist economies will not lack foreign imports: Another group of policy advisers is flying into the region, bringing in their briefcases not lessons from the West but new models from the East. Whereas during the neoliberal heyday consultants commuted directly from Cambridge to Crakow, now it seems that the preferred route reaches Budapest via Beijing, Slovenia via Seoul, and Tallinn via Taipei. If the East European patients (or their international lending agency insurers) were willing to pay for shock therapy, they are likely consumers as well of miracle cures – this time of the East Asian Miracle model.

As the policy winds shift from West to East, the new contingent of policy advisers carries a different message. Free market liberalism, they argue, places its hopes on a self-generating market. But that strategy confuses goals and means. To create markets, one cannot rely on markets. The lesson of the East Asian economies is that to strengthen the market one must first strengthen the state. If the debate was once almost exclusively about the development of capital markets or the relative merits of sequencing currency convertibility before or after price liberalization, the new discourse is about how to establish state institutions with more coherence, capacity, and cohesiveness.[2] East Asia demonstrates that the challenge for the transition in Eastern Europe is whether and how the state can fulfill its "specific, modernizing role."[3] Whereas the neoliberals held a deeply engrained antipathy to the state and were actively committed to its dismantling, the East Asianists see the need in Eastern Europe for "empowering a government bureaucracy."[4] To compete in the global economy under the current conditions of rapid technological change and capital shortage, "the need for government guidance is much greater than in the past."[5] Whereas the "Washington consensus" promoted privatization, price liberalization, and trade liberalization, the neostatists draw on the "compelling examples" of the "successful late industrializers" across East Asia to advocate activist state intervention, whether in the form of trade protection ("getting prices wrong"[6]), subsidies, investment credits, and industrial policy[7] or "public ownership."[8] "Thus, seeing the East European dilemma through the eyes of the East Asian experience suggests that if economic development is to continue, *dirigisme* cannot die."[9] Such counsel is not likely to fall on deaf ears in Yeltsin's government in Russia, or in the recently elected socialist governments in Poland, Hungary, and Bulgaria, or in governments in Belorussia, Ukraine, Slovakia, and Albania, where strongmen hold deep convictions about strong states.

The choice seems clear: free markets versus strong states. Each offers a comprehensive package of policy prescriptions to solve the problem of how to restructure the formerly socialist economies while maintaining social peace. For the one, self-generating markets can be the institutions of restructuring that, by creating self-sustaining growth, will solve the social problems of the transition. If and when problems emerge, the solution is not retreat but more markets. For the other, a transformative state is the only agent with the information and collective intelligence to direct the massive reorganization required where markets are nonexistent or weak at best. Organizationally buffered from societal interests, it alone can act with the cohesiveness needed to guide the process of economic and social transformation. If and when problems emerge, the solution is more buffering, not less, because it is precisely the transformative state's insulated autonomy that gives it the capacity to lead economic restructuring and resolve social tensions.

As our rhetoric suggests, we will argue here for an alternative conception of economic restructuring. The first task is to modulate the oscillation in intellectual trends from hierarchy to market to hierarchy. But it is not sufficient to halt the pendulum at some hypothetically virtuous middle point at which markets would be free enough and states strong enough so that each could fulfill its designated, and mutually correcting, functions. For almost 40 years, reform economists and policy analysts in the region have searched for the golden mean – the correct mix of plan and market, of public and private property. Instead of a better mix, our analysis of the past five years of economic restructuring and privatization in Central Europe suggests that strengthening markets and strengthening states requires recognizing and facilitating institutions of coordination that are neither market nor hierarchy. In this chapter, we identify and elaborate several fundamental characteristics of these institutions: They are associative (with identifiable network properties) and they are deliberative (with identifiable discursive properties). Successful economic restructuring to create self-sustaining growth and self-maintaining social peace can be achieved neither by a transformative state nor by the self-generating market but through the transformative politics[10] of deliberative association.

To make this argument, we begin with an analysis of the lack of autonomy of both states and markets under socialism. State socialism, of course, lacked developed markets, but (and this may surprise some readers) the socialist state also fundamentally lacked autonomy. We then examine how these problems were variously diagnosed, and diverse solutions prescribed, first by early strategies of liberalization, later by a fully articulated liberalism, and finally by the more recent efforts to bring the state back in. Our point of departure in elaborating an alternative strategy of development begins with an assessment of the pathbreaking concept of *embedded autonomy* advanced by Peter Evans. After clarifying the ways in which Evans's concepts must be substantially modified before they can be applied to the East European setting, we outline the major features of deliberative association. As we shall see, in place of calls to liberate the economy or to liberate the state, our advocacy of deliberation is explicitly de-liberating. But it is not illiberal. New kinds of binding agreements can promote marketization and improve economic performance. Similarly, binding agreements produced in deliberative forums constrain state executives and make them more accountable. But far from weakening the state, they can improve its capacity for formulating and implementing coherent reform programs. In Chapters 5 and 6, we elaborate the concept of deliberative association (for the fields of enterprise restructuring and economic policy, respectively) through sustained comparisons of three East Central European countries.

THE BEHEMOTH AS GULLIVER BOUND

We begin with a problem, paradoxical only on first encounter: The gigantic socialist party-state, exercising centralized control over virtually all productive assets and reserving for itself final judgment in all political, intellectual, cultural, or social questions, fundamentally lacks autonomy. In fact, we can say with little exaggeration that the field of state bureaucracy in general and the political field in particular are the least autonomous fields of activity in late state socialism.[11]

The East European socialist state did not start out in this predicament, not because it once had autonomy but because autonomy, relative or otherwise, was not a characteristic of any field. During the Stalinist period of the late 1940s and early 1950s, the societies of East Central Europe were dominated by a single logic throughout all spheres. This was the logic of *delegation by usurpation*. Through a primary act of self-delegation, the leaders of the national party-states based their rule on the claim that they alone possessed the "scientific" knowledge ("the laws of motion of history") to guide all social and economic processes.[12] Emphatically, it was not society that delegated such authority – for, according to the logic of usurpatory delegation, in the aftermath of fascism and the Second World War, it was precisely a corrupted, distrusted, and immature society that had to be tamed and trained. The satisfactions of the citizens were literally of no account. Based on its purely transcendental justification, the party-state was accountable only to the future.

Usurpatory delegation was not about interests but about will. And in the pursuit of the general will, the primitive accumulation of political capital was achieved through the physical and symbolic violence of dispossession as the state appropriated all means of production, material and symbolic. The absence of autonomous means of expression precluded particularistic interests, for none could be articulated except in the singularly general form. Absent particularisms, there were no autonomous fields. Just as the national leaders held authority delegated to them by their Soviet superiors, so, in a chain of delegation, the cadre of the party-state possessed the political capital delegated to them by their hierarchical superiors. This delegated political capital was a peculiar asset (at once singular and completely generalizable), transportable and mobilizable in any setting and universally applicable in any domain. Thus, the concept of autonomous fields was foreign to Stalinist Eastern Europe. This was a peculiarly *representative* polity: The delegate represented the party-state as the embodiment of general interests, and rewards went to those who could loyally disregard any and all particularistic interests. It was, moreover, a peculiarly *competitive* polity: Socioeconomic units at all levels (the brigade, the workshop, the firm, the locality, the region, the branch) competed with each other to demonstrate which could best re-present (make present in a particular setting) the icons and the will of the political elite. In this socialist competition, not prices but prizes were the proof, the sign, and the currency of political credit.

But the period of pure delegation was remarkably short-lived. Key to understanding the shift from totalitarian usurpation to a still far from benign paternalism is the process we might call the *dynamic of the responsibles*. In the Communist polity, the typical agenda of a given party body would be organized around the following construction: "Let us hear now the report from the comrade responsible for . . ." (followed by some bureaucratically designated category, varying according to the hierarchical level of the party body) "heavy industry," "mining," "Borsod County," "grain procurement," "outlying villages," "bread delivery," "Budapest District 22," "the press," "artists and academics," and so on. In the period of usurpation and commandism, the designated comrade is responsible for *carrying out orders*. But once primitive accumulation is underway, the delegated cadre becomes responsible for *maintaining order* within the domain of his assignment.

This redefined responsibility brings an important shift: To carry out this task, the responsible must become, at least to some extent, responsive. The *responsive responsible* thus begins to say to his or her bureaucratic superiors, "To carry out my responsibilities, I must be able to take local conditions into account." Over time, and the more the responsive responsible becomes a mediator between state and society, these interjections become "To carry out such a task, *we* must take particular conditions into account." Finally, as this mediating role is routinized, the boundary between state and society becomes expressable. Speaking as a messenger from society, the responsive responsible can address the party-state as an abstract entity: "To carry out this goal, *you* must take these particular conditions into account."

We should stress that the responsive responsible does not immediately become a *representative of* particular interests and accountable to them. As a delegate, he or she is accountable to those higher in the hierarchy and, within that accountability, finds room for maneuver: To the local interests he or she says, "See, my hands are tied." To the higher authorities he says, "To do the job, I must be free to take into account local (spatial or domain-specific) circumstances."

To understand the dynamics of the Communist polity, we need an expanded grammar and an altered syntax of the language of political representation. We cannot grasp it with the conventional categories of *interest representation*. Because the responsive responsible is responsible *for* but not responsible *to* the social actors of a particular domain, and because he or she is not authorized to speak on behalf of and in the name of particular social groups, this person does not speak for particular constituencies in the conventional sense. Yet the more decision-making bodies are explicitly composed of such responsibles who do not speak *for* but who can speak *of* designated *named places* in the social space, the more these territorial units, social groups, and specific domains become the actual constitutive units of the polity. That is, the elemental unit of the socialist polity is not the citizen, or parties, or organized groups. Precisely because it lacks *constituencies*, its basic *constitutive units* are increasingly particularistic, special interests.

These particularistic trends are exacerbated by the significant shift in the self-proclaimed legitimating principle of paternalist regimes. Whereas Stalinism was based on the explicit rejection of particular *interests*, post-Stalinist paternalism (of which Kádárism was a major variant) enunciated a new legitimation: "We care for you. We take your interests into account." But because these interests were allowed no organized representation independent of the party-state, the only way they could be brought into the polity was through the bureaucracy itself. Where the party-state was once marked by detachment, it now becomes the preeminent institution of incorporation. In this organicist conception, every leading body at any hierarchical level must be composed of those responsible agents who stand in for the particular interests in their respective policy domains. Whereas in the Stalinist period the party was *apart*, in the period of paternalism the party is nothing more than its parts. The more it fears social disruption, the more it wants to incorporate all kinds of interests without allowing their independent representation; and the more it uses its bureaucratic organs to mediate competing claims, so these combine to render more diffused and dispersed its selection criteria.[13] When the leading bodies increasingly lack leading parts, it becomes unclear what or who or how to adjudicate between the interests of "balanced growth," "dollar exports," "the solution of the housing crisis," and so on.

The particularistic tendency of the dynamic of the responsive responsibles interacts, in turn, with a process that we might call the *dynamic of the fields*. The shift from Stalinism to paternalism marks the beginning of the growing autonomization (always relative, never absolute) of various fields of activity within the society. Political loyalty is now not the only way to make a career. In fact, the best way to make a career is to combine political capital with other competencies and credentials. Whereas the party credential, as a form of political capital, was based on an esoteric knowledge that, nonetheless, had an extraordinarily immense scope of potential applicability, now careers could be based on capital with greater asset specificity, that is, by investing in skills that have a more limited applicability in a specific field (e.g., the economy, technology, science, the professions, cultural fields). There is nothing automatic or natural about this process as it is brought into play by actors in particular domains struggling to defend the boundaries of their fields and the criteria of promotion within them. The delegates responsible for these emerging fields are not immediately accountable to them, but to the extent that they begin to make careers even partially *within these fields*, they bring new principles, new accountings, new logics into the decision-making bodies of the state.

Thus, the old political capital of delegation dissipates at exactly the time that more and more claims of ever greater diversity and complexity are flooding the socialist state. At the very moment that other fields all around it are gaining their relative autonomy, the socialist state itself increasingly lacks autonomy. It continues to intervene across all boundaries; but because its own boundaries are so ill defined, it has no specific logic, no coherence, and no clear selection criteria. Like the giant Gulliver, its reach is immense; but the farther it stretches, the greater the possibility that the visible hand will be tied up by multiple particularistic claims. Within its boundaries there is bargaining aplenty; but there are no binding agreements, only a cacophony of rationalizations. It incorporates; but it is not even corporatist, for particular interests are never clearly distinct from the bureaucratic state organs that simultaneously represent and mediate them. Because there is no independent basis for assessing political support, no clear measures of political weight, the state cannot orchestrate concertation but itself becomes disconcerted. Because claims are not aggregated outside the bureaucracy by autonomous organizations that compete to *organize conflicting interests within* political programs, the party-state becomes disaggregated in the process of mediation. The party-state is not embedded in its social environment; it dissolves within it.

LIBERALIZATION AND LIBERALISM: SEVERING THE TIES THAT BIND

LIBERALIZATION

To compound the irony that the project of the all-encompassing party state results in a weakened state with little capacity to provide coherent policy direction we add another: The liberal projects of the 1990s have their antecedents in reform measures devoted to strengthening the state. Liberalization was launched, and then repeatedly refitted and relaunched, in successive waves from the late 1960s to the late 1980s by reformist technocrats within the state. Although one can find early academic proponents of the goal of liberating a market rationality for its own sake (and these voices, although occasionally vacillating, become increasingly vocal across the period), the function of market reforms for state technocrats was less a goal than a means – a means to liberate the state. The diagnosis presented in the preceding section would have come as little surprise to these reformists, for they held the view that it was the long arm of the party-state reaching into every corner of the society and the economy that was the source of the problem. If the visible hand touched less, fewer parasites would enter the body of the party-state. Market reforms were a means to unburden the state. If the state had fewer tasks to perform and fewer interests to mediate, it could perform its remaining tasks better. If, for example, it did not intervene in the microdecisions of enterprises, it would have more capacity for macroeconomic management.[14]

Concise, lucid analyses of East European liberalization are available elsewhere.[15] Suffice it to note here that these were always *partial* reforms. Firms were granted limited, never complete, autonomy. Because of this partial character, enterprise directors could always keep one hand in the state's pockets, and state bureaucrats were always ready to "correct distortions." Reforms were not simply stop-go. *Brakes* (the actual term used) were a key feature of reform designs right from the start. With constant shifting of the economic gears, it was like driving a car while stepping on the clutch, brakes, and accelerator at the same time, with a ride that was as noisy as it was jerky. Enterprise directors, moreover, were deeply ambivalent about market reforms. On the one hand, liberalization seemed to promise more room for maneuver. But managers who were skilled at hooking on to the plan, experienced in target bargaining, and adept at reading bureaucratic signals were reluctant to adjust to reading market signals alone. When and where market reforms threatened firms' soft budget constraints (if even only hypothetically), managers recoiled at the possible loss of the ability to shift responsibility upward along the ministerial hierarchies. The liberalizing technocrats could look to enterprise directors as unreliable allies at best. Indeed, the directors of the large public enterprises joined forces on several occasions to scuttle reform efforts.[16]

But liberalization was halfhearted also because the party-state bureaucracy was deeply divided about the course and consequences of marketization. Reforms were promulgated with the hope that marketization would improve economic performance and thus increase the resource base for redistribution by the party-state. But to the extent that market reforms actually took effect and increased the scope of market considerations, these reforms, of course, weakened the salience of measures other than profitability and reduced the importance of other programs, such as regional development or projects of the branch and sectoral ministries in which the state elite had a stake. Above all, reforms weakened the networks running through the large public enterprises that were the elites' principal tie to society. The more enterprises were told to look to profitability, the less they could be counted on to provide the political goods that enterprises had always been expected to deliver. "If enterprises make decisions on the basis of profitability," clamored the responsive responsibles in the offices of the county party secretaries, the trade unions, and the branch ministries, "what is to ensure that they will maintain employment levels in my district, or that less profitable consumer goods will be adequately supplied at the same level of prices, or that investment will continue to flow to my region? Automatisms might help you technocrats achieve macroeconomic balance, but they cannot be relied on to reduce social tensions. If macroeconomic stability and social stability cannot be harmonized, then what is the point of your economic rationality?" Thus, precisely because it loosened guarantees, weakened the bargaining networks, reduced direct control over the logic of production, and threatened the organizational basis of paternalism, liberalization was everywhere opposed and eventually undermined by entrenched forces within the state bureaucracy who fell back on the political use of the public enterprises.[17]

LIBERALISM

If liberalization under state socialism left a legacy of weak markets and weak states, liberalism in the immediate postsocialist period could be defined by the determination not to repeat that mistake. Marketization and economic rationality had to be ends in themselves. Given the earlier lessons, the task should not be to strengthen the state, but to break its back. The problem of the long arm of the visible hand cannot be solved merely by the state's *withdrawing* its hand from the economy. Voluntary restraints do not eliminate the possibility of involuntary reflexes at a later time. For postsocialist

liberals, the dismantling of the *party*-state would not be a sufficient correc-
tive: The behavior patterns of paternalism were so deeply ingrained throughout the bureaucracy and so widely diffused throughout the society that they
were a present danger even with the advent of competitive electoral politics.
The state must not simply withdraw its hand, it must be prevented from
being able to reach in again.[18]

To this end, in addition to the standard policies of price and import
liberalizations, the programs of the postsocialist liberal movement included
measures to cut off the helping hand. Privatization, for example, was everywhere seen as a means of marketization. But its strategic importance lay in
severing the ties of control that ran through state ownership of productive
assets. If the ministries were no longer owners, they would lose their principal means of intervening in the affairs of enterprises. In this sense, privatization was a major component of a broader *economic constitutionalism*
whose key features were a set of legal measures that prevented the state from
interfering in property relations – except in one direction: The state could
privatize, but it became constitutionally constrained from renationalization.
Similarly, the state was in all matters legally bound to property neutrality:
It could not discriminate against firms on the basis of their property form.
Through such constitutional constraints, the mix of the mixed economy
would be shaped by diffused, dispersed social agents.

But what to do with enterprises awaiting privatization? Here liberal
economists and policy makers were initially divided. Some argued that rapid
privatization would quickly dispel the problem. When initial public offerings failed to privatize all but a handful of enterprises regionwide, some
liberals argued for toleration of spontaneous privatizations as a way of getting property into private hands without getting the state into the business
of managing property sales. Others argued against such "wild" privatizations, warning that transactions perceived as illegitimate would weaken the
legitimacy of private property. Over time, positions converged on a set of
measures that together formed a package to deal with the problem of firms
remaining temporarily in state ownership. Its three components were tough
bankruptcy laws, an absolute end to all forms of state subsidies, and man-
datory *corporatization* of the public enterprises.

The intention of corporatization was to break the strongholds of the
branch ministries. Through corporatization, state-owned enterprises are
transformed into shareholding or joint stock companies, and title to these
shares is transferred to a new "owner" representing the state – a special
agency, fund, or new ministry (organizationally separated from the old ministries) with the responsibility to manage the assets and, above all, to privatize them, whether through sales or giveaways. Lest the new owner and

the transformed enterprises fall back into the old paternalist habits, the other two legs of the triad must be introduced promptly and enforced resolutely. Subsidies must be eliminated, with no false hopes of applying for new exemptions; and strict bankruptcy laws should be introduced across the board, preferably modeled on Western accounting norms and judicial practices. Together these policies must send a signal to enterprise management: If you will not or cannot swim in the emerging market, you will sink. When the state hears your siren cry, "Give me a hand, give me your hand," it must be bound to respond not simply that it should not, or that it will not, but that it cannot. Markets can emerge, and quickly – but only if all actors are legally and institutionally constrained to accept that there is no alternative.[19] The surest way to submerge the market is for the state to show any hesitation along the charted course: Markets are the ends *and the means*.[20] As for restructuring, allow markets to do the work of creative destruction. Regarding unemployment, allow liberated markets to generate growth and jobs. The problem of the unprecedentedly low levels of investment will be solved by capital markets. And the problem of enterprise governance can be coordinated by managerial markets and markets for corporate control.

THE NEOSTATISTS

By 1993, growing disillusionment with the capacities of the market as a mechanism of economic transformation led to a renewed preoccupation with the capacities of the state. The increasingly breathless reporting by *The Economist* about skyrocketing increases in production within the private sector notwithstanding, there was a widespread perception across the region that privatization (whether through privatizing firms by transferring assets or through privatizing the economy by stimulating new private entrants) was moving at a pace far below initial expectations.[21] Production had plummeted, unemployment had soared, and tax evasion and corruption were pervasive. In the view of the neostatists, marketization was strong enough to produce deleterious side effects but still too weak to ameliorate them. Across the region, liberated markets had unleashed mass demonstrations and strike waves against plant closures, wage cuts, and falling living standards. Free market programs were being rejected by electorates, leading to instability of governments, the growth of populism, and threats to democratic consolidation.[22] Bootstrapping, argued the neostatists, could not bring about the liberals' vision of a dramatic escape forward to the dominance of a market rationality. The solution to weak and inadequately functioning markets was not more markets but a stronger, more effective state.

Like the early technocratic reformers of the socialist period, the neostatists of the present share the view that the bureaucracies in Eastern Europe are weak states with only limited capacity to formulate and implement policies. But, in part because of the failures of the earlier reforms, they argue that the state will not grow stronger simply by devolving functions from hierarchies to markets or from the public to the private sector. Increased state capacity is a prerequisite for establishing the conditions for marketization. "For the creation and functioning of the market economy, a strong state is indispensable."[23] Whereas the neoliberals want to cut off the visible hand, the neostatists argue that the lesson of East Asian as well as West European development is that "the transition to capitalism required a more visible hand than neo-liberalism envisioned."[24] The postsocialist state, moreover, must not only create markets but also solve (at least in the lengthy transition period) the problems created by them. For these reasons, it is not enough to unburden or downsize the state. It must be redesigned. Proposals typically call for streamlining the administrative apparatus (with clear separation of functions, improved lines of communication, and stricter budgetary accounting), staffed by higher-paid professional bureaucrats trained in new schools of public administration.[25]

Whereas some neostatists stress the internal redesign of the state, others, especially functionaries and leading executives in the new regimes, advocate its insulation from external influences. Drawing on an ample legacy of authoritarianism in the region, this neostatist conception looks to China[26] and Latin America.[27] The prescriptions of this *transformative state* model can be described most succinctly as a direct negation of the socialist party-state as the prey of partial interests. State capacity, in this view, is an immediate function of state autonomy. Whereas the party-state was held captive by the networks of bargaining that penetrated the state and crisscrossed its bureaucracies, the transformative state will be autonomous and therefore gain capacity by insulation from these networks. If the weak bureaucracy of the late socialist state failed because it tried to mediate any and all interests, the postsocialist state will be strong to the extent that it can maximally disregard interests. At the core of this state is a team of technocrats, the *change team*, not chosen from within the state bureaucracy but from outside it and now remolding it. This is an engineering state, reshaping itself to reshape the society. The technocratic team is confident about goals, and (with salaries to match) it has the esprit de corps, selection criteria, techniques, and expertise to design the institutions and programs to achieve these goals. Ties to society, as well as connections to party politicians and even to other parts of the not yet reformed bureaucracy, are always suspect as tainted by interests. Thus, especially in times when such *information* is indistinguishable from the *noise* of social crisis, the bureaucracy must be insulated if it is to issue clear-sighted directives that will solve the pressing problems of transition.[28]

The representatives of the transformative state model do not share the optimistic assumptions of the liberals about the capacity of liberated markets to (re)generate the political basis of economic reforms via rapid economic growth. In their vision, transformative states have to cope with the problems of being surrounded by social groups with particularistic interests bound to the status quo and ready to resist any change that would threaten their status. The transformative state cannot take into account their interests, they hold, since transformative policies built on the interests of these groups would only reproduce the status quo. So, unlike the free marketeers, who think that there is no need for politics, in the transformative state model there is no place for politics. Instead, it is the strong state's task to impose the necessary transformative policies that allow for the departure from the status quo and the creation of new classes with interests already corresponding to the logic of the market economy.[29] From Yeltsin's Russia to Walesa's Poland, neostatists have attempted to establish strong executives with decree powers lacking horizontal and vertical accountability.[30] The ensuing political crises of these exemplary failures demonstrate that maximizing the capacity to disregard interests falls far short of maximizing the transformative capacity of the state.

THE DEVELOPMENTAL STATE:
TIES THAT DO NOT BIND

When asked how to restructure the postsocialist economies, neoliberals respond that the best way is to use the free market. The neostatists respond that the proper course is to use a coherent state. The problem, however, is that the societies of Eastern Europe lack both developed markets and coherent states. The nonexisting starting points of the liberals and the neostatists remind us of the joke in which an Irishman in the far countryside is asked, "What's the best way to get to Dublin?" He thinks for a minute and responds, "Don't start from here."

The Irishman's irony would not be lost on East Europeans. The *best* ways to get to capitalism started somewhere else. But those options are not available to our contemporary traveling companions. They must start the journey from here. With what institutional resources might they embark?

Postsocialist societies lack strong markets and coherent states, but they have decades of experience with strong networks. Why not start from here?

The postsocialist liberals and transformative statists are obviously reluctant to adopt such a starting point because a resolute hostility to networks is a defining feature of both perspectives. For the transformative statists, the old networks of interests are precisely the parasites against which the state must erect a thick wall of insulation, and it is their resuscitation that it must actively suppress. For the liberals, Adam Smith's principled suspicion of combinations provides the guidelines for contemporary policies to prevent networks from making links back to the state that dilute the stance of "no alternatives to the market." Each perspective is so deeply distrustful of associative ties based neither on hierarchy nor on exchange that one can well imagine either one favoring the passage of a postsocialist equivalent of the Loi le Chapelier.[31]

If we redefine the question – shifting from "What is the best way to get to capitalism?" to "What resources are available to start from here?" – with what analytic resources might we begin to address the question? For our analytic starting point, we turn to an insightful study on the state and economic development in which Peter Evans persuasively argues for the importance of social networks in shaping the capacity of the *developmental state*.[32] Whereas the theorists of the technobureaucratic transformative state conflate state autonomy and state capacity, Evans's major advance (based on a rich comparative analysis of East Asian, African, and Latin American cases) is an analytic separation of the two. For Evans, the autonomy of the developmental state derives not from its insulation from society but from its organizational coherence. The boundaries of the state are clear and well defined not because they are high and thick but because the decisions that are taken within them are governed by a logic that is clear and coherent. Evans's developmental state is autonomous when goals and means are clear: Procedural rationality guides decision making to select policies that should promote economic performance. The autonomy of the state is thus grounded on principles. Such principled autonomy is reproduced by regulating, indeed facilitating, coherent careers within it based on rigorous selection criteria bringing talent into the state and rewarding those who demonstrate that they are accountable to its principles. The developmental state can do many things in many places throughout a given territory and yet still maintain the discrete boundaries of an autonomous field because of this dual specificity – the specificity of selection criteria in decision making and the specificity of selection criteria in career making.[33] A coherent logic and a cohesive staff make possible autonomous, coherent, and cohesive policy output.

Evans's analysis, however, does not end with autonomy. Even if his coherently autonomous developmental bureaucrats know what general goals they would like to promote, they still need information. If their decisions would be no better than those of purely private actors, then they would be superfluous; and without good information, they could not make better decisions. To have better information is not simply to have better data: For that, you would not need a developmental state but only a better statistical agency and more clever forecasting. To be ahead of the trends, developmental agencies need more than statistics – they need intelligence. They must acquire situated knowledge – intimate, deeply proprietary knowledge – of present best practices and already-present futures. Autonomy in itself will not yield access to such vivid knowledge.

A merely autonomous state, moreover, cannot ensure policy implementation. Knowledge and its rational processing by talented, ambitious, and uncorruptable officials (in the best Weberian sense of the word) to produce coherent policy will be for naught if policies cannot be implemented. Implementation requires allies, partners in the economy who, far from opposition or neutrality to state policies, will look to the developmental state for guidance and actively facilitate putting policies into practice.

Because better intelligence and active implementation are the keys to state *capacity*, Evans makes a critical analytic distinction between autonomy and capacity and identifies different determinants of each. Whereas state autonomy is based on the state's organizational coherence, state capacity is based on the state's *embeddedness* in its social environment. The developmental state is embedded because it is crisscrossed with social networks that tie it closely and deeply to the economy. For Evans, bureaucrats, even the most coherent and cohesive, are not omniscient; the specific knowledge that they lack is not located within the state but situated in myriad sites throughout the economy. The developmental state must not be an impervious fortress state buffered from the economic elite. Instead, the developmental state is embedded, and its staff is intimately tied to that elite and to its business secrets. Through that mutual interchange, economic elites are privy to the agendas and policy debates within the state, and this knowledge forms a basis of alliances in policy implementation.

With this notion of embeddedness, we see that Evans turns 180 degrees from the transformative neostatists – for to insulate the state would be to eliminate the source of its capacity. In Evans's conception, the boundaries of the developmental state are not insulated but permeable. Like the membranes of a healthy cell, they allow passage of persons but not of contaminating principles. The embedded state is permeated by the personal ties of the informal networks; but because the internal operations of the state are immunized by the powerful accountability of its bureaucratic rationality, these are ties that do not bind.

It is Evans's twin concepts, *coherence* and *embeddedness*, that yield significant analytic power. And it is the corresponding twin attributes of *autonomy* and *capacity* that yield a strong, flexible state. Embeddedness increases the state's capacity for access to knowledgeable inputs. Autonomy increases the likelihood of coherent policy outputs. And again, embeddedness increases the state's capacity to realize effective policy implementation.

RETHINKING COHERENCE AND EMBEDDEDNESS

Evans's concept of the developmental state represents a major contribution to the analysis of the state and economic development. In contrast to the liberals, who have pictured the state as the source of the problem in economic development, Evans has convincingly demonstrated that state bureaucracies that are both coherent and embedded can provide the collective good of inducing investment and growth in economies in which otherwise atomized economic elites would not risk investing. Second, in contrast to both the liberals and the neostatists, who have pictured networks as rent-seeking alliances corrupting markets and/or states, Evans has convincingly argued that the network ties in which state bureaucrats are embedded can be a positive contribution to industrial transformation.

However fertile and insightful his concepts, Evans's model should not be uncritically applied to the problems of postsocialist economic development. In the discussion that follows, we indicate how the analytic categories of autonomy/coherence and capacity/embeddedness must be recast to address the specific challenges and opportunities of the East European experience. Reconsidering Evans's model in this light, we question several of his assumptions and propose other analytic dimensions that should have relevance for the study of the state and economic development in a wide range of settings. To anticipate that argument, we first point out Evans's neglect of politics and political parties: By focusing almost solely on characteristics of the field of bureaucratic administration to the neglect of important features of the political field, Evans ignores how political institutions that mediate between state and society can be a fundamental source of policy coherence. Second, we note Evans's neglect of interfirm networks: By focusing almost solely on elite networks that span the boundaries of business and state administration, Evans ignores how business networks in the economy can be a fundamental source of economic restructuring. The element common to both dimensions of our critique can thus be seen as a call for "bringing society back in" to analyze the politics of economic development.[34]

AUTONOMY/COHERENCE

In identifying the basis for the coherence of an autonomous Weberian state bureaucracy, Evans devotes little attention to politics and its institutions. His neglect of politicians, parties, and other political organizations of interest intermediation is perhaps attributable to specific structural and historical features of his exemplary developmental states. Evans explicitly acknowledges that his positive cases are either authoritarian East Asian states in which politics was excluded or regimes in which "exceptional growth, not just of output but also of real wages" had diminished the need for politics.[35] But the problems of economic development in postsocialist societies are taking place in an entirely different historical conjuncture: The recent global wave of democratization has taken place simultaneously with a contraction of the world economy. Expressed in domestic terms, in the postcommunist societies the *extension of political rights* coincides with the dramatic *increase of the social burdens* caused by economic restructuring.

A central question of the political economy of restructuring in our time becomes, therefore, how to create institutions for the mediation, coordination, and concertation of those social and political actors whose interests are threatened by reform policies and who have the capacity to block the implementation and consolidation of reforms.[36] In the concluding section of his article (and the final chapter of his book-length treatment of the developmental state), Evans recognizes that there are cases in the new historical conjuncture where both the need for and the possibility of this type of interest intermediation exist. But his proposed solution – "broader embeddedness" that connects the state bureaucracy not only to capital but also to labor and other social groups[37] – suggests that the same state bureaucrats who are responsible for carrying out a coherent reform program should also be responsible for aggregating, coordinating, and concerting broadly different group interests.

Our analysis of the late socialist state, by contrast, demonstrated that it is precisely such bureaucratic concertation that results in a disconcerted state and the loss of capacity to pursue coherent policies: A bureaucracy that attempts to mediate societal interests directly will be neither autonomous nor coherent. The lack of autonomy of the weak pre-1989 states in the region resulted much less from the qualities of their bureaucracies than from the deployment of these bureaucracies for the direct mediation of interests.

From our analysis of the "Behemoth as Gulliver Bound" we draw the fundamental lesson that the coherence of state bureaucracies requires institutions *outside the state bureaucracy* that mediate societal interests. An autonomous bureaucratic field with a distinctive organizational rationality requires an autonomous political field with distinctive selection criteria, career patterns, and forms of capital. In such an autonomous political field, other forms of capital may enter but only one is dominant: demonstration of political support. Because the selection criteria of the political field (in different parlance, the incentive structures of competitive politics) constrain politicians, parties, and organizations to maximize .political support, those criteria promote programs that encompass and incorporate broader, even conflicting interests. That is, where mediated by the political field, societal interests do not enter the state administration as fragmented, sectionalized claims that push and pull the bureaucracy hither and yon, but as interests already aggregated, coordinated, and organized into a comprehensive political program. Through this mediating role, an autonomous political field reduces the likelihood of a disconcerted state bureaucracy and increases (although never guarantees) the likelihood that it will receive relatively clear political direction.[38] Even where not fully consolidated, competitive politics and its autonomous political capital (votes for programs) give politicians a self-confidence entirely lacking in their late socialist counterparts, thereby increasing their capacity to set coherent goals for state bureaucrats.[39] In short, democratic accountability within the political field can facilitate procedurally rational accountability within the bureaucratic field.

As we elaborate more systematically in Chapters 6 and 7 (and demonstrate through sustained case comparisons), policy coherence within the political field is shaped not only by the *vertical accountability* of competitive elections but also by the institutions of *extended accountability*, whereby political authorities are monitored by other state institutions and held accountable by other organized societal actors. Extended accountability produces institutional safeguards that the citizens' "investment" in the political program of the winning party will not be squandered: Intrastate checks and balances, for example, reduce the likelihood of precipitous (and perhaps calamitous) policy swings, and institutionalized deliberations with the representatives of organized societal actors promote some confidence (or at least reduce the uncertainty) that programmatic promises about the distribution of the costs and the potential gains of economic reform can be enforced between elections. In so doing, the politics of inclusion expands the time horizons of the public.[40]

By bringing interests into the state, this transformative politics of inclusion also transforms the transformers. Extended deliberations moderate and pragmatize the programs of political elites: By constraining decision

makers to take into consideration ex ante the social and political consequences of their policies, it lengthens their time horizons and, in so doing,
increases policy coherence. Thus, in contrast to the insulationist view that
the contaminating influence of societal interests will necessarily erode state
autonomy, and in contrast to Evans's view that the state bureaucracy can
directly mediate these interests without eroding its autonomy, we argue
that the mediating institutions of the political field practicing the politics
of inclusion are a necessary source of state autonomy. Transcendental visions
that short-circuit particularistic interests in the interest of self-generating
markets will be undermined by the contentious and conflicting forces unleashed in a society undergoing economic restructuring. Paradoxically, only
by taking these societal interests into account – specifically, into the broader,
more encompassing accounts of comprehensive political programs bound to
multiple institutional channels of public accountability – can state policy
be independent of short-term, particularistic interests and pursue coherent,
long-term reform strategies.

CAPACITY/EMBEDDEDNESS

Our second criticism addresses Evans's pioneering work on the relationship
between embeddedness and the capacity for economic transformation. Our
analysis departs from Evans's, however, by shifting from network ties reaching into and out of the developmental state to focus instead on the importance of network ties as coordinating mechanisms out in the economy. In
short, it is not only the state bureaucracy but also firms and other economic
actors that are embedded in social networks.[41] This extension of the concept
of embeddedness is not a peripheral modification but addresses a core feature
of Evans's problematic – how to jump-start an economy endangered by the
stagnation of low-level equilibrium traps. Because there are circumstances
in which the *transformative capacity of social networks* can exceed the transformative capacity of the state (and contemporary Eastern Europe poses such
possibilities), we argue that the transformative capacity of an economy is
not a direct function of the personal ties of the state bureaucracy reaching
out to the business elite but must also include the strength and cohesiveness
of social networks in the economy itself.

  Evans is seemingly reluctant to acknowledge the importance of social
networks among firms and other economic actors. He is, for example, curiously silent about the role of the Japanese *keiretsu*, the South Korean *chaebol*, and the Taiwanese corporate clans even though these interenterprise
networks figure prominently in the economies where he finds successful
developmental states.[42] These lacunae are perhaps attributable to the intel-

lectual origins of the concept of the developmental state. For Gerschenkron and Hirschman, the developmental state must act as a substitute for weakly developed social networks. Evans's summary of his predecessors, in a crucial passage of his study, is instructive:

> Gerschenkron's work on late developers complements Weber by focusing on the specific contributions of the state apparatus to overcoming problems created by a disjunction between the scale of economic activity required for development and the effective *scope of existing social networks*. . . . The crux of the problem faced by late developers is that institutions that allow large risks to be spread *across a wide network of capital holders do not exist*, and individual capitalists are neither able nor interested in taking them on. Under these circumstances the state must serve as surrogate entrepreneur. . . . States that succeed in undertaking the tasks that Gerschenkron and Hirschman outline, as well as those set out by Weber, are legitimately called "developmental."[43]

But what if extensive networks of economic coordination are already in place? We shall argue here (and elaborate in greater detail in our country studies in Chapter 6) that such is the case in many postsocialist economies. Postsocialist economies are newcomers to capitalism, but they are not newcomers to industrialization. Socialism produced a gross caricature of an industrial structure, much of which must be dismantled. But it produced a structure of industrial enterprises nonetheless, much of which can be restructured to perform efficiently and effectively.

Equally important for our purposes here, socialism produced, within that industrial structure, networks of social relations of reciprocity and associative ties. These networks were unintended consequences of the attempt to "scientifically manage" an entire national economy: At the shop-floor level, shortages and supply bottlenecks led to bargaining between supervisors and informal groups; at the level of the second economy, the allocative distortions of central planning reproduced the conditions for networks of predominantly part-time entrepreneurs; and at the managerial level, the task of meeting plan targets produced dense networks of informal ties that cut across enterprises and local organizations. The existence of parallel structures in the informal and interfirm networks that got the job done under socialism means that instead of an institutional vacuum we find routines and practices, organizational forms and social ties, that can become assets, resources, and the basis for credible commitments and coordinated actions.[44]

This second element of our critique of Evans suggests that there are circumstances in which there is no need for a developmental state that *substitutes for absent networks*. But, as the first element of our critique implies, we do not conclude that the state and its coherence are irrelevant for economic development. State coherence and capacity are important – but for tasks different from those of the developmental state. Instead of coordinating economic development directly, the state can facilitate coordination in networks that spread risk not at the expense of the public good but in contribution to it. Strong networks are a resource, but they are not unproblematically so. They have the capacity to be agencies of development – or to be rent seekers depleting the public treasury and inhibiting economic growth. Under what conditions can states of relative strength recognize the coordinating capacity of networks of relative strength to unburden the state, thereby strengthening the capacity of the state to facilitate the effective monitoring of these same networks? It is to this problem that we turn.

DELIBERATIVE ASSOCIATION: NETWORKS FOR BINDING AGREEMENTS

East European capitalism is emerging under extraordinary conditions: the simultaneous extension of property rights and of political rights. Any strategy of economic development will be successful only to the extent that it addresses the problems associated with this simultaneity. First, the rapid extension of property rights creates conditions in which property boundaries are obscure, with multiple claimants for the same assets and complex interdependencies of assets across different claimants. Second, the rapid extension of political rights enfranchises the economically less advantaged at exactly the same time that restructuring exacts enormous social costs.

To restate the positions discussed earlier, but now directly in terms of this problematic: Neoliberals argue that marketization will reduce transaction costs, that an immediate clarification of property boundaries through even more rapid privatization (in effect, get the property rights "right") will reduce production costs, and that the two together will make transition costs negligible. Neostatists argue that not the boundaries of property but the boundaries of the state are the problem and the solution: Once these are properly redesigned, thoroughly insulated, or coherently embedded, the state can provide the collective good of inducing investment and growth in economies in which otherwise atomized economic elites would not risk investing.

We argue here for an alternative to the dispersed competition of markets and the hierarchical control of states, one antithetical neither to markets nor to states but that, as we shall see in our case studies, can strengthen both markets and states. This alternative perspective begins with very different assumptions about the twinned problems of property rights and political rights. Because of the objective interdependencies of assets and the network properties of liabilities, this perspective considers the possibility that fuzzy property boundaries may, in fact, be a workable solution to spread risk in a volatile economic environment with high uncertainty about returns on investment. Similarly, instead of ignoring the enfranchisement of the non-propertied classes (without shares but with stakes) or instead of viewing these as an obstacle to economic development, this perspective endorses a broader expansion of political rights, from participation at the ballot box to participation in negotiations about the disposition of assets and the distribution of liabilities. Bringing actors informed by competing evaluative principles to the negotiating table can contribute to economic development not simply by securing broader support for economic reform (through a reduction of uncertainty about the future) but also by reducing opportunities for rent seeking by opening up these negotiations to public accountability. In short, simultaneity presents opportunities as well as challenges.

Practices that recognize the network properties of liabilities and assets and that bring together in concertation interdependent shareholders, stateholders (i.e., the state as shareholder), and nonshareholding stakeholders we label *deliberative association*. In some cases, the associative or network dimension predominates; in others, the deliberative aspect is stronger. But our analysis of ongoing processes in the contemporary East European societies indicates that successful strategies combine both aspects. Before describing our country cases, we briefly outline the associative and deliberative dimensions of deliberative association.

ASSOCIATION

In the previous section, we noted that strong informal and interfirm networks were an unintended consequence of the contradictions arising from attempts to centrally manage an entire national economy. Some of these network ties dissipate in the transforming postsocialist economic environment; others are strengthened as firms, individuals, banks, local governments, and other economic agents adopt coping strategies to survive; and still others emerge anew as these same actors search for new customers and suppliers, new sources of credits and revenues, and new strategic allies.

These associative ties, we argue, suggest that the basic analytic unit for the study of economic restructuring should not be the isolated firm but networks of firms. As Gerschenkron and Hirschman were already aware, and as economic sociologists have demonstrated across the vast array of modern capitalisms, the actual unit of entrepreneurship is not the aspiring individual personality or the isolated firm but networks of persons and of firms.[45]

With few exceptions, however, the literature on postsocialist property transformation (most of it confined to privatization)[46] assumes that the *economic unit to be restructured* is the individual enterprise. But the identification of interfirm networks suggests the possibility of policies and practices in which the units to be restructured would not be isolated firms but *networks of firms*. Such an alternative strategy of restructuring would recognize that assets and liabilities have distinctive network properties.

The notion of a liability is, of course, an inherently relational, and hence network, concept: A loan appears as a liability on the books of an enterprise and as an asset on the books of the bank that extended the credit; a purchase contract registers as a scheduled payment for one firm and as a receivable for another. A number of excellent studies have recently alerted the field of postsocialist research to the fact that such dyadic asymmetries are frequently linked in complex and extended chains of debt.[47] Recognition of the *network properties of liabilities* leads, in our view, to policy implications that are in sharp contrast to the prevailing neoliberal orthodoxy. Because firms exist in networks of close interdependence, reliance on strict market criteria in which struggling firms must be allowed to fail ("each firm for itself, swim or sink") can trigger waves of business failures among their interdependent partners, resulting in a massive devaluation of otherwise well-performing assets. As we shall see in our case studies in the following chapter, this scenario is particularly likely where tough bankruptcy laws are suddenly introduced across the board. In such circumstances, an absolute hardening of budget constraints not only drives poorly performing firms into bankruptcy but can also destroy enterprises that would otherwise be quite capable of making a high-performance adjustment.[48] Wanton destruction is not creative destruction goes this reasoning, and interenterprise networks might save some of these struggling but capable firms by establishing mechanisms of risk spreading and risk sharing.[49]

Such risk spreading, moreover, can be a basis for risk taking. Extraordinarily high uncertainties of the kind we see now in the postsocialist economies can lead to low levels of investment with perverse strategic complementarities (as when firms forgo investments because they expect a sluggish economy based on the lack of investments by others).[50] By mitigating the disinclination to invest, risk spreading within affiliative networks might be one means to break out of otherwise low-level equilibrium traps. Firms in the postsocialist transformational crisis are like mountain climbers assaulting a treacherous rock face, and interorganizational networks are the safety ropes lashing them together. Neoliberals who bemoan a retarded bankruptcy rate fail to acknowledge that there might be circumstances in which this mutual binding is a precondition for attempting a difficult ascent.

This relationship between risk spreading and risk taking suggests that it would be premature in the postsocialist context to impose a rigid dichotomy between strategies of survival and strategies of innovation. Above all, we should not assume that firms will necessarily innovate when survival so seems to dictate, as if necessity in itself creates the conditions for innovation. Recent studies in organizational ecology, for example, provide strong theoretical arguments that firms are more likely to undertake the risky business of innovation (exposing themselves to the *liabilities of newness* by engaging in unfamiliar routines) not when they are pushed to the wall but when they are buffered from the immediate effects of selection mechanisms. These studies further demonstrate that interorganizational networks provide this buffering by producing the requisite organizational slack through which enterprises find the resources that make it possible to innovate.[51] Thus, these studies suggest circumstances in which the simple imperative "Innovate in order to survive" is reasonably reversed: "Survive in order to innovate."

These insights have been independently confirmed in a recent study by Barry Ickes, Randi Ryterman, and Stoyan Tenev,[52] who demonstrate, on the basis of rich survey data on Russian firms, that enterprises that are linked in interenterprise networks are more likely to engage in various forms of economic restructuring than similar firms that are not so linked. That finding, moreover, is robust: Private enterprises are not more likely to undertake restructuring than firms in state ownership or mixed property arrangements embedded in interenterprise networks.[53] In short, when we abandon the forced dichotomy of survival *versus* innovation, we can see that there are circumstances in which survival strategies can be the prelude to strategies of innovation.

A conceptual and policy shift in the unit of restructuring from the isolated enterprise to networks of firms also facilitates recognition of the *network properties of assets*.[54] The industrial structure of the socialist economy commonly grouped, within a single enterprise, assets that were incompatible (except within the logic of central planning). Merely breaking up the firm's assets or simply regrouping them within the structure of that enterprise alone precludes potentially fruitful recombinations of assets across a set of firms. Restructuring networks of firms thus opens the possibility of creating more valuable assets in their recombination. This regrouping does not necessarily imply bringing interdependent assets under the common ownership umbrella of a hierarchically organized enterprise. As we shall see, the East European cases provide examples of intercorporate networks that are alternatives to Williamson's dichotomously forced choice between markets and hierarchies. We shall see as well that creative regroupings fail to respect not only the boundaries between public and private but also the boundaries between the enterprises themselves.

Our emphasis on restructuring networks of firms, taken by itself, might suggest that we favor better industrial policy in which the state should be the dominant agent of restructuring, picking winners and losers. If that were so, we would simply be taking a step backward to join the neostatists. But here we share the view of our liberal colleagues, who question whether state bureaucrats can really possess superior knowledge to make such decisions. We depart from them when we argue that markets are not the only nonhierarchical and decentralized institutions for coordinating economic intelligence. That argument is based on recognizing the distinction between market *orientation* and market *coordination*: A broad variety of institutions of nonmarket coordination are compatible with a high-performance market orientation.[55] Acknowledging the transformative capacity of social networks in the economy itself, we argue that networks should be the units of restructuring in a *double* sense: Networks of firms should be the units to be restructured *and* considerable responsibility for carrying out this restructuring should devolve to networklike institutions.

In examining the network characteristics of the postsocialist East European economies, our analysis builds on the work of economic sociologists and legal scholars who are studying the East Asian economies from a network-centered approach in which not markets, nor states, nor isolated firms but social networks are the basic units of analysis.[56] In this perspective, the ability of the East Asian economies to adapt flexibly to changes in world markets rests in the interlocking ties characteristic of corporate groups,[57] whether these be the patterns of mutual shareholding within the Japanese *keiretsu*,[58] the ties of family ownership within the more vertically integrated South Korean *chaebol*,[59] the social ties of the more horizontally integrated Taiwanese *quanxiqiye* "related enterprises,"[60] or the dense ties that cross organizational boundaries in the buyer-driven and producer-driven networks in Hong Kong, Singapore, and elsewhere in Southeast Asia.[61] However, we do not look to Eastern Europe to find a Hungarian *keiretsu* or Czech *chaebol*. Instead, we expect to find distinctively East European forms that will differ as much from East Asian variants as the East Asian forms differ from West European capitalisms.

DELIBERATION

During both the state socialist and postsocialist periods, East European experience demonstrated that as long as official policies operate in the dichotomy of markets or hierarchy, associative networks will undermine markets and states. Lest they remain shady, these networks must be brought out of the shadows of the dominant theories and policies.[62] Where they are recognized, they can promote productive restructuring and provide a vital source of intelligence about real assets and liabilities, about mobilizable ties among organizations, and about the possible synergies of their locally coordinated projects.

The recognition of network actors in official policies must be accompanied by another recognition: the acknowledgment by local actors of their interdependencies. Because they are interdependent, they can harm each other – or they can create policies, practices, and strategies of mutual benefit. These actors may be firms with complementary assets, or large and small enterprises in a branch, or competing (but potentially cooperating) small firms in a region, or local governments, credit institutions, employees, employers, civic or church organizations, and the like. And the more complex these interdependencies and the more diverse their organizing principles, the less likely the process of reaching agreement will take the form of straightforward bargaining that results in contracts, mergers, or acquisitions. Instead, recognition of complex interdependencies can produce awareness of the need for an institutionalization of *ongoing* negotiations for spreading risk and sharing rewards and costs: The more effective these agreements, the more they change the initial circumstances that gave rise to them and prompt further negotiations.[63]

Such institutions are deliberative. Their *discursive* aspect can be distinguished from discussions about contracts (e.g., disputes over the terms of an order, such as a bill of exchange) or from discussions within a hierarchy (e.g., disputes over the meaning of an order, such as an imperative command) because they involve negotiations across ordering principles. Deliberations cannot harmonize interests or make them compatible because, if they indeed involve multiple logics, there is no single common principle of equivalence;[64] but they can promote integration and coordination among competing, coexisting, and diverse evaluative principles and organizational logics. The *recursive* aspect of deliberative association can be distinguished from pacts, which typically involve peak associations constructing one-time stabilizing agreements about the numbers (e.g., wage indexing, levels of investment). Pacts can facilitate more recursive negotiations if and when national-level agreements act as a catalyst to bring together regional and local networks that institutionalize ongoing deliberations.

As those familiar with the work of Philippe Schmitter and Wolfgang Streeck will have already recognized, our notion of deliberative association bears strong affinities to their concept of *associative orders*.[65] But our cases (and our concept of negotiation) differ from the advanced industrial democracies analyzed by Streeck and Schmitter, whose corporative associations are much more formalized – "shaped and constrained by established, licensed, oligopolistic (or even monopolistic) organizational structures."[66] The actors of Streeck and Schmitter's "organizational concertation" are typically already Associations – formal organizations with licenses, charters, offices, and functionaries. Although they emphasize that identities and interests can be modified in the process of concertation, their actors do enter negotiations with given organizational identities and sharply articulated interests. As we shall see, in Eastern Europe identities and interests are much less clearly defined; in fact, identities and interests often emerge in the process of deliberation.

With this emphasis on emergent identities and interests, our conception of deliberation corresponds more closely to the kinds of processes that Charles Sabel identifies within the institutions he labels *developmental associations*. Sabel explicitly adopts this term, in contrast to that of *developmental state*, because, similar to our own view, no state (regardless of how coherent it is) has knowledge superior to that of economic actors that would justify its intervention to centrally direct economic processes. Moreover, such intervention is unnecessary where strong bonds of affiliation, like those of Sabel's regional developmental associations,[67] can coordinate restructuring. For Sabel, it is the associations, not the state, that do the developing. The Sabelian state does not direct; it "monitors," acts as a "superintendent," and "sets the rules of economic transactions."[68] To do so in ways that facilitate rather than impede developmental associations, it must be strong and coherent.[69]

The forms of deliberative association that we identify in Eastern Europe are typically initiated in cases where either states are not as coherent or networks not as cohesive as Sabel's cases of developmental association. This relative weakness presents obstacles to and opportunities for deliberative association in the postsocialist cases. On the one hand, states in Eastern Europe can perceive associative life as relatively weak and use this perception to justify recurrent interventions. And the more these states lack coherence, the more prone they are to interventionism in the first place. Some state sponsorship may be necessary to facilitate deliberative association, but persistent intrusions into associational life can weaken its development. In the worst case, negotiating forums become mere outposts of central state authority, and direct budgetary ties allow responsibility to be once again shifted up a hierarchy.[70] On the other hand, the fiscal crises of most East European states create circumstances in which many local and regional economic and political actors are left of necessity to search for growth strategies unburdened by central budgetary ties. Where interorganizational networks form the basis for deliberative association, outcomes can unburden the state not only in fiscal terms but also in the scope of its decision-making requirements. Where they function most effectively, negotiating forums operate with state oversight but not direct intrusion, and deliberative associations develop their own selection criteria to cut losses, identify unrecognized resources, and reallocate and recombine their assets. In the process of such virtuous circles, states *and* associative networks can shift from initial starting positions to gain legitimacy and strength.

Thus, whereas Hirschman's developmental state *disequilibrates*, associative networks and their interdependents can *deliberate* to move beyond the status quo. Whereas the neoliberals advocate freeing markets to liberate the economy and the transformative statists propose insulating the bureaucracy to liberate the state, we examine processes that "de-liberate." It is through deliberations that interdependent actors, learning from each other, can recognize the goals and means that can best serve their distinct and mutual interests. The political task of a reform strategy, it follows, should be not the liberation of the actors of the economic transformation from each other but the encouragement to create institutions of deliberation among them. From country to country in the region we find cases where deliberative association produces binding agreements – sometimes of shorter duration, elsewhere longer-lasting agreements to continuing (re)negotiations. It is these binding ties that can unbind the state and unbind markets.

Although there are no simple formulas, the research findings that we present in Chapters 5 and 6 indicate that deliberative association functions most productively where heterogeneous types of social actors enter negotiations. Homogeneity increases opportunities for collusion and rent seeking. Heterogeneity in itself does not, of course, preclude an expanded circle of collusion, but it improves the chances that deliberations will have some degree of publicity and increases the likelihood of exposing egregious rent seeking. In short, networks monitoring networks increase accountability.

Taking as a theoretical background our discussion of deliberative associations as alternatives to markets and hierarchies, we now turn to examine recent developments in Germany, Hungary, and the Czech Republic. In Chapter 5, we focus on the associative ties of restructuring networks in these postsocialist *economies*, with attention as well to the processes of deliberation within them. In Chapter 6, we focus on the deliberative institutions of extended accountability in the *polities* of our three countries, with attention to the associative ties within them.

RESTRUCTURING NETWORKS IN EAST EUROPEAN CAPITALISM

To what extent are networks the units and the agents of economic restructuring in East Central Europe? Our presentation of each of the country cases (Germany, Hungary, and the Czech Republic) begins with a brief description of some important starting conditions, in particular the initial strength and cohesiveness of social networks in the economy and the initial orientations of policy makers in the government. From these starting points, we chart changes in the course of economic restructuring according to whether and how policy makers (and other economic actors) acknowledge the network properties of assets and of liabilities. We will see how institutional innovations, some of which resemble the configurations of deliberative association we discussed in the previous chapter, are facilitated or hindered by the particular ways in which policy makers in each case manage (or fail to manage) the interdependencies of assets and the chains of debt in the postsocialist setting.

GERMANY

Economic restructuring in the lands of the former GDR, or the *new Länder*, as they are now referred to in Germany, begins in a context in which a transplanted state administration and weak networks interact with strong markets. Among our three cases, interfirm networks were weakest in the old GDR. Unlike Hungary, where partial reforms had opened opportunities for firms to cultivate a range of supply links and engage in subcontracting with private and semiprivate subcontractors, the large *Kombinate* of East

German industry were extraordinarily autarchic, and where they did rely on an outside supplier, the source was strictly designated by the planning authorities.[1] Unlike Czechoslovakia, where managers had enough autonomy to capture mesolevel industrial associations (and even restore these after they were abolished from above), the German *Kombinate* were entirely the creatures of a centralized administrative apparatus.

It was with a similarly centralized administrative apparatus that Germany set out to reorganize the East German economy: The gigantic state holding, the Treuhandanstalt, was single-handedly responsible for the rapid conversion of some 12,000 formerly state-run companies into private enterprises modeled on West German corporate law.[2] Headquartered in Berlin, the agency assembled a staff of 4,000, consisting of retrained East German clerical and professional staff augmented by itinerant West Germans with previous experience in management, consultancy, or finance. Younger, less experienced managerial cadre were especially eager to chalk up track records of successful turnarounds to facilitate their reentry on the German managerial market as specialists in corporate restructuring. Under the no-nonsense leadership of Birgit Breuel, the Treuhand approximated more than any other postsocialist case a well-functioning Weberian bureaucracy – not by accident in Weber's homeland.

This combination of weak networks and a cohesive bureaucratic agency placed the starting point of German restructuring close to circumstances most favorable for a neostatist strategy. State-directed restructuring, however, was not in the cards. Neither the federal government nor the Treuhand was ready to create a large-scale program of centralized industrial policy requiring even larger expenditures than the ruling Conservatives were willing to accept and fostering the kinds of rent-seeking alliances they opposed. The acceptable solution was to rely on the market, one ready at hand, for who could doubt that the West German market economy was among the strongest and most competitive in the world? The Treuhand's mandate, thus, was not to orchestrate reorganization but, through rapid privatization, to promote the spontaneous and massive inflow of West German capital that would then direct restructuring.

CREATING LIABILITIES

However, instead of solving problems, the economic unification that accompanied political unification produced a new set of problems for the new lands. First, the unification of Germany marked the collapse of the old COMECON markets: The enterprises of the former GDR would have to face immediate restructuring, with no temporary cushion provided by a gradual phasing out of the export of their inferior products to the East. In this first respect, of course, East Germany did not differ from Hungary and Czechoslovakia, but there were two other factors, each a product of its distinctive path of extrication from state socialism, that further complicated the German experience. Thus, second, economic unification indeed brought the enterprises of the former GDR into contact with West German firms – not, however, in the first instance in the form of a capital influx but in the form of intense market competition. The West German market economy was powerful, and when its goods flooded the eastern lands, the result was a powerful market shock: Industrial output in the new *Länder* declined by 50% between the first half of 1990 and the first half of 1991 and continued to fall until it stabilized at about one-third of its original level.[3] Meanwhile, between 1989 and 1992, the number of jobs decreased by 4.5 million, or 46% of the pretransition level (Gerlin, 1993; Roesler, 1994). Third, as if East German firms did not suffer enough from the lack of managerial talent, marketing experience, and advanced technologies, they were further hampered in this enforced market competition by the politically motivated wage increases designed to bring the compensation packages of East German employees to parity with those of their West German counterparts. Although stepped in (and later stepped up in response to union pressure) and although still lower than those of the West Germans, the wages of the East Germans were accelerating much faster than any increases in productivity.[4]

The political economy of unification thus produced an organizational crisis for the Treuhandanstalt: Although it had started out as a centralized manager of assets, within only a year of its functioning it had become the centralized manager of liabilities. Taking into account the market potential and the levels of wages and productivity, the overwhelming majority of firms in the Treuhand's portfolio were of negative value.[5] The strong market, it seemed, had left the strong state bureaucracy with a bundle of worthless enterprises.

SUBSIDIZING PRIVATIZATION

At its inception, the Treuhand was chartered for a straightforward task – rapid privatization alone. But the unintended market shock began to produce pressures for it to accomplish everything that the invisible hand could not: to reduce unemployment and create jobs, to halt deindustrialization, to guarantee the viability of privatized firms, to take responsibility for regional or sectoral reorganization, and so on. Moreover, it had to accomplish those tasks without greatly exceeding its budget and within the severe constraints of the politics of unification. If net transfers across the two former territories were eventually to exceed 12 times the level of the Marshall Plan, such expenditures could be politically justified only as cost sharing *among German citizens*, never as transfers from West German taxpayers to the old state enterprises of the East.

After selling the obviously easy breweries, food processing firms, distribution chains, and smaller "jewels" in machining and related industries, the Treuhand confronted a dilemma: Not only were the value of and the demand for its remaining assets declining, but these assets (taken on a firm-by-firm basis) typically existed as arbitrary collections assembled as an "enterprise" according to the logic of the socialist economy. Worthless within the wreck of the planned economy, these assets were nonetheless of value provided that the *Kombinate* and other larger enterprises could be broken up and then recombined. But because of the scale of these operations, it was not enough to reassemble assets and then wait for a buyer. The challenge was made even more complicated by the expanded social and political tasks of the Treuhand (e.g., providing guaranteed employment levels), especially given budgetary constraints. And while taking on these new tasks, the Treuhand could not be perceived as straying from its mandate of rapid privatization.

With what resources could the Treuhand accomplish these diverse assignments? The brittle interfirm networks of the old socialist economy had snapped under the first pressure of the combined market collapse to the East and the market shock from the West. Firms with only a few suppliers and perhaps even as few as one designated customer in the days of planned deliveries were left isolated virtually overnight.[6] Informal and interorganizational networks based on personal ties were similarly decimated as the personnel of the trade unions, political parties, local government, and public administration were replaced in *die Wende*, the *turning*.

The Treuhand's answer was to maneuver through and around its organizational charter in an organized but not organizationally self-conscious search for new practices and policies.[7] As its goals and tasks shifted from selling properties with positive values to making arrangements for reorganizing the assets and liabilities of firms with doubtful value, the organization was reorganized. In this process of organizational learning under uncertainty,[8] the Treuhand became inserted into a set of deliberative institutions involving (among others) regional governments, trade unions, and employers' associations. Like the Tennessee Valley Authority (TVA), a similarly large-scale governmental development agency, the Treuhand was partially opened to the interest groups of its environment. And, as with the TVA, this cooptation of outside actors partially resolved its legitimacy problems. On the one hand, the meddling of outside institutions in the work of the

Treuhand continually complicated its mission. On the other, this network of external relations provided an arena for transferring its ever-growing responsibilities.[9]

Deliberations thus provided a means to solve some of the Treuhand's coordination problems as the agency sought to connect actors who had a potential stake in the longer-term viability of assets and induce them to work out and implement a joint strategy of restructuring. With information provided by the Treuhand but without a preconceived solution proposed by that agency, it was up to the various actors around the table (banks, firms, trade associations, trade unions, ministry officials, and local governments) to identify the particular assets that could be viably recombined, arrange financing, link the new entities to customers and suppliers, and win approval of the design from the Treuhand.

But the networks of these deliberative forums were peculiarly lacking in dense, extensive, and cohesive ties within and among the social actors variously assembled. Typically, it was the Treuhand itself that linked the feeble policy network together. As such, the Treuhand gained room for maneuver and systematically exploited its intermediary role between the federal government and the governments of the new *Länder*. In such a *tertius gaudens* role (the third who benefits), it was often the Treuhand, and not the East German economy, that was the beneficiary. The Treuhand's expanded deliberations did shift the organization from its previously disastrous course of creating liabilities; but the weakness of the preexisting social networks and the artificial character of the networks that came into existence (often as creatures of the Treuhand) created a policy structure attuned to the network properties of liabilities without recognizing the network properties of assets.

Thus, without straying from its principled commitment to rapid privatization, the Treuhand became involved in the business of preserving assets without necessarily restructuring or recombining them. This was most typical where, because of concentration in a single *Land* (state, province), a given industry was extraordinarily important for the economic health of a given region – shipbuilding in Mecklenberg Vorpommern, steel in Brandenburg, and chemicals in Sachsen-Anhalt, for example. Privatizations in these cases were highly politicized, with the *Land* government, the federal government, and the Treuhand as partners – and sometimes not the most powerful ones – in a complex network of actors including the Commission of the European Community, organized labor, and the representatives of big business as potential investors. With some exceptions,[10] these asset-preserving measures did not involve creating new forward and backward linkages as a creatively recombinant industrial policy. Instead, the resulting privatizations were more or less contingent outcomes of bargaining processes whose economic viability remains questionable in many cases. With government subsidies as their precondition, the big privatization deals in the steel, shipbuilding, and chemical industries cost the taxpayer between 500,000 and 1,200,00 marks for every job saved.[11]

Emblematic of the Treuhand's general disregard for the network properties of assets was the experiment with the so-called *Management-Kommanditgesellschaften* (MKGs), which began in 1992. The miniholdings of the MKGs were an attempt to move away from the principle of privatizing individual firms or plants toward that of restructuring groups of firms. The typical portfolio of an MKG miniholding consisted of about 20 firms. However, one of the criteria in selecting firms for the MKGs was that they should not be linked in terms of technology or buyer–supplier relations. In other words, the logic of these portfolios precluded the identification of organizational synergies. Fearful that these synergies could turn out to be simply a synonym for the interfirm dependencies of the *Kombinate* era and careful to prevent criticism that the Treuhand was insidiously engaging in industrial policy, the Treuhand managers deliberately obstructed the synergistic recombination of assets.[12] As it became embedded in a set of deliberative institutions, the Treuhand moderated its earlier course of transforming assets into liabilities. But because these deliberations occurred in a context in which social networks in the economy lacked extensivity, depth, and vitality, the network properties of assets remained unrecognized. Whereas in Germany strong deliberations were not matched by strong associative ties, in Hungary, strong associative ties were not matched by robust deliberations. It is to this latter case that we turn.

HUNGARY

To what extent did the reform strategy in Hungary, where enterprise-level networks were the most fully developed and cohesive among our country cases, recognize the network properties of assets and liabilities? Robust economic networks in Hungary were a legacy of partial reforms under state socialism through which the managers of public enterprises gained considerable autonomy to choose among suppliers and to construct dense and extensive horizontal ties among themselves. The rapid expansion of the second economy during the 1970s and throughout the 1980s, moreover, further diversified the repertoire of action of these enterprise managers as they sought out business partners among small entrepreneurs and subcontracted production to semiautonomous "partnerships" inside their own firms.

In its electoral campaign and in its early official pronouncements after taking office in the summer of 1990, the government of József Antall created a picture of a nation of middle-class proprietors in a social-market economy. Rejecting all shock therapies, the government stated that the gradual course toward this goal would be directed by the sure and steady hand of a state that would reclaim property rights usurped by enterprise directors. Through centralized agencies, the state would not only control the speed but would also direct every aspect of the process of property transformation through which it would designate the new owners of privatized assets.

NETWORK PROPERTIES OF ASSETS

From its inception, the State Property Agency (SPA) adopted the official policy that privatization in Hungary would be conducted on a strictly case-by-case, firm-by-firm basis. The SPA never considered assets as interdependent and thus regroupable across firms or that networks of firms could be the units to be restructured. Such, of course, was also the public policy in Germany's Treuhandanstalt, but as we saw there, restructuring often did precede privatization despite all the ideological statements to the contrary. In Hungary, policy pronouncements and organizational practice remained harmonious. Externally, the SPA legitimated its activities by emphasizing the bottom line – revenues brought into the state treasury from the eventual sale of the individual firms. Internally, incentives matched these goals as the SPA's transaction officers were officially rewarded and promoted according to the criterion of revenue from sales. During our interviews in the SPA, we encountered (as typical of a pattern) a transaction officer responsible for the privatization of a firm manufacturing steel cable who was completely ignorant of the work of the other transaction officers down the hall who were dealing with the cable firm's upstream supplier in basic metallurgy and with its downstream customer in the manufacture of electric motors.

Although SPA policy makers were hostile and its transaction officers indifferent to the systematic regrouping of assets, autonomous actors out in the economy were nonetheless cognizant of the network properties of assets and were restructuring accordingly. Some of this property transformation resulted in privatization in the conventional meaning of the term. Other cases resulted in novel forms of interorganizational ownership that blurred the boundaries of public and private, as well as the boundaries between the enterprises themselves. It is to these Hungarian forms of recombinant property that we turn.

Interenterprise Ownership

To cope with the uncertainties of volatile change in their economic environments and to respond to the state's injunction that state-owned enterprises must be privatized, many large Hungarian firms adopted the strategies of institutional ownership discussed in Chapter 2. That is, they acquired shares in other firms and they made arrangements for other enterprises to become their new shareholders. To assess the prevalence of such interenterprise ownership, Stark compiled and analyzed a data set on the ownership structure of the largest 200 Hungarian corporations (ranked by sales).[13] These firms compose the *Top 200* of the 1993 listing of *Figyelö*, a leading Hungarian business weekly. Like their *Fortune* 500 counterparts in the United States, the *Figyelö* 200 firms are major players in the Hungarian economy, employing an estimated 21% of the labor force and accounting for 37% of total net sales and 42% of export revenues. The data also include the top 25 Hungarian banks (ranked by assets). Ownership data were obtained directly from the Hungarian Courts of Registry, where corporate files contain not only information on each company's officers and board of directors but also a complete list of the company's owners as of the 1993 annual shareholders' meeting. The data analyzed here are limited to the top twenty shareholders of each corporation.[14] In the Budapest Court of Registry and the nineteen County Registries we located ownership files for 195 of the 200 corporations and for all of the 25 banks, referred to subsequently as the Top 220 firms.

Who holds the shares of these 220 largest enterprises and banks? We found some form of state ownership – with shares held by the ÁV-Rt (the State Holding Corporation), the SPA, or the institutions of local government (which had typically exchanged their real estate holdings for enterprise shares) – in the overwhelming majority (71%) of these enterprises and banks. More surprisingly, given the relatively short time since the system change in 1989–90, we found thirty-six companies (i.e., more than 16% of this population) under majority foreign ownership. Hungarian private individuals (summed down the top twenty owners) hold at least 25% of the shares of only twelve of these largest enterprises and banks.

Most interesting from the perspective of our argument here is the finding of eighty-seven cases in which another Hungarian company is among the 20 largest shareholders. In forty-two of these cases the other Hungarian companies together hold a clear majority (50% plus one share). Thus, by the most restrictive definition, almost 20% of our Top 220 companies are unambiguous cases of interenterprise ownership, and we found some degree of interenterprise ownership in almost 40% of these large companies.

Network 1

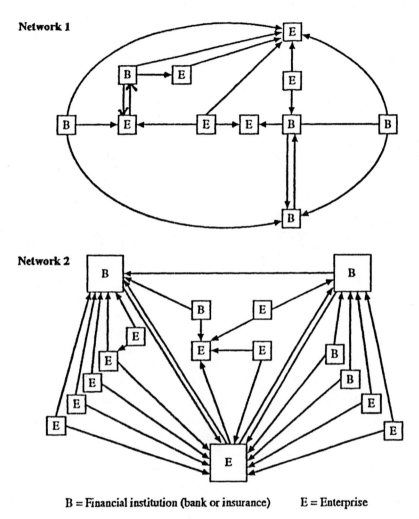

Network 2

B = Financial institution (bank or insurance)   E = Enterprise

Figure 3. Two interenterprise ownership networks among large Hungarian firms (based on data gathered from corporate files of the 200 largest enterprises and top 25 banks in Hungarian Courts of Registry).

Figure 3 presents two discrete networks formed through such interenterprise ownership. Arrows indicate the direction in which a given firm holds shares in another large enterprise. Weak ties (shareholdings with other firms that do not have at least one other tie, whether as owner or as owned, to any other firm in the network) are not displayed. The relations depicted in the figure, we emphasize, are the direct horizontal ties among the very largest enterprises – the superhighways, so to speak, of Hungarian corporate networks. From the vantage point of these corporate thoroughfares linking the large enterprises we will now examine the local byways linking spin-off properties within the gravitational field of large enterprises.

Corporate Satellites

Out attention thus focuses on limited liability companies (*korlátolt felelöségü társaságok* or KFTs), the corporate form that experienced the most dramatic growth during the postsocialist period, increasing from only 450 at the end of 1988 to almost 80,000 by the end of 1994. Some of these KFTs are genuinely private entrepreneurial ventures. But many of them are not entirely distinct from the transformed shareholding companies examined earlier. In fact, the formerly socialist enterprises have been active founders and continue as current co-owners of the newly incorporated units. This pattern is exemplified by the case of one of Hungary's largest metallurgy firms, represented in Figure 4. As we see in that figure, "Heavy Metal," an enormous shareholding company in the portfolio of the State Holding Corporation, is the majority shareholding of twenty-six of its forty corporate satellites.

Like Saturn's rings, Heavy Metal's satellites revolve around the giant corporate planet in concentric orbits.[15] Near the center are the core metallurgy units, hot-rolling mills, energy, maintenance, and strategic planning units held in a kind of geosynchronous orbit by 100% ownership. In the next ring, where the corporate headquarters holds roughly 50–99% of the shares, are the cold-rolling mills, wire and cable production, oxygen facility, galvanizing and other finishing treatments, specialized castings, quality control, and marketing units. As this list suggests, these satellites are linked to each other and to the core units by ties of technological dependence. Relations between the middle-ring satellites and the company center are marked by the center's recurrent efforts to introduce stricter accounting procedures and tighter financial controls. These attempts are countered by the units' efforts to increase their autonomy – coordinated through personal ties and formalized in the biweekly meetings of the "Club of KFT Managing Directors."

The satellites of the outer ring are even more heterogeneous in their production profiles (construction, industrial services, computing, ceramics, machining) and usually have lower levels of capitalization. Units of this outer ring are less fixed in Heavy Metal's gravitational field: Some have recently entered and some seem about to leave. Among the new entrants are some of Heavy Metal's domestic customers. Unable to collect receivables, Heavy Metal exchanged interenterprise debt for equity in its clients, preferring that these meteors be swept into an orbit rather than be lost in

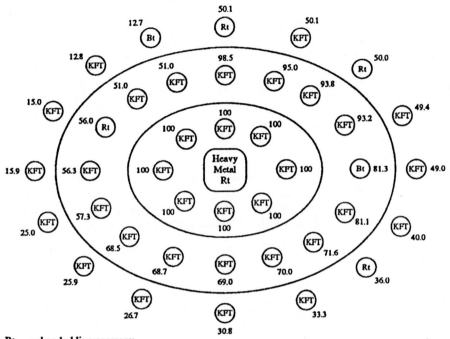

Rt   = shareholding company
KFT = limited liability comapny
Bt   = partnerships

Figure 4. Corporate satellites at Heavy Metal (based on data from internal company records).

liquidation. Among those satellites launched from the old state enterprise are some for which Heavy Metal augments its less than majority ownership with leasing arrangements to keep centrifugal forces in check.

The corporate satellites among the limited liability companies are, thus, far from unambiguously private ventures, but neither are they unmistakably statist residues of the socialist past. Property shares in most corporate satellites are not limited to the founding enterprise. Top and mid-level managers, professionals, and other staff can be found on the lists of founding partners and current owners. Such private persons rarely acquire complete ownership of the corporate satellite, preferring to use their insider knowledge to exploit the ambiguities of institutional co-ownership. The corporate satellites are thus partially a result of the hedging and risk-sharing strategies of individual managers. We might ask why a given manager would not want to acquire 100% ownership in order to obtain 100% of the profit, but from the perspective of a given manager the calculus instead is "Why acquire 100% of the risk if some of it can be shared with the corporate center?" With ambiguous interests and divided loyalties, these risk-sharing (or risk-shedding) owner-managers are organizationally hedging.[16] As these managers are joined by ownership stakes on the part of other limited liability companies spinning around yet other large enterprises, we see that this new property form thus finds horizontal ties of cross-ownership intertwined with vertical ties of nested holdings.

Recombinets

The recombinant character of Hungarian property is a function not only of the direct (horizontal) ownership ties among the largest firms and of their direct (vertical) ties to their corporate satellites but also of the network properties of the full ensemble of direct and indirect ties linking entities, irrespective of their attributes (large, small, or of various legal forms) in a given configuration. The available data do not allow us to present a comprehensive map of these complex relations. Records in the Courts of Registry include documents on the owners of a particular firm, but enterprises are not required to report the companies in which they hold a stake. However, on the basis of enterprise-level field research, examination of public records at the SPA, and interviews with bankers and executives of consulting firms, we have been able to reconstruct at least partial networks, which are represented in Figure 5.

For orientation in this graphic space, we position Figure 5 in relation to Figures 3 and 4. Figure 3 presents interenterprise ownership networks formed through horizontal ties directly linking large enterprises. Figure 4 zooms in on the corporate satellites of a single large enterprise. With Figure 5 we pull back to examine a fragment of a broader interenterprise ownership network, bringing into focus the ties that link corporate satellites to each other and that form the indirect ties among heterogeneous units in a more loosely coupled network.[17]

We label this emergent form a *recombinet*. Here we see that the limited liability companies that began as corporate spinoffs are oriented through ownership ties either to more than one shareholding company and/or to other limited liability companies. In the recombinet, actors recognize the network properties of their interdependent assets and regroup them across formal organizational boundaries. These creative regroupings are, indeed, examples of property transformation, but they cannot be grasped under the simple rubric of privatization – for they fail to respect not only the boundaries between public and private but also the organizational boundaries of the enterprises themselves. Restructuring via the recombinet thus opens the

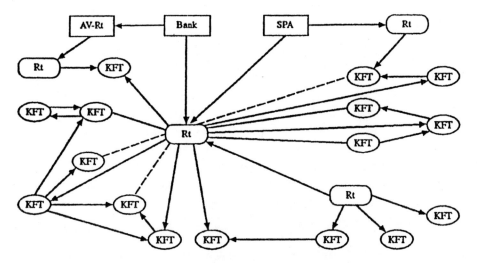

Figure 5. A Hungarian recombinet (based on data from internal company records, SPA files, and corporate files at the Budapest Court of Registry).

possibility of increasing the value of existing assets through their recombination. This regrouping does not necessarily imply bringing interdependent assets under the common ownership umbrella of a hierarchically organized enterprise. Hungarian recombinant property thus provides examples of intercorporate networks that are alternatives to a forced choice between markets and hierarchies.

NETWORK PROPERTIES OF LIABILITIES

While economic actors across enterprises were recombining chains of assets, the SPA was still insisting on privatization on a case-by-case basis. Meanwhile, other ministries and agencies of the Hungarian state were similarly devising policies addressing debt on a case-by-case basis, failing to recognize the network properties of liabilities.

Taking the Last Small Steps

The liabilities management story begins in 1991, when the Hungarian government fundamentally modified three important laws regulating the accounting of assets and liabilities in an attempt to maintain its lead in regional competition for foreign investments and international credits. Hungary's comparative advantage, it appeared, was its gradualism, which, across the 1970s and 1980s, had yielded a full range of marketlike institutions. Admittedly, these were not the institutions of a market economy, but they were close; and so, the government reasoned, why not take the last small steps? As the pioneer attempt to bring postsocialist practice into full conformity with Western accounting and banking standards, the new measures could be cast as a bold move when appealing to international lending agencies. But because they were not big steps, the new measures could gain external legitimation without creating a domestic shock.

Thus, the new Accounting Law of 1991 (which took effect on January 1, 1992) required enterprises to switch to Western-style accounting principles. A simultaneously enacted tough new Western-style Bankruptcy Act similarly contained stiff personal penalties for directors of enterprises that failed to file for bankruptcy after the accountants (using the new accounting principles) sounded the alarm. At the same time, the new Act on Financial Institutions introduced in December 1991 was designed to put Hungary's commercial banks on a Western footing. In particular, the reserve requirements for measuring capital-adequacy ratios were modified, and the securities and other financial instruments for provisioning against qualified loans were respecified.

The last small steps proved to be a leap into the abyss. Already reeling from the collapse of the Council for Mutual Economic Assistance (CMEA) markets, enterprise directors now learned from their accountants that the new accounting practices were coloring the companies' books even redder than expected. By the end of 1992, over 10,000 bankruptcies and liquidation proceedings had been initiated – a figure ten times higher than during the previous year, when enterprises had experienced the worst shock of the collapsed East European markets.[18] With one-third to one-half of enterprises in the red, the loss-making firms began to stop payment on their bank credits. By the end of 1992, the overdue loan stock of the banking system was 127 billion forints ($1.5 billion), up 90 percent from the previous year.[19]

With thousands of firms filing for bankruptcy, the banks were forced by the new banking law to reclassify loans. The subsequent dramatic increase in the new legally required provisionings against poorly performing loans cut deeply into bank profits, slashed dividends and tax revenues from the banking sector to the state treasury, and turned the banks' capital-adequacy ratios from positive to negative. The banking system was in crisis – first announced, no less, in the *Financial Times*.[20]

From Small Steps to Big Bailouts

The same government that had administered an unintended financial shock now initiated a bold plan to save the banks. In its 1992 loan consolidation program, the government bought 104.9 billion forints (about $1 billion) of qualified debt (almost all in the bad-debt category) involving 14 banks and 1,885 companies. In a related move in early 1993, the government purchased the bank debt of eleven giant enterprises (the so-called dirty dozen) for roughly $300 million. But the loan consolidation and enterprise recapitalization programs did not restore stability in the banking sector. By September 1993, only nine months later, financial experts were estimating that loans in arrears had once again soared to 20% of total loan portfolios. And the 10 largest banks were again hovering at or below the 0% capital-adequacy ratio (technical insolvency).

For the government, the new banking rules did not rule out bailing out banks and enterprises again and again. But the big bailout of 1993 had a new twist. Instead of buying the debt from the banks, this time the government adopted a two-stage strategy of first recapitalizing the banks and then using the banks to work out the enterprise debt. By injecting enormous sums of fresh capital into the banks, the Ministry of Finance became the dominant shareholder of the large commercial banks. The first stage of the strategy, then, could be summarized in a phrase: Don't acquire the debt; acquire the banks.

The second stage of the strategy was designed to harness the expertise of the banks in the service of the state. Because it was the banks, and not the state, that would be left holding the qualified debt, the banks would have an incentive to collect that debt, or at least the part they had not already written off their books. And they would do so, this time, not with the state as their sometime partner but with the state as their majority owner. But efforts to exercise control through direct ownership do not equal more effective state capacity. The conservative–nationalist government seemed determined to learn the lesson of the "trap of centralization" from its own experience. The banks have shown almost no willingness to use the consolidation funds for actively restructuring firms; and despite the assumption that the Ministry of Finance's ownership would yield control of the banks, the government has been almost entirely ineffective in monitoring how the banks use the recapitalization funds.

The massive bailout programs were not, of course, without effects: At 300 billion forints ($3 billion) – amounting to 10% of the Hungarian GDP and 18.3% of the 1994 national budget (i.e., proportionally more than the U.S. savings and loan bailout) – the bailouts created a long line of banks and firms with their hands out, reaching for the state's pocketbook. Ignored, the networks nonetheless existed, and now in light of the state's largesse they began augmenting their strategy of risk sharing with the strategy of risk shedding.[21]

AN ANTIDEVELOPMENTAL STATE?

Our examination of debt consolidation thus suggests a new basis of paternalism in Hungary: Whereas in the state socialist economy paternalism was based on the state's attempt to centrally manage assets,[22] in the first years of the postsocialist economy paternalism was based on the state's attempt to centrally manage liabilities.

The Hungarian bank bailout/debt consolidation program stands in marked contrast to the organizational learning we saw in the German experience. Although the Treuhandanstalt seemed constrained to adopt a similar role in the centralized management of liabilities, in fact it switched course to facilitate decentralized, deliberative forums to work out the liabilities. These decentralized institutions pooled the local knowledge not only of banks but of a broader range of economic and social actors who could find, in the mountains of liabilities, assets that could be preserved and recombined. In Hungary, by contrast, the *consolidation committees* established to manage enterprise debt brought together only claimants. And where they reached agreement at all, they functioned more as streamlined bankruptcy courts than as agents of restructuring: Relatively sophisticated instruments such as debt–equity swaps, debt rescheduling, and bond issues were almost never the result of this bargaining among the claimants. These bodies gave such a thin patina of legitimacy to debt forgiveness that even they were scuttled – leaving the claimants to fend for themselves and leaving firms that might have been profitably restructured with nowhere to turn.

With a price tag of over $3 billion, the bank bailout/debt consolidation program failed to restructure the banking system, failed to restructure enterprises, and failed to alter the structure of incentives at the level of banks and enterprises – except to reinforce dependency on the newly paternalistic state. Nor was the crisis seized as an opportunity to create national, branch, sectoral, regional, or local deliberative forums that, by bringing together actors around the assets (banking, business, labor, communities), could thereby alter expectations about the future and devise strategies of coordinated action that might remove the state from further crisis management. Instead, the major result of the centralized management of liabilities was to add an enormous burden to the already overstressed state budget.

With its policy swing from unintended market shock to interventionist state bailouts, the Antall government had turned Hungary into what we might call the *antidevelopmental state*. In contrast to the developmental state, which mobilizes and channels resources to high-growth sectors and firms, the antidevelopmental state siphons resources out of the economy. Unlike the socialist state, which redistributed resources among its centrally managed assets, the antidevelopmental state redistributes resources from society to finance its centralized management of liabilities.

In so doing, the antidevelopmental Hungarian state is crowding out profitable firms from credit markets. To finance its deficits, the state sells bonds to the banks. The state's competition with enterprises for credit raises interest rates and makes new investment funding more expensive for the business sector in any case, but it is especially debilitating under conditions of a weak banking system where bankers see uncertainty everywhere – except in the government's treasury notes. Hardest hit are the new entrepreneurs of smaller firms, who are at a loss to find bank financing for expansion. Such crowding out had already begun in the early postsocialist period, but it was exacerbated by the wave of bankruptcies in 1992–3 (which drove many small firms out of business and made the banks all the more risk averse regarding this sector). The $3 billion debt consolidation made the state's crowding out of credit markets almost complete, causing some to wonder whether the banking system could still claim the function of financial intermediation.[23]

To cover its looming deficits, the antidevelopmental state increasingly looks to foreign financing. And the greater the state's external debt, the more it cuts off resources from profit-making firms, squeezes consumption, and cuts social services to meet its cumulatively mounting interest payments. Antidevelopmental, it neither stimulates consumption nor promotes profitability; its policies are anti–demand side and anti–supply side.

In short, during its four years in office, the nationalist-conservative government had temporarily solved the financial crisis by creating a long-term fiscal crisis. The government triggered a wave of enterprise bankruptcies in its rush to the market. The statist measures it later adopted to forestall the collapse of the banking system had precipitated the impending bankruptcy of the state.

THE CZECH REPUBLIC

We turn now to the Czech case (first as part of Czechoslovakia and later, after the January 1993 *Velvet Divorce* from Slovakia, as the Czech Republic), where networks at the enterprise level were less developed and cohesive than in Hungary. Unlike Hungary, where partial reforms in the 1970s and 1980s had facilitated the rapid growth of a second economy of small-scale producers and allowed enterprises to seek out their own business partners, Czechoslovakia was marked by the absence of extensive networks of horizontal ties and direct enterprise-to-enterprise contacts. By comparison with their Hungarian counterparts, Czechoslovak firms had extremely limited autonomy. It was not the case, however, that the state in the old regime had held unlimited property rights. The Czechoslovak state was repressive, but its sovereignty in the economic field was limited – not by assertive enterprises but by the strong networks of *mesolevel* Industrial Associations. That is, unlike Hungary, where reforms in the old regime devolved considerable property rights to the level of firms, or unlike the former GDR, where the large *Kombinate* were always kept under tight state control, in the old Czechoslovak regime, industrial associations had acquired increasing latitude and responsibility for organizing production and contracting among firms belonging to the same branch or located in the same geographic area.[24] As we shall see, it is at this similarly mesolevel that new networks of cross-ownership and economic coordination are most dense in the contemporary postsocialist Czech economy.

If Hungary's government in 1991 and 1992 thought it could win legitimation as the best student in the East European reform school, it faced stiff competition in Vaclav Klaus, finance minister of postsocialist Czechoslovakia and currently prime minister of the Czech Republic. This economist-turned-politician so confidently wore the cloak of Adam Smith that he could lecture Western leaders on the virtues of free-market liberalism and chastise them for straying from the straight and narrow. Here was a student who could pick up the chalk and correct the teacher's sums.

In the early speeches and policy pronouncements in which Klaus articulated his neoliberal vision, *privatization* was almost invariably modified by the adjectives *rapid* and *massive*, and *price liberalization* and *foreign trade liberalization* were typically preceded by *merciless*. For Klaus, the greatest enemies of allocative efficiency were the ties that bind – the subsidies binding firms to the state, the interenterprise credits binding firms to each other, and the informal attachments that link firms to localities. Because they are the major obstacles to risk taking, they must be destroyed. No one in 1991 could mistake Klaus for a developmental statist: In the neoliberal vision that he outlined, investment and growth could not be stimulated by reducing, spreading, or sharing risk. Instead, risk taking should be forced through the abolition of risk-sharing networks.

NETWORK PROPERTIES OF LIABILITIES

It was thus, amid such ideological fanfare, that Klaus's partisans in the Czechoslovak parliament passed a stringent new Bankruptcy Law in October 1991. Although Klaus's Bankruptcy Law was many rhetorical decibels louder than its Hungarian counterpart, the two differed in a more fundamental respect: The Czech law was not put into practice. By the spring of 1992, only months after it was enacted and even before the new bankruptcy courts were staffed with judges, the law was suspended for one year and was then postponed again.[25] Instead of aggressive bankruptcy measures, the Czech government has pursued an active *anti*bankruptcy policy. That policy has been coordinated among key institutions: The Fund for National Property has used receipts from privatization to subsidize public firms preparing for privatization; the Konsolidacni Banka was created to buy much of the old enterprise debt inherited from the socialist period and continues to channel funds to roll over enterprise debt through the largest commercial banks (which have been reluctant to initiate bankruptcy or liquidation proceedings and at whose urging the Bankruptcy Law was postponed); and the Ministry of Trade and Industry has repeatedly intervened to guide multilateral deliberations to prevent the bankruptcy of dozens of large enterprises with poor prospects for privatization.[26] So aggressive was this antibankruptcy policy that between November 1992 and October 1993, in roughly the same period when over 10,000 bankruptcy and liquidation proceedings were initiated in Hungary, only 993 bankruptcies (mostly of small private enterprises) were filed in the Czech Republic and not a single sizable state-owned enterprise was liquidated.[27]

What accounts for the dramatic differences in the consequences of bankruptcy legislation in our two cases? First, Klaus and his coterie pragmatically saw that the bankruptcy measures would jeopardize their privatization strategy if enterprises designated for their voucher program could be forced into bankruptcy proceedings prior to being privatized. Simply speaking, the government could not allow large state enterprises to fail while undergoing privatization. And because voucher privatization has taken longer to prepare and administer than anticipated in the early Klausian vision, state subsidies have been more protracted in the process. These considerations were clearly articulated by Tomas Jezek, then chairman of the National Property Fund, in his annual report of the fund's activities during 1992: "The greatest financial operation of the Fund was the emission of obligations for indebted firms . . . so that the joint stock companies privatized through vouchers would live through the relatively long period before the real owners took charge."[28]

But the Czech antibankruptcy policy was not driven by the privatization strategy alone. It derived as well from the fact that Czech policy makers were much more cognizant of the network properties of liabilities. This greater awareness can be seen in the decision of the Ministry of Industry and Trade to fund systematic research on the networks of interenterprise debt. This well-financed project developed a system for the computerized matching of payables and receivables, with the aim of identifying closed chains of debt (e.g., firm A owes B, B owes C, C owes A) that might be settled through simple accounting procedures. In the first round, only 9.1% of declared receivables could be so matched.[29] The success of the program was not limited, however, to this administratively canceled debt: The computerized representations of the networks of liabilities dramatically illustrated (1) the extraordinary degree to which firms were acknowledging their interdependencies and extending interenterprise credit to keep their strategic partners afloat and (2) that long chains of debt could ripple into tidal waves of bankruptcy that could threaten the banking system.[30]

Although the Czech economy was not plagued by the hyperinflation that had so racked Poland and was unburdened by the staggering foreign debt that afflicted Hungary, its health was nonetheless threatened by a weak banking system. In 1991 the Organization for Economic Cooperation and Development (OECD) estimated that Czechoslovak debt to banks totaled 66% of gross domestic product (GDP) compared to 46% in Hungary and 30% in Poland.[31] If the proportionately higher mountain of outstanding loans made Czech bankers acutely aware of the financial interdependencies of their debtors, the more oligopolistic character of Czech manufacturing made Ministry of Industry and Trade officials more acutely aware of production interdependencies. In that highly oligopolistic structure, bankruptcies could eliminate the sole domestic suppliers of critical inputs. Because of production interdependencies, aggressive action against the liabilities of one firm could devalue the assets of another. "Why turn assets into liabilities?" they argued as they lobbied together with the banks for the suspension of the Bankruptcy Law.

That these efforts could succeed required a third factor: Klaus saw that massive bankruptcies would not only threaten his plans for rapid privatization but would also undermine popular support for his broader reforms. Closing or rapidly downsizing firms, and the possible domino effects across the tight links among the limited number of customers and suppliers, could create large pockets of unemployment in many localities. As McDermott notes, "with the rise of local political groups, such as in the Silesian–Moravian region, the government feared such actions could result in a severe political backlash against itself and economic reform."[32] The Czech Republic's antibankruptcy policy has, thus, also been a proemployment policy, and its low unemployment rate cannot be understood without it.[33] In the narrow field of party politics Vaclav Klaus gives no quarter, but in his interactions in the broader societal field he has consistently avoided direct confrontations.

Our two cases thus offer an intriguing contrast in the management of liabilities. In Hungary the Antall government, despite its rhetoric about a "social market economy," launched such a rapid withdrawal of the state from the economy that the consequences provoked it to extraordinary intervention. In the Czech case, despite the Klaus government's neoliberal rhetoric, the state did not withdraw but has pursued a much more moderated policy always geared to securing social peace and maintaining political support for its programs. In the Czech case, however, the relationship between ideology and practical policy has not been a simple discrepancy or self-contradiction. Vaclav Klaus has a vision; but, as he himself insists, he does not have a blueprint. Unconstrained by a blueprint, he has adjusted flexibly and pragmatically. Insistent that he has a vision, Klaus is positioned to translate the support generated by the pragmatic turns and flexible twists into political credit. Support is won by specific policies. But, in Klaus's translation, it is not won for these specific policies alone but for the vision. Pragmatism is thus guided by the program and advances it: Pragmatism engenders a tolerance among the public for existing policies, and Klaus, in turn, interprets this tolerance as validation for his broader programs and support for further policy initiatives.[34]

If Klaus's is a pragmatism in the name of a program, that pragmatism, however, has not left the program unmodified. These changes can be seen in a recent essay by Klaus, titled (with characteristic immodesty) "The Ten Commandments Revisited."[35] The 10 commandments proclaimed in the first part of the essay read like a "Greatest Hits" of the neoliberal starting point, but their revisiting, as we see in the following passages, indicates that Klaus's vision is now more revisionist:

> Unless the political situation dictates otherwise, gradualism can work. Government regulatory interventions have an important role to play during the transitional period.
>
> Creating opportunities for non-state enterprises, including small-scale private businesses, and improving corporate governance of *state-owned enterprises* is more important than privatization as such.
>
> The basic reform strategy should be based on a maximum degree of sharing of non-trivial transformation costs. The concept of sharing is necessary for social reasons (to make it possible to advocate the inevitably growing income and property disparities) as well as for economic reasons.[36]

If we did not know that Mr. Klaus was a committed neoliberal, we might think that these passages, and others in the essay, had been written by a developmental statist commenting on the East Asian experience. And, indeed, after concluding his new Decalogue, Klaus presents six "valuable lessons" from the "transitional Asian economies." Favorably contrasting the "cautious and pragmatic approach" in East Asia with the "big bang price

decontrol" implemented in Eastern Europe, Klaus praises Chinese and Viet-
namese policy makers for learning an "indirect approach" from Korea and
Taiwan that recognizes the "inevitability of industrial dualism" in which
"traditional state enterprises continue to receive subsidized credit from state
banks" while the central government directs a set of "export promotion
policies."[37]

NETWORK PROPERTIES OF ASSETS

In Klaus's original vision, a speedy if unorthodox privatization scheme
would separate property from the state, from other stakeholders, and from
any considerations other than caring for profitability. One of the goals of
the privatization program was to create sovereign owners with clear property boundaries, thereby avoiding the mixed property forms and blurred
organizational boundaries so characteristic of the Hungarian experience.
The much vaunted voucher-auction scheme was to be the means to this
end.

By transferring assets of the state enterprises through a voucher-auction,
the Czech policy makers appeared to favor a kind of popular capitalism with
millions of citizen investors and a clear separation of public and private
property. Until just a few months before the first wave of computerized
auctions, however, only several hundred thousand citizens had entered the
privatization lottery by paying 1,000 crowns (about $35) to register the
investment points of their voucher coupon books. The problem of low participation was solved when *investment funds* (an afterthought in the initial
program) began to promise citizens who signed over their investment points
a 1,000% return, payable a year and a day following the transformation of
their points into shares. Czechs and Slovaks responded on the basis of years
of socialist conditions: Averse to risk, they were unwilling to play the investors' game, but they recognized a guaranteed income when they saw it.
Millions signed up.

The consequence of the voucher privatization was not to make popular capitalism but to make Vaclav Klaus popular. Klaus was named prime
minister following an election held just weeks after millions had registered their investment points by signing their names next to his signature
(as finance minister) on their voucher coupon booklets. The outcome,
moreover, has not been a people's capitalism but a strange kind of finance
capitalism.[38] During the first wave of privatization, only 28.1% of inves-
tible points were held by individual citizen investors; 71.9% were held by
the 429 Investment Privatization Funds (IPFs). When we aggregate the
voucher points obtained by the multiple IPFs founded by the same in-

vestment company, we find that 48.5% of all available voucher points in the first wave were held by the nine largest investment firms. That is, almost half of all the investment points were held by fewer than 10 investment companies.[39] This concentration of investment points, moreover, still understates the predominant position of the largest investment companies because individual voucher holders are almost never represented (and the smaller IPFs are underrepresented) on the boards of directors of the nominally privatized enterprises, where board seats are typically distributed to the largest blockholders.[40]

In this Czech finance capitalism, voucher privatization did not sever the ties between state and economic institutions; it reorganized them. The investment companies are not unambiguously private: The founders of six of the nine largest funds are predominantly state-owned financial institutions (banks and insurance companies).[41] For example, four of the five largest investment companies were founded by the largest banks – institutions in which the National Property Fund holds the controlling interest (44% of Komerční Banka, 45% of Vseobečna Uverova Banka, 45% of Investiční Bank, and 40% of Česka Spovřitelna). The same fund, moreover, still owns about 20% of the book value of the "privatized" companies and directly holds seats on the boards of many enterprises. Meanwhile, the Ministry of Finance controls the Konsolidační Banka, which is the major creditor of 80% of all medium-sized and large firms in the Czech Republic.[42]

Most important, as we see in Figure 6, banks and investment funds are cross-owned and the investment companies are interlocked in dense networks of related holdings. That is, investment companies, founded by the major banks, in turn, acquired shares of the banks through the voucher privatization. As John Coffee documents, sizable stakes in the major commercial, investment, and savings banks were acquired by investment funds established by these same financial institutions.[43] In the typical case, a large investment fund holds shares in its sponsoring financial institution,[44] as well as in one or more of the other major banks. In addition to their ties through their co-ownership of the banks, Czech investment funds are linked to each other through their enterprise holdings. Regulations of the voucher-auction prohibiting an investment fund from acquiring more than 20% of a given enterprise virtually ensured that the typical firm becomes a node at which investment funds intersect. Thus, one of the most important outcomes of voucher "privatization" is that the largest investment funds and the largest banks are crisscrossed by ties of ownership in networks whose density, in all likelihood, surpasses that of even the Japanese *kerietsu*.

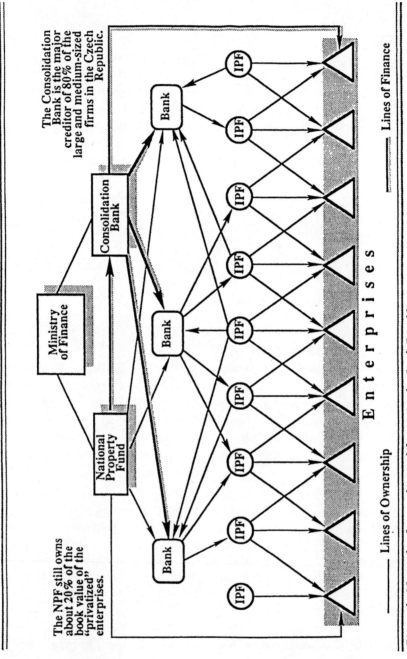

The Consolidation Bank is the major creditor of 80% of the large and medium-sized firms in the Czech Republic.

The NPF still owns about 20% of the book value of "privatized" enterprises.

E n t e r p r i s e s

——— Lines of Ownership   ——— Lines of Finance

Figure 6. Networks of ownership and finance in the Czech Republic.

FINANCE CAPITAL OR CAPITAL MARKETS?

We conclude our discussion of the Czech case with a brief account of an ongoing debate about the relationship between banks, investment companies, and enterprises. The outcome of that debate will have important consequences for the shape of Czech economic institutions. Will the Czech economy continue to evolve in the direction of a finance capital model or will it move toward the more Anglo-American model of capital markets?

The proximate issues in the debate concern whether investment funds should be limited in the shares they can hold in a given enterprise and limited in the seats they can occupy on its board of directors. In the ad hoc administrative measures regulating the participation of investment funds in the voucher privatization program, any particular fund was prohibited from holding more than 20% of the shares in a given privatized enterprise. At the same time, no restrictions were placed on the funds' participation on the board of directors of an enterprise. Both of these questions (limitations on shares and limitations on board membership) are addressed in the current debate, in which we can identify three policy positions: The first position advocates no changes in the current regulations; the second position argues for eliminating all restrictions; and the third position recommends eliminating the 20% shareholding limitation while simultaneously excluding investment funds from board membership (although allowing them to hold seats on the less powerful supervisory committees) and excluding bank-affiliated investment funds from participation in any enterprise governing bodies (whether boards of directors or supervisory committees).

Behind this debate on lifting or tightening restrictions (with consequences for tightening or loosening the ties between investment funds and enterprises) are fundamental policy differences on the future course of the Czech economy. The first, "no-change" position is an implicitly *managerialist* perspective. Its major proponents, not surprisingly, are the managers of the large enterprises, who publicly justify their stance with the argument that there is no reason to change a structure that seems to be working well. Indeed, it may be that the current 20% shareholding limitation works well enough to give enterprise managers more room for maneuver among a multiplicity of investment funds. From the enterprise manager's perspective, moreover, having more than one investment fund represented on the company's board of directors gives the enterprise more opportunity to *represent its interests* upward through the funds to the banks and outward to various state institutions. In Hirschman's terms, this managerialist stance is making claims for the positive role of *voice* within economic institutions.

The second, "eliminate all restrictions," position finds strong advocates in the Finance Ministry, the banks, and the investment funds themselves. Proponents of this *finance capital* perspective argue that the funds should have a free hand to acquire firms, to intervene or not intervene in their management when and how they see fit, and to coordinate the activities of a variety of enterprises within the extended network of the investment fund. Good corporate governance, they argue, will ensure that the banks are not the captives of the firms to which they are linked both by credit and (indirectly through the funds) through ownership. Arguing for tightening the connections between firms, funds, and banks and for facilitating career patterns in which managers can be transferred laterally across firms or vertically up the intercorporate managerial hierarchy, this perspective downplays voice and signals the importance of *loyalty*, not to particular firms but to the megacorporate, finance capital grouping.

Proponents of the third policy stance ("lift limitations on the funds' shareholdings and disallow board membership") argue that opportunities for voice or the constraints of loyalty mitigate the possibilities of *exit*. Supporters of this *capital markets* perspective within the National Bank and among liberal members of parliament contend that the presence of fund representatives on boards of directors diminishes the signals of price as it increases the salience of voice. Indeed, funds should have a free hand, they argue, but not one free to manage. Freed from all loyalties, the funds' portfolio managers should be free to sell when the price of shares (or their dividends) so indicates. The desired course is not better corporate governance, but more efficient capital markets. Lest they evolve in the direction of German banks, special restrictions must be imposed on bank-affiliated funds; lest they evolve in the direction of East Asian corporate groupings, the investment companies should be institutionally constrained to behave as mutual funds in smoothly operating capital markets uncontaminated by voice or loyalty.

Although the implicitly finance capital position (backed by the Ministry of Finance) seems, at this point, the likely victor, the debate is still ongoing; and we are likely to see several more surprising developments[45] before it is decisively concluded. But whatever the outcome of this particular debate, we can draw one conclusion from our analysis of property transformation in the Czech Republic: Voucher privatization did not eliminate the ties that bind; it rearranged them. The result is a web of connections through which a multiplicity of actors are renegotiating not simply contractual ties but also their mutual claims on interdependent assets. Within that web, firms, banks, investment companies, local governments, and parts of the state bureaucracy identify firms that should be saved, devise strategies for restructuring assets, bargain about the allocation of resources, and renegotiate the rules and governing institutions for resolving disputes among them.[46]

The Czech state did not create these ties, but it participates in them. That is, unlike the developmental state, the Czech state does not substitute for absent ties. It is neither the spider that created the web nor (at least not yet) the fly that is caught within it. It is a part of the network.

A COMPARATIVE REPRISE

Are the Hungarian interenterprise ownership networks the East European counterparts of Taiwanese related enterprises? Are the cross-owning banks/investment companies Czech versions of the Japanese *keiretsu* or the Korean *chaebol*? The question suggests a comparative study of corporate groupings in modern economies. But before making comparisons across regions, we must consider another question: How do the network patterns of the German, Hungarian, and Czech cases differ?

Our analysis of East Germany revealed a case in which economic transformation began in the context of weakly developed networks connecting firms and the almost total absence of subcontracting ties between the *Kombinate* and private or semiprivate producers. Such fragile ties as did exist, moreover, were eliminated by the market shock immediately following unification. In managing the liabilities that it inherited (and also contributed to making), the Treuhandanstalt was eventually given new instructions to acknowledge regional bodies charged with the responsibility of restructuring groups of enterprises. But although the deliberative element was strong, it could not fully compensate for the absence of cohesive economic networks. In consequence, the economy of contemporary East Germany shows little sign of the vibrant associational life linking networks of producers through lines of competition and cooperation such as those that characterize the "third Italy," Silicon Valley, or Baden-Württemberg.[47] With the lines of purchase and supply linking enterprise transplants in East Germany more to firms in western Germany than to their immediate environment, regional economies remain undeveloped, prompting one close observer of the East German economy to label these new facilities "cathedrals in the desert."[48] Although German political leaders were able to make a coherent adjustment of the Treuhand's policy, the East German economy still bears the mark of its pathway from state socialism.

In Hungary and the Czech Republic, by contrast, we find dense and extensive networks in both economies. But the shape and patterns of these networks are distinctive in each economy, and consequently, the structures of corporate groupings are likely to differ. Our analysis indicates that Hungarian networks are formed predominantly through enterprise-to-enterprise links, sometimes involving banks but lacking ties between banks and intermediate-level institutions such as investment companies. The Czech case is the exact opposite. There, ownership networks are formed predominantly through ties at the mesolevel among banks and investments funds, but direct ownership connections among enterprises themselves are rare. Restated in the language of network analysis, *whereas Hungarian networks are tightly coupled at the level of enterprises but loosely coupled at the mesolevel, Czech networks are loosely coupled at the level of enterprises and tightly coupled at the mesolevel.*

As in East Germany, the distinctive patterns of the Czech and Hungarian ownership networks also bear the marks of their differing pathways from state socialism. As we have shown, each configuration has been directly shaped by distinctive policies of property transformation, themselves shaped by contingent institutional choices at early junctures in the transformation process. These economic strategies, moreover, could not be dictated or imposed on the blank features of a postsocialist institutional vacuum. Instead, they interacted with the strategies of actors within the economy who possessed distinctive organizational resources and who were well practiced in distinctive repertoires of action, themselves shaped by the distinctive character of their preexisting network ties.

Through partial economic reforms in Hungary during the 1970s and 1980s, enterprises were already gaining considerable autonomy, enjoying greater flexibility in choosing other enterprises as supply partners, and constructing networks of small-scale protoentrepreneurial producers at (and even within) the boundaries of the firm. Moreover, as we saw in Chapter 2, legislation facilitating property transformation (the Company Law of 1988, which established conditions for creating limited liability companies, and the Law on Transformation of early 1989) was in place *before* the system change and *during* the political hiatus between the opening of negotiations in June 1989 for changing the rules of the political system and the installation of the first democratically elected government in May 1990. As a consequence, firms already had direct enterprise-to-enterprise contacts and a legal framework in which these horizontal ties could be transformed into the interenterprise ownership networks of the present.

Czech enterprises, of course, had not enjoyed such autonomy under state socialism. But they were not without their own network resources in their ongoing conflicts with the industrial ministries of the old regime. The difference with Hungary was that these networks operated not through direct enterprise-to-enterprise ties but at a mesolevel within the Industrial Associations organized along branch or regional lines. So resilient were these mesolevel associations that they survived or resurfaced after several attempts at their elimination by the Communist authorities.[49] It is at this similarly mesolevel, as opposed to direct enterprise-to-enterprise ties, that the networks of cross-ownership are most dense in the contemporary Czech economy.

In both cases, property relations are being transformed – but *within structures whose network features exhibit continuity even as their ownership content is altered.* In neither case is property transformation a simple transition from public to private. In both, it results in the blurring of the properties of public and private. And in both, we find the trespassing of organizational boundaries in "moebius-strip organizations"[50] and strategies of "recombinant property" in which actors diversify their portfolios of assets of very heterogeneous character in attempts to maneuver through situations where organizational survival is fragile, not simply because of the uncertainties of the market but also because the criteria of success, the measures of worth, and the selection mechanisms are themselves uncertain.

In Hungary, where the state has attempted to privatize assets and manage liabilities on a case-by-case basis, we see recombinations of assets at the level of firms in chains of interenterprise ownership. In the Czech Republic, we see a state that has recognized the network properties of liabilities and that participates in mesolevel networks for renegotiating the recombination of assets. In both cases, the invisible hand gets a hand not from the long arm of the state but from the associative ties of interorganizational networks. Recalling our Irishman's joke, it might not be the best, but it is a way to start from here.

6

ENABLING CONSTRAINTS: INSTITUTIONAL SOURCES OF POLICY COHERENCE

How shall we assess the reform projects in our three East Central European cases? One obvious method would be to adopt the perspective of the reigning liberal orthodoxy. As we saw in the previous chapter, each of our national cases departed dramatically from neoliberal policy prescriptions. Despite their protest that they never swerved from the commitment to "privatize first, reorganize later," the managers of the German Treuhandanstalt, in fact, became involved in deliberative forums in which networks of shareholders and stakeholders restructured assets prior to privatization. Czech policy makers made even more radical departures. Although from ideological pronouncements alone we might have predicted that they would follow Adam Smith's prescriptions to "destroy the combinations," in fact they acknowledged network properties – adopting antibankruptcy policies and job creation measures while giving priority to restructuring over price liberalization. Their privatization measures were unorthodox not simply because they developed the novel (and, at the time, still untested) voucher formula but because they resulted in new combinatory property forms with dense networks of interorganizational ownership. And what could be more unorthodox than the radical swings from market shock to paternalistic state and back again that characterize Hungarian policy?

An alternative method of assessing these reform projects is not to apply some external yardstick but to use the comparative analytic strategy we have adopted throughout this book. The most striking comparative difference in our cases is the degree of policy coherence, ranging from relative stability in principles and practices to almost frantic swings from one policy course to another. Once they recognized that mercilous exposure to market competition had transformed assets into liabilities, German policy makers established new restructuring institutions while persisting on a course of rapid privatization. Czech policy makers were even more coherent – avoiding tidal waves of bankruptcy from the first. In effect, Klaus and his colleagues rejected speed as a guiding principle, for the pace of change alone could be no guarantor of coherence. Instead, they operated with relatively clear selection criteria, believing that restructuring (always in the broad and loosely defined direction of privatization) should occur within frameworks that protected fixed assets, preserved human capital, and saved the network properties that reside in interorganizational ties. By these standards, Hungarian policy cannot be characterized as either consistent or coherent. Not only were its privatization and property management agencies woefully out of touch with the actual practices of decentralized reorganization, but its broader economic policies lurched from extreme to extreme. Whereas German and Czech policy makers made *adjustments* when confronting the consequences of their policies, the Hungarian scene, by contrast, more closely resembled the pattern of *regulation by crisis* (so familiar from the days of state socialism[1]). In that mode, each policy current is dogmatically pursued right up to the moment that the crisis it produces makes it no longer sustainable, at which point it is replaced by an antithetical policy current whose political half-life is measured by the crisis tendencies inherent in it. As our discussion of the Hungarian case suggests, although decision makers claim that they are applying *policies of crisis management*, it would be more accurate to speak of *the crisis management of policies*.

How should we account for these differences in policy coherence across our cases? How can we explain the differential ability to produce coherent policies that can be adjusted rather than abandoned?

Neostatists who advocate the creation of East European schools of public administration to promote greater professionalism among the bureaucratic staff[2] would point to the German case to support their claim that policy coherence is a function of the quality of the state bureaucracy. Indeed, there can be little doubt that the Treuhand's staff had solid professional credentials and considerable esprit de corps. That professional ethos and enthusiasm, however, were probably less a function of importing bureaucrats from the formerly West German state than of staffing the Treuhand with young professional consultants anxious to acquire credentials in corporate restructuring to make careers in German banking. In any case, the argument about the quality of state bureaucracy falters with the Czech–Hungarian comparison, for it is highly unlikely that, within just a few months, the quality of the Czech state bureaucracy equaled or surpassed that of its Hungarian counterparts. If anything, the Hungarian state bureaucracy was more likely to have inherited from the Kádárist reform era a more competent (by professional standards) staff than that inherited from the deep freeze of the Husak years lasting until the moment of collapse of the old regime in Czechoslovakia. The quality of the state bureaucracy cannot explain policy coherence in the Czech Republic and policy incoherence in Hungary.

Some might argue that the Czech case is evidence that strong ideas make for policy coherence. Not the quality of state bureaucracy but the internal consistency of the guiding ideas behind the economic programs is the key factor in explaining cohesive policy formulation and effective implementation. In this view, uncompromising pursuit of these ideas is the best strategy for success. But as our discussion in the previous chapters has shown, ideological pronouncements and visionary principles were rarely tightly coupled with actual policy programs. There we saw how the Hungarian advocates of a social market economy implemented unintended and then intentional market shocks, whereas Friedmanite advocates of "a market economy without an adjective" in the Czech Republic are candidates for designation as the most dedicated social democrats in the region. That is, in contrast to the view that coherence follows where ideology faithfully guides policy, we saw that Klaus's actual practice was most marked by an ability to make unorthodox departures from his orthodox ideology. Not economic dogmatism but political realism was the key to Klausian pragmatism.

Not ideas but institutions, some would argue, are the key to explaining policy coherence. Indeed, the broad comparative study of the relationship between political change and economic reform is rapidly converging on a new consensus that the single most important factor in the success or failure of economic reforms is strong executive authority.[3] From this perspective, our attention should be drawn to the relations among state (and other political) institutions: Where institutional configurations fragment, impede, restrict, challenge, check, or constrain executive authority, there economic reforms will stumble.

This new consensus view restates several of the recurring themes in the development literature. First, whereas Evans had posited that coherence (in his terms, coherence of selection criteria in the double sense of staffing and policy) yields autonomy, advocates of the unconstrained executive model argue that such a view posits as an independent variable (coherence) exactly the relevant outcome that we need to explain as the *dependent* variable. When we get our analytic priorities straight, we can see that it is not coherence that explains autonomy but autonomy that delivers coherence. But the new perspective does not simply regress to an earlier point in the debate because, second, it shifts attention from the autonomy of the state writ large to the *autonomy of executive authority* more specifically. In so doing, it reformulates policy management of economic reform as a coordination problem.[4] Thus, whereas the problem of economic reform had formerly been formulated as the need to keep *societal interests* from coming into the state and subverting economic reforms, here it is reformulated as the problem of how to structure the *interests of state actors* in the face of potential institutional entanglements (internal to the state) that dissipate executive authority.[5] Institutional configurations (constitutional restrictions, multiparty coalition governments, fragmented party systems, and the like) that constrain the discretionary authority of the executive increase coordination problems; conversely, concentrated executive authority minimizes institutional friction, facilitating smooth coordination.[6] Institutional entanglements that limit executive authority confound the rationalization of policy formulation, thereby eroding policy coherence and corroding effective implementation.[7]

The institutional focus of the strong executive model is congruent with our own assessment that the critical question in the debate is not that of the relationship between democracy and economic reform, but whether and how different *kinds of democracies* differ in their capacity to cope with the complexities of economic transformation. That is, what we find most fascinating in the strong executive position is the precise attention to different *institutional* configurations and whether or not they constrain the unilateral prerogatives of executive authority.

With that emphasis in mind, we can produce a rough test of the strong executive framework by ranking our cases according to concentrated/unconstrained executive authority, on the one hand, and policy coherence, on the other. The results indicate a definite correlation. The problem for the unconstrained executive theory, however, as we shall see, is that the sign is negative. That is, our examination of the East Central European cases suggests that institutional configurations that constrain executive authority are more likely to yield coherent formulation and implementation of economic reforms. Conversely, the least constrained are the least coherent.

In the following sections, we examine the institutional configurations that succeed (or fail) in placing limitations on the unilateral prerogatives of central executive authority in the Hungarian, German, and Czechoslovak (later, Czech) cases and we indicate, in a preliminary way, how these constraints enable more coherent policies. As we shall see, in the Hungarian case we find relatively few constitutional and institutional limitations on concentrated executive authority, nor are Hungarian policy makers constrained by deliberations with organized social actors. As a consequence, policies are neither coherent nor sustainable as they swing from extreme to extreme. By contrast, in the Czechoslovak (and, later, Czech) case, where central executives' room for maneuver is more limited by societal deliberations and by intrastate checks and balances, the resulting moderated policy course has been more coherent and sustainable. Germany, as we shall see, is an intermediate case in which the relatively extreme policies adopted during the exceptionalist period (when the institutional rules of the game of German politics were temporarily nullified by Chancellor Kohl's assumption of concentrated executive authority in pursuit of his unification strategies) were later moderated after federal and corporatist institutions took root in the new *Länder* of eastern Germany. Following a detailed presentation of these cases in this chapter, we move in the concluding chapter from the language of critique to specify, in a positive sense, the types of beneficial constraints (*extended accountability*) that increase authority to carry out projects of economic reform.

HUNGARY

BASIC INSTITUTIONAL FEATURES

Of the three cases we examine here, executive authority has been least constrained, constitutionally and conjuncturally, in Hungary. Hungary's president, elected by Parliament and with limited constitutional powers, is, of course, not strong. Instead, executive authority is concentrated in the office of the prime minister, whose broad constitutional powers are strengthened by the feature of a "positive vote of no confidence."[8] Under this system, Parliament can register a vote of no confidence only in the unlikely circumstance that it can simultaneously propose a new government. The constitutional features that render the Hungarian prime minister chancellor in all but name are reinforced by such institutional features as the electoral law, whose rules for translating votes into parliamentary seats make it possible (and even likely) that a leading party that captures only one-third of the votes will have near-majoritarian standing in Parliament. Such a majority was attained by Gyula Horn's Socialist Party, with only 36% of the vote in the 1994 elections, and was nearly attained by Antall's Democratic Forum in the 1990 elections. The results in both cases were coalition governments in which the party of the prime minister could govern with few concessions to (and only occasional consultations with) its junior coalition partners. The result of these constitutional, institutional, and conjunctural factors was that Parliament became an abstract debating society and not a venue for deliberations that secured broadly encompassing agreements across contending policy positions. In such a setting, it is perhaps not surprising that Prime Ministers Antall and, later, Horn strove to centralize decision-making authority in almost personal terms.

This centralization of policy making, moreover, was relatively unchallenged by organized social actors in other institutional arenas. Hungary's interorganizational networks, to be sure, could embark on enterprise restructuring, but only as decentralized reorganizations in the domain of corporate strategy. But these networks have not given rise to strong employer associations articulating forceful positions on matters of national economic policy. In this they mirror the deficiencies of organized labor, whose weak and fragmented trade unions[9] have neither mounted sustained challenges to government polices nor been counted as reliable allies in policy initiatives. Unhindered by the Central Bank (whose independence under both governments was severely questioned), unchecked by its coalition partners, unresponsive to Parliament, and unconstrained by ex ante deliberations with representatives of labor and business, Hungary's strong executive had nearly free rein – to make policies without taking into account their economic and social consequences, to reverse course without charting coordinates, to lurch from self-inflicted crisis to crisis. Concentrated executive authority expanded the room for maneuver and thereby magnified the costs of error and amplified the swings in policy. Save for a Constitutional Court[10] that demonstrated its independence by opposing aspects of the nationalists' restitution law, blocking Antall's attempts to subordinate Hungarian television to the office of the prime minister, and overturning some of the Socialists' plans to dismantle social welfare programs, these policy swings would have been even wilder.

DELIBERATIONS PROPOSED

If weak institutions mediating societal interests and the relative absence of constitutional and other institutional limitations on executive authority fostered the national-conservatives' erratic policy course of oscillation between market and statist policies, these same institutional deficiencies also eroded policy coherence under the Socialist Party following its victory in the 1994 elections.

With the national-conservative coalition disintegrating in its waning months, Hungarian opposition parties had approached the 1994 parliamentary campaign with optimism – and with the sure knowledge that electoral victory would be followed by enormous challenges. Harsh measures would have to be introduced to stop the deterioration of the budget, and these measures would necessarily be accompanied by a rapid increase in the social costs of transition borne by society. To prepare for this situation, each of the three major opposition parties campaigned on the promise that, if it came to power, it would handle these problems through wage pacts or encompassing social agreements negotiated in tripartite (business, labor, government) deliberative institutions.[11]

In their run for elections, the reconstructed Socialists showed the society a Janus face. On one side, the liberal wing of the party under the leadership of László Békesi campaigned as the prophets of doom. Whereas the FIDESZ economic policy advisers advocated a half turn, with measures that would not be overly restrictive, Békesi argued strenuously that stabilization would require a full turnabout, and he elaborated in detail the extraordinary social burdens that would accompany it. For his liberal wing of the party, the major purpose of negotiations for a broad socioeconomic agreement would be to *educate the public* that there was no alternative. On the other side, Gyula Horn, president of the Socialist Party (and former foreign minister in the last Communist government), campaigned as the caretaker of social burdens. If Békesi was the prophet of doom, Horn was the balm of Gilead that would make the wounded whole. With a set of assurances that were all the more vague as they were all the more inclusive, Horn's message to society was in essence: As the party that cares for your problems, we will be the government of social dialogue. National-level negotiations will be the means for *you to educate a socially responsible government* about your sufferings, which we will devise measures to treat.

Capturing the votes of those who believed that a Socialist government would reduce the agonies of transition, the Socialists won a resounding electoral victory with 54% of the seats in parliament. Although they were themselves a parliamentary majority party, the Socialists chose to enter into a coalition with the liberal Free Democrats, with whom they hammered out a detailed socioeconomic program in the early summer of 1994. The 72% majority that the new coalition government commanded was the most decisive parliamentary control of any postsocialist government in the region. With both coalition parties having campaigned for socioeconomic pacting, with an elaborated program to deal with the economy and the impending budgetary crisis, with an unchallengeable position in parliament, with their political capital and popular support at near record levels, with the dominant federation of trade unions in the Socialist camp, and with the well-oiled negotiating machinery of the National Council of Reconciliation already in place, it seemed that tripartite deliberations were just around the corner.

DELIBERATIONS REJECTED

But leadership to launch the coalition's program and inaugurate negotiations was not forthcoming. In his initial pronouncements as prime minister, Horn assured the foreign business community that Hungary would not stray from the path of market reforms. The reformed Socialists, he observed, however, would chart a distinctive course to the market that would not neglect the impoverished, the aged, the young, and the unemployed. Like reform Communists in an earlier epoch who had attempted to craft "socialism with a human face," the Socialists would provide a transition with a human face – in short, capitalism with a heart. But for nine months the country was kept waiting for the program that would embody such a strategy as the new government neither brought major legislation to the Parliament nor placed its program on the agenda for negotiations in the National Council of Reconciliation.

Meanwhile, the state's indebtedness, and with it the country's external debt, were racing out of control. With a budget deficit at 10% of GDP in the fourth quarter of 1994, the Socialist–Liberal coalition had one of the worst government records in the world. By the beginning of 1995, Hungary's national debt approached $30 billion, with a $600 million shortfall in the balance of payments. But the more Békesi, now finance minister, broadcast an impending catastrophe, the more Horn sounded the themes of caring and compassion while taking steps to politically kill the messenger of bad tidings.[12] Unable to ignore the fact that Horn's war of maneuver had turned into a war against his position, Békesi resigned as finance minister in February 1995.

Victorious in the field of internecine politics, Horn could now approach the field of economic policy with the three most strategic positions (finance minister, privatization minister, and presidency of the National Bank) at his disposal. The political class was stunned, therefore, when Horn signaled his 180 degree political turn toward Békesi's policy by appointing two outspoken liberals, Lajos Bokros and György Surányi, as finance minister and president of the National Bank, respectively.[13] Moreover, the public was stunned when Bokros almost immediately announced a bold (some would say, frenzied) plan to rapidly slash the budget deficit by 165 billion forints ($1.4 billion). With some 40 items of expenditure cuts (e.g., health, social services, salaries and staffing in the public sector) and about the same number of revenue increases (e.g., a sharp increase in import taxes, tuition fees for college students.), the stabilization program seemed, almost as if by design, to impinge on nearly every social group the Socialists had campaigned to protect. The Socialist-led transition, it seemed, would be to capitalism with a broken heart.

Both the public and the political class could not but be startled by the Bokros Plan because the new change team had done nothing to prepare them for its content. The stabilization program was announced by Horn, Bokros, and Surányi at a hastily called Sunday evening press conference following a secret retreat. The new shock therapy was deliberately not the product of deliberations: Horn had not consulted even his own Socialist members of parliament. Excluded from the discussions and not warned about the new measures, the trade union leaders in the Socialist camp were ill prepared with arguments to defend the plan – had they been, however now unlikely, inclined to do so.

Bokros displayed the same contempt for deliberations when, two weeks later, the tripartite National Council of Reconciliation was taken from its nine-month deep freeze. The new finance minister concluded his opening remarks emphatically: We invite your comments about details, but the program itself is nonnegotiable. Because Hungary was in a deep economic crisis,[14] the only cure was drastic deficit reduction; and about his specific prescription there could be no negotiations.[15] In every forum and media outlet, Bokros defined the situation as life in the emergency room. In normal times, the surgeon might seek a second opinion and perhaps even discuss procedures with the patient, but in an emergency he must be in absolute command. Deliberative forums might be appropriate for normal times but not during crises.[16] Two weeks after its convocation, the Reconciliation Council met again and adjourned within an hour when the participants reached agreement – that there was no mutual basis for negotiations.

In the early summer of 1995, the Bokros team revealed that the stabilization phase of their program would be followed neither by measures of Keynesian fiscal stimulus nor by the guidance of a developmental state. For the second phase of their strategy, they proposed to reduce taxes on business so that profitable firms would have higher retained earnings to finance new investment internally. To ensure that this supply-side solution would not contribute to further budget deficits, they proposed that these business tax cuts be offset by a renewed round of even deeper cuts in social expenditures. Whereas the earlier unintended market shock of the Antall government had been a form of destruction that wiped out viable firms along with the bad, the intended market shock of the first phase of the Bokros program would stabilize the economic environment. The subsequent social shock of the second phase of the program would, they contended, free up resources for expansion led by spontaneous market actors, not government direction.

From the paternalistic state of the nationalist–conservatives, the Hungarian Socialists had turned to an orthodox liberal position in an exclusive belief in the transformative capacity of the market. Taking a page from the playbook of Newt Gingrich, they had made balanced budget deficit reduction the sole plank of their economic platform. Whereas in the parliamentary campaign the Socialists (like the other opposition parties) had been actively searching for a formula that combined economic and political rationality, once in office Horn had attempted to buy patience by avoiding reforms for almost a year. Later, with unparalleled concentration of executive authority, he turned the tables even on his own party and spurned deliberations that might have secured patience through politics. Economically irresponsible in the first period, his government was politically foolhardy in the next.

The Hungarian Socialists, it seems, have reversed the course of the antidevelopmental state, but at the price of securing long-term support for real and lasting economic reforms. At the first signs of success in deficit reduction and economic growth, the populist bloc of the party is likely to clamor for the ouster of the neoliberals and push the pendulum in the other direction as Hungary continues in its zigzag course of oscillation between market and statist policies.

GERMANY

At the national level, the relations among state institutions in Germany are not markedly different from those in Hungary – in part because those in postsocialist Hungary are broadly modeled after Germany's. Like the Occupying Powers in postwar Germany who, fearing Weimar instability, had designed institutions with clear lines of authority,[17] the architects of the new constitutional arrangements in Hungary had opted for governability over accountability, thereby ensuring a strong executive. In fact, the Hungarians had gone one step further, introducing a set of electoral rules that were even more disproportionate than those of the German system. Nonetheless, the structure of parliament–government relations was broadly similar in these two cases. As we shall see, where Germany differs from Hungary is in its federal structure and the strength of its most important interest associations.

THE EXCEPTIONALIST PERIOD

During the months following German unification in October 1990, East Germans witnessed a process that we can describe without hyperbole as colonization: Political, economic, and social institutions across the board were replaced with those of the former Federal Republic of Germany (and often staffed with personnel of West German origin).[18] The federalist and quasi-corporatist institutions that had characterized the postwar politics of the Federal Republic of Germany did not, however, come immediately into play in postunification East Germany. Campaigning in the 1990 elections with the message that the market mechanisms of a second *Wirtschaftwunder* (economic miracle) would restore prosperity in East Germany, just as they had in West Germany during the 1950s, Chancellor Helmut Kohl scored impressive victories in the West and East. With his broad constitutional powers conjuncturally reinforced by the electoral successes following his stunning diplomatic triumph in negotiating reunification, the German chancellor "assumed the position of an unconstrained sovereign decision-maker,"[19] operating as if the usual rules of the game[20] no longer applied in such extraordinary circumstances. It was within this political matrix that state bureaucracies such as the Treuhandanstalt set out to remake East Germany. In this project, they were initially unchecked by regional and local civil institutions in the East. As if the pathetic legacy of an abysmally weak civil society was not disparaging enough, East Germans saw what little was left of their possibly defensive institutions disappear as municipal and local government administrations were dismantled and the old trade unions scrapped.

Given this relative absence of constraining institutions, we might expect that, as in Hungary, highly centralized and tightly concentrated decision-making structures would yield an unmoderated course. Indeed, initially, they did. As we described in the previous chapter, unmitigated exposure to market competition triggered not an economic miracle but an economic nightmare – whose consequences were as rapidly apparent as the market competition was strong. Moreover, because the sources of the problem were more transparent and the political promises more grandiose,[21] in Germany economic crisis carried the danger of political crisis. The signs were soon manifest: the assassination of the Treuhand's chief executive, demonstrations in the city seats of *Länder* parliaments, and strike waves in the East, where workers held dozens of factories and citizens occupied the state parliament in Schwerin, capital of Mecklenberg-Vorpommern.[22]

However, unlike the wild swings of policy makers in Hungary, the response of German policy makers to the political and economic crisis was more incremental and moderated. The explanation for this difference lies in the emergence of countervailing state structures and societal/political institutions that restrained the strong executive, constrained its agents in the state bureaucracies, and moderated their policy course. These institutional arrangements were also the legacy of colonization: Along with the executive arm of the federal government, reunification also brought to East Germany the West German institutions of *federalism* (with autonomous *Länder* government as the critical component) and *corporatism* (with strong trade unions as the crucial feature).[23] These institutions could be quickly transplanted in the autumn of 1990, but it was only with the spring rains of looming economic collapse and impending political crisis that they would take effect.

FEDERALISM RESURGENT, DELIBERATIONS RESTORED

Confronted by unprecedented levels of unemployment, bankruptcy, and decline in growth, the recently elected prime ministers of the new *Länder* in the formerly East German territory did not sit by passively in the face of resurgent opposition. Within the German federal system, they were not the agents of the Bund (the federal government) but had independent mandates from their respective electorates. As politicians whose political careers were at stake, they began, in the early months of 1991, to strongly criticize the privatization policies of the Treuhand agency. And as heads of state governments covetous of part of the administrative action in the field of economic restructuring (with enormous consequences for their jurisdictions), they demanded the dismantling of the Treuhand into regional agencies – responsibility for which would devolve to the respective *Länder* governments.[24]

At the same time, the institutional transfer of West German trade union structures to East German territories was taking hold.[25] From the fall of 1989 to March 1990, West German officials of the German Trade Union Federation (Deutscher Gewerkschaftsbund, or DGB) had adopted a policy of not meddling in trade union affairs in East Germany, preferring to wait and see whether and how the unions of the Free German Trade Union Federation (Freier Deutscher Gewerkschaftsbund, or FDGB) would engage in a self-cleansing process of democratization in anticipation of possible amalgamation at some point two to four years in the future. But after the landslide election victory of the Christian Democratic Union (CDU)–led East German *Allianz für Deutschland* in late March 1990, the takeover strategy of Bonn was matched by a takeover strategy by the DGB as its unions threw massive resources into creating an organizational basis for new unionism in the East.[26] "Don't wait – expand" became the operational slogan; and by the fall of 1991, the organizational expansion of the 16 unions that composed the DGB was essentially completed. At the end of 1991 some 4.2 million union members had been registered in the new *Länder*, surpassing the goals of the recruitment drive by almost 600,000 (with almost half as many members as in West Germany, but from a much smaller base of employees).[27]

It was in the midst of this organizational drive, in early 1991, that the leaders of many of these trade unions began (in tandem with the *Länder* politicians) to challenge the policies of the Treuhand, calling for state-controlled *reconstruction* instead of accelerated privatization. While East German enterprises were being forced to compete with the firms of one of the strongest economies in the world, East German workers were gaining representation by one of the strongest trade unions in the world – precisely at the time that economic crisis was being translated into political crisis.

Thus, by the spring of 1991, strong executive authority within the German state was no longer unconstrained, and it could not pursue further elaboration and implementation of its policies without taking into account the new state and societal actors that were the institutionalized creatures of reunification. Federal politicians soon entered into intensive negotiations with the *Länder* governments and the trade unions. The result was the broad program of *Aufschwung Ost* ("Revival of the East"), embodied in a set of agreements struck among representatives of the federal government, *Länder* governments, trade unions, and business associations from March to July 1991,[28] followed by further deliberations over the "Solidarity Pact" for which, during a six-month period starting in September 1992, over 40 rounds of negotiation were held in the chancellor's office alone.[29]

In Germany, deliberations constrained executive authority and moderated its course of action. But the frequent lack of economic rationale for public subsidies to private firms that we saw in the previous chapter suggests that German institutions went only halfway toward developing a policy of coherent restructuring. Three factors explain why Germany would have moved toward but not fully embraced a course of recognizing the potential for network-led restructuring. First, in contrast to Hungary, where we found associative ties in the absence of deliberative institutions, in Germany we found the reverse: deliberative institutions in the absence of associative ties. Second, in contrast to the Czech Republic, where (as we shall see) the institutions of tripartite negotiations have their roots in society, in Germany the shallow roots of corporatist institutions were a product of their transplantation to the East German setting.

Third, under conditions of political unification, in Germany decision makers had a policy choice: They could restructure assets or they could redistribute resources. Unlike the other postsocialist countries, Germany could afford to decouple the protection of people from the restructuring of firms. Such redistribution took several forms. Through the less visible channels of the social insurance system (health, pension, and unemployment provisions, for example), by 1994 transfer payments accounted for 40% of household disposable income in East Germany.[30] Resources were also redistributed through the somewhat more politically visible public budget as the new *Länder* governments were partially pacified by consolidated integration into the general system of tax redistribution. Thus, the political problems of the new *Länder* governments and those of the union leadership in East Germany were at least partially solvable without active restructuring efforts. Moreover, redistribution found constituencies not only in the East but also in the West, as West German unions and West German employers had a common interest in impeding East German competition in the commodity market as well as in the labor market. Faced with the option of restructuring or redistributing, German policy makers did some of both. Such a choice was not available in the Czech Republic, where deliberative and associative elements were both robust.

THE CZECH REPUBLIC

As in Hungary, the president of the Czech Republic is elected by parliament. Although the current president, Vaclav Havel, enjoys considerable moral authority, the office is largely ceremonial and has limited constitutional powers. But unlike Hungary, with its quasi-chancellorian prime minister, in the Czech Republic unilateral executive authority is constitutionally, institutionally, and conjuncturally more constrained.

Unlike Hungary, where, as we saw in Chapter 1, the formation of political parties preceded the dissolution of the old regime and where electoral competition was itself the path of extrication from state socialism, in Czechoslovakia the Velvet Revolution of November 1989 brought movements, not parties, into government as the Civic Forum (in the Czech lands) and the Public Against Violence (in Slovakia) assumed office following the founding elections in June 1990. These broad social and political movements split into parties during 1991. During 1992, following the June parliamentary elections, the leaders of the two strongest Czech and Slovak parties (Vaclav Klaus and Vladimir Meciar, respectively) negotiated the "Velvet Divorce" culminating in the independence of the Czech and Slovak republics that took effect on January 1, 1993. The timing of these political developments must be underscored in their relationship to economic policy making: In Czechoslovakia, the decisive *formation of policy paths* in the economic field (concerning privatization, bankruptcy, employment, wages, and the like) took place precisely during the period in which executive authority was held by politicians/policy makers who were grappling with the *formation of parties and the separation of the two republics.*

INSTITUTIONAL CONSTRAINTS, RESTRAINED POLICIES

Thus, in contrast to the Hungarian prime ministers, Antall and Horn, who could govern the country by leading their majoritarian (or near-majoritarian) parties, Vaclav Klaus assumed the position of finance minister as a politician without a party. With that political deficit he was not long-suffering: With no regard for the previous delicacies with which political differences had been largely unspoken within the dissident community, he declared to his colleagues in the Civic Forum that the days of dilettantism were over. He would have a political party, an unabashedly right-wing party, and it would be his. But even as Klaus, the party politician, was drawing the heavy ideological lines that would lead to the split of the Civic Forum and the creation of his Civic Democratic Party in late February 1991, Klaus, the finance minister, was already practicing the politics of pragmatism.

The strong executive was constrained, first, by the fact that parliament was not his to command. If the neoliberals could secure support for stabilization through restrictive monetary policy, there was no guarantee that their precarious majority in parliament would hold for the more ambitious program of privatization at the top of their priorities.[31] Second, the strong executive was further constrained by the fact that the government was not his to command. Within this same formative period, the labor and social portfolios within the government were largely in the hands of the social democratic wing of the Civic Forum.[32] With entirely free rein, it is not inconceivable that Klaus might have willfully ignored the network properties of liabilities and assets; but the need for accommodation with parliament and other government ministries tempered these policies by bringing broader social issues into account. As a consequence, Klaus's program of property transformation came into the world with a twin – for this bold plan was entwined with a cautious policy that included antibankruptcy features, active labor market policies, and social welfare measures. Together these fraternal (not identical) policy twins comprised a more coherent strategy of economic restructuring.[33]

One might suppose that these policies would change after Klaus's electoral victory and his ascension to prime minister following the elections in June 1992. With his own disciplined and victorious party and, as prime minister, able to choose his cabinet ministers, Klaus had surmounted the initial conditions that restrained him from pursuing an even bolder plan of attack. But the fundamentals of the policy path that had been set in place during 1991 remained in place throughout 1992 and 1993 because Klaus remained constrained by a further set of constitutional and conjunctural factors.

As a result of the June 1992 parliamentary elections, Klaus's Civic Democratic Party (ODS) became the largest party in each of the three chambers in which it sat. But it was no parliamentary giant. Unlike the Hungarian Socialists, who could win roughly 34% of the vote on the party lists and, nonetheless, obtain (through a combination of the disproportionate electoral rules and the ability to win enough single-member districts) 53% of the seats in a unicameral parliament, the ODS's room for parliamentary maneuver was constrained by a different set of electoral rules and by the constitutional limits of Czechoslovakia's federal structure. For the Republic's Parliament, winning 30% of the votes yielded the ODS 38% of the seats (76 of 200) in the Czech National Council. But for the two houses of the Federal Assembly, it obtained only 32% (48 of 150) of the seats in the Assembly of People and only 25% (37 of 150) of the delegates to the Assembly of Nations.

The multicameral structure of Czechoslovak federal parliamentarism, we should note, had a distinctly antimajoritarian feature. Although Slovakia accounted for about one-third of the population of Czechoslovakia, seats in the upper house of the Federal Assembly (the Assembly of Nations) were not so apportioned. Instead, half of the delegates were elected by the citizens of Slovakia and half by the citizens of the Czech lands. As a consequence, despite their minority status in the lower federal chamber (the Assembly of People), the Slovak parties, which were far less enthusiastic about rapid economic reforms, could use the upper house to effectively block any federal legislation on economic transformation.

Thus, throughout the entire period in which he was formulating and beginning to implement his economic strategy, Klaus (whether as finance minister or as prime minister) had to secure wide political agreement to ensure legislative passage of his programs. Prior to the Velvet Divorce, it was impossible to divorce the "Slovak question" from questions of economic policy. Slovak politicians, who were most likely to be the first to feel the political pressures of rising unemployment, for example, would be more likely to endorse economic restructuring if it was packaged with an active labor market policy. The active antibankruptcy policy, similarly, was conceived in no small part in an effort to avoid the predictably explosive situation of Czech banks initiating bankruptcy proceedings against Slovak companies.[34] As in Germany, in Czechoslovakia federal structures placed constitutional limits on executive authority and, by establishing a more varied range of mechanisms for cross-institutional accountability and by providing forums for more encompassing deliberations, thereby moderated its policies.[35]

Following the legal separation of the Czech and Slovak republics on January 1, 1993, we again might suppose that Klaus, now free of the Slovak problem and of its federalist constraints, would finally take off the gloves and bring policy practice into alignment with ideological strictures. But the postindependence period has not seen dramatic departures from the earlier policy course. To be sure, bankruptcy legislation was removed from its two-year deep freeze, but its implementation remained extremely selective and highly cautious.[36] On the social front, job.creation subsidies were not dismantled,[37] and instead of price liberalization, Czech residents continued to enjoy liberal subsidies for housing and public utilities.[38] If realignment occurred, the method, as we saw in the "Ten Commandments *Revisited*" in the previous chapter, has brought ideological pronouncements in line with practice. To date, as one reads Klaus's public statements, the standardized formula fairly jumps off the page: So inseparable are the terms *vision* and *pragmatism* that if the first appears, the second will typically do likewise – often in the same sentence.[39]

This institutionalization of policy pathways was reinforced by a final set of constraints (less constitutional than conjunctural) on the strong executive in the postindependence period. Whereas formerly Klaus had to shepherd economic policy legislation through three parliamentary chambers, now he had to contend with only one legislative body: the Czech National Council. But the parliamentary majority of his multiparty coalition government was not overwhelming. Klaus's ODS–KDS electoral alliance had gained him 76 seats in the Czech Parliament; the CDU-People's Party held 15 seats; and the Civic Democratic Alliance had 14 delegates. Together the coalition government held a slender 52% majority.[40] With only 105 out of 200 delegates, Klaus was in no position to ignore his coalition partners: if only 6 representatives among his junior partners switched allegiances, he would find himself in the minority and lose his government. As a consequence, the Czech Parliament has remained a genuinely deliberative body, and the ministries held by Klaus's junior coalition partners enjoy considerable authority. When we factor into the equation a truly independent Central Bank, we see that the Czech situation has been one in which the Parliament, the Finance Ministry, the Ministry of Industry and Trade, and the Central Bank have been cooexisting as relatively autonomous policy centers.

Again, the comparison to Hungary is most telling. With the Hungarian Democratic Forum (MDF) occupying 42.5% of the parliament and his coalition government composing a 60% parliamentary majority,[41] Prime Minister József Antall could centralize authority with much greater disregard for the positions of the junior parties in his coalition government – for he could well afford (and actually did witness) a considerable drop in support from their parliamentary delegates. Similarly, Gyula Horn's centralization rested on his Socialist Party's 53% absolute majority and the qualified (two-thirds) majority it enjoyed together with its coalition partner, the Free Democrats. The contrast to the Czech case is instructive because the Hungarian *electorate* was not more enthusiastic for the MDF in 1990 or for the Socialists in 1994 than the Czech electorate was for Klaus's Civic Democrats in 1992.[42] The major difference was in the *electoral rules* and their institutional outcomes. In Hungary, electoral rules aiming for greater governability systematically over-reward the party that secures the largest number of votes; in the Czech Republic, by contrast, electoral rules favoring greater representativeness increase the possibility that more parties will have a voice in governance. Whereas the former favors the party with a simple *plurality*, the latter fosters a more complex and diverse *pluralism*.

GOVERNMENT AND LABOR: MUTUAL RESTRAINT, CONFLICTUAL CONSENSUS

A similar inclusiveness marks the Czech government's relations with the trade unions. Czech unions, of course, have not been as strong as the powerful German DGB, nor have corporatist institutions been as decisive in the Czech case as in the German. But the strength of the Czech trade unions and the salience of corporatist intermediation are not wanting, especially when measured against the yardstick of the experiences of the other societies in postsocialist Eastern Europe: The Czechoslovak Confederation of Trade Unions (and later the Czech and Moravian Chamber of Trade Unions) has been the only unitary trade union federation in the region, postsocialist Czechoslovakia was the first in the region to establish tripartite institutions, and these institutions have maintained their vitality in the postindependence period. From the outset to the present, the relationship between the government and organized labor has shown a consistent pattern of mutual restraint. Faced with persistent trade union defense of the basic rights of organized labor, the government has avoided frontal attacks on the unions. Faced with the government's insistence that it will not compromise the basic principles of its program of economic reform, the trade unions have refrained from mobilizing against that program. Even with threats and counterthreats, the result has been the conflictual production of social harmony as institutionalized negotiations repeatedly reproduce a growth strategy based on low wages, low unemployment, and robust trade union rights.

The prehistory of postsocialist Czech labor politics has one relevant date: November 27, 1989. On that day, grass-roots committees led the general strike that delivered the final blow to the Communist regime.[43] The only such general strike in the "revolutions of 1989," this collective action survives in the collective memory: The present trade unions owe their legitimacy to this successful strike.

During the early months of 1990, new labor activists under the leadership of the National Association of Strike Committees quickly took over the old trade unions from below and gained government recognition of their right to divide among the new trade unions the property (buildings, clubs, vacation resorts, etc.) of the old regional councils.[44] At the All-Union Congress on March 3, 1990, the delegates of the 50 new unions formally dismantled the 17 industrial unions of the old regime's Revolutionary Trade Union Movement and established the Czechoslovak Confederation of Trade Unions, with the actual management of trade union activity to be coordinated separately in the Chambers of Trade Unions formed in the Czech and Slovak republics.[45]

With just enough time to move into their new offices, the new trade unions quickly learned in the summer of 1990 that Finance Minister Vaclav Klaus would not launch his career in postsocialist politics as an undying friend of organized labor. Although the new federal government set up after the first postcommunist elections in June 1990 had proclaimed in its program the "desirability of consolidated strong trade unions" as a "social partner" for "negotiations on labor and social conditions,"[46] that same government, at nearly the same moment, introduced to the new parliament a draft bill on strikes. Noting that the draft bill resembled an earlier bill that the Communist Federal Assembly had considered in 1989 but lacked time to ratify, the trade unions condemned it as an antistrike law. With the successful general strike that had toppled a government still fresh in their memories, the neoliberals withdrew the bill.

Similar skirmishing continued throughout 1990 as labor mounted an active campaign around the Labor Code (with the Metalworkers Union gathering 600,000 signatures in four days on a petition protesting the first draft of the new code) and threatened to strike when dissatisfied with drafts of the Collective Bargaining Act.[47] But while such charges and countercharges were being aired before the public, the trade unions were heavily involved in drafting labor legislation and, with the active participation of the International Labor Organization (ILO),[48] the result was a system of labor law generally favorable to the trade unions. Through the Act on Wages of 1991, the amended Labor Law, and the 1991 Act on Collective Bargaining, Czech trade unions secured strong organizational rights: Employers, for example, cannot hire replacement workers during a strike; unions' rights to bargain and to strike are protected in accordance with the norms of the ILO; Czech workers enjoy relatively strong protection against job dismissal; and dismissed employees are eligible for fairly generous redundancy pay.[49]

But the Czechoslovak (and, later, Czech) trade unions have not only defended and then institutionalized their organizational rights and interests;

together with the government, they have established an institutional framework for interest mediation. On October 10, 1990, the Coordination Council representing the confederation of business associations, the Czechoslovak Confederation of Labor, and the government agreed to establish the tripartite Council of Economic and Social Accord. The agreement requires the government to bring all important legislation affecting employees and trade unions (as well as other matters of social policy) to the council *prior to submitting it to Parliament*. In addition to these intermittent policy deliberations, the council has an agenda-setting function: It is responsible for producing a General Agreement on employment and wage policies for the next year.[50]

The Council on Economic and Social Accord, thus, provided the forum for the complex negotiations that produced the Labor Code and the Law on Collective Bargaining. Similarly, it was through tripartite deliberations in the council that organized labor successfully blocked the government's attempt in late 1993 to ban public sector unions and collective bargaining in the state administration.[51] Tripartite deliberations have not always run smoothly (the unions withdrew from negotiations in July 1991, for example, in protest against the government's refusal to raise the minimum wage to the level required in the General Agreement)[52] and have sometimes been acrimonious (as when Klaus denounced the peaceful trade union demonstration in Prague's central plaza on March 23, 1994, by comparing it to the demonstration in 1948 in which Klement Gottwald proclaimed the Communist coup),[53] but in these and similar cases, both sides returned to the negotiating table and resolved their differences.[54] Low-level maneuvers to gain limited tactical advantages rather than frontal attacks to strategically disarm the opponent seems the modus operandi in this process of conflictual consensus.

Along with its work in institutionalizing trade union rights, the Council on Economic and Social Accord has been instrumental in securing the low-wage/low-unemployment growth strategy characteristic of the Czech economy in the postsocialist period. Total wage costs in the Czech Republic are considerably lower than those in Hungary and Poland. At the same time, unemployment in the Czech Republic is not only lower than in the other postsocialist economies but is, at around 3%, the lowest in Europe. The low level of Czech unemployment is, in part, explained by the fact that much of the shock of the collapse of the export markets to the former socialist economies was borne by Slovakia (where the unemployment rate was almost 15% at the end of 1994); similarly, the ability to exploit its great potential for tourism (which grew by almost 50% from 1992 to 1994) has been a bonanza, providing new employment in services and hotel construction, especially in Prague.[55] But these one-time events are only a partial explanation. In fact, low wages and low unemployment have been part of an explicit policy strategy.

Czech(oslovak) trade unions have made full employment a central theme in their programs since 1991. Toward that goal, they have accepted low wages as a cost of economic restructuring. These costs are acceptable, first, because the unions acknowledge that low wages can contribute to low unemployment. As Rutland observes, "labor costs are so low that companies can afford to keep workers on the payroll, and private entrepreneurs find it cheap to hire new staff."[56] Second, organized labor has signed on to the General Wage agreements in the tripartite council because, in return for that wage restraint, the government has maintained its commitment to move cautiously in the area of bankruptcy (hence forestalling layoffs) and to pursue active labor market policies. The job-preserving aspect of the former is difficult to estimate, but Orenstein notes that the employment gains from the latter are significant: "In 1992–93, at any given time the number of people employed through the various job programs ranged from 100,000 to 140,000, making up about 2% of total employment. The Czech government spent 1.7 billion crowns ($58 million) on active labor market policies in 1992."[57]

Thus, institutionalized deliberations made it possible for the trade unions to shift their time horizons as, for example, when Vladimir Petrus, who led the Czech Trade Union Chamber from 1992 to 1994, explicitly acknowledged the government's reform strategy as "the key to prosperity that could make the unions' *long-term objectives* realizable."[58] At the same time that tripartite structures moderated trade union demands, they moderated the policies of the government and altered its time horizons as well. Despite his initial antipathy to the trade unions, Klaus came to learn through the process of negotiations that labor could be an ally, and tripartite deliberations an instrument, in crafting a consensus on policies of economic restructuring.[59]

Here, too, the comparison to Hungary is illuminating.[60] There the Antall government's strategy of dividing and conquering labor succeeded: It succeeded in excluding labor from policy formulation, thereby preventing it from exercising a moderating influence on policy and on its own members. The results were damaging both to labor and to the national economy, with sharp leaps and drops in the real value of wages and greater unpredictability in the behavior of business, labor, and the government throughout the period.[61] The greater inclusiveness of Czech policy toward organized labor appears all the more remarkable when contrasted with the policy of the Hungarian Socialists in 1994–5. Having scored their electoral victory with

considerable help from the Socialist trade unions, one might have expected
that Gyula Horn and his team would activate the existing tripartite institutions and redress the overtly antilabor features of the legislation passed
by their predecessors. Instead, by treating them as mere palliatives to be
used after the fact and matter of factly, they have debased the institutions
of social deliberation. To date, the Socialists have introduced no legislation
to modify the Hungarian Labor Code and its provisions on strikes and
collective bargaining.[62] Without an allied political party, the Czech trade
unions were, nonetheless, *strong enough* to secure a set of institutional rights
to defend their organizational interests. With his vitriolic outbursts still
proof that it is not attitudes but institutions that provide moderation, Vaclav Klaus was, nonetheless, *constrained enough* to learn that he had more to
gain by making an offer to his opponents than by attempting to disarm
them. It has been the neoliberal Prime Minister Klaus, not the politician
of labor, who has utilized the institutions of tripartite deliberations and, in
so doing, been moderated by them.

Our examination of the three Central European cases yields a central finding
squarely at odds with the core thesis of the unconstrained executive model,
for we have seen that where institutional structures placed the strongest
constraints on executive authority, there policies were more coherent. Relatively unconstrained executives (in Hungary, throughout the period, under
conservatives and Socialists alike; in Germany during the immediate aftermath of unification) were more likely to produce policies whose unantici-
pated consequences created crises and provoked policy reversals (recklessly
in Hungary, modulated in Germany). Relatively constrained executives (in
Czechoslavakia from 1990 to 1992; in the Czech Republic after separation;
in Germany after the institutions of federalism and corporatism took effect)
were more likely to produce coherent policies that could be adjusted rather
than abandoned. Our finding of a negative correlation between concentrated
executive authority and policy coherence leads us to reject the unconstrained
executive model. In the concluding chapter, we draw on our case studies to
elaborate an alternative theoretical framework in which to understand the
institutional sources for sustainable policies of economic transformation.

EXTENDED ACCOUNTABILITY

What implications do the findings from the case studies in the previous chapter have for our understanding of the relationship between political structures and reform policies? In particular, what is the relationship between public accountability and authority to carry out reform projects? The unconstrained executive model, of course, involves a widely held assumption in political theory[1] about a trade-off between authority and accountability: The less accountable the reforming center is, the more capable it is of representing the general will; the less connected it is, the more it is capable of coordinating its program. Unrestrained by ties that bind, the unconstrained executive can behave responsibly because it has full authority to undertake the difficult tasks that the situation demands.

By contrast, our analysis suggests an organizational phenomenon, paradoxical only on first encounter: Executive capacity, understood here as the capacity to formulate and implement coherent reform programs, can be increased by limitations on the unilateral prerogatives of executive authority. Executives that are held accountable by other state institutions and held in check by organized societal actors are not necessarily weaker executives; in fact, their policies can be more effective. In this view, policy coherence for sustainable economic reforms is an outcome of extended accountability.

By *extended accountability* we mean the embeddedness of the decision-making center in networks of autonomous political institutions that limit the arbitrariness of incumbents. Extended accountability differs, first, from the vertical accountability of periodic elections, for it *extends accountability horizontally* in a set of relations through which executives are held accountable by other state institutions. By exposing policies to greater institutional scrutiny, extended accountability reduces the possibility that executives will make enormous miscalculations in rash, extreme policies.[2] Extended accountability differs, second, from simple electoral accountability because, in contrast to the episodic character of the latter, it is *extended in time*. Extending accountability as a continuous, ongoing process reduces the possibilities that executives can appeal to a "crisis" in attempts to legitimate and expand their delegative electoral authority.[3] As our analysis of the Czech and German cases suggests, far from impeding state coordination, such extended deliberation in networks of autonomous institutions that accompanies the formulation and implementation of policies actually increases the possibilities for ex ante coordination among them.

Along these first two (axial and temporal) dimensions, extended accountability bears obvious affinities to the concept of *horizontal accountability*, employed so forcefully by Guillermo O'Donnell in his critique of *delegative democracy* in the recently established but poorly consolidated democracies of Latin America. Deploring the vicious cycle of decisional frenzy that erodes trust while claiming ever-more authority for a central executive at once curiously omnipotent and impotent,[4] O'Donnell advocates horizontal accountability across state institutions. Our notion of extended accountability subsumes this feature of O'Donnell's model but goes on to *extended accountability in scope* to include not only *intra*state institutions but also other political institutions – in particular, other organized societal actors – in the networks of accountability.

In this extension of scope, our conception of extended accountability bears a family resemblance to Peter Evans's concept of expanded embeddedness. In the conclusion of *Embedded Autonomy: States and Industrial Transformation*, Evans speculates about the future prospects of the developmental state. The problem that he poses for his own previous analysis is that the very success of the developmental state in stimulating industrial transformation might pose obstacles to its further development. Successful industrialization creates new social classes with their own agendas potentially capable of challenging the state itself. Painfully aware that his model of state–society links is limited to ties between the state bureaucracy and industrial elites, Evans calls for an expanded embeddedness that includes consultations with organized labor and other subordinate groups in a more broadly defined set of state–society links.[5]

Evans's emphasis on inclusion, although consistent with his view that autonomy is not a function of insulation, marks an important new departure in his analytic framework, with broad applicability in the postsocialist setting. The party-states of the Soviet bloc were not developmental, and the industrialization that they directed was far from successful. But from Gdansk to Vladivostock they succeeded in creating an industrial working class now capable of challenging the reform policies of the new postsocialist states in the region. As Evans's more general argument suggests and our own analysis indicates, their political inclusion in policy networks is a fundamental condition for robust and adaptive programs of economic transformation. Expanding network ties beyond industrial elites and extending accountability beyond intrastate institutions to include a broader range of interests and intelligence in decision-making centers, we argue, further contributes to the *coherence* of reform policies.

Such a view is, of course, entirely implausible from the standpoint of the unconstrained executive model. Within its logic, the experts who have been delegated authority by the popularly elected executives already possess the necessary intelligence in the double meaning of the term: They have the requisite information and the enlightened intelligence to know what needs to be done. If horizontal checks and balances would confound coordination problems within the state, the inclusion of societal interests would doubtless be a source of policy pollution. Extended accountability could only dilute their authority and erode policy coherence. But our analysis of the Czech and German cases suggests the opposite: However imperfect, relative political inclusion of subordinate societal interests actually buttressed political authority and enhanced policy coherence. Extending accountability to regional bodies in which labor enjoyed prominent representation and extending deliberations in tripartite institutions of business, labor, and the state did not result in damaging compromises. Instead, these were major institutional channels for keeping policies on course.[6] Bringing society back into politics at the time of policy formulation meant that decision makers did not confront society only at the time of policy implementation. Instead, these deliberations increased the intelligence of policy makers, providing critical inputs that helped them anticipate the future economic, political, and social consequences of their policy actions. Extended accountability thus *extended the time horizons of key state actors*, correcting political miscalculations in advance and encouraging them to think several steps ahead in the strategic games of reform politics. Because deliberations forced them to be responsive ex ante, the resulting policy currents were already shaped in coherent and cohesive ways that facilitated a rapid response and responsible adaptations in changing circumstances. Extensive deliberation did not "soften" policies; it tempered policies, making them more durable because they were more resilient. Extended accountability did not compromise politicians; it made their visions more pragmatic.

Our conception of extended accountability thus combines aspects of

O'Donnell's horizontal accountability and Evans's expanded embeddedness. Like O'Donnell, we highlight the process of accountability in shaping policy coherence; and, like Evans, we emphasize the need to include
societal actors in the policy-making networks. But our theoretical elaboration is not merely additive, for our extension of the notion of accountability requires an important modification of Evans's framework. Simply
expanding the range of network ties linking state bureaucrats to society
risks an erosion of policy coherence. As our analysis of the Behemoth as
Gulliver Bound (in Chapter 4) indicated, the incoherence of the socialist
party-state was directly attributed to such unmediated links between state
bureaucrats and societal interests. There we saw that the more bureaucrats
attempted to take into account an ever-expanding set of particular interests, the less the state was capable of policy concertation. In the absence of
mediating institutions providing mechanisms of accountability, such taking into account meant that the state was taken captive by policy partic-
ularism. For this reason, our choice of terminology is deliberate: *Extended
accountability* is not simply a different name for Evans's concept but connotes a process that differs from expanding the personal embeddedness of
the state bureaucratic administrators.

Among our cases, the German Treuhandanstalt comes closest to
Evans's conception of the "pilot agency" of a developmental state, a "su-
peragency"[7] in the economic arena. Moreover, in its later development, it
most closely resembles Evans's call for expanded embeddedness with the
incorporation of the trade unions in the widened circle of network ties
reaching to the Treuhand bureaucrats who directed and coordinated policy. As we demonstrated, political inclusion of subordinate interests did
place the Treuhand on a more even course. But, as we also saw, the limitations of these new policies rested precisely in the extent to which the
network ties of the new deliberative institutions were centered too closely
on the Treuhand. Making the Treuhand accountable was difficult in a situation in which the various societal interests were too often linked to each
other only through the ties of the Treuhand managers themselves. Compared to Hungary, in Germany the transplanted trade union structures
and the federal institutions of the *Länder* governments provided some
check on the megalomania of central executives. But the new policies still
floundered precisely because expanding the immediate ties of the Treuhand's bureaucrats (in line with Evans's prescriptions for expanded embeddedness) threatened to dissolve the agency in a sea of particular
interests. Our conception of extended accountability thus shifts the analytic focus from the personal ties of the state bureaucracy to the institutional features of the political field.

AUTHORITY AND ACCOUNTABILITY

How can heterogeneous societal interests be brought into the state without compromising ambitious programs for economic reform? The danger of bringing such interests directly into a broadly embedded but nonetheless disaggregated state bureaucracy is that reform policy might become disaggregated. Not unlike the dynamic of the responsive responsibles under state socialism, policy coherence would be dissipated in a multiplicity of bureaucratic side dealings, so fractured and fragmentary that the state administration escapes accountability.

As our explication thus far of the concept of extended accountability has implied, and as we here make explicit, the answer to this problem rests in extending our analysis from the field of the state bureaucracy and from the domain of intrastate institutions to *properties of the political field*. In a first and rough approximation of its contours, we can say that, when and where it functions relatively effectively, the *outputs* of this field are generalized principles and guidelines, and that its internal dynamics are shaped by ongoing contests over specific forms of *credit*. Its central actors are politicians vying for claims of creditworthiness; and its key organizations are political parties competing over political programs and interacting with state institutions, as well as with other organizations mediating societal interests.[8]

What do reform politicians do? More specifically, how do they engage in a transformative politics that contributes to extended accountability? To examine the work of politicians, we employ the notion of *accounts*.[9] Etymologically rich, this term simultaneously connotes bookkeeping and narration. Both dimensions entail evaluative judgments, and each implies the other: Accountants prepare story lines according to established formulas, and in the accountings of a good storyteller we know what counts. Politics is a distinctive form of social accountancy. Politicians "open accounts" and they "make accounts." Politicians open accounts when they appeal to the electorate: "Put your credit on my account," they say. "Credit me, invest in me, authorize me to act on your account." But politicians who simply take myriad interests into account will be penalized within the framework of competitive politics. To compete successfully, parties must gain the support of social groups with widely different, even conflicting, interests and rationalities. Winning strategies submerge these particular interests in the aggregated, overarching accounts known as *political programs*.

In preparing such programs as specific forms of accounting/narration, politicians exploit the doubly associative character of resources – as ties among groups and as links within the *networks of categories*[10] that make up legitimating principles. The work of forging and maintaining a political program always involves regrouping political resources – rearranging social ties among groups and making new associations among the cognitive/political categories through which society is represented. In making these new associations, politicians do not represent interests (simply making present in the political field already given and fixed positions) so much as reconfigure them by establishing novel, and sometimes counterintuitive, connections among them. Stated differently, the accounts of a political program do not simply represent interests; they reshape identities. Political programs are therefore doubly associative: In making claims to represent, to speak on behalf of named social groups (e.g., "We are the party of labor *and* small business"), they attempt to create alliances; in making the case for a particular course of action, they attempt to modify the *chains of association* representing how society functions and how it can be transformed (e.g., "Moderate wage demands can raise profitability and export performance, thereby increasing levels of investment and securing government revenues, thereby upgrading infrastructure and investment in human capital, leading to stabilization of employment and increases in wages").

Thus, political parties compete in *systems of representation* not only in their delegatory claims to speak for designated social groups but also in their deliberate efforts to alter the contours of the cognitive maps on which society is represented. Successful political programs do not rest with existing associative ties but deliberately attempt to mold new associations that break the boundaries of previously fixed social groupings. Representational politics is a struggle over the divisions *and the visions* of the social world. In reform politics, parties and politicians offer competing visions of societal transformation.

But as our case studies have demonstrated, the decisive challenge for transformative politics is how to present such a vision without becoming a visionary. And here we argue, also on the basis of our case studies, that the answer to this question lies in the institutions of extended accountability.

In the standard view, it is precisely the *episodic* character of electoral accountability that gives politicians the room for maneuver to forcefully pursue the winning program that it has offered to the electorate. In fact, some have argued that the longer the time period between elections, the greater is the possibility that incumbents will be able to take a long-term perspective and undertake difficult tasks, knowing that they are buffered from accountability in the meantime.[11] From that perspective, a long-term vision, together with the authorization to pursue it, exist in a trade-off with short-term accountability.

From the perspective of extended accountability, by contrast, authorization is a continuous process; and successful reform politicians recognize that selling the vision requires ongoing accreditation.[12] They know that the more ambitious the program and the more difficult the reform tasks, the greater the uncertainty among societal actors about the present and the future. And so, while continuing to project their vision of the future, they engage in the work of producing an ongoing account, making associations between present concerns and that transformative vision. Precisely because the stakes are big and the uncertainties high, successful politicians know that they cannot rest by simply claiming "By your votes you have invested in me, and now, wearing the vestments of my vision, I plan for your future." Instead, they work to demonstrate their responsiveness and battle for continued public support on an almost daily basis.

Under transformative politics, political investment is a multifaceted process. On the one hand, it resembles an initial public offering supervised by the Electoral Commission (like a Securities and Exchange Commission) and underwritten by a political party (like a lead investment bank). Only with a convincing program (prospectus) can the party gain enough investors to cover its points. But that is not the only appropriate analogy to be drawn from the world of finance. For on the other hand, under reform conditions of high uncertainty, political investment resembles a fragile savings bank whose managers must reassure the numerous depositors that their investments are secure, lest a run on the bank prove disastrous for the bank and depositors alike. Recognizing that public support can be withdrawn between elections, the successful reform politician continuously engages in the work of political translation: pointing to support for particular policies as evidence of the soundness of the broader strategic vision, linking short-term sacrifices to long-term returns, and reassuring the public of effective stewardship of the political resources so entrusted. In short, the politician points to a diverse set of "proofs" of his or her *ongoing creditworthiness*.

But this political alchemy is not enough to ensure that the individual investors will feel that their deposits are secure. Even the most skillful accountings cannot assure the public that their accounts are properly managed and their interests protected. In fact, such representations alone can lead to a mobilizing frenzy: rallies, demonstrations, and the proliferation of top-down associations as proof of continued support; overt manipulation of the press; and populist demagoguery that short-circuits the chains of association between present and future. At its worst, mobilization risks preempting the decisive role of elections. At the least, because it typically results in spiraling mistrust, it always threatens a collapse of investor confidence and a run on the bank of political credit (i.e., defection in favor of parties opposing the reform policies).

Necessary but not sufficient, the ongoing pursuit of creditworthiness

by politicians and political parties is only one aspect of extended accountability. Because a political program is not like a long-term bond with a
delayed but fixed rate of return, it requires more than an immediate, personal bond between the politician and the public. It is the intrastate and
extrastate institutions of extended accountability, we argue, that convince
the individual depositors to keep their credit with the reform politicians.
Through the increased public scrutiny of the institutions of horizontal accountability (state institutions monitoring other state institutions), citizens
acquire some guarantees that their *investment in a reform program* is not an
authorization of capricious actions precipitating disasters. Through the ex-
tensions of accountability in time and in scope to include other organized
representations of societal interests, citizens acquire some guarantees that
their social burdens are registered as accounts payable.

Extending accountability (horizontally to other state institutions, laterally to other institutions of political representation, temporally to ongoing
monitoring) provides the *institutional safeguards* to assure the depositors that
the political brokers are not squandering their resources. And the more
effective these safeguards are, the more the depositors are able to recognize
that the lines at the bank are not runs on the bank but normal deposits and
withdrawals (as the political program undergoes the normal process of losing
and gaining supporters between elections). Institutional safeguards thus
promote investor confidence. They make it possible for the public to credit
reforms. In short, extended accountability *extends the time horizons of societal
actors*.

In the standard view, the greater the time interval between episodes of
accountability, the greater the Archimedean leverage for the reform politician to "move the world." By contrast, extended accountability shortens the
period between episodes of accountability. Yet, as we have seen, it extends
the time horizons of politicians and the public, suggesting a political variant
of Zeno's paradox: Just as the ancient Greek mathematicians approached
infinity by slicing the fractions into ever-smaller increments, incremental
monitoring provides the political basis for longer-term strategies. In the
standard view, the greater the concentration of authority, the more the
executive is able to engineer change. By contrast, extended accountability
results in a network of distributed authority. Yet, paradoxically, when the
central executive is embedded in a set of autonomous, mutually monitoring
institutions, this very distribution of authority strengthens the coherence
and effectiveness of reform policies. It does so by multiplying the leverage
points throughout the political field. Transformative politics is leveraged
not simply by lining up the longest chains of allies but by utilizing institutional antagonists. Not by a smooth transition but by using institutional

friction[13] at multiple fulcrum points does transformative politics build credibility with the public and gain authorization for change. The neo-Hobbesians are mistaken. Authority and accountability are not necessarily in a trade-off. Extended accountability can extend authority to undertake reforms.

RETHINKING COHERENCE

Through the binding agreements of extended deliberations, politicians are de-liberated. So bound, they are free to offer their institutionally pragma-tized visions: "I am bound to my program, and I am bound in a network of distributed authority. You can authorize me to act because I am con-strained from acting precipitously." It is this peculiar double bind that opens the space for transformative politics – for it is the distinctive com-bination of vision and constraint, of program and pragmatism, that yields successful reform policies. Purely pragmatic, reform politics risks stumbling against entrenched interests. Purely programmatic, reform politics risks be-coming the captive of its own representations (*illusio*). It is the double bind of extended accountability (binding the executive in a network of distrib-uted authority and binding the executive to the systematic accountings of a reform program) that yields a programmatic pragmatism.

The notion of extended accountability and its attendant programmatic pragmatism has implications for our understanding of coherence. In the conventional view, policy coherence is judged by qualities of the internal consistency, precision, and all-encompassing character of reform design. The more clear, precise, and thoroughly specified the policy blueprint, the more coherent will be the actual policy course. Some economic policy designers are beginning to question this view, at least to the extent of shunning the notion of fixed sequencing.[14] In place of the architectural metaphor of the blueprint, in these cases reform design draws on cybernetic models with feedback loops and built-in correctives. Like a sophisticated computer pro-gram with a series of simultaneous "if . . . then" subroutines, the designer continuously monitors a vast array of economic indicators in a process of ongoing recalibration of the major parameters of the model.

Transformative politics builds on this departure from design as blue-print. But in addition to using the indicators of economic processes (level of inflation, wage rates, export performance, and the like), it recognizes that the longer-term viability of a reform program depends on such noneconomic factors as levels and forms of public support, business confidence, voting behavior, and the like. The institutions of extended accountability provide this critical feedback. Through deliberative associations, politicians and the public alike recalibrate the parameters of change. As the "institutionalization of practical reason," they implement John Dewey's "pragmatic rule" that "in order to discover the meaning of an idea, ask for its consequences."[15] In such a programmatic pragmatism, ends and means are in a relation of reciprocal or mutual causality. Goals do not dictate means, for it is only in pursuing our goals that we discover the full meaning of the initial idea and, through this learning about the implications of our goals, recalibrate both the instruments of vision and the practical tools for a further stage of experimentation.[16] Transformative politics is experimental – not because society is the subject of a grand fixed design but because deliberations educate the educator, they transform the transformer. In pragmatizing the vision, they do not limit the field of vision. Instead, they open it up, they reveal goals, and invite revision, not as a looking back but as a turning toward new perceptions of the possible.

Programmatic pragmatism thus not only questions the fixed sequencing of various policy measures in a reform program but goes beyond that to challenge the sequencing of reform design and policy implementation.[17] As such, it resembles the recent reorganization of production in some of the most fast-growing sectors of advanced economies characterized by rapid technological advances and extraordinary market volatility. As identified by Charles Sabel,[18] these new developments have two distinctive features. First, because of strong first-mover advantages in which the first actor to introduce a new product (especially one that establishes a new industry standard) captures an inordinately large market share by gaining increasing returns to scale, firms that wait to begin production until design is completed will be penalized in competition. In these settings, successful strategies integrate conception and execution, with significant aspects of the production process beginning even before the design is finalized. Second, these new systems of production are also often characterized by *simultaneous engineering*. Whereas conventional design is sequential, with central subsystems designed in detail first and setting the boundary conditions for the design of lower-ranking components, in simultaneous engineering separate project teams develop all the subsystems concurrently. In such concurrent design, the various project teams engage in ongoing mutual monitoring, as innovations produce multiple, sometimes competing, proposals for improving the overall design.[19] Success in simultaneous engineering, Sabel argues, depends on this "learning by monitoring" and requires an acute organizational reflexivity that sustains rather than squashes ambiguity throughout the entire process.

This conception of design as deliberation within leading sectors of advanced economies corresponds closely to our conception of the sources of coherence of reform strategies in the postsocialist economies. In this view, policy coherence is a direct function not of the thoroughness and precision of initial design but rather of the integration of design and implementation. And like simultaneous engineering, transformative politics sustains ambiguity for the purpose of clarifying goals through deliberation. Neither aimless nor rigid, the iterative, deliberative process through which goals are established and their implications recognized facilitates learning from the changing circumstances brought about by reform efforts. Policy coherence is thus the product of reflexive learning.

The reader should not be misled to believe, however, that by invoking the concepts of learning we have in mind a process of quiet contemplation. In fact, as our cases, especially the most successful ones, reveal, the process of extended accountability is noisy and discordant. Where deliberations are real, interests are not easily harmonized. They sing in different keys, they calculate with different measures of evaluation, they appeal to different legitimating principles. Deliberative forums are not domains for suppressing these differences but for expressing them. The strategy of exclusion stills that noisy clash but sacrifices policy coherence. The strategy of inclusion may appear discordant, but it promotes the organizational reflexivity that is the basis of long-term adaptability.[20]

EXTENDING ACCOUNTABILITY TO ECONOMIC ACTORS

In this chapter, we have addressed questions of the authority and accountability of state actors. In these concluding pages, we briefly discuss the possibility of extending accountability to economic actors. In the conventional view, performance and accountability in the economic field (parallel to authority and accountability in the political field) involve a trade-off. More accurately, this view holds that performance and accountability do not involve a trade-off – provided that accountability involves a single principle of accounting: the logic of profit maximization. The introduction of other principles of accountability will, perhaps regrettably yet inevitably, weaken competitive performance. The prescriptions are clear. As in the political field, where in order to eliminate a crisis, it is necessary to maximize authority by liberating the executive from institutional constraints, in the economic field, in order to solve a crisis, it is necessary to give maximum authority to the owners/managers of property by liberating them from any other principle than the logic of profitability.

Political economists, however, are not unanimous in agreeing that the single-minded pursuit of profitability is the surest route to long-term competitive performance. Writing on the German economy, Wolfgang Streeck, for example, has been a forceful proponent of the concept of *beneficial constraints*.[21] Similarly, on Japan, Ronald Dore draws our attention to the importance of *flexible rigidities*.[22] At the core of this alternative conception is the notion that the imposition of constraints (limitations on the mobility of capital, on the ability to lay off employees, and the like) can increase long-term competitive performance. Studies by Dore, Streeck, and others demonstrate, for example, that employers who are constrained by employment norms and/or by industry-level collective bargaining from firing workers will be more likely to upgrade the skills of their permanent staff. Higher skills, in turn, create incentives for firms to compete for the higher end of market segments where quality counts. Constraints (the introduction of social logics other than profitability), in this view, can improve performance; rigidities can be a source of flexibility. The logic of efficiency is not always and everywhere at odds with social integration; in fact, the latter can establish conditions for realizing the former.

In challenging the conventional view that nonmarket rationalities will inevitably erode performance, these studies are not suggesting that all rigidities will contribute to enhanced competitiveness or that owners or managers will always adopt a limited perspective of short-term profit maximization unless constrained to do otherwise. The question for the postsocialist economies is whether corporate governance (in the narrow sense) alone can yield strategies for long-term competitiveness. The message of beneficial constraints and flexible rigidities seems especially relevant for contemporary Eastern Europe in the face of pressures for quick adaptation to world markets – for these pressures carry the danger that "successful" short-term *adaptation* will undermine the bases for long-term *adaptability*.[23] East European firms might succeed, for example, in eliminating research and development, firing engineers and skilled employees, and turning to minimally skilled operations that subcontract to large multinationals – only to find that this strategy is a dead-end street that cuts them off from international markets in the next round of competition.

In our view, sustained competitiveness depends on the ability to recombine resources adaptively: Strategies of innovation are strategies that recognize the complex and changing interdependencies of assets and actors. Severing these ties by granting unconstrained authority to the owners of property promotes "liberation" as the ideology of unaccountable economic agents (whether isolated firms or networks of enterprises) that prevents the potential forms of cooperation among interdependent actors that could yield longer-term flexibility and adaptability. For this reason, our rejoinder to the neoliberals' appeals to "liberate the market" and to the neostatists' call to "liberate the state" cannot be to "liberate the networks" but to search for institutional arrangements to make the networks accountable.

Should the state, then, be the agent that directs that accountability? Should it impose social logics other than profitability, rewarding and punishing the networks according to their performance based on heterogeneous principles? This would reproduce the bureaucratic failures of state socialism under which firms were forced to produce multiple accounts to their administrative superiors indicating their accountability not only for production but also for community welfare, kindergartens, night courses for credentialism, levels of party membership among their staff, and ritual displays of loyalty to socialist internationalism.

But if the state should not be the agency to which the networks are accountable, it does have a specific, if more limited, role to play in extending accountability to economic actors. Without directly intruding on enterprise affairs, the state can facilitate decentralized institutions that constrain the networks to take into account long-term interdependencies. It should not regulate *content*, but it can regulate the *context* of enterprise governance through legislation that weakens or strengthens the ability of social actors to negotiate about these interdependencies. Not by issuing directives or by setting substantive targets, but by shaping the environment of procedural rights, the state can facilitate the deliberations that lengthen time horizons.

Thus, because competitive performance in highly profitable sectors depends on skilled labor, the state need not micromanage the content of job skills — but it can facilitate the right of organized labor to bargain collectively for the security of employment that creates incentives for employers to improve and utilize their skills. Because competitiveness depends on stability of labor relations, the state need not micromanage the employment contract — but it can aid in establishing institutions of interest intermediation. Because competitiveness in world markets depends on cooperation across firms, the state need not micromanage industrial policy — but it can facilitate industry-level employer associations. Because long-term adaptability depends on vibrant localities that sustain dense networks across universities, firms, and local government, the state need not micromanage regional development — but it can facilitate the rights of localities and municipal authorities vis-à-vis enterprises. By so extending the conditions *for accountability*, the state does not determine outcomes; these can only be derived through the work of deliberations in which not only the business networks but also the representatives of labor and localities can be held responsible within the institutions of extended accountability.

Within the framework of extended accountability, the state does not direct the networks. Instead it is the web of mutually binding agreements that de-liberates them. It is not the state that extends its accountability over the networks, but rather the institutions of deliberative association that extend accountability through the economy. The state is not the site of a metarationality or the carrier of some superreflexivity; its limited intelligence can only establish the conditions whereby localized intelligence can broaden the organizational reflexivity that is the basis for the self-organization of society.

NOTES

INTRODUCTION

1 For examples of these kinds of comparisons see Ivan Szelenyi, Social Inequalities in State Socialist Redistributive Economies, *Theory and Society*, 1978, 1–2: 63–87; and David Stark, Rethinking Internal Labor Markets: New Insights from a Comparative Perspective, *American Sociological Review*, 1986, 51:492–504.

2 Suzanne Berger and Ronald Dore, eds., *National Diversity and Global Capitalism*, Ithaca, NY: Cornell University Press, 1995; John Zysman, How Institutions Create Historically Rooted Trajectories of Growth, *Industrial and Corporate Change*, 1994, 2(1):243–83; S. R. Clegg and S. G. Redding, eds., *Capitalism in Contrasting Cultures*, Berlin: Walter de Gruyter, 1990; J. Rogers Hollingsworth and Robert Boyer, eds., *Contemporary Capitalism: The Embeddedness of Institutions*, New York and Cambridge: Cambridge University Press, 1997.

3 Luiz Carlos Bresser Pereira, José María Maravall, and Adam Przeworski, *Economic Reforms in New Democracies: A Social-Democratic Approach*, Cambridge: Cambridge University Press, 1993; Stephen Haggard and Robert R. Kaufman, *The Political Economy of Democratic Transitions*, Princeton, NJ: Princeton University Press, 1995; Larry Diamond and Marc F. Plattner, eds., *Economic Reform and Democracy*, Baltimore: Johns Hopkins University Press, 1995; and Juan J. Linz and Alfred Stepan, *Problems of Democratic Transition and Consolidation: Southern Europe, South America, and Post-Communist Europe*, Baltimore: Johns Hopkins University Press, 1996. For insightful overviews of the issues in this vast literature, see Larry Diamond, Democracy and Economic Reform: Tensions, Compatibilities, and Strategies for Reconciliation, in *Economic Transition in Eastern Europe and Russia: Realities of Reform*, ed. Edward P. Lazear, Stanford, CA: Hoover Institution Press, 1995, pp. 107–158; and Diamond, Is the Third Wave Over?, *Journal of Democracy*, 1996, 7(3): 20–37.

4 Edward Friedman, *The Politics of Democratization: Generalizing the East Asian Experience*, Boulder, CO: Westview Press, 1996; Peter Evans, *Embedded Autonomy:*

States and Industrial Transformation, Princeton, NJ: Princeton University Press, 1995.

5 Scott Mainwaring, Guillermo O'Donnell, and J. Samuel Valenzuela, eds., *Issues in Democratic Consolidation: The New South American Democracies in Comparative Perspective,* Notre Dame, IN: University of Notre Dame Press, 1992; Stephan Haggard and Robert R. Kaufman, eds., *The Politics of Economic Adjustment: International Constraints, Distributive Conflicts and the State,* Princeton NJ: Princeton University Press, 1992; and Joan Nelson, ed., *Precarious Balance: Democracy and Economic Reforms in Latin America,* Washington, DC: Overseas Development Council, 1994.

6 Edward Friedman, *National Identity and Democratic Prospects in Socialist China,* Armonk, NY: M. E. Sharpe, 1995, pp. 188–207; Andrew Walder, Local Governments as Industrial Firms: An Organizational Analysis of China's Transitional Economy, *American Journal of Sociology,* 1995, 101(1):263–301; and Victor Nee and Sijin Su, Institutions, Social Ties, and Commitment: In China's Corporatist Transformation in *Reforming Asian Economies: The Growth of Market Institutions,* ed. John McMillan and Barry Naughton, Ann Arbor: University of Michigan Press, 1996, pp. 111–34.

7 Linz and Stepan, *Problems of Democratic Transition;* Mark R. Beissinger, The Persisting Ambiguity of Empire, *Post-Soviet Affairs,* 1995, 11(2):149–84; Rogers Brubaker, *Nationalism Reframed: Nationhood and the National Question in the New Europe,* New York: Cambridge University Press, 1996; Michael McFaul, State Power, Institutional Change, and the Politics of Privatization in Russia, *World Politics,* 1995, 47(2):210–43; McFaul, Russia's Rough Ride, in *Consolidating the Third Wave Democracies: Regional Challenges,* ed. Larry Diamond, Marc F. Plattner, Yun-han Chu, and Hung-mao Tien, pp. 64–94, Baltimore: Johns Hopkins University Press, 1997; and Steven Fish, *Democracy from Scratch: Opposition and Regime in the New Russian Revolution,* Princeton, NJ: Princeton University Press, 1995.

8 See the fascinating debate in the recent pages of the *Slavic Review.* Terry Lynn Karl and Philppe C. Schmitter, The Conceptual Travels of Transitologists and Consolidologists: How Far to the East Should They Attempt to Go? *Slavic Review,* Spring 1994, 53(1):173–85; Valerie Bunce, Should Transitologists Be Grounded? *Slavic Review,* Spring 1995, 54(1):111–27; and Karl and Schmitter's rejoinder, From an Iron Curtain of Coercion to a Paper Curtain of Concepts: Grounding Transitologists or Confining Students of Postcommunism? *Slavic Review,* Winter 1995, 54(4): 965–78.

9 For other studies that take national cases as the unit of analysis in systematic explanations of variation *within* Eastern Europe, see especially Ellen Comisso, Political Coalitions, Economic Choices, *Journal of Economic Affairs,* Summer 1991, 45(1):1–29; Comisso, The Economic Consequences of Democracy's Ambiguities, paper presented at the Conference on Ethnographies of Transition: The Political, Social and Cultural Dimensions of Emergent Market Economics in Russia and Eastern Europe, University of California, Berkeley, March 22–4, 1996; Herbert Kitschelt, The Formation of Party Cleavages in Post-Communist Democracies, *Party Politics,* 1995, 1(4):447–72; Gil Eyal, Ivan Szelenyi, and Eleanor Townsley, Making Capitalism without Capitalists: Class Formation and Elite Struggles in Post-Communist Central Europe, unpublished manuscript, Department of Sociology, UCLA, 1997; József Böröcz and Ákos Róna-Tas, Small Leap Forward:

Emergence of New Economic Elites in Hungary, Poland, and Russia, *Theory and Society*, 1995, 24:751–81; and Grzegorz Ekiert and Jan Kubik, Strategies of Collective Protest in Democratizing Societies: Hungary, Poland, and Slovakia Since 1989, paper presented at the Tenth International Conference of Europeanists, Chicago, March 1996.

10 Merton J. Peck and Thomas J. Richardson, eds., *What Is to Be Done?: Proposals for the Soviet Transition to the Market*, New Haven, CT: Yale University Press, 1992; John Williamson, Democracy and the "Washington Consensus," *World Development*, 1993, 21(8):1329–36; Jeffrey Sachs, Life in the Economic Emergency Room, in *The Political Economy of Policy Reform*, ed. John Williamson, Washington, DC: Institute for International Economics, pp. 501–24; and Jeffrey D. Sachs and Andrew M. Warner, Economic Reform and the Process of Global Integration, *Brookings Papers on Economic Activity*, 1995, 1: 1–118.

11 Michael Burawoy, Industrial Involution: The Dynamics of the Transition to a Market Economy in Russia, paper presented to the Social Science Research Council Workshop on Rational Choice Theory and Post-Soviet Studies, New York: Harriman Institute, December 1994, pp. 2–3.

12 Michael Burawoy and Pavel Krotov, The Soviet Transition from Socialism to Capitalism: Worker Control and Economic Bargaining in the Wood Industry, *American Sociological Review*, 1992, 57:34.

13 Burawoy, Industrial Innvolution, p. 28 (emphasis added).

14 Burawoy, The State and Economic Involution: Russia Through a China Lens, *World Development*, 1996, 24(6):1108. The same view is held in some policy circles in international lending institutions such as the World Bank and the International Monetary Fund, though it is usually expressed more cautiously. Former U.S. Secretary of the Treasury Lloyd Bentsen, for example, observes: "Russia is an experiment to see whether it is possible to build democratic institutions before a functioning market economy is in place. China is an experiment as to whether it is possible to develop a thriving free-market economy without democratic political reform." Bentsen is quoted by Edward Friedman in an informative and thoughtful piece on China and Russia, Is China a Model of Reform Success? in Friedman, *National Identity and Democratic Prospects*, p. 189.

15 Burawoy, Industrial Involution, p. 18, emphasis in the original. Discussing the Chilean and Chinese cases as favorable models for the postsocialist societies, John Gray similarly concludes: "Stated in its most general terms, my argument has been, first, that the human and social costs of transition to a market economy are for most of the post-Communist states so great that it is foolish to suppose that the transition can be conducted under liberal democratic institutions. Or, to put the same point in other terms, the preconditions of a market order in most of the post-Communist states are incompatible with those of liberal democracy." Gray proposes "a Hobbesian peace, imposed by governments." John Gray, From Postcommunism to Civil Society: The Reemergence of History and the Decline of the Western Model, in *Liberalism and the Economic Order*, Ellen Frankel Paul, Fred D. Miller, Jr., and Jeffrey Paul, Cambridge: Cambridge University Press, 1993, p. 44.

16 The general thrust of Burawoy's argument is reflected in his views of specific events as well. Most telling, for example, is his observation about the national

strike of miners in Russia in 1989: "Failure to repress this strike marked the beginning of the end of the Soviet state." *Russia Through a China Lens*, p. 1109.

17 We see the concept of rebuilding states not simply *on* the ruins of the old order but *with* the institutional ruins following revolutions as the key analytic insight of Theda Skocpol's *States and Social Revolutions*, Cambridge: Cambridge University Press, 1979.

18 Luc Boltanski and Laurent Thévenot, *De la Justification: Les Économies de la Grandeur*, Paris: Gallimard, 1991; Harrison White, *Identity and Control: A Structural Theory of Social Action*, Princeton, NJ: Princeton University Press, 1992; White, Values Come in Styles, Which Mate to Change, in *The Origins of Values*, ed. Michael Hechter, Lynn Nadel, and Richard E. Michod, New York: Aldine de Gruyter, 1993, pp. 63–91; and Wolfgang Streeck and Philippe C. Schmitter, Community, Market, State – and Associations?: The Prospective Contribution of Interest Governance to Social Order, in *Private Interest Government: Beyond Market and State*, ed. Streeck and Schmitter, Beverly Hills, CA: Sage, 1985, pp. 1–29.

19 Micheal Piore and Charles F. Sabel note that viable organizational innovations often appear to be monstrous because they fail to conform to existing categories. *The Second Industrial Divide: Possibilities for Prosperity*, New York: Basic Books, 1984; see also Sabel, Möbius-Strip Organizations and Open Labor Markets: Some Consequences of the Reintegration of Conception and Execution, in *Social Theory for a Changing Society*, ed. Pierre Bourdieu and James Coleman, Boulder, CO, and New York: Westview Press and Russell Sage Foundation, 1990, pp. 23–54; and Charles F. Sabel and Jane E. Prokop, Stabilization through Reorganization?: Some Preliminary Implications of Russia's Entry into World Markets in the Age of Discursive Quality Standards, in *Corporate Governance in Central Europe and Russia*, Volume II: *Insiders and the State*, ed. Roman Frydman, Cheryl W. Gray, and Andrzej Rapaczynski, Budapest and London: Central European University Press, 1996, pp. 151–91.

20 Zysman, How Institutions Create Trajectories. Ruth Berins Collier and David Collier similarly write on critical junctures. See especially Chapter 1 of their *Shaping the Political Arena: Critical Junctures, the Labor Movement, and Regime Dynamics in Latin America*, Princeton, NJ: Princeton University Press, 1991.

21 Joseph A. Schumpeter, *The Theory of Economic Development*. Cambridge, MA: Harvard University Press, 1934; Richard R. Nelson and Sidney G. Winter, *An Evolutionary Theory of Economic Change*, Cambridge, MA: Harvard University Press, 1982; Bruce Kogut and Udo Zander, Knowledge of the Firm, Combinative Capabilities, and the Replication of Technology, *Organization Science*, 1992, 3(3):383–97; Charles F. Sabel and Jonathan Zeitlin, Stories, Strategies, Structures: Rethinking Historical Alternatives to Mass Production, in *Worlds of Possibilities: Flexibility and Mass Production in Western Industrialization*, ed. Sabel and Zeitlin, Cambridge: Cambridge University Press, 1997, pp. 1–33; and David Stark, Recombinant Property in East European Capitalism, *American Journal of Sociology*, 1996, 101(4):993–1027.

22 See Guillermo O'Donnell, Philippe C. Schmitter, and Laurence Whitehead, eds., *Transitions from Authoritarian Rule: Prospects for Democracy*, Baltimore: Johns Hopkins University Press, 1986; Adam Przeworski, The Games of Transition, in

Issues in Democratic; Consolidation, ed. Scott Mainwaring, Guillermo O'Donnell, and J. Samuel Valenzuela, Notre Dame, IN: University of Notre Dame Press, 1992, pp. William H. Sewell, Jr., A Theory of Structure: Duality, Agency, and Transformation, *American Journal of Sociology*, 1992, 98: 1–29; and Sewell, Three Temporalities: Toward an Eventful Sociology, in *The Historic Turn in the Human Sciences*, ed. Terence J. McDonald, Ann Arbor: University of Michigan Press, 1996, pp. 245–80.

23 Evans, *Embedded Autonomy*; and Evans, The State as Problem and Solution: Predation, Embedded Autonomy and Structural Change, in *Politics of Economic Adjustment*, ed. Haggard and Kaufman, pp. 139–81. We also draw on recent work by economic sociologists on the network structures of East Asian economies, for example, Marco Orru, Nicole Wolsey Biggart, and Gary G. Hamilton, Organizational Isomorphism in East Asia, in *The New Institutionalism in Organizational Analysis*, ed. Walter W. Powell and Paul J. DiMaggio, Chicago: University of Chicago Press, 1991, pp. 361–89; Richard D. Whitley, The Social Construction of Business Systems in East Asia, *Organization Studies*, 1991, 12(1):1–28; and James R. Lincoln, Michael L. Gerlach, and Christina L. Ahmadjian, Keiretsu Networks and Corporate Performance in Japan, *American Sociological Review*, 1996, 61(1):67–88.

24 Charles F. Sabel, Constitutional Ordering in Historical Perspective, in *Games in Hierarchies and Networks*, ed. Fritz W. Scharpf, Boulder, CO: Westview Press, 1993, pp. 65–123; Learning by Monitoring: the Institutions of Economic Development, in *Handbook of Economic Sociology*, ed. Neil Smelser and Richard Swedberg, New York and Princeton, NJ: Russell Sage Foundation and Princeton University Press, 1994, pp. 137–65; and Design, Deliberation, and Democracy: On the New Pragmatism of Firms and Public Institutions, paper presented at the Conference on Liberal Institutions, Economic Constitutional Rights, and the Role of Organizations, European University Institute, Florence, December 1995. See also Streeck and Schmitter, Community, Market, State, and Associations.

25 Gary G. Hamilton, William Zeile and Wan-Jin Kim, The Network Structures of East Asian Economies, in *Capitalism in Contrasting Cultures*, ed. S. R. Clegg and S. G. Redding, Berlin: de Gruyter, 1990, pp. 105–29; and Eun Mee Kim, The Industrial Organization and Growth of the Korean Chaebol: Integrating Development and Organizational Theories, in *Business Networks and Economic Development in East and Southeast Asia*, ed. Gary Hamilton, Hong Kong: Centre for Asian Studies, Occasional Papers and Monographs, no. 99, University of Hong Kong, 1991, pp. 272–99.

26 In formulating the concept of extended accountability, we draw on Guillermo O'Donnell, Transitions, Continuities, and Paradoxes, in *Issues in Democratic Consolidation*, ed. O'Donnell et al., pp. 17–56; and O'Donnell, Delegative Democracy, *Journal of Democracy*, 1994, 5(1):55–69; see also Richard L. Sklar, Developmental Democracy, *Comparative Studies in Society and History*, 1987, 29: 686–714; and Sklar, Towards a Theory of Developmental Democracy, in *Democracy and Development: Theory and Practice*, Adrian Leftwich, ed., Cambridge: Polity Press, 1996, pp. 25–44.

27 Wolfgang Streeck, Beneficial Constraints: On the Economic Limits of Rational Voluntarism, in Hollingsworth and Boyer, eds, *Contemporary Capitalism*, in press.

CHAPTER 1

From László Bruszt and David Stark, Remaking the Political Field in Hungary: From the Politics of Confrontation to the Politics of Competition, in *Eastern Europe in Revolution*, ed. Ivo Banac, Ithaca, NY: Cornell University Press, 1992, pp. 13–55. Copyright © 1992 by Cornell University Press. Used by permission of the publisher, Cornell University Press.

1 These were states, moreover, with limited sovereignty due, by 1989, not to direct control by Moscow but to dependence on foreign creditors and international lending institutions in Washington and Berlin.

2 The concept of civil society under state socialism here refers to the self-organization of society in spheres of activity relatively autonomous from the state. Civil society would be more or less strong, depending on the level of development of social and economic autonomy, independent political organization, and civic values. On the concept of civil society, see John Keane, ed., *Civil Society and the State*, London: Verso, 1988; and especially Andrew Arato, Revolution, Civil Society, and Democracy, *Cornell Working Papers on Transitions from State Socialism*, 1990, no. 90–3. On the second economy as a sphere of relative autonomy, see David Stark, Bending the Bars of the Iron Cage: Bureaucratization and Informalization under Capitalism and Socialism, *Sociological Forum*, 1990, 4(4):637–64.

3 For a more comprehensive discussion of this literature, see David Stark and László Bruszt, Negotiating the Institutions of Democracy: Strategic Interactions and Contingent Choices in the Hungarian and Polish Transitions, *Cornell Working Papers on Transitions from State Socialism*, 1990, no. 90–5. This interactionist framework draws on the work of Guillermo O'Donnell, Adam Przeworski, and Philippe Schmitter. See Guillermo O'Donnell, Philippe C. Schmitter, and Laurence Whitehead, eds. *Transitions from Authoritarian Rule: Prospects for Democracy*, Baltimore: Johns Hopkins University Press, 1986; and Adam Przeworski, The Games of Transition, in *Issues in Democratic Consolidation: The New South American Democracies in Comparative Perspective*, ed. Scott Mainwaring, Guillermo O'Donnell, and J. Samuel Valenzuela, Notre Dame, IN: University of Notre Dame Press, 1992, pp. 105–52.

4 In the language of comparative methodology, purely structuralist comparative explanations using the methods of similarity or difference are inappropriate here because the country cases are not independent.

5 See, for example, Valerie Bunce and Dennis Chong, The Party's Over: Mass Protest and the End of Communist Rule in Eastern Europe, paper presented at the annual meeting of the American Political Science Association, San Francisco, August 1990. For another review of the countries of Eastern Europe as cases of contagion, see Adam Przeworski, The Political Dynamics of Economic Reform, in his *Democracy and the Market: Political Reform in Eastern Europe and Latin America*, New York: Cambridge University Press, 1991, pp. 136–61.

6 Our perspective should similarly be counterposed to views of the East European case as a unitary phenomenon in which "Gorbachev pulled the plug and the water ran out" (personal communication from a prominent area specialist). Our analysis of the Hungarian case in light of the comparison with Poland and other countries

in the region indicates that there was no single "Gorbachev effect" striking each of the countries with the same resonance.

7 For a provocative discussion of the multiple modes of transition, see Terry Karl and Philippe C. Schmitter, Modes of Transition and Types of Democracy in Latin America, Southern and Eastern Europe, *International Social Science Journal*, 1990, 128:269–84; and Juan Linz and Alfred Stepan, *Problems of Democratic Transition and Consolidation*, Baltimore and London: Johns Hopkins University Press, 1996.

8 Figure 1, it should be stressed, demarcates the varying responses of the old elite. Although free and fair elections are the eventual *outcomes* in each of the East Central European societies, it is only in some of the cases that elections are conceived by the old elite as a *means* of attempting to salvage their power.

9 The geopolitical differences include the full range of changing relations in the region, not only the relationship to the Soviet Union under Gorbachev but also the weight of economic dependence on, and increasing political pressure from, the West. The peaceful character of the revolutions (Romania excepted, but see note 10) is one distinctive feature of the East European cases as a set. Discovery of an explanation for the absence of force (Gorbachev's unwillingness to send repressive assistance, the Communists' shattered morale, etc.) across the cases should not be mistaken for a demonstration of the unitary character of these upheavals.

10 It might be objected that Romania does not belong in the same major East European category of "no decisive use of force against society." Our reading of studies by Vladimir Tismaneanu, Gail Kligman, and Katherine Verdery leads us to see Romania as a case of intraelite violence. That is, Bulgaria and Romania are similar as countries where one part of the elite orchestrated a coup against the old guard. Unlike Bulgaria's palace coup, Romania's was not peaceful and was coordinated with a popular uprising that itself lacked leadership and organization.

11 Our analysis of the Hungarian case is based on interviews we conducted with the leaders of the major opposition parties, as well as with numerous high officials in the Hungarian Socialist Workers' Party, including all members of the party's Presidium, the minister of foreign affairs, the minister of internal affairs, and the heads of the party's delegations to the Round Table negotiations; transcripts of the Round Table negotiations; detailed minutes of the opposition's umbrella strategy sessions; and data from public opinion surveys conducted throughout the transition period. Data collection was supported by a grant from the National Science Foundation.

12 On the removal of Kádár see George Schöpflin, Rudolf Tökés, and Iván Völgyes, Leadership Change and Crisis in Hungary, *Problems of Communism*, September–October 1988: 23–46. For the best analytic description of change in the Hungarian economy during the Kádár era and criticism of the limitations of reform economics, see János Kornai, The Hungarian Reform Process: Visions, Hopes, and Reality, in *Remaking the Economic Institutions of Socialism: China and Eastern Europe*, ed. Victor Nee and David Stark, Stanford, CA: Stanford University Press, 1989, pp. 32–94.

13 Imre Pozsgay began his career as a party apparatchik in a provincial county. By the 1970s, he had become a reformist minister of education and culture and had

established close ties to the populist writers (who later created the Hungarian Democratic Forum) and to some reformist intellectuals. Later, as the leader of the Patriotic Front, a satellite organization of the MSzMP, he offered shelter to some newly emerging independent initiatives. By the second half of the 1980s, he was appealing to selective aspects of the legacy of Imre Nagy, who had identified the Patriotic Front as an institution for societal consultation. By the end of the decade, he was moving publicly to appropriate the mantle of Imre Nagy, prime minister and Communist Party leader in the revolution of 1956.

14 In mid-1988 the number of alternative organizations was still under 10, but by the end of that year more than 50 organizations were listed in the first book that tried to map the alternative scene, and many more were starting to form. Although some organizations had several thousand members, most had only a few dozen. The majority of these new organizations, movements, circles, clubs, networks, and independent trade unions were organized by Budapest-based intellectuals, and their organizations did not extend beyond Budapest and several larger provincial cities.

15 One precursor of compromise solutions was offered by reform economists inside and outside the Ministry of Finance. Their *Fordulat és Reform* (Turnabout and Reform), published in *Medvetánc* no. 2, was initiated in a series of semipublic debating forums under the auspices of the Popular Front. Political scientists and sociologists were quick to follow, with detailed blueprints of institutional changes centering on parliament and related constitutional questions. See, for example, Béla Pokol, A politikai rendszer reformjáról (On the Reform of the Political System), *Valóság*, 1986, no. 12: 32–45; and László Bruszt, A többszólamu politikai rendszer felé (Toward a Polyphonic Political System), *Valóság*, 1987, no. 5: 87–95.

16 János Kis, Ferenc Köszeg, and Ottília Solt, *Társadalmi Szerzödés (Social Contract)*, *Beszélö*, Special Issue, June 1987.

17 János Berecz in *Népszabadság*, November 19, 1988, p. 5.

18 Gorbachev and other Soviet leaders explicitly rejected the Brezhnev Doctrine and articulated the Sinatra Doctrine ("Do it your way") several times throughout 1988–9. But the first clear test of the end of the Brezhnev Doctrine was the Soviets' acceptance of the non-Communist Mazowiecki government in Poland.

19 Hard-liners in the MSzMP based their plans, similar to those of Bulgarian, Romanian, Czechoslovak, and East German leaders, on the hope of Gorbachev's fall. Their hope was dashed when Ligachev lost his game against Gorbachev at the meeting of the Central Committee of the Communist Party of the Soviet Union in October 1988.

20 Kis, Köszeg, and Solt, Társadalmi Szerzödés.

21 Throughout the 1980s, the government revoked each of its programs for economic stabilization because it feared the social tensions they would produce. The first program of stabilization to bring real results was the one endorsed by the opposition parties at the end of 1989 – three months after the signing of an agreement establishing free elections.

22 It was during this period that the hard-line ideologist János Berecz (quoted earlier) referred to himself in an interview as the "Hungarian Ligachev" (*Reform*, 1988, no. I). See also the infamous speech in which the party chief, Károly Grósz, referred to the opposition as portending the danger of "white terror."

23 In addition to their general moderating influence, foreign governments, creditors, and other international agencies often directly expressed their policy preferences to the Hungarian leadership. In part, the protests of international trade union federations and intensive negotiations between the Hungarian government and the ILO and the U.S. Department of Labor curbed the hard-liners' attempt to pass new regulations that would have restricted the right to strike and organize trade unions. For example, extending the protection of the Overseas Private Investment Corporation (OPIC) to U.S. investors in Hungary required certification by the AFL-CIO that the Hungarian labor code protected trade union pluralism.

24 For a more elaborated discussion of defensive liberalization, see László Bruszt, Hungary's Negotiated Revolution, *Social Research*, 1990, 57(2):365–87.

25 The Western media misinterpreted this decision when they called it a decision about "giving up the monopoly of power" of the Communist Party. In fact, the decision more closely resembled the following calculation: If our North Korean or East German comrades are able to thrive with multiparty systems, why can't we make such accommodations?

26 On the concept of paternalism as applied to state-socialist political systems, see Ferenc Fehér, Paternalism as a Mode of Legitimation in Soviet-Type Societies, in *Political Legitimation in Communist States*, ed. T. H. Rigby and Ferenc Fehér, New York: St. Martin's Press, 1982, pp. 64–81.

27 The Hungarian Democratic Forum was founded in 1987 by 160 moderate intellectuals, especially populist writers, many of whom had strong ties to the leading reform Communist, Imre Pozsgay (who himself attended the founding meeting at Lakitelek). The MDF reorganized itself as a political party in mid-1989. The Alliance of Free Democrats was the organizational offspring of the Network of Free Initiatives created by radical Budapest intellectuals, many of whom were outspoken dissidents in the 1970s.

28 By late 1988 there were over 50 organized independent groups. These included such organizations as the Federation of Young Democrats (Fiatal Demokraták Szövetsége, or FIDESZ), founded by young law school students in March 1988 as the first independent group to declare itself a political organization. The first independent white-collar trade unions were created by scientific and cultural employees in the early summer of 1988, and the League of Independent Trade Unions was established in December of that year. The changing political field also saw the reemergence of parties that traced their lineage to some of the pre-1948 political parties. The Independent Smallholders' Party was organized in September 1988, the Social Democratic Party of Hungary in December 1988, and the Christian Democrats in early spring 1989.

29 The precondition for cooperation within the EKA was acceptance of the principle that the relative levels of support of the various opposition parties could be determined only by free elections. That is, only free elections could adjudicate among the competing claims to speak in the name of society. Acceptance of this principle, of course, could not entirely suppress the problem of measuring the relative power of organizations within the opposition. In the absence of free elections, other tests of strength could be attempted; but they were illegitimate in terms of explicit self-conception of the Opposition Round Table.

30 At the time of their negotiations from February to April, the Polish opposition

still did not trust the "End of Yalta," and the formation of their strategies was shaped by considerations of some of the imperatives of the empire. Late in the spring, leaders of the Hungarian opposition (encouraged in part by Gorbachev's apparent toleration of the Polish developments) shaped their strategy on the assumption that they were – at least temporarily under Gorbachev – "outside Yalta." Whereas the Polish opposition spoke about "self-Finlandization," the slogan in Hungary was "Back to Europe!"

31 The continued existence and growing legitimacy of the opposition parties were further strengthened when, starting in early 1989, Western delegations (presidents, prime ministers, party leaders, and parliamentarians) officially invited by the Hungarian government also held meetings with representatives of the opposition organizations. Increasingly as the spring progressed, such foreign delegations scheduled meetings with their Hungarian opposition-party counterparts *before* meeting with representatives of the government.

32 Miklós Németh was a leading representative of a new generation of young technocrats, mainly economists, who worked for rapid marketization of the economy but made compromises with the party apparatchiks in the 1980s by accepting important positions in the state and party bureaucracies. His public realignment with the party's reform faction was a dramatic indication of the party's crumbling hold on state institutions.

33 Károly Grósz had agreed to the reburial as a "humanitarian gesture" after repeated questioning by reporters during his visit to the United States in 1988. The results of complex negotiations between the Committee for Historical Justice and the authorities about a reburial were publicly announced on May 24, 1989.

34 On the meaning of Poszgay's efforts to recategorize 1956, see László Bruszt, The Negotiated Revolution of Hungary, in *Post-Communist Transition: Emerging Pluralism in Hungary*, ed. András Bozóki, András Körösönyi, George Schoepflin, New York: St Martin's Press, 1989, pp. 45–60.

35 Although the party hard-liners (represented by the Central Committee's secretary, György Fejti) refused permission for a public reburial, the *government* (represented by Prime Minister Németh) endorsed the reburial and cooperated with the organizers of the public ceremony. In exchange for this cooperation, the government was able to send three senior representatives of the reform wing to Heroes Square. In his speech there, Viktor Orban, the leader of the Federation of Young Democrats, commented on their presence: "We young people are unable to comprehend that those who not so long ago were reviling in chorus the revolution and its prime minister have suddenly come to realize that *they* are the continuers of Imre Nagy's reform policies. We also fail to comprehend that those party and government leaders who had decreed that we be taught from textbooks which falsified the revolution are now practically scrambling to touch these coffins, almost as talismans that will bring them good luck" (*Magyar Nemzet*, June 17, 1989, p. 4).

36 Although the reform Communist leaders were clearly in the ascendance by late May 1989, they had not yet succeeded in removing hard-line conservatives from their midst. Károly Grósz, for example, remained a member of the party's four-person Presidium, and his close associate, György Fejti, was one of the leaders of the party's delegation in the negotiations.

37 As Lech Walesa stated during the Round Table negotiations: "None of us want these elections. They're the terrible, terrible price we have had to pay in order to get our union back" (quoted in Lawrence Weschler, Reporter at Large (Poland), *The New Yorker*, vol. 53, no. 13 (November 13, 1989), p. 64. After the June defeat of the Polish Communists, Walesa similarly observed: "by a stroke of bad luck, we won the elections" (quoted in Adam Przeworski, The Choice of Institutions in the Transition to Democracy: A Game Theoretical Approach, *Sisyphus*, 1992, (1):7–40.

38 It should not be forgotten that Walesa had faced critics inside and outside Solidarity who opposed the compromise and even the negotiations themselves (e.g., Gwiazda's Fighting Solidarnosc faction). Walesa had succeeded in marginalizing these critics, but the Hungarian opposition was not optimistic that they would have the means to do the same.

39 László Bruszt and János Simon, "Politikai orientációk Magyarországon a redszerváltás évében" (Political Attitudes in Hungary in the Year of the Regime Change), in Bruszt and Simon, *A Lecsendesített többség* (*The Soothed Majority*), Budapest: Társadalomtudományi, 1990, pp. 33–75.

40 According to various surveys conducted in the spring and early summer of 1989, the opposition parties were scarcely known to the public. Typically, one-third of the survey respondents could not name a single opposition organization, and another third could name only one or two.

41 In exit interviews conducted during the recall elections in the summer of 1989, the majority of those who declared that they had voted for the Communist candidates told surveyers that they distrusted the MSzMP. Similarly, more than half of those who voted for the candidates of the opposition declared that they did not trust the opposition parties. According to these same surveys, conducted while the Round Table negotiations were in progress, only 13% of the respondents agreed with the statement that the EKA represented the interests of society.

42 Adam Przeworski, Democracy as a Contingent Outcome of Conflicts, in *Constitutionalism and Democracy*, ed. Jon Elster and Rune Slagstad, Cambridge: Cambridge University Press, 1988, pp. 59–80.

43 The opposition parties' relative passivity in the economic subcommittees is not, of course, due to their lack of interest in economic changes. Committed to marketization yet without a mandate to decide the precise arrangements for institutionalizing markets, they (and the representatives of the MSzMP) reached agreement about a most important economic question – but did so outside the economic subcommittees within the political subcommittee on constitutional questions. There they agreed to remove from the constitution the paragraph consecrating the dominant role of state ownership in the Hungarian economy.

44 As the reform Communists jettisoned the paternalistic principles of the party's past in favor of the competitive principles of its future, the qualitative differences in legitimating claims (with fundamentally different scales for measuring the validity of their stature and weight) that had separated rulers and opposition gave way to the anticipation of a time when their relative strengths could be weighed by a common measure, a unitary political capital, a single currency – the number of votes received from the electorate.

45 A condition for talks had been that all sides desist from any further mobilization; with good reason, it could be seen that escalating the game of counting dem-

onstrators would only interfere with reaching agreement on the electoral rules for counting votes. After the well-publicized inauguration of the talks, no further plenary sessions (and no subcommittee meetings) were conducted before television cameras, and neither side made serious efforts to inform the public about the details of the talks.

46 Parties that expected to receive only a small number of parliamentary seats, for example, wanted lower percentage thresholds on exclusion rules. Similarly, parties that inherited historical names known to the public favored national or regional party lists over local, single-member elections. But such calculations would be especially speculative in a case such as the Hungarian one in 1989, when none of the parties had any previous experience on which to base their electoral expectations.

47 John Rawls, *A Theory of Justice*, Cambridge, MA: Belknap Press of Harvard University Press, 1971.

48 The Social Democrats signed the agreement with the qualifier that they disagreed with the creation of the presidency. They, and later the Independent Smallholders, who had signed the agreement, joined the "front of rejection" in campaigning for the referendum.

49 These problems had been left unsolved because the MDF and MSzMP reformers had not wanted to waste time in fights with party hard-liners. The Németh government moved promptly to abolish the workers' guards, remove the party cells from the workplace, and clarify the party's assets before the plebiscite, but it was already too late.

50 Juan Linz, Presidential or Parliamentary Democracy: Does It Make a Difference? in *The Failure of Presidential Democracy*, ed. Juan J. Linz and Arturo Valenzuela, Baltimore: Johns Hopkins University Press, 1994, pp. 3–87; and Arend Lijphart, Presidentialism and Majoritarian Democracy: Theoretical Observations, ibid., pp. 91–105.

51 If not active support then at least passive acceptance was crucial for the Polish government's crash stabilization program (until mid-1991, the first and only such effort in Eastern Europe). The presidential election and the end of 1990 marked a new epoch in the Polish transition. The surprisingly strong showing of Stanislaw Tyminski in the first round of those elections indicated the limits of such passive acceptance and pointed to the future volatility of Polish politics. For an argument that we need new categories to understand the next phase of developments in Poland, see Andrzej Rychard, Passive Acceptance or Active Participation? The Ambiguous Legacies of Societal Opposition in Poland, *Cornell Working Papers on Transitions from State Socialism*, 1991, no. 91–3.

52 Timothy Garton Ash, *The Magic Lantern: The Revolution of '89 Witnessed in Warsaw, Budapest, Berlin and Prague*, New York: Random House, 1990, p. 78.

CHAPTER 2

From David Stark, Privatization in Hungary: From Plan to Market or from Plan to Clan? *East European Politics and Societies*, 1990, 4(3):351–920 © 1990 by the American Council of Learned Societies. Reprinted from *East European Politics and Societies*, Vol. 4. No. 3, pp. 351–92, by permission.

1 The contrast with Poland's Round Table negotiations is obvious but worth

noting, if only to suggest one of the major differences in the dynamics of nego-tiations in both countries. On politics and privatization in Poland, see especially Jadwiga Staniszkis, *The Dynamics of the Breakthrough in Eastern Europe. The Polish Case, 1988–89.* Berkeley: University of California Press, 1991.

2 For an account of the plan-market discourse and its continued legacy despite rhetorical shifts in the contemporary period, see János Mátyás Kovács, Reform Economics: The Classification Gap, *Daedalus*, (Winter 1990), 119(1):215–48. The first major critical salvo against the assumptions of reform economics was fired by István Gábor in Reformok, második gazdaság, államszocializmus: A 80-as évek tapasztalatainak fejlődéstani és összehasonlító gazdaságtani tanulságairól (Reforms, Second Economy, State Socialism: Speculation on the Evolutionary and Comparative Economic Lessons of the Hungarian Eighties), *Valóság*, 1986 6: 32–48. János Kornai further challenged the illusions of reform economics but re-frained from making the link between markets and private property in The Hungarian Reform Process: Visions, Hopes and Reality, in *Remaking the Economic Institutions of Socialism: China and Eastern Europe*, ed. Victor Nee and David Stark, Stanford, CA: Stanford University Press, 1989, pp. 32–94. The fundamental question of ownership was raised in the scholarly literature by Márton Tardos, A tulajdon (Ownership), *Közgazdasági Szemle*, 1988, 35(12):1405–22 (which has appeared in English as Economic Organizations and Ownership, *Acta Oeconomica*, 1989, 40(1–2):(17–37) and by János Kornai, A tulajdonformák és koordinációs mechanizmusok affinitása, *Valóság* 1990, 33(1):1–15 (available in English as The Affinity between Ownership Forms and Coordination Mechanisms, in *Highway and Byways*, ed. Kornai, Cambridge, MA: MIT Press, 1995, pp. 35–56).

3 Materials for this discussion are drawn from the Hungarian business press, from lengthy conversations with Hungarian economists, from interviews with man-agers and employees at several large Hungarian enterprises conducted in January 1990 (in collaboration with János Lukács), and from interviews with ministers in the outgoing Socialist government, leading officials in the Hungarian Socialist Party, and leading figures in the major opposition parties conducted in January and April 1990.

4 Some combinations of positions along the various dimensions are logically or practically improbable. A particular policy package favoring foreign owners through state-directed privatization yielding ownership by private persons in a highly dispersed ownership structure, for example, is highly unlikely.

5 Accordingly, we present that stylized debate in the ethnographic present.

6 *Magyar Nemzet*, July 21, 1988, and *Figyelő*; September 22, 1988.

7 See *Figyelő*, February 16, 1989, for this list and for interviews with apparently startled enterprise directors who claimed to have learned that their firms were marked for sale through radio reports or from telephone calls from their West European customers or suppliers.

8 This unfamiliarity leads to repeated calls in the daily press to establishing fair prices for selling state enterprises through competitive bidding – as if a deal in the hundreds of millions of dollars (for which there is typically only one actually interested, qualified buyer) could be conducted in the same way as the auction of farm equipment.

9 The conception of social fields (of many varieties, not simply the economy) as

organized around distinctive forms of capital and the notion that these forms can be converted from one social form to another are key components of the social theory of Pierre Bourdieu. See for example, his *Homo Academicus*, Stanford, CA: Stanford University Press, 1988; and Forms of Capital, in *Handbook of Theory and Research for the Sociology of Education*, ed. John G. Richardson, New York: Greenwood Press, 1986, pp. 241–58. For a creative elaboration of this idea for the contemporary East European setting see Elemér Hankiss, *East European Alternatives: Are There Any?* Oxford, Clarendon Press, 1990.

10 Critics also fear that the spontaneous privatization that characterized the first wave of selling state enterprises also ultimately threatens Hungary's ability to attract foreign capital. Public outcry at the disclosures of insider deals (e.g., the now infamous cases of the ÁPISZ stationery chain and the HungarHotels chain) forced state authorities to cancel these contracts. Such episodes increase the risk calculation of the potential foreign buyer. Privatization that is legitimate, because more controlled, will increase rather that weaken the business confidence of foreign investors.

11 Some proponents of institutional ownership advocate endowments in which 50–100% of the institution's operating funds are generated by its shareholdings. Such proposals ignore the long evolution of the most visibly successful endowed institutions – the elite private universities of the United States. Such institutions have very diversified holdings, but they also have very diversified sources of revenue. Income from endowments typically covers about 25% of the annual budget of elite private universities, with the remainder generated by alumni contributions, student tuition, large donations, and grants from the federal government and private foundations. Such institutions can have an interest in the *long-run* profitability of their endowment because they "walk on many legs."

12 Intellectual guidance in the concept of institutional ownership came from Márton Tardos, the leading reform economist of the previous decades. In the more recent phase of transformation, he has provided leadership as founder and director of the consulting firm Financial Research Incorporated, as the leading economist for the Alliance of Free Democrats, and as cochairman of the International Blue Ribbon Commission. Tardos is currently a member of parliament and chair of its Economic Committee.

13 A clause in the law establishing the State Property Agency might further stimulate such cross-ownership: Share capital issued but not purchased within three years after the transformation of a state enterprise automatically becomes an asset of the agency. To avoid assets falling into the hands of the agency, firms could exchange these shares for the shares of some other enterprise.

14 The most articulate critic of institutional ownership and the most fervent advocate of natural ownership is Hungary's leading economist, János Kornai. See *The Road to a Free Economy: Shifting from a Socialist System, the Example of Hungary*, New York: W. W. Norton, 1990. This book, Kornai's first major policy statement (following numerous books of analytic criticism of the state socialist economy) was published as a "passionate pamphlet" in Hungary in 1989. Too liberal for the more statist, nationalist circle around the Democratic Forum, too statist for the more pro-spontaneity circle around the Free Democrats, and too brilliantly independent for just about everyone else, the book was immediately attacked from almost every quarter.

15 János Lukács, A gazdaság demokratizálási utjai: a munkavállaók részvénytulaj-
donlásáról a magyar piacgazdaságban (Ways of Democratization of the Hun-
garian Economy: On Employee Stock Ownership Plans in the Emerging
Hungarian Market Economy), unpublished manuscript, Hungarian Academy of
Sciences. Lukács's paper includes the precise income levels and the basis for the
estimate cited previously. See also János Lukács, Vertical Disaggregation and
Privatization in Hungary: Organizational Consequences, paper presented at the
Conference On the Social Economies of Inter-Firm Cooperation, Social Science
Center, Berlin, June 1990.

16 See Ivan Szelenyi, Eastern Europe in an Epoch of Transition: Toward a Socialist
Mixed Economy? in *Remaking the Economic Institutions of Socialism*, pp. 208–32;
ed. Victor Nee and David Stark; *Socialist Entrepreneurs: Embourgeoisement in Rural
Hungary*, Madison: University of Wisconsin Press, 1988; and Alternative Futures for Eastern Europe: The Case of Hungary, *East European Politics and Society*,
1990, 4(2): 231–54.

17 We should note here a terminological difference in the literature on privatization. Whereas scholars studying East Central Europe use the term to refer to
the transformation of state enterprises into private assets, Sovietologists use it
to refer to the growth of a private sector (cooperatives and other, typically
smaller-scale ventures) alongside the centrally directed economy. East European
scholarship has not agreed on a single term for this latter process (*privatization*
is not used in this sense), and the expressions utilized are typically more cumbersome (*expansion of the traditional private sector, transformation of the second economy*,
etc.). To the extent that such development indirectly transfers resources from
state-controlled to privately controlled activities and significantly alters their
relative proportions, one might meaningfully speak of privatization of the economy. Such conceptual problems cannot be resolved by terminological fiat. But
the two processes should not be confused. The analytic distinction is useful, if
only to highlight that it is possible for privatization with the second meaning
to occur without a fundamental transformation of property relations in the state
sector and, similarly, that privatization with the first (East European) meaning
might take place without unfettered development of small-scale entrepreneurial
activity.

18 The leading proponent of ESOPs in the Hungarian setting has been János Lukács, an industrial sociologist at the Academy of Sciences, who carried out field
investigations at the employee-owned Wierton Steel factory in West Virginia
after being introduced to the ESOP concept while on leave at the Institute of
Industrial Relations at Berkeley. Together with a group of lawyers and economists, Lukács established a foundation, *Rész-vétel* (the artificial hyphen creates a
double meaning in Hungarian as *shareholding* and *participation*) in early 1990 to
disseminate information about employee ownership and to provide technical
advice to managers and workers interested in establishing ESOP schemes.

19 The most comprehensive survey of the literature on ESOPs in the United States
so concludes. See Michael A. Conti and Jan Svejnar, The Performance Effects of
Employee Ownership Plans, in *Paying for Productivity: A Look at the Evidence*, ed.
Alan S. Blinder, Washington, DC: The Brookings Institution, 1990, pp. 143–
81.

20 The major proponent of universal share grants in Hungary is István Sík-Laky,

an economist who was an earlier devotee of the schemes of entrepreneurial socialism of the iconoclast Tibor Liska.

21 Kornai, *The Road to a Free Economy*, p. 82.

CHAPTER 3

From David Stark, Path Dependence and Privatization Strategies in East Central Europe, *East European Politics and Societies*, 1992, 6(1): 17–53. © 1992 by the American Council of Learned Societies. Reprinted from *East European Politics and Societies*, Vol. 4, No. 3, pp. 17–53, by permission.

1 See, for example, Olivier Blanchard, Rudiger Dornbusch, Paul Krugman, Richard Layard, and Lawrence Summers, *Reform in Eastern Europe*, Cambridge, MA: Harvard University Press, 1991.

2 Peter Murrell, Conservative Political Philosophy and the Strategy of Economic Transition, *East European Politics and Society*, 1992, 6(1): 3–16.

3 See especially Michael T. Hannan and John H. Freeman, *Organizational Ecology*, Cambridge, MA: Harvard University Press, 1989; Richard Nelson and Sidney Winter, *An Evolutionary Theory of Economic Change*, Cambridge, MA: Harvard University Press, 1982; Paul David, Understanding the Economics of QWERTY: The Necessity of History, in *Economic History and the Modern Historian*, ed. W. Parker, London: Blackwell, 1986, pp. 30–49; and Brian W. Arthur, Competing Technologies and Lock-in by Historical Events: The Dynamics of Allocation under Increasing Returns, *Economic Journal*, 1989, 99:116–31.

4 Sensitivity to these differences is obscured by the very events that brought so much attention to the region. The 1989 phenomenon was a double conjuncture: both in the near simultaneity of events across the countries of the region and in the rapid acceleration and increasingly reciprocal effects of changes across political, economic, and social domains. But 1989 will prevent us from understanding developments in the region if we take it as a universal beginning or culmination. That is, we must begin to disaggregate *the transition*, perhaps even dispense with it as a concept, and undertake the difficult research work of understanding how changes in the different countries and domains have very different temporalities. Change in social institutions, for example, is not simply slower but might well have been taking place long before more easily observable political developments. If the pace and timing differ across domains, we should also not assume that changes within them necessarily move in the same directions.

5 Unlike the designer's schemes, in which the actions and preferences of subordinate social groups are a hindrance to the speedy enactment of the prescribed formulas, in the perspective adopted here the institutionalized interactions between state and society play a formative role in shaping actual strategies.

6 Theda Skocpol, *States and Social Revolutions*, Cambridge: Cambridge University Press, 1979.

7 As our emphasis on paths of extrication in the preceding paragraphs should indicate, by *path dependence* we are not referring to processes whereby the societies of Eastern Europe are seen to return to the natural historical trajectories of the interwar period from which they had temporarily deviated (see, e.g., the argument of Ivan Szelenyi in *Socialist Entrepreneurs*, Madison: University of Wisconsin

Press, 1988). Unlike these notions of already existing roads or the concept of *trajectory*, in which one can calculate the destination from knowledge of the initial direction and thrust, the concept of *path dependence* is not that of a vector.

8 Our conception of institutions as embodied routines, and our emphasis on practices instead of preferences and on predispositions instead of rational calculations, draw on the work of Pierre Bourdieu, especially *The Logic of Practice*, Stanford, CA: Stanford University Press, 1990. For a similar conception of institutions not as simply constraining but also as enabling, see Paul DiMaggio and Walter Powell's introductory essay in *The New Institutionalism in Organizational Analysis*, Chicago: University of Chicago Press, 1991.

9 Although the first phase of transformation is now completed, to convey the sense of open-ended reforms as experienced by policy makers at the time, our exposition maintains the use of the present tense in each of our country cases. The reader can trace further developments in actual practices (and of our analytic categories) in subsequent chapters.

10 For the use of a similar comparative methodology see David Stark, Rethinking Internal Labor Markets: New Insights from a Comparative Perspective, *American Sociological Review*, 1986, 51(4):492–504; and Stark, Bending the Bars of the Iron Cage: Bureaucratization and Informalization under Capitalism and Socialism, *Sociological Forum*, 1990, 4(4):637–64.

11 Rather than explicating these dimensions as a strictly logical deductive exercise, we give the analytic categories content in terms of the specific historical and social setting that is contemporary East Central Europe. The Weberian notion of historically grounded concepts should be familiar to most sociologists. Our method here is antithetical to the hollow antinomies of "deduction versus induction" or "theory versus historicism" resuscitated in the recent rational choice literature, e.g., Kaiser and Michael Hechter, The Role of General Theory in Comparative-historical Sociology, *American Journal of Sociology*, 1991, 97(1):1–30.

12 On relational contracting and other forms of coordination between firms that lie between (or outside) the dichotomy of markets and hierarchies, see Oliver Williamson, *The Economic Institutions of Capitalism: Firms, Markets, and Relational Contracting*, New York: Free Press, 1985; and Rogers Hollingsworth and Wolfgang Streeck, Countries and Sectors: Concluding Remarks on Performance, Convergence, and Competitiveness, in *Governing Capitalist Economies: Performance and Control of Economic Sectors*, ed. Hollingsworth, Schmitter, and Streeck, New York: Oxford University Press, 1994, pp. 270–300.

13 Strategies of justification thus lie at the heart of strategies of privatization. Although we raise these issues explicitly in this subsection, processes of justification are an important aspect of each of our three dimensions. Our intention here is not to unmask them as after-the-fact ideologies that rationalize or mystify some underlying injustice but rather to see how the specific work of justification can vary from case to case as shaped by the broader transformative politics. On strategies of justification in the transitional period on the shop floor, see David Stark, La valeur du travail et sa rétribution en Hongrie, *Actes de la recherche en sciences sociales*, 1990, no. 85:3–19 (available in English as Work, Worth, and Justice in the Hungarian Mixed Economy, *Working Papers on Central and Eastern Europe*, Center for European Studies, Harvard University, 1990, no. 5). For an

ambitious theory of justifications, see Luc Boltanski and Laurent Thevenot, *La justification: Les economies de la grandeur*, Paris: Gallimard, 1991.

14 We think obviously here of the work of Pierre Bourdieu on different forms of capital in modern societies. See, e.g., his Forms of Capital in *Handbook of Theory and Research for the Sociology of Education*, ed. John G. Richardson, Westport CT: Greenwood Press, 1986, pp. 241–58.

15 The old political capital suffered a massive devaluation and, in the current period, the publication of memoirs is one of the few remaining avenues of such direct conversion. In fact, there are good reasons to expect that in the current period monetary rather than positional resources will be a more important avenue to ownership for those former apparatchiks whose earlier assets were exclusively political (i.e., whose political capital had not already been combined with certain forms of cultural capital to yield *economic* positions in the managerial ranks).

16 A more comprehensive examination would also have to address the disposition of real estate and the question of the *reprivatization* of property. Restitution or compensation of former owners is an important question with significant implications for the timing, pace, and methods for privatizing the large public enterprises. In particular, uncertainties about reprivatization can pose serious obstacles that inhibit potential buyers and delay privatization in the state sector.

17 For example, our location of Hungary in the lower-left-hand cell indicates that policy makers there have designed ownership restructuring around corporate owners, through bargaining processes favoring positional resources. It does not imply, for example, that financial/monetary resources are not mobilizable in Hungary or that positional resources are not mobilizable in Germany. Similarly, the use of citizen vouchers in Poland and Czechoslovakia does not exclude incorporated actors from participation in privatization in those economies – although it is interesting to note that the governments of Germany and Hungary have, thus far, excluded the principle of citizenship from their strategies for privatization.

18 *The World Bank/CECSE*, 1991, 2(5):3.

19 For a description of the work of the Treuhand in its first months of operation and a balanced analysis of the difficult problems facing it in the near future, see Roland Schönfeld, Transformation and Privatization in East Germany: Strategies and Experience, in *Transforming Economic Systems in East-Central Europe*, ed. Roland Schönfeld, Munich: Südosteuropa-Gesellschaft, 1993, pp. 159–170.

20 Such short-term work was originally scheduled to expire on June 30, 1991, prompting some estimates that there would be 3.5 to 4 million unemployed (as many as 45% of the active earners in 1989) by the end of the summer of 1991. See Schönfeld, Privatization in East Germany. These worst nightmares were not realized, in part, because short-term work was extended beyond that deadline. By the late fall of 1991, high-level Treuhand officials acknowledged an effective unemployment rate of about 30%. See Horst Kern and Charles F. Sabel, Between Pillar and Post: Reflections on the Treuhand's Uncertainty About What to Say Next, paper presented at the Conference on the Treuhandanstalt, Harvard University, November 1991, and comments by Treuhand officials at that conference.

21 János Lukács, Organizational Flexibility, Internal Labor Market, and Internal

Subcontracting, Hungarian Style, in *Economy and Society in Hungary*, ed. Rudolf Andorka and László Bertalan, Budapest: Karl Marx University of Economics, 1986, pp. 15–34; and Stark, Rethinking Internal Labor Markets.

22 Schönfeld, Privatization; and Kern and Sabel, Between Pillar and Post.

23 Kern and Sabel, Between Pillar and Post.

24 The voucher-auction scheme was formulated prior to the breakup of Czechoslovakia, and the first round was launched in both republics. We focus on the Czech Republic in this chapter because the voucher method has been the hallmark of its privatization strategy.

25 The first round of voucher auctions was opened in 1992, but further rounds are still underway. Our exposition adopts the present tense both to express this ongoing character and to capture the extraordinary uncertainties confronting Czech policy makers at the time they launched such an untested experiment in property transformation. We present the outcomes of the voucher privatization program in Chapter 5.

26 By late 1991, the ministry had received 3,588 privatization projects from some 900 enterprises. Some 2,800 of these projects conformed with the requirements of the voucher scheme. We are grateful to Gerald McDermott for providing these figures.

27 We might also observe that the kind of auction Klaus is proposing somewhat resembles the schemes of Oscar Lange for setting prices through a *simulated market* within a socialist economy.

28 The Czech leadership, moreover, appears prepared to accept relatively high transition costs (the voucher-auction will be complicated and costly) in the distribution of shares in its privatization strategy in anticipation that these one-time *transition costs* will quickly reduce overall *transaction costs* in the newly privatized economy.

29 To the problem that the citizens might not have *information about the market* the Czech strategists also seem to have a market solution in mind: Investors who take risks will want better information; the demand for information will stimulate some of them to get into the business of gathering and selling it. The simulated market, they believe, will help to set in motion the secondary institutions (brokerage houses, market analysis, firms, etc.) required for smoothly functioning capital markets.

30 Who among the Czech citizens will have money to speculate on the stock exchange that is to be the product of the voucher-auction? Prominent among them will be former Communist officials and black marketeers. The cynicism of the architects of the Czech privatization strategy is undisguised: "It's sure that there is dirty money here," said Tomas Jezek, Czech minister of privatization. "But the best method for cleaning the money is to let them invest it." *New York Times*, January 27, 1991, p. 10.

31 See Jan Szomburg, Poland's Privatization Strategy, paper presented at the Conference on Transforming Economic Systems in East Central Europe, Munich, June 1991. For an overview of the ambitious goals but limited achievements of the early privatization efforts in Poland, see Tomasz Gruszecki, Privatisation in Poland in 1990, *Communist Economies and Economic Transformation*, 1991, 3(2): 141–54.

32 Lewandowski and Szomburg had proposed a stock distribution plan as early as

1988. See their Uwlaszczenie jako fundament reformy spoleczno-gospodarczej (Property Change as a Fundamental Aspect of Socio-Economic Reform) in *Propozyce Przeksztalcen Polskiej Gospodarki*, Warsaw: Polish Economics Association, 1989, pp. 63–81. A similar program of mass privatization was later elaborated by David Lipton and Jeffery Sachs in Privatization in Eastern Europe: The Case of Poland, *Brookings Papers*, 1990, no. 2, pp. 293–341.

33 Ownership claims coming from the Workers' Councils spring in some places from strong bargaining positions and in others from weakness. For an excellent analysis of reorganization at the level of enterprises, see Janusz Dabrowski, Michal Federowics, and Anthony Levitas, Stabilization and State Enterprise Adjustment: The Political Economy of State Firms After Five Months of Fiscal Discipline, *Working Papers on Central and Eastern Europe*, Harvard University, 1990.

34 Szomburg, Privatization Strategy.

35 See, e.g., Janusz Lewandowski and Jan Szomburg, The Strategy of Privatization, Gdansk: Research Centre for Marketization and Property Reform, October 1990.

36 The distinction beteen credit-based and capital market-based (roughly, banks versus a stock exchange) financial systems is presented in John Zysman, *Government, Markets, and Growth*, Ithaca, NY: Cornell University Press, 1983.

37 By late 1991, Poland's program of mass privatization showed signs of unraveling. The 400 firms scheduled for the voucher program had been reduced to 230, and the program was under attack from all quarters. See Ben Slay, Privatization and De-Monopolization in Poland, unpublished manuscript, Research Institute, Radio Free Europe/Radio Liberty, November 1991. If citizen vouchers recede in importance, we should expect that the locus of privatization/reorganization will shift even more to the level of firms and localities and especially to the Workers' Council – one of the most important institutional legacies in the economic realm of Poland's extrication from state socialism. For an excellent analysis of decentralized reorganization in Poland, see Anthony Levitas, Rethinking Reform: Lessons from Poland, in *Changing Political Economies: Privatization in Post-Communist and Reforming Communist States*, ed. Vedat Milor, Boulder, CO: Lynne Rienner, 1994, pp. 99–114; also Janusz M. Dabrowski, Michal Federowicz, and Anthony Levitas, Polish State Enterprises and the Properties of Performance: Stabilization, Marketization, Privatization, *Politics and Society*, 1991, 19(4):403–37.

38 The *continuing nature* of these relational contracts sets them apart from the use of *spot markets* (auctions) in the Czech case.

39 Such a restructuring would require preparation of a comprehensive transformation program, under the guidelines of the 1989 Law on Transformation, with the direct involvement of the SPA.

40 We are grateful to László Neumann and Éva Voszka for providing these data.

41 The term *VKFT* is not the authors' invention but comes from workers whom Stark interviewed (in collaboration with János Lukács) in January 1990 during field work in several Hungarian factories. With that acronym these workers were alluding to an earlier hybrid organizational form, the VGMK (enterprise work partnership), involved in a primarily internal system of subcontracting. Although they were free to make contracts, and had significant autonomy in

organizing production and allocating their "entrepreneurial fees," in the VGMK form ownership of fixed assets remained in the hands of the parent enterprise. With the term *VKFT* these workers were denoting the *semi*autonomous character of the new limited liability companies spinning around the enterprise. On the VGMK as a hybrid organizational form and a precursor of new mixed property forms, see David Stark, Coexisting Organizational Forms in Hungary's Emerging Mixed Economy, in *Remaking the Economic Institutions of Socialism: China and Eastern Europe*, ed. Victor Nee and David Stark, Stanford, CA: Stanford University Press, 1989, pp. 137–68.

42 See especially the important study by Éva Voszka, *Tulajdon–reform (Property– Reform)*, Budapest: Financial Research Institute, 1991; and also her From Twilight to Twilight, paper presented at the Congress of Hungarian Sociology, Budapest, June 1991. For an excellent case study of such reorganization, see Éva Voszka, Rope Walking: Ganz Danubius Ship and Crane Factory Transformed into a Company, *Acta Oeconomica*, 1990, 43(1–2):285–302; see also Mária Móro, Az állami vállalatok (ál)privitizációja (Pseudoprivatization of State Enterprises), *Közgazdasági Szemle*, 1991, 38(6):565–84.

43 From January 1990 to June 1991, the creation of new economic units increased 2.5 times but the number of corporations grew 17 times (Voszka, Twilight to Twilight, 1991). If we preferred to measure by capitalization instead of counting units, the new semi-autonomous corporate forms would be even more preponderant.

44 In this phase, as Éva Voszka succinctly describes, on issues of privatization the government was much more preoccupied with the question of who should be the *seller* rather than who should be the new *owner*. Voszka, Rope Walking.

45 Voszka, Rope Walking; Móro, Pseudoprivatization; and László Neumann, Labour Conflicts of Privatization in Hungary, Budapest: Institute for Labour Studies, 1991.

46 In this scenario, the debt–equity swaps so prevalent in the first round of reorganization could play an important role in the second round. The overwhelming problem of enterprise debt (owed to banks, as well as in the disguised form of interenterprise debt as firms increasingly delay paying their suppliers in the state sector) is resulting in the problem of insolvency in the banking sector.

47 In such a scenario, the relationship between enterprises and the state would take the form of *bargaining* and would reflect the continuity of ambiguous property relations in Hungarian state enterprises from the 1968 reforms to the present. But there would be discontinuities as well: In place of the earlier *plan bargaining* and the later *regulatory bargaining*, under decentralized reorganization and re-consolidation of state ownership the new relationship would be characterized as *dividend* bargaining. For a discussion of the continuities and discontinuities in these bargaining relations, see Erzsébet Szalai, A hatalom metamorfózia? (The Metamorphosis of Power?), *Valóság*, 1991, 6:1–26.

48 Encouraging but limiting such privatization would be consistent with a policy choice that sought to rationalize the state's ownership role (trimming its assets) while consolidating its ability to intervene in the economy as an (indirect) owner.

49 In the Czech Republic, trade unions, for example, bear little trace of the pre-1989 unions – in contrast to those in Hungary, where the old official union

remains the largest (if tired) trade union federation, and in Poland, where both Solidarity and the OPZZ are the continued legacy of the 1980s.

50 On the concepts of different types of capitalism and different types of democracy, see the insightful work of Phillipe Schmitter, Modes of Sectoral Governance: A Typology, unpublished manuscript, Stanford University; and Terry Karl and Philippe Schmitter, Modes of Transition and Types of Democracy in Latin America, Southern and Eastern Europe, *International Social Science Journal*, 1991, no. 128:269–84.

51 The reader who suspects exaggeration here would benefit from reading, e.g., Werner Gumpel's The Mentality Problem in the Transition Process from Centrally Planned Economy to Market Economy, paper presented at the Conference on Transforming Economic Systems in East-Central Europe, Munich, June 1991. We have paraphrased Professor Gumpel in the preceding passage. To quote him directly: "These people must be made to unlearn most of what they were brought up with."

52 The rapidity with which some innovation packages have become institutionalized (that is, come to be taken for granted) is extraordinary. No one was shocked, for example, when Yeltsin announced shock therapy for the Russian economy. On diffusion across national boundaries, see David Strang and John W. Meyer, Institutional Conditions for Diffusion, *Theory and Society*, 1993, 22:487–511.

53 On the decoupling of formal structures celebrating institutionalized myths from actual organizational practices, see especially John W. Meyer and Brian Rowan, Institutionalized Organizations: Formal Structure as Myth and Ceremony, in *The New Institutionalism in Organizational Analysis*, ed. Walter W. Powell and Paul J. DiMaggio, Chicago: University of Chicago Press, 1991, pp. 41–62.

54 Murrell, Conservative Political Philosophy.

55 See especially the research presented in *Governing Capitalist Economies,* ed. J. Rogers Hollingsworth, Philippe C. Schmitter, and Wolfgang Streeck, New York: Oxford University Press, 1994; Philippe C. Schmitter, Modes of Sectoral Governance: A Typology, unpublished manuscript, Stanford University; Robert Boyer, The Transformations of Modern Capitalism in Light of the Regulation Approach and Other Theories of Political Economy, paper presented at the Conference on Comparative Governance of Economic Sectors, Bellagio, Italy, June 1989; and Walter Powell, Neither Market nor Hierarchy: Network Forms of Organization, in *Research in Organizational Behavior*, ed. B. Straw and L. L. Cummings, Greenwich, CT: JAI Press, 1990, pp. 295–336. The key analytic move in this new literature is to shift from the preoccupation with micro or macro phenomena to a mesolevel focus on *sectors*. These studies suggest an exciting agenda for similar mesoanalysis of sectors and localities in contemporary Eastern Europe.

56 On the polysemy of the term *market*, see the excellent paper by Robert Boyer, Markets within Alternative Coordinating Mechanisms: History, Theory and Policy in the Light of the Nineties, presented at the Conference on the Comparative Governance of Sectors, Bigorio, Switzerland, April 1991.

57 Michael T. Hannan and John Freeman, *Organizational Ecology*, Cambridge, MA: Ballinger, 1989, esp. p. 3; and David Stark, Coexisting Organizational Forms, esp. p. 168.

CHAPTER 4

1 Jeffrey Sachs, The Reformers' Tragedy, *The New York Times*, January 23, 1994; *The Boston Globe*, January 21, 1994.
2 Argued most forcefully by Alice H. Amsden, Jacek Kochanowicz, and Lance Taylor in *The Market Meets Its Match: Restructuring the Economies of Eastern Europe*, Cambridge, MA: Harvard University Press, 1994; see also Jeffrey Henderson, Against the Economic Orthodoxy: On the Making of the East Asian Miracle, *Economy and Society*, (1933), 22:200–17; Jacek Kochanowicz, Reforming Weak States and Deficient Bureaucracies, in *Intricate Links: Democratization and Market Reforms in Latin America and Eastern Europe*, ed. Joan M. Nelson, Jacek Kachanowicz, Kálmán Mizsei, and Oscar Munoz, New Brunswick, NJ: Transaction Books, 1994, pp. 195–227; and Jacek Kochanowicz, Transition to Market in a Comparative Perspective: A Historian's Point of View, in *Stabilization and Privatization in Poland: An Economic Evaluation of the Shock Therapy*, ed. Kazimierz Poznanski, Boston: Kluwer, 1993, pp. 233–50.
3 Kochanowicz, Reforming Weak States, p. 198.
4 Amsden et al., *The Market Meets Its Match*, p. 206.
5 Ibid., p. 14.
6 Alice H. Amsden, Can Eastern Europe Compete by "Getting the Prices Right"? Contrast with East Asian Structural Reforms, in *Rebuilding Capitalism: Alternative Roads after Socialism and Dirigisme*, ed. Andres Solimano, Osvaldo Sunkel, and Mario I. Blejer, Ann Arbor: University of Michigan Press, 1994, pp. 81–107.
7 Jene Kwon, The East Asia Challenge to Neoclassical Orthodoxy, *World Development*, 1994, 22:4:635–44; and Sanjaya Lall, The East Asian Miracle: Does the Bell Toll for the Industrial Strategy?, *World Development*, 1994, 22(4):645–54.
8 Paul Bowles and Xiao-yuan Dong, Current Successes and Future Challenges in China's Economic Reforms, *New Left Review*, 1994, 208: 49–76.
9 Amsden, Can Eastern Europe Compete? p. 104.
10 On transformative politics, see Charles F. Sabel, Ambiguities of Class and the Possibility of Politics, in *The Future of Socialism in Europe*, ed. Andre Liebich, Montreal: Interuniversity Centre for European Studies, 1979, pp. 257–79; and Charles F. Sabel, *Work and Politics*, New York: Cambridge University Press, 1982, especially The End of Fordism? pp. 194–231.
11 On the concept of field, see Pierre Bourdieu and Loic Wacquant, The Logic of Fields, in Bourdieu and Wacquant, *An Invitation to Reflexive Sociology*, Chicago: University of Chicago Press, 1992, pp. 115–40; and Bourdieu, The Genesis of the Concepts of Habitus and of Field, *Sociocriticism*, 1985, 2(2):11–24.
12 Pierre Bourdieu writes on delegation and usurpation in *Language and Symbolic Power*, Cambridge, MA: Harvard University Press, 1991, pp. 171–219. The concept of legitimating claims based on teleological knowledge is central to Konrad and Szelenyi's theory of state socialism. György Konrád and Ivan Szelenyi, *Intellectuals on the Road to Class Power*, New York: Harcourt Brace Jovanovich, 1979.
13 László Bruszt, A centralizáció csapdája és a politikai rendszer reformalternatívái (The Trap of Centralization and the Reform-Alternatives of the Political Sys-

tem), *Medvetánc*, 1988, 1:171–95; László Bruszt, Reforming Alliances: Labor, Management, and State Bureaucracy in Hungary's Economic Transformation, in *Strategic Choice and Path Dependency in Post-Socialism: Institutional Dynamics in the Transformation Process*, ed. Jerzy Hausner, Bob Jessop, and Klaus Nielsen, London: Edward Elgar, 1994, pp. 261–87.

14 László Antal, *Gazdaságirányítás és pénzügyi rendszerünk a reform útján*, Budapest: Közgazdasági és Jogi Könyvkiadó, 1985; and Bruszt, A centralizáció csapdája.

15 See especially János Kornai, The Hungarian Reform Process: Visions, Hopes and Reality, in *Remaking the Economic Institutions of Socialism: China and Eastern Europe*, ed. Victor Nee and David Stark, Stanford, CA: Stanford University Press, 1989, pp. 32–94.

16 See especially Erzsébet Szalai, *Gazdasági mechanizmus, reformtörekvések és nagyvállalati érdekek (Economic Mechanism, Reform Efforts and Corporate Interests)*, Budapest: Gazdasági és Jogi Könyvkiadó, 1989.

17 Attila K. Soós, Béralku és selmi politika adalékok a mechanizmus reform 1969 évi elsö megtorpanásának magyarázatához (Wage Bargaining and the Politics of Grievances: Notes to the Explanation of the First Halt of the Reform of the Economic Mechanism in 1969), *Medvetánc*, 1984, no. 2–3:227–45; Mária Csanádi, Függöség, konszenzus és szelekció (Dependence, Consensus and Selection), Budapest: Pénzügykutatási Intézet Kiadványai, 1986; and Bruszt, A centralizáció csapdája.

18 János Kornai, *The Road to a Free Economy*, New York: Norton, 1990; Leszek Balcerowicz, Understanding Postcommunist Transitions, in *Economic Reform and Democracy*, ed. Larry Diamond and Marc F. Plattner, Baltimore: Johns Hopkins University Press, 1995, pp. 86–100; and Jeffrey Sachs, Building a Market Economy in Poland, *Scientific American*, March 1992, pp. 34–40.

19 Jeffrey Sachs, Life in the Economic Emergency Room, in *The Political Economy of Policy Reform*, ed. John Williams, Washington, DC: Institute for International Economies, 1994, pp. 501–24.

20 "I am convinced that Adam Smith supplies us with a vision of where to go that needs no correction. . . . All of that is of utmost importance in our part of the world just now because you will still be able to find that there are dreams of a paternalistic state. . . . Adam Smith knew that the market and its evolution is a spontaneous process that can't be planned, organized, or constructed. We are, in our part of the world, under permanent pressure to create markets first and to 'use' them after that. Everybody (especially our opponents) wants to see perfect reform blueprints based on a detailed sequencing of individual reform measures first. They do not want to participate actively in the often difficult and traumatic transformation process. They used to think in terms of 'building socialism' and now they want to 'build' markets. They want, therefore, to introduce the invisible hand of the market by means of a visible and omnipotent hand of a government bureaucrat. The Adam Smith message is, however, clear: We have to liberalize, deregulate, privatize at the very early stage of the reform process, even if we are confronted now and will be confronted with rather weak and, therefore, not fully efficient markets." Vaclav Klaus, delivering the Adam Smith Address to the 34th Annual Meeting of the National Association of Business Economists in Dallas, Texas, September 13, 1992.

21 For details, see David Stark, Networks of Assets, Chains of Debt: Recombinant Property in Hungary, in *Corporate Governance in Central Europe and Russia:* Volume II: *Insiders and the State*, ed. Roman Frydman, Cheryl W. Gray, and Andrzej Rapaczynski, Budapest and London: Central European University Press, 1996, pp. 114–26.

22 Jerzy Hausner, *Populist Threat in Transformation of Socialist Society*, Friedrich Ebert Foundation Series on Economic and Social Policy no. 29, Warsaw, 1992; Grzegorz Ekiert and Jan Kubik, Strategies of Collective Protest in Democratizing Societies: Hungary, Poland and Slovakia since 1989, paper presented at the Tenth International Conference of Europeanists, Chicago, March 14–16, 1996; Béla Greskovits, Demagogic Populism in Eastern Europe? *Telos*, 1995, no. 102: 91–106; Greskovits, Is the East Becoming South? Where Do Threats to Reform Come From?, paper presented at the XVIth World Congress of the International Political Science Association, Berlin, August 21–5, 1993; Greskovits, Hungerstrikers, the Unions, the Government and the Parties: A Case-Study of Hungarian Transformation, *Occasional Papers in European Studies No. 6*, Essex, U.K.: Essex University Center for European Studies, 1994; and Máté Szabó, A társadalmi mozgalmak szektora és a tiltakozás kultúrája Magyarországon (Social Movements and the Culture of Social Protest in Hungary), *Politikatudományi Szemle*, 1993, 3:45–70.

23 Jacek Kochanowicz, Reforming Weak States and Deficient Bureaucracies, in *Intricate Links: Democratization and Market Reforms in Latin America and Eastern Europe*, ed. Joan M. Nelson, Jacek Kachanowicz, Kálmán Mizsei, and Oscar Munoz, New Brunswick, NJ: Transaction Books, 1994, p. 196.

24 Amsden, Kochanowicz, and Taylor, *Market Meets Its Match*, p. 16. According to the neostatists, although already industrialized, the postsocialist economies share with "late industrializers" structural features such as difficulties in achieving market access, problems of product design, and relatively backward technology. None of these problems can be solved, argues Amsden, by foreign investment, currency devaluation, or lowering wages. "Barring divine intervention, therefore, and for want of a better alternative, the solution to these bottlenecks lies with government intervention, much as it did in East Asia." Growth requires "systematic, disciplined state intervention, at all development stages, to help selected firms overcome their low quality and productivity problems." Amsden, Can Eastern Europe Compete? pp. 103–4.

25 Kochanowicz, Reforming Weak States; The World Bank, *Governance and Development*, Washington, DC: The World Bank, 1992.

26 Michael Burawoy, The State and Economic Involution: Russia Through a China Lens, *World Development*, 1996, 24(6):1105–170.

27 "[W]e have no historical examples of a command economy on anything resembling the scale of the post-Soviet states being transformed into a market economy, without either an accompanying dictatorship, as in Chile, or the destruction of its supportive totalitarian polity in war as in National Socialist Germany. . . . The Chilean model of capitalist development under authoritarian dictatorship has been, and continues to be, discussed in several post-Communist states, including Poland and Russia, and an attempt to emulate it, in one or more of these states, is highly likely." John Gray, From Post-Communism to Civil Society: The Reemergence of History and the Decline of the Western

Model, in *Liberalism and the Economic Order*, ed. Ellen Frankel Paul, Fred D. Miller, Jr., and Jeffrey Paul, Cambridge: Cambridge University Press, 1993, pp. 28, 43.

28 Jadwiga Staniszkis, Dilemmata der Demokratie in Osteuropa, in *Demokratischer Umbruch in Osteuropa*, ed. Robert Deppe and Honel Dubiel, Frankfurt: Suhrkamp Verlag, 1990, pp. 326–47.

29 Burawoy, The State and Economic Involution; Gray, From Post-Communism.

30 Guillermo O'Donnell, On the State, Democratization and Some Conceptual Problems: A Latin American View with Glances at Some Postcommunist Countries, *World Development*, 1993, 21(8):1355–69; see also O'Donnell, Delegative Democracy, *Journal of Democracy*, 1994, 5(1):55–69. We explore problems of accountability further in Chapters 6 and 7.

31 The Loi le Chapelier, passed in 1791 by the French National Constituent Assembly, banned combinations and explicitly prohibited public officials from consorting with them: "Since the abolition of all kinds of corporations of citizens of the same occupation and profession is one of the fundamental bases of the French Constitution, re-establishment thereof under any pretext or form whatsoever is forbidden. . . . All administrative or municipal bodies are forbidden to receive any address or petition in the name of an occupation or profession, or to make any response thereto. . . . If, contrary to the principles of liberty and the Constitution, some citizens associated in the same professions, arts, and crafts hold deliberations or make agreements among themselves tending to refuse by mutual consent or to grant only at a determined price the assistance of their labor, such deliberations and agreements, whether accompanied by oath or not, are declared unconstitutional, in contempt of liberty and the Declaration of the Rights of Man, and noneffective; administrative and municipal bodies shall be required to declare them." In John Stewart, ed., *A Documentary Survey of the French Revolution*, New York: Macmillan, 1951, p. 165.

32 Peter Evans, *Embedded Autonomy: States and Industrial Transformation*, Princeton, NJ: Princeton University Press, 1995; Evans's general argument was introduced in article form in The State as Problem and as Solution in *The Politics of Economic Adjustment*, ed. Stephan Haggard and Robert Kaufmann, Princeton, NJ: Princeton University Press, 1992, pp. 139–81.

33 Evans cites Weber, but his insights on autonomy also have striking similarities to Bourdieu's concept of *field*. See Pierre Bourdieu, Rethinking the State: Genesis and Structure of the Bureaucratic Field, *Sociological Theory*, 1994, 12(1):1–18; and Bourdieu and Wacquant, *Invitation to Reflexive Sociology*, pp. 94–114.

34 Roger Friedland and Robert R. Alford, Bringing Society Back In: Symbols, Practices, and Institutional Contradictions, in *The New Institutionalism in Organizational Analysis*, ed. Walter W. Powell and Paul J. DiMaggio, Chicago: University of Chicago Press, 1991, pp. 232–63.

35 Evans, The State as Problem and as Solution, p. 181.

36 Stephan Haggard and Robert R. Kaufman, eds., *The Politics of Economic Adjustment. International Constraints. Distributive Conflicts, and the State*, Princeton, NJ: Princeton University Press, 1992; Ellen Comisso, Steven Dubb, and Judy McTigue, The Illusion of Populism in Latin America and East-Central Europe, in *Flying Blind. Emerging Democracies in East-Central Europe*, ed. György Szoboszlai, Yearbook of the Hungarian Political Science Association, Budapest:

Hungarian Political Science Association, 1992, pp. 27–57; Joan M. Nelson, ed., *Fragile Coalitions: The Politics of Economic Adjustment*, Oxford: Transaction Books, 1989; Nelson, Organized Labor, Politics and Labor Market Flexibility in Developing Countries, *The World Bank Research Observer*, 1991, 6(1):37–56; Adam Przeworski, *Democracy and the Market*, Cambridge: Cambridge University Press, 1991; Przeworski, ed., Sustainable Democracy, unpublished manuscript, Department of Political Science, University of Chicago, 1992.

37 Evans, *Embedded Autonomy*, pp. 17, 227–50.

38 In other words, Evans's rich interpretation of Weber on bureaucracy must be complemented by an updated reading of Weber on politics. Whereas the former addresses questions of procedural rationality, the latter points to the problem of setting substantive political goals. Max Weber, *Politics as a Vocation*, New York: Fortress Press, 1965.

39 For empirical evidence, see Karen Remmer's insightful studies Democracy and Economic Crisis: The Latin American Experience, *World Politics*, 1990, 42:315–35; and The Political Economy of Elections in Latin America, 1989–1991, *American Political Science Review*, 1993, 12:393–407.

40 If the interests that potentially threaten the course of economic reforms are brought into the political arena, such deliberations increase the possibility that social actors whose interests are taken into account will invest in the future, e.g., with moderate wage demands on one side and effective capital investment on the other. See especially Peter Lange, Unions, Workers and Wage Regulation: The Rational Bases of Consent, in *Order and Conflict in Contemporary Capitalism*, ed. John H. Goldthorpe, Oxford: Oxford University Press, 1984, pp. 98–123; and Nelson, Organized Labor, Politics.

41 Mark Granovetter, Economic Action and Social Structure: The Problem of Embeddedness, *American Journal of Sociology*, 1985, pp. 91:481–510. See also Gernot Grabher, Rediscovering the Social in the Economics of Interfirm Relations, *The Embedded Firm: On the Socioeconomics of Industrial Networks*, ed. Grabher, London and New York: Routledge, 1993, pp. 1–31.

42 Gary G. Hamilton, William Zeile, and Wan-Jin Kim, The Network Structures of East Asian Economies, in *Capitalism in Contrasting Cultures*, ed. S. R. Clegg and S. G. Redding, Berlin: de Gruyter, 1990, pp. 105–29; Michael L. Gerlach, *Alliance Capitalism: The Social Organization of Japanese Business*, Berkeley: University of California Press, 1992; and Gerlach, The Japanese Corporate Network: A Blockmodel Analysis, *Administrative Science Quarterly*, 1992, 37:105–39.

43 Evans, The State as a Problem, pp. 146–7 (emphasis added).

44 For a more detailed discussion, see David Stark, From System Identity to Organizational Diversity: Analyzing Social Change in Eastern Europe, *Contemporary Sociology*, 1992, 21:299–304.

45 Granovetter, Economic Action and Social Structure; Walter Powell, Neither Market Nor Hierarchy: Network Forms of Organization, in *Research in Organizational Behavior*, ed. B. Staw and L. L. Cummings, Greenwich, CT: JAI Press, 1990, pp. 295–336; Walter Powell, Inter-Organizational Collaboration in the Biotechnology Industry, *Journal of Institutional and Theoretical Economics*, 1996, 152:197–225; Nitin Nohira and Robert G. Eccles, eds., *Networks and Organizations: Structure, Form, and Action*, Cambridge, MA: Harvard Business School

Press, 1992; and Günther Teubner, The Many-Headed Hydra: Networks as Higher-Order Collective Actors, in *Corporate Control and Accountability: Changing Structures and the Dynamics of Regulation*, ed. Joseph McCahery, Sol Picciotto, and Colin Scott, Oxford: Clarendon Press, 1993, pp. 41–51.

46 Notable exceptions are Horst Kern and Charles Sabel, Between Pillar and Post – Reflections on the Treuhand's Uncertainty About What to Say Next, unpublished manuscript, MIT, 1991; and Charles Sabel and Jane Prokop, Stabilization through Reorganization? Some Preliminary Implications of Russia's Entry into World Markets in the Age of Discursive Quality Standards, in *Corporate Governance in Central Europe and Russia*, Volume II: *Insiders and the State*, ed. Frydman, Gray, and Rapaczynski, pp. 151–191. See also Stark, Recombinant Property.

47 See especially the informative and insightful essays by Barry W. Ickes and Randi Ryterman, Roadblock to Economic Reform: Inter-Enterprise Debt and the Transition to Markets, *Post-Soviet Affairs*, 1993, 9(3):231–52; and From Enterprise to Firm: Notes for a Theory of the Enterprise in Transition, in *The Postcommunist Economic Transformation*, ed. Robert W. Campbell, Boulder, CO: Westview Press, 1994, pp. 83–104.

48 See especially Zhiyuan Cui, A Schumpeterian Perspective and Beyond, unpublished manuscript, Department of Political Science, MIT, 1994.

49 By dampening the performance of the stronger firms and facilitating the survival of the weaker ones in the interfirm networks, these mechanisms would, of course, impede creative destruction in the conventional sense.

50 On strategic complementarities in the postsocialist economies, see John Littwack, Strategic Complementarities and Economic Transition, Discussion Paper, Institute for Advanced Study/Collegium Budapest, 1994; and Eric J. Friedman and Simon Johnson, Complementarities and Optimal Reform, unpublished manuscript, Duke University, 1995.

51 Anne Miner, Terry L. Amburgey, and Timoth M. Stearns, Interorganizational Linkages and Population Dynamics: Buffering and Transformational Shields, *Administrative Science Quarterly*, 1990, 35:689–713. For an extended discussion of buffering in the postsocialist setting, see Gernot Grabher and David Stark, Organizing Diversity: Evolutionary Theory, Network Analysis, and Postsocialist Transformations, in *Restructuring Networks in Postsocialism: Legacies, Linkages, and Localities*, ed. Grabher and Stark, London and New York: Oxford University Press, 1997, pp. 1–32. Charles Sabel writes on organizational hedging in Möbius-Strip Organizations and Open Labor Markets: Some Consequences of the Reintegration of Conception and Execution in a Volatile Economy, in *Social Theory for a Changing Society*, ed. Pierre Bourdieu and James Coleman, Boulder, CO, and New York: Westview Press and Russell Sage Foundation, 1990, pp. 23–54.

52 Barry Ickes, Randi Ryterman, and Stoyan Tenev, On Your Marx, Get Set, Go: The Role of Competition in Enterprise Adjustment, unpublished manuscript, The World Bank, September 1995.

53 In a related study on innovation in the Hungarian economy, sociologist Pál Tamás found that purely private and purely state-owned enterprises were less likely to have innovated by introducing new technologies or bringing out new products than firms involved in the organizationally hedging strategy of

mixed ownership. Pál Tamás, Innovációs teljesítmények és vállalati stratégiák (Achievements in Innovation and Company Strategies), Working Paper, Budapest: Institute for Social Conflicts, 1993. For an analysis of risk sharing in the networks of the Japanese *keiretsu*, see James R. Lincoln, Michael L. Gerlach, and Christina L. Ahmadjian, Keiretsu Networks and Corporate Performance in Japan, *American Sociological Review*, 1996, 61(1):67–88. See also Powell, Inter-Organizational Collaboration.

54 Our use of network concepts here departs dramatically from a recent tendency to introduce network variables into the analysis of status attainment or enterprise strategy. In that view, social capital is a new individual-level variable that interacts with other assets (financial capital, human capital, etc.) in the process of career mobility or entrepreneurship. The problem with this egocentric conception of network capital is that it introduces a new (seemingly network) variable in a manner that neglects the relational dimension that is the fundamental insight of network analysis. Networks become, in that view, a new kind of property in the possession of an individual or an enterprise. In our analysis of interdependent assets, by contrast, attention shifts from *networks as property* to the *properties of networks*; that is, it highlights how different kinds of networks have different types of characteristics. We shall see in the following chapter how interorganizational networks differ in density, in shape, and in the patterns of tight and loose coupling across our country cases.

55 Philippe Schmitter, Sectors in Modern Capitalism: Modes of Governance and Variations in Performance, paper presented at the Conference in honor of Ezio Tarantelli on Markets, Institutions and Cooperation, 1988; Robert Boyer, Markets within Alternative Coordinating Mechanisms: History, Theory, and Policy in Light of the Nineties, paper presented at the Conference on the Comparative Governance of Sectors, Bigorio, Switzerland, 1991; and Luiz Carlos Bresser Pereira, The Crisis of the State Approach to Latin America, discussion paper no. 1., São Paulo: Instituto Sul-Norte, 1993.

56 Gilson and Roe, for example, "take as the Japanese structure not a single Japanese corporation in isolation, but the keiretsu structure – the interlocking webs of firms, which loom so large in the Japanese economy." (Ronald J. Gilson and Mark J. Roe, Understanding the Japanese Keiretsu: Overlaps Between Corporate Governance and Industrial Organization, *The Yale Law Journal*, 1993, 102:871–906.) Economic sociologists Hamilton and Feenstra (Varieties of Hierarchies and Markets: An Introduction, *Industrial and Corporate Change*, 1995, 4(1):51–87), offer a similar but more general argument: "Inter-firm networks that rest on strongly normative bonds are better understood as economic organizations in their own right instead of a residual or intermediate category. Embedded networks become units of economic action rather than the firms that constitute them. . . . The network linkages are stronger than the firms that make up the networks. Firms come and go, but the networks persist over time."

57 For the most concise and insightful comparative treatments of the characteristic differences among the East Asian cases, see Marco Orrú, Nicole Woolsey Biggart, and Gary G. Hamilton, Organizational Isomorphism in East Asia, in *The New Institutionalism in Organizational Analysis*, ed. Walter W. Powell and Paul J. DiMaggio, Chicago: University of Chicago Press, 1991, pp. 361–89; and Richard D. Whitley, The Social Construction of Business Systems in East Asia,

Organization Studies, 1991, 12(1):1–28. For an overview of corporate groups including but not limited to the East Asian economies, see Mark Granovetter, Business Groups, *Handbook of Economic Sociology*, ed. Neil Smelser and Richard Swedberg, Princeton, NJ: Princeton University Press, 1994, pp. 453–75.

58 Gerlach, *Alliance Capitalism*; Takeo Hoshi, The Economic Role of Corporate Grouping and the Main Bank System, in *The Japanese Firm: The Sources of Competitive Strength*, ed. Masahiko Aoki and Ronald Dore, London and New York: Oxford University Press, 1994, pp. 285–309.

59 Eun Mee Kim, The Industrial Organization and Growth of the Korean Chaebol: Integrating Development and Organizational Theories, in *Business Networks and Economic Development in East and Southeast Asia*, ed. Gary Hamilton, Hong Kong: Centre of Asian Studies, Occasional Papers and Monographs, no. 99, University of Hong Kong, 1991, pp. 272–99; Hamilton and Feenstra, Varieties of Hierarchies and Markets. Kim sets out to correct the neostatist reading of South Korean economic development in which "the *chaebol* was portrayed as being entirely created, maintained, and managed by the Korean state, and was therefore treated as an enterprise that is not very different from a public one, an enterprise with limited autonomy" (p. 273).

60 Ichiro Numazaki, The Role of Personal Networks in the Making of Taiwan's *Guanxiqiye* (Related Enterprises), in *Business Networks*, ed. Hamilton, pp. 77–93.

61 Gereffi's *global commodities chain* approach, for example, "looks at the configuration of economic and social networks, rather than the structure and strategy of isolated firms, as a key to understanding new patterns of global competition. . . . In summary, the transnational governance structures that define buyer-driven and producer-driven GCCs make conventional boundaries between firms, industries, and countries obsolete" (Stephanie Fonda, Gary Gereffi, and Lynn Nonnemaker, Tapping the Global Economy: An Analysis of Globalization Strategies Among U.S. Apparel and Retail Companies, paper presented at the Conference on the New Institutionalism in Economic Sociology, Comparative Societal Analysis Program, Cornell University, 1994); see also Gary Gereffi, The Organization of Buyer-Driven Global Commodity Chains: How U.S. Retailers Shape Overseas Production Networks, in *Commodity Chains and Global Capitalism*, ed. Gary Gereffi and Miguel Kornzeniewicz, Westport, CT: Greenwood, 1994, pp. 95–122; and State Policies and Industrial Upgrading in East Asia, in *Revue d'Economie Industrielle*, 1995, no. 71:79–90.

62 On the conceptual problems for legal theory of recognizing networks as new moral actors, see the insightful work of Günther Teubner, Beyond Contract and Organization?: The External Liability of Franchising Systems in German Law, in *Franchising and the Law: Theoretical and Comparative Approaches in Europe and the United States*, ed. Christian Joerges, Baden-Baden: Nomos Verlagsgesellschaft, 1991, pp. 105–32; Michael Hutter and Günther Teubner, The Parasitic Role of Hybrids, *Journal of Institutional and Theoretical Economics*, 1993, 149(4): 706–15; and Richard M. Buxbaum, Is "Network" a Legal Concept? *Journal of Institutional and Theoretical Economics*, 1993, 149(4): 698–705.

63 Charles Sabel, Constitutional Ordering in Historical Perspective, in *Games in Hierarchies and Networks*, ed. Fritz W. Scharpf, Boulder, CO: Westview Press, 1993, pp. 65–123.

64 On the notion of equivalence and the multiplicity of ordering principles in modern societies, see especially Luc Boltanski and Laurent Thevenot, *La justification: Les économies de la grandeur*, Paris: Gallimard, 1991.

65 Wolfgang Streeck and Philippe C. Schmitter, Community, Market, State–and Associations? The Prospective Contribution of Interest Government to Social Order, in *Private Interest Government: Beyond Market and State*, ed. Streeck and Schmitter, Beverly Hills, CA: Sage, 1985, pp. 1–29.

66 Streeck and Schmitter, Community, Market, State, p. 19.

67 For Sabel's views on regional development, see especially his discussion of Western European cases (in Studied Trust: Building New Forms of Cooperation in a Volatile Economy, in *Industrial Districts and Local Economic Regeneration*, ed. Frank Pyke and Werner Sengenberger, Geneva: ILO, 1992, pp. 215–49) and of Pennsylvania (in Constitutional Ordering).

68 Sabel, Learning by Monitoring and Constitutional Ordering.

69 Streeck and Schmitter similarly emphasize the "strength and continuing relative autonomy of the state" lest its role in "regulated self-regulation" results in "agency capture" by the strong corporative associations (Community, Market, State – and Associations?, pp. 1–29, 16, 20).

70 On these dangers, see especially Jerzy Hausner, Tadeusz Kudlacz, and Jacek Szlachta, Regional and Local Factors in the Restructuring of South-Eastern Poland, in *Restructuring Networks in Postsocialism: Legacies, Linkages, and Localities*, ed. Gernot Grabher and David Stark, Oxford and New York: Oxford University Press, 1997, pp. 200, 206.

CHAPTER 5

1 Gernot Grabher, Eastern Conquista. The Truncated Industrialization of East European Regions by Large West European Corporations, in *Regional Development and Contemporary Industrial Response. Extending Flexible Specialization*, ed. H. Ernste and V. Meier, London: Belhaven Press, 1992, pp. 219–33.

2 In mid-1990, some 8,500 enterprises and over 60% of the surface area of the former GDR came under Treuhand auspices. Breaking up the *Kombinates* and splitting other large enterprises increased the number of firms to around 12,100. By July 1994, 97% of these had been sold, privatized, municipalized, or liquidated. Wolfgang Seibel, Privatization by Means of State Bureaucracy?: The Treuhand Phenomenon in Eastern Germany, in *Restructuring Networks in Postsocialism: Legacies, Linkages, and Localities*, ed. Gernot Grabher and David Stark, London and New York: Oxford University Press, 1997, p. 285; Jörg Roesler, Privatization in Eastern Germany – Experience with the Treuhand, *Europe-Asia Studies*, 1994, 46(3):505–17; Wendy Carlin, Privatization and Deindustrialization in East Germany, unpublished manuscript, Department of Economics, University College, London, 1993.

3 By the first quarter of 1991, industrial output in East Germany had fallen to 30% of the level of the fourth quarter of 1989. Seibel, Privatization . . . in Eastern Germany, p. 290.

4 Although producer prices in East Germany fell rapidly, wages steadily increased. East German labor productivity was only 31% of the West German level (rising to 49% in 1994). As a consequence, unit labor costs in East Germany reached

158% of their West German counterparts in 1991 and were still 135% in 1994. Wolfgang Seibel, Nicht-intendiert wirtschaftliche Folgen politischen Handelns. Die Transformationspolitik des Bundes in Ostedeutschland seit 1990, in *Regierungssystem und Verwaltungspolitik*, ed. Arthur Benz and Wolfgang Seibel, Opladen: Westdeutscher Verlag, 1995, pp. 214–49 (available in English as Unintended Consequences of Political Action: The Privatization of the East German Economy as Political Coping, *Working Paper of the Center for German and European Studies*, University of California–Berkeley, 1995, p. 16).

5 G. A. Akerloff et al., East Germany in from the Cold: The Economic Aftermath of Currency Union, *Brookings Papers for Economic Activity*, 1991, I:1–101.

6 For a detailed description based on case studies, see Horst Albach, The Transformation of Firms and Markets: A Network Approach to Economic Transformation Processes in East Germany, *WZB Discussion Papers* FS IV 93–1, Berlin: Wissenschaftszentrum Berlin für Sozialforschung, 1993.

7 On search, see especially Richard Nelson and Sidney Winter, *An Evolutionary Theory of Economic Change*, Cambridge, MA: Harvard University Press, 1982; for a concise and insightful survey of recent work on organizational learning, see John F. Padgett, Learning from (and about) March, *Contemporary Sociology*, 1992, 21(6):744–9. Kern and Sabel's argument (in Between Pillar and Post – Reflections on the Treuhand's Uncertainty about What to Say Next, unpublished manuscript, MIT, 1992) that the Treuhand muddled through to innovative solutions without changing its explicit organizational ideology was indirectly supported by Brigit Breuel's remarks that the Treuhand's official policy has never strayed from its fundamental opposition to reorganization before privatization (Conference on the Treuhandanstalt, Center for European Studies, Harvard University, 1991).

8 Wolfgang Seibel, Lernen unter Unsicherheit: Hypothesen zur Entwicklung der Treuhandanstalt und der Staat-Wirschaft-Beziehungen in den neuen Bundesländern, in *Verwaltungsreform und Verwaltungspolitik im Prozess de deutschen Einigung*, ed. Wolfgang Seibel, Arthur Benz, and Heinrich Mäding, Baden-Baden: Nomos, 1993, pp. 359–70.

9 Roland Czada, *Policy Networks and the Transition from Socialism to Capitalism: The Treuhand Complex*, Cologne: Max-Planck-Institut für Gesellschaftsforschung, 1994.

10 The decomposition, recombination, and privatization of the large chemical firms in the so-called chemical triangle is the most notable exception. See the study by Horst Kern and Ulrich Voskamp, Bocksprungstrategien: Überholende Modernisierung zur Sicherugn ostdeutscher Industriestandorte? Munich: SOFI-Mitteilungen Nr. 21, 1994, 98–138. For an examination of the potential (briefly recognized but ultimately unexploited) of regional network structures in the machine tool industry in Sachsen-Anhalt, see Katharina Bluhm, Regionale Unterstützungsnetzwerke in der ostdeutschen Industrie: Der Interessenverband Chemnitzer Maschinenbau, in *Einheit als Interessenpolitik: Studien zur sektoralen Transformation Ostdeutschlands*, ed. Helmut Wiesenthal, Frankfurt: Campus, 1995, pp. 160–193.

11 Wolfgang Seibel, Strategische Fehler oder erfolgreiches Scheitern? Zur Entwicklungslogik der Treuhandanstalt, *Politische Vierteljahresschrift*, 1994, 35:3–39.

12 Ibid.

13 Such data collection is not a simple matter where capital markets are poorly developed. There is no Hungarian *Moody's* and certainly no corporate directory equivalent to *Industrial Groupings in Japan* or *Keiretsu no Kenkyu* (see, e.g., Michael L. Gerlach and James R. Lincoln, The Organization of Business Networks in the United States and Japan, in *Networks and Organizations*, ed. Nitin Nohira and Robert G. Eccles, Cambridge, MA: Harvard Business School Press, 1992, pp. 491–520). The labor-intensive solution has been to gather these data directly from the Hungarian Courts of Registry. We thank Lajos Vékás, rector of the Institute for Advanced Study Collegium Budapest, for his interventions to secure access to these data, as well as Szabolcs Kemény and Jonathan Uphoff for assistance in data collection.

14 This 20-owner limitation is a convention adopted in research on intercorporate ownership in East Asia (Gerlach and Lincoln, The Organization of Business Networks; Takeo Hoshi, The Economic Role of Corporate Grouping and the Main Bank System, in *The Japanese Firm: The Sources of Competitive Strength*, ed. Masahiko Aoki and Ronald Dore, London and New York: Oxford University Press, 1994, pp. 285–309). In the Hungarian economy, where only 37 firms are traded on the Budapest stock exchange and where corporate shareholding is not widely dispersed among hundreds of small investors, the 20-owner restriction allows us to account for at least 90% of the shares held in virtually every company.

15 Heavy Metal is one of six Hungarian enterprises in which Stark conducted field research in 1993–4 in collaboration with László Newmann.

16 Many of these midlevel managers had experiences in the 1980s with an organizational precursor of the present recombinant forms – the intraenterprise partnership – in which semiautonomous subcontracting units used enterprise equipment to produce goods or services during the off hours. Like second economy producers who continued to hold a job in state enterprises, these entrapreneurial units were a widespread result of hedging strategies in the Hungarian economy. Some of these partnerships were scarcely disguised rent-seeking schemes that privatized profit streams and left expenses with the state-owned enterprise. Others creatively redeployed resources from diverse parts of the shop floor and regrouped, as well, the informal norms of reciprocity with the technical norms of professionals. See David Stark, Rethinking Internal Labor Markets: New Insights from a Comparative Perspective, *American Sociological Review*, 1986, 51:492–504; and Coexisting Organizational Forms in Hungary's Emerging Mixed Economy, in *Remaking the Economic Institutions of Socialism: China and Eastern Europe*, ed. Victor Nee and David Stark, Stanford, CA: Stanford University Press, 1989, pp. 137–68.

17 The recombinet is not a simple summation of the set of horizontal and vertical ties: To categorically label the ties between a given KFT and a given RT as vertical would be to ignore the ways the KFTs are recombining properties. To the extent that genuinely network properties emerge in the recombinet, the terms *horizontal* and *vertical* should give place to more appropriate descriptors such as *extensivity, density, tight or loose coupling, strong or weak ties, structural holes,* and the like. For lucid presentations of these network concepts, see Ronald L. Breiger and Philippa Pattison, Cumulated Social Roles: The Duality of Persons and Their Algebras, *Social Networks*, 1986, 8(3):215–56; and Ronald Burt, *Struc-*

tural Holes, Cambridge, MA: Harvard University Press, 1992. On the potential benefits and problems of loosely coupled networks in transforming economies, see Gernot Grabher and David Stark, Organizing Diversity: Evolutionary Theory, Network Analysis, and Postsocialist Transformations, in Grabher and Stark, eds., *Restructuring Networks in Postsocialism,* pp. 1–32.

18 Lajos Bokros, Privatization and the Banking System in Hungary, in *Privatization in the Transition Process. Recent Experiences in Eastern Europe*, ed. László Szamuely, Geneva: United Nations Conference on Trade and Development and KOPINT-DATORG, 1994, pp. 305–20.

19 National Bank of Hungary, *Annual Report*, Budapest, 1992, p. 109.

20 Nicholas Denton, Two Hungarian Banks Said to Be Technically Insolvent, *Financial Times*, May 20, 1993.

21 For more on the background and consequences of the Hungarian bank bailout and debt consolidation program, see David Stark, Networks of Assets, Chains of Debt: Recombinant Property in Hungary, in *Corporate Governance in Central Europe and Russia:* Volume II: *Insiders and the State*, ed. Roman Frydman, Cheryl W. Gray, and Andrzej Rapaczynski, Budapest and London: Central European University Press, 1996, pp. 133–43.

22 For the classic statement, see János Kornai, *Contradictions and Dilemmas*, Cambridge, MA: MIT Press, 1986, especially pp. 52–61. For his treatment of these issues in the postsocialist context, see Kornai, *Highways and Byways: Studies on Reform and Post-Communist Transition*, Cambridge, MA: MIT Press, 1995, pp. 107–60.

23 István Ábel and John Bonin, State Desertion and Financial Market Failure: Is the Transition Stalled?, *Budapest Bank Working Papers*, 1993, no. 5.

24 See Gerald McDermott, Renegotiating the Ties That Bind: The Limits of Privatization in the Czech Republic, in *Restructuring Networks*, ed. Grabher and Stark, pp. 70–106. Our argument here contrasts with that of Frydman and Rapaczynski, who, ignoring the Industrial Associations, present the Czech case as one where a strong state held all property rights, which it could then distribute at its discretion. (Roman Frydman and Andrzej Rapaczynski, *Privatization in Eastern Europe: Is the State Withering Away?*, Budapest and London: Central European University Press, 1994.) As we shall see, the Hungarian and Czech cases do differ – not because the Hungarian state was weak vis-à-vis enterprises while the Czechoslovak state was strong but because the types of dense networks of countervailing power differed in the two economies under the old regime.

25 Karla Brom and Mitchell Orenstein, The Privatized Sector in the Czech Republic: Government and Bank Control in a Transitional Economy, *Europe-Asia Studies*, 1994, 46(6):899.

26 Miroslav Hrncir, Reform of the Banking Sector in the Czech Republic, in *The Development and Reform of Financial Systems in Central and Eastern Europe*, ed. John P. Bonin and István P. Székely, London: Edward Elgar, 1994, pp. 221–56; John Ham, Jan Svejnar, and Katherine Terrell, Czech Republic and Slovakia, in *Unemployment, Restructuring, and the Labor Market in Eastern Europe and Russia*, ed. Simon Commander and Fabrizio Coricelli, Washington, DC: The World Bank, 1995, pp. 91–146; and McDermott, Rethinking Ties.

27 Brom and Orenstein, The Privatized Sector, p. 899; and Peter Rutland,

Thatcherism, Czech-Style: Transition to Capitalism in the Czech Republic, *Telos*, Winter 1993, 94:114.

28 Quoted in Brom and Orenstein, The Privatized Sector, p. 898.

29 Ibid., p. 902.

30 McDermott, Rethinking Ties, pp. 83–7.

31 Ibid., p. 85.

32 Ibid., p. 86.

33 So the leading analysts of Czech labor markets conclude: "While the Czech Republic has so far been extremely successful in keeping unemployment down, this good record to date has hinged on the government's willingness to use privatization revenues to keep firms afloat through the banking system, as well as its ability to stimulate the growth of the private sector and create a large number of temporarily financed 'socially purposeful jobs.' An increasing number of firms are on the brink of bankruptcy, but the government and the small number of colluding banks have so far prevented bankruptcies from occurring on a significant scale." (Ham, Svejnar, and Terrell, Czech Republic and Slovakia, pp. 143–4.)

34 Klaus's politics are examined in more detail in the following chapter.

35 Václav Klaus, The Ten Commandments Revisited, *The International Economy*, September–October 1993, pp. 36–9, 70–2.

36 Ibid., pp. 70–2, emphasis added.

37 Ibid., pp. 70–2.

38 Rudolf Hilferding's classic study of Central Europe is again applicable to the region: Hilferding. *Finance Capital: A Study of the Latest Phase of Capitalist Development*, ed. Tom Bottomore, trans. Morris Watnick and Sam Gordon, London and Boston: Routledge & Kegan Paul, 1981.

39 PlanEcon, Inc., Results of Czechoslovak Voucher Privatization, *PlanEcon Report*, 1992, VIII: 8–9.

40 Brom and Orenstein, The Privatized Sector, p. 908, estimate that the 13 largest investment companies hold about 75% of the board seats won in the first wave of voucher privatization.

41 Of the remaining three, two were founded by foreign (German and Austrian) banks. The third is the largest independent investment company, Harvard Capital and Consulting.

42 Hrncir, Reform of the Banking Sector; Josef Kotrba, Privatization in the Czech Republic: An Overview, Discussion Paper No. 18, Prague: Center for Economic Research and Graduate Education (CERGE), 1993.

43 John Coffee, Institutional Investors in Transitional Economies: Lessons from the Czech Experience, in *Corporate Governance in Central Europe and Russia*, ed. Frydman, Gray, and Rapaczynski, Volume I, pp. 146–90.

44 By creating subsidiary funds, investment companies easily circumvented the loose regulations that technically prohibited an investment fund from acquiring shares in the bank that founded it.

45 In a recent market shakeup, for example, the aggressive raiding by the Motoinvest group to take over several large investment funds controlled by the big banks was halted only when the National Bank stepped in to challenge the renegade and forced the banks to buy back their shares at inflated prices.

46 McDermott, Rethinking Ties, pp. 88–97.

47 Richard Locke, *Remaking the Italian Economy*, Ithaca, NY: Cornell University Press, 1995; AnnaLee Saxenian, *Regional Advantage: Culture and Competition in Silicon Valley and Route 128*, Cambridge, MA: Harvard University Press, 1994; and Gary B. Herrigel, Power and the Redefinition of Industrial Districts: The Case of Baden-Württemberg, in *The Embedded Firm: On the Socioeconomics of Industrial Districts*, ed. Gernot Grabher, London and New York: Routledge, 1993, pp. 227-52.

48 Gernot Grabher, Adaptation at the Cost of Adaptability? Restructuring the Eastern German Regional Economy, in *Restructuring Networks in Postsocialism*, ed. Grabher and Stark, pp. 126-9.

49 McDermott, Rethinking the Ties That Bind, pp. 77-9.

50 Charles Sabel, Möbius-Strip Organizations and Open Labor Markets: Some Consequences of the Reintegration of Conception and Execution in a Volatile Economy, *Social Theory for a Changing Society*, ed. Pierre Bourdieu and James Coleman, Boulder, CO, and New York: Westview Press and Russell Sage Foundation, 1990, pp. 23-54; Zhiyuan Cui, Particular, Universal, and Infinite: Transcending Western Centrism and Cultural Relativism, in *Progress: Fact or Illusion?*, ed. Leo Marx and Bruce Mazlish, Ann Arbor: University of Michigan Press, 1996, pp. 141-52.

CHAPTER 6

1 Jadwiga Staniszkis developed the concept of management by crisis in her analysis of the cyclical changes in state-socialist economic policies. See Jan T. Gross, ed., *Poland's Self-Limiting Revolution*, Princeton, NJ: Princeton University Press, 1984, pp. 249-77.

2 Jacek Kochanowicz, Reforming Weak States and Deficient Bureaucracies, in *Intricate Links: Democratization and Market Reforms in Latin America and Eastern Europe*, ed. Joan M. Nelson, Jacek Kachanowicz, Kálmán Mizsei, and Oscar Munoz, New Brunswick, NJ: Transaction Books, pp. 212-19.

3 John Williamson, In Search of a Manual for Technopols, in *The Political Economy of Policy Reform*, ed. Williamson, Washington, DC: Institute for International Economics, 1994, pp. 11-28; Barbara Geddes, *Politician's Dilemma: Building State Capacity in Latin America*, Berkeley: University of California Press, 1994; Stephan Haggard and Robert R. Kaufman, *The Political Economy of Democratic Transitions*, Princeton, NJ: Princeton University Press, 1995; Stephen Holmes, The Postcommunist Presidency, *East European Constitutional Review*, 1993, 2(3): 36-41; Holmes, Superpresidentialism and Its Problems. *East European Constitutional Review*, 1993, 4(1):123-6; and Thomas Callaghy, Africa: Back to the Future? in *Economic Reform and Democracy*, ed. Larry Diamond and Marc F. Plattner, Baltimore: Johns Hopkins University Press, 1995, pp. 140-52.

4 As such, this literature stresses *incentive structures* (e.g., security of tenure) for incumbents. See Geddes, *Politician's Dilemma*, esp. p. 190; Stephan Haggard and Steven B. Webb, Introduction in *Voting for Reform*, ed. Haggard and Webb, New York: Oxford University Press, 1994, pp. 1-36; and Alberto Alesina, Political Models of Macroeconomic Policy and Fiscal Reforms, ibid., pp. 37-61.

5 Barbara Geddes presents a clear and forceful statement of this reformulation in

Challenging the Conventional Wisdom, in *Economic Reform and Democracy*, ed. Diamond and Plattner, pp. 59–73. Joel Hellman expresses this shift as one from the "participation dilemma" to the "contestation dilemma." Hellman, Political Power and Economic Reform in the Post-Communist Transitions, unpublished manuscript, Harvard University, 1995.

6 Geddes (*Politician's Dilemma*), for example, emphasizes presidential authority and notes its limitations by fragmented party systems, undisciplined government coalitions, and incompetent or disloyal bureaucrats.

7 Haggard and Kaufman (*Political Economy of Transitions*) emphasize the need for strong executive authority in the *initiation* of reforms. Once reforms are underway and begin to deliver benefits, it is possible (and, they argue, even desirable) to include major social groups in policy making.

8 The present features of Hungarian parliamentarianism were strongly shaped by the so-called Parliamentary Pact struck in the spring of 1990 between the MDF (the winner of the first free elections) and the SzDSz (the strongest opposition party). In exchange for the presidency (elected by Parliament and occupied by the SzDSz candidate, Árpád Gönz), the Free Democrats ceded their right to challenge the government on a broad set of social and economic measures by renouncing the clause requiring a qualified (two-thirds) majority parliamentary vote on such legislation. The constitutional consequence of the pact was that Hungary opted for parliamentarianism in place of a presidential regime. With governability given clear priority over participation, the new institutional arrangements not only abolished the two-thirds clause that would have given de jure veto power to the parliamentary opposition but also, by introducing the positive vote of no confidence, weakened parliament's controlling powers and strengthened the central position of the prime minister. On the functioning of the Hungarian parliamentary regime, see the interesting debate initiated by the editorial board of *Politikatudományi Szemle* in 1994. See, e.g., Péter Kende, Mü-ködik-e a demokrácia intézményrendszere Magyarországon (Do the Institutions of Democracy Function in Hungary?), *Politikatudományi Szemle*, 1994, 4:126–38; Attila Ágh, A demokratikus átmenet feltételrendszere (The Conditions of the Democratic Transition), *Politikatudományi Szemle*, 1994, 4:139–45; and comments by Andrew Arato (ibid., 146–51) and Gábor Halmai (ibid., 1995, 1:125–31).

9 In contrast to the Czech Republic, where a unitary trade union confederation represents labor interests, in Hungary there are seven trade union confederations that organize about 25–30% of the labor force, i.e., they have roughly half the level of the organization of the Czech unions. In Hungary the reformed trade union confederation (MSZOSZ) from the Communist era remains the strongest confederation, organizing mainly in the sectors hardest hit by market reforms. Two splinter organizations of the former unitary Communist trade unions represent different groups of white-collar workers, and a third unites the chemical workers and some other smaller sectoral trade unions that did not want to join MSZOSZ. Three new trade union confederations were formed after 1988, the Democratic League of Independent Trade Unions being the strongest. Together with the Worker Councils and the much smaller Solidarity Confederation, the new confederations organize about 15–20% of Hungarian labor. László Bruszt, Reforming Alliances: Labor, Management, and State Bureaucracy in Hungary's

Economic Transformation, in *Strategic Choice and Path Dependency in Post-Socialism: Institutional Dynamics in the Transformation Process*, ed. Jerzy Hausner, Bob Jessop, and Klaus Nielsen, London: Edward Elgar, 1994, pp. 261–87; András Tóth, Great Expectations and Fading Hopes, Trade Unions and System Change in Hungary, in *Parties, Trade Unions and Society in East-Central Europe*, ed. Michael Waller and Martin Myant, Ilford, U.K.: Frank Cass, 1994, pp. 176–97; and László Neumann, A Deficiency of the Transition: Lack of Effective Institutionalization of Wage Bargaining and Labor Conflicts in Hungary, paper presented at the Tenth International Conference of Europeanists, Chicago, March 1996.

10 Herman Schwartz, The New East European Constitutional Courts, in *Constitution-Making in Eastern Europe*, ed. A. E. Dick Howard, Baltimore: Johns Hopkins University Press, 1993, pp. 163–207; Andrew Arato, Constitution and Continuity in the East European Transitions, Part II. The Hungarian Case, *Constellations*, 1994, 1(2):306–25; and Ferenc Majoros, Ungarische Verfassungsgerichtsbarkeit seit 1990, Berlin: Bundesinstitut fur Ostwissentschaftliche und Internationale Studien, 1993.

11 The Young Democrats (FIDESZ), campaigning under a new label as a "national-liberal" party, emphasized the problem of inflation and proposed a national-level wage pact as its cure. To combat inflation, FIDESZ economic advisers proposed to alter expectations through negotiations – to convince labor to restrain wage demands, with the expectation that inflation would be curbed and to convince business that they could place their confidence in a competent government. Their hope was that restored business confidence (resulting from a successfully negotiated wage pact) would translate into higher levels of investment, leading to noninflationary growth that would curtail the length and depth of social burdens on wage earners. In the assessment of the Free Democrats (SzDSz), the nature of the crisis was more severe and hard times were likely to be more protracted. To convince society to tolerate further hardships, with the expectation that it would also benefit from these sacrifices, they proposed tripartite negotiations to secure much broader socioeconomic agreements not limited to wage issues but including as well issues of social policy, safety nets for the hardest hit, trade union rights, and the like.

12 During the fall of 1994, that attack on Békesi intensified when Horn, in rapid succession, (a) forced the resignation of the nominally independent president of the National Bank well before the expiration of his six-year term, adding that a replacement would be sought from among one of "our men"; (b) directly intervened, against the counsel of the finance minister, to cancel the finalized contract to sell the Hungar Hotel chain to an American buyer; and (c) forced the resignation of the president of the SPA with an announcement that he was creating a new Ministry of Privatization that would not report to the Ministry of Finance.

13 Bokros, who had published dissident articles during the Kádár era under the pseudonym David Ricardo, had served as the first chairman of the Budapest Stock Exchange before becoming CEO of Budapest Bank. Surányi was no stranger to the National Bank, having served as its president before being ousted from this independent post by the Antall government. Together they had studied under the economist László Antal and had continued under his tutelage in

the research department of the Ministry of Finance. Each was well known and respected by the World Bank and the IMF.

14 Of the character of the crisis there was little doubt. After nine months of inaction regarding the staggering foreign debt, balance of payments shortfalls, and soaring budget deficits, the Hungarian government's standing among foreign investors, financial markets, and international lending institutions was in free fall: Prices on the secondary market for Hungarian government bonds were plummeting; to attract buyers of new government bonds, yields once pegged at several percentage points above comparable U.S. Treasury bonds quickly rose up to 10 percentage points higher; Moody's adjusted their ratings downward; and, triggered by the collapse of the peso, prices tumbled on the Budapest Stock Exchange, with shares of Fotex, a company long close to the Socialists, falling by more than 50% when foreign investors (who, in the aggregate, did not desert the Czech, Polish, or Turkish emerging markets) pulled their capital from the Budapest Exchange.

15 Sándor Nagy, president of the largest federation of trade unions, responded that the same 165 billion forint deficit reduction target could be achieved with an alternative plan (presented in detailed items and figures) that was less burdensome to some groups in society and less likely to threaten the economy with deeper recession. Bokros expressed his gratitude to the trade union leader/Socialist MP for providing such a detailed list, noting that his staff at the Finance Ministry would study it appreciatively when it came time to make the *next* round of budget cuts. The representatives of business welcomed deficit reduction but argued that the Bokros program fell far short of a long-term growth strategy.

16 Advocates of tripartite social agreements, of course, argued that broad negotiations are not needed in normal times but rather during abnormal times such as these. Bokros and his advisers countered: The danger you do not see is that social negotiations with our domestic partners will lower our credibility in the eyes of our foreign partners. If we credit society, we lose external credits. Negotiation might yield short-term credibility, but if it erodes external credibility, we lose some means to bring about the economic results necessary to keep long-term credibility. Society must simply accept that there is no alternative.

17 On the origins of the postwar German political system, see Daniel Rogers, Transforming the German Party System: The United States and the Origins of Political Moderation, *Journal of Modern History*, 1993, 65(3):512–32; and Kathleen Bawn, The Logic of Institutional Preferences: German Electoral Law as a Social Choice Outcome, *American Journal of Political Science*, 1993, 37(4):965–91.

18 On the lively debate among German scholars about whether the notion of colonization is an appropriate characterization of the unification process, see Andreas Pickel, Jump-Starting a Market Economy: A Critique of the Radical Strategy for Economic Reform in the Light of East German Experiences, *Studies in Comparative Communism*, 1992, 25(2):177–91; and Michael Brie, Die Ostdeutschen auf dem Wege vom "armen Bruder" zur organisierten Minderheit?, Working Papers Series of the Arbeitsgruppe Transformationsprozesse, 94/4, Berlin: Max-Planck-Gesellschaft.

19 Writing on this period of exceptionalism in postwar German political

institutions, Gerhard Lehmbruch, a leading observer, notes: "What happened in early 1990 was the temporary breakdown of the quasi-'corporatist' linkage structure of the West German policy network. Under the unusual circumstances of 1990, the party system cut its communication channels to other corporate actors in the West German polity and assumed the position of an *unconstrained sovereign decision-maker*. This had the further consequence that its peculiar belief systems, which normally serve integrative rather than operative purposes, came to govern its operative policy choices. The belief system that dominated not only the electoral discourse in 1990 but also the decisions of the government was the myth of the 'social market economy' in an extremely simplified version." Gerhard Lehmbruch, The Institutional Framework of German Regulation, in *The Politics of German Regulation*, ed. Kenneth Dyson, Aldershot, U.K.: Dartmouth, 1992, pp. 45-6 (emphasis added). See also Klaus von Beyme, The Effects of Reunification on German Democracy, *Government and Opposition*, 1992, 27(2):158-177.

20 On the interlocking policy networks of the postwar (but preunification) period that precluded the *semisovereign state* from making unilateral decisions and obliged it to negotiate the content of public policy, see Peter J. Katzenstein, *Policy and Politics in West Germany: The Growth of a Semisovereign State*, Philadelphia: Temple University Press, 1987.

21 Unlike Hungary and the rest of the postsocialist world, where miracles were never credible and hence never fostered, East Germany had been assured that the social costs of restructuring would not be great and West Germany had been assured that fiscal cost sharing would not be inordinate. For a comprehensive discussion of the politics of unification costs, see Wolfgang Seibel, Nichtintendiert wirtschaftliche Folgen politischen Handelns. Die Transformationspolitik des Bundes in Ostdeutschland seit 1990. In *Regierungs system und Verwaltungspolitik*, ed. Arthur Benz and Wolfgang Seibel, pp. 214-49, Opladen: Westdeutscher Verlag, 1995.

22 Wolfgang Seibel, Privatization by Means of State Bureaucracy?: The Treuhand Phenomenon in Eastern Germany, in *Restructuring Networks in Postsocialism: Legacies, Linkages, and Localities*, ed. Gernot Grabher and David Stark, London and New York: Oxford University Press; Denis McShane, IG Metall – Ossis Fight Back, *New Statesman and Society*, (1993), 6(252):10-12.

23 Razeen Sally and Douglas Webber, The German Solidarity Pact: A Case Study in the Politics of the Unified Germany, *German Politics*, 1994, 3(1):27-53.

24 Wolfgang Seibel, Privatization . . . in Eastern Germany, pp. 290-1.

25 Richard Hyman, Institutional Transfer: Industrial Relations in Eastern Germany, unpublished manuscript, University of Warwick, 1996; and Ettle Wilfried and Helmut Wiesentahl, Tarifautonomie in de-industrialisierten Gelande. Analyse eines institutionentransfers in Prozess der deutschen Einheit, *Kölner Zeitschrift für Soziologie und Sozialpsychologie*, 1994, 40(3):425-52.

26 Michael Fichter, A House Divided: A View of German Unification as It Has Affected Organized Labour, *German Politics*, 1993, 2(1):21-39; and Michael Fichter and Hugo Reister, *Zum Stand der Gewerkschaftsentwicklung in Den neuen Bundeslandern: Afbau-Struktur-Politik*, research report prepared for the Committee for the Research on Social and Political Changes in the New German *Länder*, Berlin, 1995.

27 Michael Fichter, Institutional Transfer and Institutionalization in Unified Germany: The Case of the Unions, paper presented at the Conference on the Political Economy of the New Germany, Cornell University, October 1994, p. 16. Hyman, however, reports that union membership fell in subsequent years, declining to 2.6 million (a loss of 38% of its peak membership) by the start of 1995. Hyman, Institutional Transfer, p. 20.

28 These included, among others, the Grundsätze zur Zusammenarbeit von Bund, neuen Ländern, und Treuhandantalt (Guidelines for Cooperation among the Federal State, New *Länder*, and the Treuhand), issued March 14, 1991, which established regular meetings between the heads of the Treuhand and the ministers of the East German state governments; the Gemeinsame Erklärung of the DGB, the German White-Collar Union, and the Treuhand on April 13, 1991; and the agreement with the Societies for Work Promotion, Employment, and Structural Development reached on July 17, 1991. Seibel, Privatization . . . in Eastern Germany, pp. 292–3.

29 Sally and Webber, German Solidarity Pact, p. 30.

30 Seibel, Unintended Consequences, p. 14.

31 Although it did not reach majority status, Klaus's new party was rapidly able to claim a plurality in Parliament. The problem, however, was that even though the ODS was able to gain increasing support among the parliamentary members, it still lacked the electoral legitimacy to make a direct and decisive assault against the Socialists, social democrats, and "sixty-eighters" (political activists from the Prague Spring of 1968) who together composed a majority of the government in this early postsocialist phase.

32 Peter Rutland, Workers' Responses to the Market Transition: The Czech Case, Working Paper, National Council for Soviet and East European Research, 1994. Mitchell Orenstein, The Czech Tripartite Council and Its Contribution to Social Peace, unpublished manuscript, Yale University, November 1994, p. 14.

33 Orenstein argues that the "social-liberal hybrid character" of the early reform package was the outcome of a compromise between the two groups within the government: "While Vaclav Klaus and his team of neo-liberals in the Finance Ministry planned mass privatization, liberalization of prices, and currency stabilization, actual existing social democrats in the Ministry of Labor planned and implemented a social dimension of reform." Mitchell Orenstein, Out of the Red: Building Capitalism and Democracy in Post-Communist Europe, Ph.D. dissertation, Yale University, May 1996, p. 84.

34 Karla Brom and Mitchell Orenstein, The Privatized Sector in the Czech Republic: Government and Bank Control in a Transitional Economy, *Europe-Asia Studies*, 1994, 46(6):894.

35 Barry Weingast presents a forceful case for the benefits of federalism in economic transformation in The Economic Role of Political Institutions: Market-Preserving Federalism and Economic Growth, *Journal of Law, Economics, and Organization*, 1995, 11:1–31. See also Gabriella Montinola, Yingyi Qian, and Barry R. Weingast, Federalism, Chinese Style: The Political Basis for Economic Success in China, *World Politics*, 1995, 48(1):50–81.

36 See, e.g., We Cannot Allow a Wave of Bankruptcies (interview with Karel Dyba, minister for Economic Policy and Development), *Zemedelske Noviny*, January 29, 1993, p. 6; and Bankruptcies Under Supervision: The Law on Bank-

ruptcies and Settlements to Be Softened, *Hospodarske Noviny*, February 12, 1993, pp. 1–2 (in Joint Publications Research Service, *East European Reports* JPRS-EER-93-021-S, March 19, 1993. See also Aydin Haryi and Gerald A. McDermott, Restructuring in the Czech Republic: Beyond Ownership and Bankruptcy, unpublished manuscript, CERGE-EI, Prague, April 1995.

37 Orenstein, Czech Tripartite, p. 12.

38 Peter Rutland notes that rents cover only about 20% of maintenance costs and that heating and electricity are heavily subsidized. In this situation, the mining industry is lobbying to raise the price of coal, utilities are clamoring for higher rates, and the new private owners of apartment blocks acquired through property restitution are demanding the right to charge market-level rents to their tenants. "Despite these diverse pressures for price liberalization (all of impeccable Thatcherite logic), Klaus has only permitted a gradual increase in rents, for fear of igniting social protests. In 1992, subsidies amounted to 4.8 billion crowns. In December 1993, a new program was introduced providing K250 ($8) a month subsidies for around half a million low-income tenants." Rutland, Workers' Responses, p. 11.

39 "The key factor in our success has been a clear *vision* of the future we wanted to achieve and a *pragmatic*, feasible reform strategy capable of winning the support of the majority of the population." Vaclav Klaus, interview, *OECD Transition Brief*, No. 2, Winter 1996, p. 3 (emphasis added). See also Klaus, The Experience with Radical Economic Reforms in the Czech Republic, *The Brown Journal of World Affairs*, Spring 1994, 123–7.

40 Under the 5% exclusion rule (according to which parties that received less than 5% of the vote were excluded from holding parliamentary seats), the coalition government had reached this 52% majority with 42% of the votes (*East European Constitutional Review*, Spring 1994, 3(2), Special Issue, Designing Electoral Regimes, p. 65). On the particular features of the Czechoslovak electoral law, see the insightful paper by David M. Olson, The Sundered State: Federalism and Parliament in Czechoslovakia, presented at the Conference on Comparative Parliamentary Development in Eastern Europe and the Former USSR at the Center for Soviet, Post-Soviet, and East European Studies, Emory University, Atlanta, April 9–10, 1993.

41 Országos Választási Bizottság Közleménye az Országgyülési Képviselök Választásról, *Magyar Közlöny*, 1990, no. 44, pp. 3–12.

42 On the 1990 and 1994 Hungarian elections, see Szonja Szelényi, Iván Szelényi, and Winifred R. Poster, Interests and Symbols in Post-Communist Political Culture: The Case of Hungary, *American Sociological Review*, 1996, 61(3):466–77; Barnabás Rácz, Political Pluralization in Hungary: The 1990 Elections, *Soviet Studies*, 1991, 43(1):107–36; Bob Dent, Letter from Budapest, *New Statesman and Society*, 1994, 7(303):11–16; and Edith Oltay, The Former Communists' Electoral Victory in Hungary, *Radio Free Europe–Radio Liberty Research Reports*, 1994, 3.1–6, J2. 24.

43 Bernard Wheaton and Zdenek Kavan, *The Velvet Revolution: Czechoslovakia, 1988–1991*, Boulder, CO: Westview Press, 1992, pp. 95–8.

44 Rutland, Workers' Responses, p. 6, notes that in the process of this reorganization, union locals were granted considerable autonomy, retaining 70% of collected union dues, for example. Whereas in Czechoslovakia the new trade

unions promptly obtained the right from the government to divide among themselves the property of the old Communist trade unions, in Hungary the government delayed, for several years, a decisive settlement of the question of the (substantial) trade union assets and skillfully exploited the debate among the old and new unions to deepen the division among the six competing trade union confederations. Union property was finally divided only in 1993. See András Tóth, Great Expectations; and László Bruszt, The Antall Government, the Labour Unions, and the Employers' Associations, in *Lawful Revolution in Hungary: 1989–1994*, ed. Béla Király and András Bozóki, Boulder, CO: Social Science Monographs, 1995, pp. 369–95.

45 Martin Myant, Czech and Slovak Trade Unions, in *Parties, Trade Unions and Society in East-Central Europe*, ed. Michael Waller and Martin Myant, Essex, U.K.: Frank Cass, 1994, p. 61; Ludek Rychetnik, Can the Czech Republic Develop a Negotiated Economy?, in *Strategic Choice and Path Dependency in Post-Socialism: Institutional Dynamics in the Transformation Process*, ed. Jerzy Hausner, Bob Jessop, and Klaus Nielsen, Aldershot, U.K.: Edward Elgar, 1995, p. 242; and Rutland, Thatcherism, Czech-Style, p. 119.

46 Quoted in Rychetnik, Negotiated Economy, p. 244.

47 See Myant, Trade Unions, pp. 64–7, for a discussion of labor mobilization during this period.

48 About this international role, Rutland notes: "In several respects the new code fell below the minimum provisions for the protection of workers' interests recommended by the International Labour Organization. Letters from the ICFTU and Lane Kirkland of the AFL-CIO helped to persuade the government to modify the code." Rutland, Thatcherism, Czech-style, p. 122.

49 Orenstein, Czech Tripartite, pp. 6, 8; Rutland, Workers' Responses, pp. 13–14; Rychetnik, Negotiated Economy, pp. 242–4. As added confirmation of our earlier argument that the formation of economic and social policies should not be analyzed in isolation from the question of the Czech–Slovak separation, we should note that these rights were further solidified in the run-up to the Velvet Divorce. In the period immediately prior to the formal separation on January 1, 1993, the new Czech constitution had to be drafted and quickly ratified to provide a legal framework for the emergent state. Such ratification required a qualified (two-thirds) majority. In exchange for its support, the Czech Social Democratic Party demanded that the European Charter of Rights and Freedoms be incorporated in the new constitution. That document, providing a large number of social rights, was indeed appended to the Czech constitution. Orenstein observes, "[W]hile Thatcher's Britain steadfastly opted out of the European 'social chapter,' the European Charter of Rights and Freedoms is now law in the Czech Republic. As Czech social democrats were fond of saying at the time, 'we are in the middle of Europe, not in the British Isles.'" Orenstein, Out of the Red, p. 98. The legacy of separation thus continues to shape social and economic policy.

50 For an example of one such agreement worked out by the Council of Economic and Social Accord, see the full text of the General Agreement of the Czech Republic for 1993 in Joint Publication Research Service, *East European Reports* (JPRS-EER-93-030-S), April 13, 1993, pp. 9–12.

51 On January 14, 1994, the tripartite council announced its agreement that "the

government will not insist on the prohibition of trade union organizations in the state administration when it sends its law to parliament. Instead, it will prepare a draft law that sets out conditions for their activity specifically" (Orenstein, Czech Tripartite, p. 17).

52 Rychetnik, Negotiated Economy, p. 243. See Myant, Trade Unions, pp. 68–72, for a discussion of tensions within the tripartite body, claims by labor that the government failed to keep its side of the agreements, and various warning strikes to get negotiations back on track.

53 Orenstein, Tripartite Council, p. 20.

54 In 1992, the chair of the Council on Economic and Social Accord, Vice-Premier Pavel Hoffmann, summarized the council's first two years' experience: "it was apparent that the envisaged changes in the economy required at least elementary social consensus and it asked for more than just a decision by the government. The government needed . . . to lead a dialogue with the social partners. . . . It worked well whenever a desire to find a sensible solution prevailed over a priori positions." Quoted in Rychetnik, Negotiated Economy, p. 244.

55 Economist Intelligence Unit, *Country Profile: Czech Republic and Slovakia, 1995–6*, unemployment figures, pp. 14 and 41; tourism figure, p. 22. The dramatically low unemployment figures in the Czech Republic are also partially explained by the very restrictive eligibility criteria and limited benefits (in duration and in levels) for the unemployed. In Hungary, by contrast, unemployment benefits are more substantial and the costs of employment are greater due to the extraordinarily high social security taxes paid by the employer. In Hungary, one out of two dismissed workers is registered as unemployed compared to only one out of three in the Czech Republic. This said, it should also be noted that dismissal rates have been far lower in the Czech Republic: From 1990 to 1994, employment in Hungary fell by 26% compared to about 10% in the Czech Republic. Moreover, because new workplaces have been created and total wage costs kept relatively low, long-term unemployment is significantly lower in the Czech Republic, and the reemployment rate is six times higher in the Czech Republic than in Hungary. See Jenö Koltay, Munkanélküli és foglalkoztatáspolitika Közép és Kelet Európban (Unemployment and Employment Policies in Central and Eastern Europe), *Közgazdasági Szemle*, no. 2:142–67; Raphael Shen, *Economic Reform in Poland and Czechoslovakia: Lessons in Systemic Transformation*, Westport, CT: Praeger, 1993; and Marek Gora, Central and Eastern European Labour Markets in Transition: Can We Draw Common Conclusions on Their Behaviour?, unpublished manuscript, Warsaw University of Economics, 1996.

56 Rutland, Workers' Responses, p. 10.

57 Orenstein, Tripartite Council, p. 12.

58 Quoted in Myant, Czech and Slovak Trade Unions, p. 76 (our emphasis). Myant, pp. 75–80, presents an excellent overview of different levels of support for the government's reform program across segments of the labor movement.

59 Just weeks after his flight of hyperbole against the trade union mobilization in the spring of 1994, Klaus accepted an invitation to give the keynote speech at the trade union congress by offering the following olive branch: "The government seeks a basic consensus of the citizens in the fundamental issues of the present and the future and it is conscious of the fact that the trade unions play

in this an exceptionally important role. Therefore we respect the existence of the Council of Economic and Social Accord and we will try also in the future to negotiate in this context, even though the role of the government (and the state) as an employer, thanks to privatization, is changing in a fundamental way. We will continue to make suggestions for further changes and shifts in the tripartite negotiations, but I would like here, before you, to emphasize that we are not calling for a revolution, nor for radical changes. Further differences of opinion in these matters are therefore not, in my opinion, necessary to dramatize." (Quoted in Orenstein, Tripartite Council, pp. 20–1.)

60 We are well aware of the possible structuralist objections to our institutionalist account. The former view argues that policy differences in the Hungarian and Czech cases are more parsimoniously explained by differences in economic background conditions, such as the extraordinarily high foreign debt in the Hungarian case and its absence in the Czech case. But that explanation falters because the outcomes we might predict from its logic are at odds with the actual developments. With the Czechs' greater economic room for maneuver, we might have expected them (especially given their initial policy preferences) to move with much greater haste and fortitude; nonetheless, their behavior has been moderate. With the Hungarians facing more severe economic constraints, we might have expected them (especially with their initial gradualist proclivities) to proceed with caution; nonetheless, they moved precipitously, provoking a severe financial crisis that exacerbated their foreign debt. Similarly, from the unreformed character of the old socialist economy in the Czech Republic, we might have anticipated greater structural problems of adjustment – higher levels of dismissal and unemployment, for example, than in Hungary, where microeconomic conditions at the level of firms seemed more auspicious. Our point here is that policies cannot be read directly from economic structural endowments. Our effort throughout this chapter has been to explain *policies* based on the characteristics of the *polities* that produced them.

61 Bruszt, The Antall Government and the Unions.

62 Our Hungarian–Czech comparison finds an interesting Antipodean counterpoint. During the past decade, Labor governments in both Australia and New Zealand introduced sweeping neoliberal reforms. But as with their Eastern European counterparts, the institutional features of the two polities exhibit important differences. As in Hungary, executive authority in New Zealand is highly concentrated and relatively unconstrained (with a unicameral parliament and a winner-take-all plurality voting system). Moreover, as in Hungary, Labor politicians in New Zealand moved unilaterally, rejecting consultations with organized labor. By contrast, the greater checks and balances of Australia's bicameral parliament and federal division of powers produced (as in the Czech Republic) more moderate and incremental policies resting on formalized cooperation agreements between the government and the Australian Council of Trade Unions. Not surprisingly, from the point of view of our general argument, whereas in Australia economic reforms have been sustainable, in New Zealand they have been constantly threatened with electoral reversal. Only with the 1996 elections, 12 years after the reform process began, can economic reforms in New Zealand be said to have won general acceptance. See the fascinating set of studies in Francis G. Castles, Rolf Gerritsen, and Jack Vowles, eds., *The Great Experi-*

ment: Labour Parties and Public Policy Transformation in Australia and New Zealand, Auckland: Auckland University Press, 1996.

CHAPTER 7

1 Hanna Pitkin presents a lucid contrast between the *authorization view* of Hobbes and the *accountability view* in *The Concept of Representation*, Berkeley: University of California Press, 1967, pp. 55–9; for an updating of these issues, see James G. March and Johan P. Olsen, *Democratic Governance*, New York: Free Press, 1995, pp. 141–81.

2 As Guillermo O'Donnell, almost paraphrasing the *Federalist Papers*, argues in defense of horizontal accountability: "Because policies are carried out by a series of relatively autonomous powers, decision-making in representative democracy tends to be slow and incremental and sometimes prone to gridlock. But, by this same token, those policies are usually *vaccinated against gross mistakes*, and they have a reasonably good chance of being implemented; moreover, responsibility for mistakes tends to be widely shared." Guillermo O'Donnell, Delegative Democracy, *Journal of Democracy*, 1994, 5(1):62.

3 As we saw in the Hungarian case and as Yeltsin's increasingly delegative (rule by decree) style exemplifies, such efforts to use crisis itself as legitimation for expanded executive power is endemic in societies lacking extended accountability. O'Donnell's observations about delegative democracy in Latin America might have been written about these postsocialist cases: "[A deep social and economic] crisis generates a strong sense of urgency and provides fertile terrain for unleashing the delegative propensities that may be present in a given country. Problems and demands mount up before inexperienced governments that must operate through a weak and disarticulated (if not disloyal) bureaucracy. Presidents get elected by promising that they – being strong, courageous, above parties and interest, *machos* – will save the country. Theirs is a 'government of saviors' (*salvadores de la patria*). This leads to a 'magical' style of policy making: the delegative 'mandate' supposedly bestowed by the majority, strong political will, and technical knowledge should suffice to fulfill the savior's mission – the 'packages' follow as a corollary." O'Donnell, Delegative Democracy, p. 65.

4 "In delegative democracy, we witness a decision-making frenzy, what in Latin America we call *decretismo*. Because such hasty, unilateral executive orders are likely to offend important and politically mobilized interests, they are unlikely to be implemented. In the midst of a severe crisis and increasingly popular impatience, the upshot is usually new flurries of decisions which, because of the experience many sectors have had in resisting the previous ones, are even less likely to be implemented." O'Donnell, Delegative Democracy, pp. 66–7.

5 "Re-examining the developmental state means rethinking embedded autonomy. Can embedded autonomy also be built around ties to other groups? Are alternative constructions more or less politically stable than the original version? The basic argument . . . is that expanding the scope of state–society links to include a broader range of groups and classes, however difficult that might be to accomplish, should result in a more politically robust and adaptive version of embedded autonomy." Peter Evans, *Embedded Autonomy: States and Industrial Transformation*, Princeton, NJ: Princeton University Press, 1995, p. 228.

6 In Hungary, by contrast, where the interests of labor and localities were ex-cluded, policies turned into crises with a rapidity proportionate to the speed of decision making. There business interests, likewise excluded from open and public participation in policy formation, later found the back door to bankrupt the state when it reversed course.

7 Evans, *Embedded Autonomy*, p. 52.

8 Pierre Bourdieu, Political Representation: Elements for a Theory of the Political Field, and Delegation and Political Fetishism, in Bourdieu, *Language and Symbolic Politics*, Cambridge, MA: Harvard University Press, 1991, pp. 171–220. For an analysis of the pathologies of the democratic political field that corrects the relative neglect of the habitus and practices of politicians, see especially Guillermo 'J'Donnell, On the State, Democratization, and Some Conceptual Problems: A Latin American View with Glances at Some Postcommunist Countries, *World Development* 1993, 21(8):1355–69. Herbert Kitschelt presents a comparative analysis of the properties of postcommunist political fields in The Formation of Party Cleavages in Post-Communist Democracies, *Party Politics*, 1995, 1(4):447–72; see also Kitschelt, Post-Communist Democracies: Do Party Systems Help or Hinder Democratic Consolidation? paper presented at the Conference on Democracy, Markets, and Civil Societies in Post-1989 East Central Europe, Center for European Studies, Harvard, May 17–19, 1996; and László Bruszt applies the concepts of credit and political capital to the study of postcommunist politics in Miert tamogatnak a kapitalizmust a Kelet-Europaiak (Why on Earth Would East Europeans Support Capitalism), *Politikatudományi Szemle*, 1995, no. 3:81–107.

9 David Stark, Recombinant Property in East European Capitalism, *American Journal of Sociology*, 1996, 101:993–1027.

10 Those analysts who tend to focus on *strong ties* in an ideational network – that is, where the constituent idea-blocks of a form are tightly coupled and linked in dense patterns – call these forms *ideologies* (for the classic statement, see Reinhard Bendix, *Work and Authority in Industry*, Berkeley: University of California Press, 1956). Those analysts who emphasize the comprehensible, as op-posed to comprehensive, quality of forms focus on the *weak ties* in an ideational network, as stressed in their employment of the term *stories* and their attention to narrative structure (Harrison C. White, *Identity and Control*, Princeton, NJ: Princeton University Press, 1992; Charles Sabel and Jonathan Zeitlin, Stories, Strategies and Structures: Rethinking Historical Alternatives to Mass Production, in *Worlds of Possibilities: Flexibility and Mass Production in Western Industrialization*, ed. Sabel and Zeitlin, Cambridge: Cambridge University Press, 1997, pp. 1–33. Ideologies are like road maps, demonstrating the comprehensive connections; stories are like sketched pathways, telling how one got from there to here through a particular chain of connections.

11 Stephan Haggard and Robert R. Kaufman, *The Political Economy of Democratic Transitions*, Princeton, NJ: Princeton University Press, 1995, pp. 156–9; and Barbara Geddes, *Politician's Dilemma: Building State Capacity in Latin America*, Berkeley: University of California Press, 1994, p. 190.

12 Commenting on a conversation with Leszek Balcerowicz, Vaclav Klaus notes his own engagement in day-to-day politics: "When he last visited me . . . I asked him how many times a week he traveled around Poland and spoke on the

town squares, in the cultural centers, in the sports halls, in order to gain the greatest mass support for his plan. He revealed that he preferred to sit in his study and prepare documents. I have been going to meetings on average about two times a week, and now, before the elections, let's say six times. I think that Poland is paying above all for the inability of certain politicians to gain such marked support of the voters that they have enough power to continue with the reforms." Vaclav Klaus quoted in Mitchell Orenstein, Out of the Red: Building Capitalism and Democracy in Post-Communist Europe, Ph.D. dissertation, Yale University 1996, p. 73.

13 On the notion of institutional friction as a source of innovation, see Gernot Grabher and David Stark, Organizing Diversity: Evolutionary Theory, Network Analysis, and Postsocialist Transformations, in *Restructuring Networks in Postsocialism: Legacies, Linkages, and Localities*, ed. Grabher and Stark, New York and London: Oxford University Press, 1997, pp. 21–2.

14 See especially Peter Murrell, The Transition According to Cambridge, Mass., *Journal of Economic Literature*, 1995, 33:164–78, for a fascinating discussion of these issues.

15 John Dewey, *Reconstruction in Philosophy* (1920), in *John Dewey: Middle Works*, Volume 12, Carbondale: Southern Illinois University Press, 1982, p. 173. The concept of *institutionalization of practical reason* is from Charles Sabel, Design, Deliberation, and Democracy: On the New Pragmatism of Firms and Public Institutions, paper presented to the conference on Liberal Institutions, Economic Constitutional Rights, and the Role of Organizations, European University Institute, Florence, December 1995.

16 Sabel, Design, Deliberation, and Democracy, p. 28.

17 Vaclav Klaus: "It is also important to keep in mind that reform is not a theoretical issue. It takes place in real conditions, it affects real and vital interests of particular groups and strata of the population, and those interests are reflected in politics. It means that attempts to follow a master-minded ideal blue-print of reform are simply not feasible in the real world. . . . I never thought in terms of 'very best' or 'second best' policies. It is a theoretical, unrealistic construction. We knew that neither a perfect reform strategy nor an optimal set of policies can be invented in advance and then simply introduced." Interview with Vaclav Klaus, in Mario I. Blejer and Fabrizio Coricelli, eds., *The Making of Economic Reform in Eastern Europe: Conversations with Reformers in Poland, Hungary, and the Czech Republic*, Aldershot, U.K.: Edward Elgar, 1996, pp. 79, 91.

18 Charles F. Sabel, Moebius-Strip Organizations and Open Labor Markets: Some Consequences of the Reintegration of Conception and Execution in a Volatile Economy, in *Social Theory for a Changing Society*, ed. Pierre Bourdieu and James S. Coleman, Boulder, CO, and New York: Westview Press and Russell Sage Foundation, 1990, pp. 23–54; Sabel, Intelligible Differences: On Deliberate Strategy and the Exploration of Possibility in Economic Life, paper presented to the 36th annual meeting of the Societá Italiana degli Economisti, Florence, October 1995; Sabel and Jane E. Prokop, Stabilization Through Reorganization?: Some Preliminary Implications of Russia's Entry into World Markets in the Age of Discursive Quality Standards, in *Corporate Governance in Central Europe and Russia*, Volume II: *Insiders and the State*, ed. Roman Frydman, Cheryl W. Gray, and Andrzej Rapaczynski, Budapest and London: Central European Uni-

versity Press, 1994, pp. 151–91; and Sabel, Design, Deliberation, and Democracy.

19 Sabel, Design, Deliberation, and Democracy, p. 24.

20 Stark, Recombinant Property, pp. 1021–2.

21 Wolfgang Streeck, Beneficial Constraints: On the Economic Limits of Rational Voluntarism, in *Contemporary Capitalism: The Embeddedness of Institutions*, ed. J. Rogers Hollingsworth and Robert Boyer, New York and Cambridge: Cambridge University Press, 1997.

22 Ronald Dore, *Flexible Rigidities: Industrial Policy and Structural Adjustment in the Japanese Economy, 1970–80*, Stanford, CA: Stanford University Press, 1986.

23 Grabher and Stark, Organizing Diversity, pp. 1–3.

REFERENCES

Ábel, István and John Bonin. 1993. State Desertion and Financial Market Failure: Is the Transition Stalled? *Budapest Bank Working Papers* no. 5.

Ágh, Attila. 1994. A demokratikus átmenet feltételrendszere (The Conditions of the Democratic Transition). *Politikatudományi Szemle* no. 4.: 139–45.

Akerloff, G. A., A. K. Rose, J. L. Yellen, and H. Hessenius. 1991. East Germany in from the Cold: The Economic Aftermath of Currency Union. *Brookings Papers for Economic Activity* I: 1–101.

Albach, Horst. 1993. The Transformation of Firms and Markets: A Network Approach to Economic Transformation Processes in East Germany. *WZB Discussion Papers* FS IV 93-1. Berlin: Wissenschaftszentrum Berlin Für Sozialforschung.

Alesina, Alberto. 1994. Political Models of Macroeconomic Policy and Fiscal Reforms. In *Voting for Reform*, ed. Stephan Haggard and Steven B. Webb, pp. 37–61. New York: Oxford University Press.

Altmann, Franz-Lothar. 1993. The Transformation of Property Rights in Czechoslovakia. In *Transforming Economic Systems in East Central Europe*, ed. Roland Schönfeld, pp. 155–8. Munich: Südosteuropa-Gesellschaft.

Amsden, Alice H. 1994. Can Eastern Europe Compete by "Getting the Prices Right"? Contrast with East Asian Structural Reforms. In *Rebuilding Capitalism: Alternative Roads after Socialism and Dirigisme*, ed. Andres Solimano, Osvaldo Sunkel, and Mario I. Blejer, pp. 81–107. Ann Arbor, MI: University of Michigan Press.

Amsden, Alice H., Jacek Kochanowicz, and Lance Taylor. 1994. *The Market Meets Its Match: Restructuring the Economies of Eastern Europe*. Cambridge, MA: Harvard University Press.

Arato, Andrew. 1990. Revolution, Civil Society, and Democracy. *Cornell Working Papers on Transition from State Socialism* no. 90–5.

1994. Constitution and Continuity in the East European Transitions, Part II. The Hungarian Case. *Constellations* no. 1–2: 306–25.

Arthur, Brian W. 1989. Competing Technologies and Lock-in by Historical Events: The Dynamics of Allocation under Increasing Returns. *Economic Journal* 99: 116–31.

Ash, Timothy Garton. 1990. *The Magic Lantern: The Revolution of '89 Witnessed in Warsaw, Budapest, Berlin, and Prague*. New York: Random House.

Balcerowicz, Leszek. 1995. Understanding Postcommunist Transitions. In *Economic Reform and Democracy*, ed. Larry Diamond and Marc F. Plattner, pp. 86–100. Baltimore: Johns Hopkins University Press.

Bawn, Kathleen. 1993. The Logic of Institutional Preferences: German Electoral Law as a Social Choice Outcome. *American Journal of Political Science* 37(4): 965–91.

Beissinger, Mark R. 1995. The Persisting Ambiguity of Empire. *Post-Soviet Affairs*, 11(2): 149–184.

Bendix, Reinhard. 1956. *Work and Authority in Industry*. Berkeley: University of California Press.

Berger, Suzanne, and Ronald Dore, eds. 1996. *National Diversity and Global Capitalism*. Ithaca, NY: Cornell University Press.

von Beyme, Klaus. 1992. The Effects of Reunification on German Democracy. *Government and Opposition* 27(2): 158–77.

Blanchard, Oliver, Rudiger Dornbusch, Paul Krugman, Rychard Layard, and Lawrence Summers. 1991. *Reform in Eastern Europe*. Cambridge, MA: Harvard University Press.

Blejer, Mario I., and Fabrizio Coricelli, eds. 1996.*The Making of Economic Reform in Eastern Europe: Conversations with Reformers in Poland, Hungary, and the Czech Republic*. London: Edward Elgar.

Bokros, Lajos. 1994. Privatization and the Banking System in Hungary. In *Privatization in the Transition Process. Recent Experiences in Eastern Europe*, ed. László Szamuely, pp. 305–20. Geneva: United Nations Conference on Trade and Development and KOPINT-DATORG.

Boltanski, Luc, and Laurent Thevenot. 1991. *La justification: Les économies de la grandeur*. Paris: Gallimard.

Böröcz, József, and Ákos Róna-Tas. 1995. Small Leap Forward: Emergence of New Economic Elites in Hungary, Poland, and Russia. *Theory and Society* 24: 751–81.

Bourdieu, Pierre. 1985. The Genesis of the Concepts of Habitus and of Field. *Sociocriticism* 2(2): 11–24.

—— 1986. Forms of Capital. In *Handbook of Theory and Research for the Sociology of Education*, ed. John G. Richardson, pp. 241–58. Westport, CT: Greenwood Press.

—— 1988. *Homo Academicus*. Stanford, CA: Stanford University Press.

—— 1990. *The Logic of Practice*. Stanford, CA: Stanford University Press.

—— 1991. *Language and Symbolic Power*. Cambridge, MA: Harvard University Press.

—— 1994. Rethinking the State: Genesis and Structure of the Bureaucratic Field. *Sociological Theory* 12(1): 1–18.

Bourdieu, Pierre, and Loic Wacquant. 1992. The Logic of Fields. In Bourdieu and Wacquant, *An Invitation to Reflexive Sociology*, pp. 115–40. Chicago: University of Chicago Press.

Bowles, Paul, and Xiao-yuan Dong. 1994. Current Successes and Future Challenges in China's Economic Reforms. *New Left Review* 208: 49–76.

Boyer, Robert. 1989. The Transformations of Modern Capitalism in Light of the Regulation Approach and Other Theories of Political Economy. Paper presented at the Conference on Comparative Governance of Economic Sectors, Bellagio, Italy.

1991. Markets within Alternative Coordinating Mechanisms: History, Theory, and Policy in Light of the Nineties. Paper presented at the Conference on the Comparative Governance of Sectors, Bigorio, Switzerland.

Breiger, Ronald L., and Philippa Pattison. 1986. Cumulated Social Roles: The Duality of Persons and Their Algebras. *Social Networks* 8(3): 215–56.

Bresser Pereira, Luiz Carlos. 1993. The Crisis of the State Approach to Latin America. Discussion paper no. 1, Instituto Sul-Norte, São Paulo, Brazil.

Bresser Pereira, Luiz Carlos, José María Maravall, and Adam Przeworski. 1993. *Economic Reforms in New Democracies: A Social-Democratic Approach.* Cambridge: Cambridge University Press.

Brom, Karla, and Mitchell Orenstein. 1994. The Privatized Sector in the Czech Republic: Government and Bank Control in a Transitional Economy. *Europe-Asia Studies* 46(6): 893–928.

Brubaker, Rogers. 1996. *Nationalism Reframed: Nationhood and the National Question in the New Europe.* New York: Cambridge University Press.

Bruszt, László. 1987. A többszólamú politikai renszer felé (Toward a Polyphonic Polity). *Valóság* no. 5: 87–95.

1988. A centralizáció csapdája és a politikai rendszer reformalternatívái (The Trap of Centralization and the Reform Alternatives of the Political System). *Medvetánc* 1: 171–95.

1990. Hungary's Negotiated Revolution. *Social Research* 57(2): 365–87.

1992. Transformative Politics: Social Costs and Social Peace in East Central Europe. *East European Politics and Societies* 6(1): 55–72.

1994. Reforming Alliances: Labor, Management, and State Bureaucracy in Hungary's Economic Transformation. In *Strategic Choice and Path Dependency in Post-Socialism: Institutional Dynamics in the Transformation Process*, ed. Jerzy Hausner, Bob Jessop, and Klaus Nielsen, pp. 261–87. London: Edward Elgar.

1995. Miert tamogatnak a kapitalizmust a Kelet-Europaiak (Why on Earth Would East Europeans Support Capitalism?) *Politikatudományi Szemle* no. 3: 81–107.

1995. The Antall Government, the Labor Unions, and the Employers' Associations. In *Lawful Revolution in Hungary, 1989–94*, ed. Béla Király and András Bozóki, pp. 369–95. Boulder, CO.: Atlantic Research and Publications Social Science Monographs.

Bruszt, László, and János Simon. 1990. *A lecsendesített többség (The Soothed Majority).* Budapest: Társadalomtudományi Intézet.

1993. The Great Transformation – Theoretical Conceptions and Public Opinion on Democracy and Capitalism in Eastern Europe. In *Flying Blind*, ed. György Szoboszlai, pp. 37–75. Budapest: Institute of Political Science.

Bunce, Valerie. 1995. Should Transitologists Be Grounded? *Slavic Review* 54(1): 111–27.

Bunce, Valerie, and Dennis Chong. 1990. The Party's Over: Mass Protest and the End of Communist Rule in Eastern Europe. Paper presented at the annual meeting of the American Political Science Association, San Francisco.

Burawoy, Michael. 1994. Industrial Involution: The Dynamics of the Transition to a Market Economy in Russia. Paper presented for the Social Science Research Council Workshop on Rational Choice Theory and Post-Soviet Studies. New York, Harriman Institute, December.

1996 The State and Economic Involution: Russia Through a China Lens. *World Development* 24(6): 1105–17.

Burawoy, Michael, and Pavel Krotov. 1992. The Soviet Transition from Socialism to Capitalism: Worker Control and Economic Bargaining in the Wood Industry. *American Sociological Review* 57: 16–38.

Burt, Ronald. 1992. *Structural Holes*. Cambridge, MA: Harvard University Press.

Buxbaum, Richard M. 1993. Is "Network" a Legal Concept? *Journal of Institutional and Theoretical Economics* 149(4): 698–705.

Callaghy, Thomas. 1995. Africa: Back to the Future? In *Economic Reform and Democracy*, ed. Larry Diamond and Marc F. Plattner, pp. 140–52. Baltimore: Johns Hopkins University Press.

Carlin, Wendy. 1993. Privatization and Deindustrialization in East Germany. Unpublished manuscript, Department of Economics, University College, London.

Castles, Francis G., Rolf Gerritsen, and Jack Vowles (eds.). 1996. *The Great Experiment: Labour Parties and Public Policy Transformation in Australia and New Zealand*. Auckland: Auckland University Press.

Clegg, S. R., and S. G. Redding (eds.). 1990. *Capitalism in Contrasting Cultures*. Berlin: Walter de Gruyter.

Coffee, John. 1996. Institutional Investors in Transitional Economies: Lesson from the Czech Experience. In *Corporate Governance in Central Europe and Russia*: Volume I: *Banks, Funds and Foreign Investors*, ed. Roman Frydman, Cheryl W. Gray, and Andrzej Rapaczynski, pp. 111–86. Budapest: Central European University Press.

Collier, Ruth Berins, and David Collier. 1991. *Shaping the Political Arena: Critical Junctures, the Labor Movement, and Regime Dynamics in Latin America*. Princeton, NJ: Princeton University Press.

Comisso, Ellen. 1991. Political Coalitions, Economic Choices. *Journal of International Affairs* 45:1–29.

1996. The Economic Consequences of Democracy's Ambiguities. Paper presented at the Conference on Ethnographies of Transition: The Political, Social, and Cultural Dimensions of Emergent Market Economies in Russia and Eastern Europe, University of California, Berkeley, March 22–4.

Comisso, Ellen, Steven Dubb, and Judy McTigue. 1992. The Illusion of Populism in Latin America and East-Central Europe. In *Flying Blind. Emerging Democracies in East-Central Europe*, ed. György Szoboszlai, pp. 27–57. Yearbook of the Hungarian Political Science Association. Budapest: Hungarian Political Science Association.

Conti, Michael A., and Jan Svenjnar. 1990. The Performance Effects of Employee Ownership Plans. In *Paying for Productivity: A Look at the Evidence*, ed. Alan S. Blinder, pp. 143–81. Washington, DC: The Brookings Institution.

Csanádi Mária. 1986. Függőség, konszenzus és szelekció (Dependence, Consensus and Selection). Budapest: Pénzügykutatási Intézet Kiadványai.

Cui, Zhiyuan. 1994. A Schumpeterian Perspective and Beyond. Unpublished manuscript, Department of Political Science, MIT.

——— 1996. Particular, Universal, and Infinite: Transcending Western Centrism and Cultural Relativism. In Progress: Fact or Illusion?, ed. Leo Marx and Bruce Mazlish, pp. 141–52. Ann Arbor: University of Michigan Press.

Dabrowski, Janusz M., Michal Federowicz, and Anthony Levitas. 1991. Polish State Enterprises and the Properties of Performance: Stabilization, Marketization, Privatization. Politics and Society 19:403–37.

David, Paul. 1986. Understanding the Economics of QWERTY: The Necessity of History. In Economic History and the Modern Historian, ed. W. Parker, pp. 30–49. London: Blackwell.

Dewey, John. 1982 [1920]. Reconstruction in Philosophy. In John Dewey: The Middle Works, 1800–1924, ed. Jo Ann Boydston, pp. 80–201. Carbondale: Southern Illinois University Press.

Diamond, Larry, 1995. Democracy and Economic Reform: Tensions, Compatibilities, and Strategies for Reconcilation. In Economic Transition in Eastern Europe and Russia: Realities of Reform, ed. Edward P. Lazear, pp. 107–58. Stanford, CA: Hoover Institution Press.

——— 1996. Is the Third Wave Over? Journal of Democracy 7(3): 20–37.

Diamond, Larry, and Marc F. Plattner, eds. 1995. Economic Reform and Democracy. Baltimore: Johns Hopkins University Press.

DiMaggio, Paul, and Walter Powell. 1991. Introduction. In The New Institutionalism in Organizational Analysis, ed. P. DiMaggio and W. Powell, pp. 1–38. Chicago: University of Chicago Press.

Dore, Ronald. 1986. Flexible Rigidities: Industrial Policy and Structural Adjustment in the Japanese Economy, 1970–80. Stanford, CA: Stanford University Press.

Ekiert, Grzegorz, and Jan Kubik. 1996. Strategies of Collective Protest in Democratizing Societies: Hungary, Poland and Slovakia since 1989. Paper presented at the Tenth International Conference of Europeanists, Chicago, March 14–16.

Elster, Jon. 1990. When Communism Dissolves. London Review of Books, 12(January 25): 3–6.

Evans, Peter. 1992. The State as Problem and as Solution: Predation, Embedded Autonomy, and Structural Change. In The Politics of Economic Adjustment, ed. Stephan Haggard and Robert Kaufmann, pp. 139–81. Princeton, NJ: Princeton University Press.

——— 1995. Embedded Autonomy: States and Industrial Transformation. Princeton, NJ: Princeton University Press.

Eyal, Gil, Ivan Szelenyi, and Eleanor Townsley. 1997. Making Capitalism without Capitalists: Class Formation and Elite Struggles in Post-Communist Central Europe. Unpublished manuscript, Department of Sociology, UCLA.

Fehér, Ferenc. 1982. Paternalism as a Mode of Legitimation in Soviet-Type Societies. In Political Legitimation in Communist States, ed. T. H. Rigby and Ferenc Fehér, pp. 64–81. New York: St. Martin's Press.

Fichter, Michael. 1993. A House Divided: A View of German Unification as It Has Affected Organized Labour. German Politics 2(1): 21–39.

1994. Institutional Transfer and Institutionalization in Unified Germany: The Case of the Unions. Paper presented at the Conference on the Political Economy of the New Germany, Cornell University, Ithaca, NY, October.

Fichter, Michael, and Michael Kurbjuhn. 1993. *Spurensicherung: Der DGB und seine Gewerkschaften in den neuen Bundeslandern 1989–91.* Düsseldorf: Hans-Boeckler-Stiftung.

Fish, Steven. 1995. *Democracy from Scratch: Opposition and Regime in the New Russian Revolution.* Princeton, NJ: Princeton University Press.

Friedland, Roger, and Rober R. Alford. 1991. Bringing Society Back In: Symbols, Practices, and Institutional Contradictions. In *The New Institutionalism in Organizational Analysis,* ed. Walter W. Powell and Paul J. DiMaggio, pp. 232–63. Chicago: University of Chicago Press.

Friedman, Edward. 1995. *National Identity and Democratic Prospects in Socialist China.* Armonk, NY: M. E. Sharpe.

1996. *The Politics of Democratization: Generalizing the East Asian Experience.* Boulder, CO: Westview Press.

Friedman, Eric J., and Simon Johnson. 1995. Complementarities and Optimal Reform. Unpublished manuscript, Duke University.

Frydman, Roman, and Andrzej Rapaczynski. 1994. *Privatization in Eastern Europe: Is the State Withering Away?* Budapest, London, and New York: Central European University Press.

Gábor, István R. 1986. Reformok, második gazdaság, államszocializmus: A 80-as évek tapasztalatainak fejlödéstani és összehasonlitó gazdaságtani tanulságairól (Reforms, Second Economy, State Socialism: Speculation on the Evolutionary and Comparative Economic Lessons of the Hungarian Eighties). *Valóság* 6: 32–48.

1990. On the Immediate Prospects for Private Entrepreneurship and Reembourgeoisement in Hungary: A Pessimistic Meditation in the Wake of Ivan Szelenyi's Prognosis of Continuity and Janos Kornai's Program of Discontinuity. *Cornell Working Papers on Transitions from State Socialism* no. 90–3.

1994. Modernity or a New Type of Duality?: The Second Economy Today. In *Transition to Capitalism?: The Legacy of Communism in Eastern Europe,* ed. János Mátyás Kovács, pp. 3–21. New Brunswick, NJ: Transaction Books.

Gambetta, Diego. 1993. *The Sicilian Mafia: The Business of Private Protection.* Cambridge, MA: Harvard University Press.

Geddes, Barbara. 1994a. Challenging the Conventional Wisdom. In *Economic Reform and Democracy,* ed. Larry Diamond and Marc F. Plattner, pp. 59–73. Baltimore: Johns Hopkins University Press.

1994b. *Politician's Dilemma: Building State Capacity in Latin America.* Berkeley: University of California Press.

Gereffi, Gary. 1994. The Organization of Buyer-Driven Global Commodity Chains: How U.S. Retailers Shape Overseas Production Networks. In *Commodity Chains and Global Capitalism,* ed. Gary Gereffi and Miguel Kornzeniewicz, pp. 95–122. Westport, CT: Greenwood.

1995. State Policies and Industrial Upgrading in East Asia. *Revue d'Economie Industrielle* no. 71: 79–90.

Gerlach, Michael L. 1992a. *Alliance Capitalism: The Social Organization of Japanese Business.* Berkeley: University of California Press.

——— 1992b. The Japanese Corporate Network: A Blockmodel Analysis. *Administrative Science Quarterly* 37: 105–39.

Gerlach, Michael L., and James R. Lincoln. 1992. The Organization of Business Networks in the United States and Japan. In *Networks and Organizations*, ed. Nitin Nohira and Robert G. Eccles, pp. 491–520. Cambridge, MA: Harvard Business School Press.

Gilson, Ronald J., and Mark J. Roe. 1993. Understanding the Japanese Keiretsu: Overlaps Between Corporate Governance and Industrial Organization. *The Yale Law Journal* 102: 871–906.

Grabher, Gernot. 1992. Eastern Conquista. The Truncated Industrialization of East European Regions by Large West European Corporations. In *Regional Development and Contemporary Industrial Response. Extending Flexible Specialization*, ed. H. Ernste and V. Meier, pp. 219–33. London: Belhaven Press.

——— 1993. Rediscovering the Social in the Economics of Interfirm Relations. In *The Embedded Firm: On the Socioeconomics of Industrial Networks*, ed. Gernot Grabher, pp. 1–31. London and New York: Routledge.

——— 1994. The Dis-Embedded Economy. Western Investment in Eastern German Regions. In *Holding Down the Global: Possibilities for Local Economic Prosperity*, ed. Ash Amin and Nigel Thrift, pp. 177–96. Oxford: Oxford University Press.

——— 1997. Adaptation at the Cost of Adaptability? Restructuring the Eastern German Regional Economy. In *Restructuring Networks in Postsocialism: Legacies, Linkages, and Localities*, ed. Gernot Grabher and David Stark, pp. 107–34. Oxford and New York: Oxford University Press.

Grabher, Gernot, and David Stark, 1997. Organizing Diversity: Evolutionary Theory, Network Analysis, and Postsocialist Transformations. In *Restructuring Networks in Postsocialism: Legacies, Linkages, and Localities* , ed. Gernot Grabher and David Stark, pp. 1–32. London and New York: Oxford University Press.

Granovetter, Mark. 1985. Economic Action and Social Structure: The Problem of Embeddedness. *American Journal of Sociology* 91:481–510.

——— 1994. Business Groups. In *Handbook of Economic Sociology*, ed. Neil Smelser and Richard Swedberg, pp. 453–75. Princeton, NJ: Princeton University Press.

Gray, John. 1993. From Post-Communism to Civil Society: The Reemergence of History and the Decline of the Western Model. In *Liberalism and the Economic Order*, ed. Ellen Frankel Paul, Fred D. Miller, Jr., and Jeffrey Paul, pp. 26–50. Cambridge: Cambridge University Press.

Greskovits, Béla. 1993. Is the East Becoming South? Where Do Threats to Reforms Come From? Paper presented at the XVIth World Congress of the International Political Science Association, Berlin, August 21–5.

——— 1994. Hungerstrikers, the Unions, the Government and the Parties: A Case-Study of Hungarian Transformation. *Occasional Papers in European Studies No. 6.* Essex, U.K.: Essex University Center for European Studies.

——— 1995. Demagogic Populism in Eastern Europe? *Telos* no. 102:91–106.

Gruszecki, Thomasz. 1991. Privatization in Poland in 1990. *Communist Economies and Economic Transformation* 3(2):141–54.

Haggard, Stephan, and Robert R. Kaufman, eds. 1992. *The Politics of Economic Adjustment. International Constraints, Distributive Conflicts, and the State.* Princeton, NJ: Princeton University Press.

1995. *The Political Economy of Democratic Transitions.* Princeton, NJ: Princeton University Press.

Haggard, Stephan, and Steven B. Webb, eds. 1994. *Voting for Reform.* New York: Oxford University Press.

Ham, John, Jan Svejnar, and Katherine Terrell. 1995. Czech Republic and Slovakia. In *Unemployment, Restructuring, and the Labor Market in Eastern Europe and Russia,* ed. Simon Commander and Fabrizio Coricelli, pp. 91–146. Washington, DC: The World Bank.

Hamilton, Gary G., and Robert C. Feenstra. 1995. Varieties of Hierarchies and Markets: An Introduction. *Industrial and Corporate Change* 4(1): 51–87.

Hamilton, Gary G., William Zeile, and Wan-Jin Kim. 1990. The Network Structures of East Asian Economies. In *Capitalism in Contrasting Cultures,* ed. S. R. Clegg and S. G. Redding, pp. 105–29. Berlin: de Gruyter.

Hankiss, Elemér. 1990. *East European Alternatives.* Oxford: Clarendon Press.

Hannan, Michael T., and John H. Freeman. 1989. *Organizational Ecology.* Cambridge, MA: Harvard University Press.

Hartl, Jan. 1995. Social Policy: An Issue for Today and the Future. *Czech Sociological Review* 3(2): 209–19.

Haryi, Aydin, and Gerald A. McDermott. 1995. Restructuring in the Czech Republic: Beyond Ownership and Bankruptcy. Unpublished manuscript. Prague: Center for Economic Research and Graduate Education.

Hausner, Jerzy. 1992. *Populist Threat in Transformation of Socialist Society.* Warsaw: Friedrich Ebert Foundation Series on Economic and Social Policy no. 29.

1993. Imperative vs. Interactive Strategy of Systemic Change in Central and Eastern Europe. Unpublished manuscript, Cracow Academy of Economics.

Hausner, Jerzy, Tadeusz Kudlacz, and Jacek Szlachta. 1997. Regional and Local Factors in the Restructuring of South-Eastern Poland. In *Restructuring Networks in Postsocialism: Legacies, Linkages, and Localities* , ed. Gernot Grabher and David Stark, pp. 190–208. Oxford and New York: Oxford University Press.

Hellman, Joel. 1995. Political Power and Economic Reforms in the Post-Communist Transitions. Unpublished manuscript, Harvard University.

Henderson, Jeffrey. 1993. Against the Economic Orthodoxy: On the Making of the East Asian Miracle. *Economy and Society* 22:200–17.

Henderson, Jeffrey, Richard Whitley, and György Lengyel. 1994. Bureaucracies and Agencies: Contradiction and Chaos in the Hungarian State's Route to Industrial Capitalism. Unpublished manuscript, Manchester School of Business, Manchester, U.K.

Herrigel, Gary B. 1993. Power and the Redefinition of Industrial Districts: The Case of Baden-Württemberg. In *The Embedded Firm: On the Socioeconomics of Industrial Districts,* ed. Gernot Grabher, pp. 227–52. London and New York: Routledge.

Hollingsworth, J. Rogers, and Robert Boyer, eds. 1997. *Contemporary Capitalism:*

The Embeddedness of Institutions. New York and Cambridge: Cambridge University Press.

Hollingsworth, J. Rogers, Philippe Schmitter and Wolfgang Streeck, eds. 1994. *Governing Capitalist Economies: Performance and Control of Economic Sectors.* New York: Oxford University Press.

Holmes, Stephen. 1993. The Postcommunist Presidency. *East European Constitutional Review* 2(3): 36–41.

Hoshi, Takeo. 1994. The Economic Role of Corporate Grouping and the Main Bank System. In *The Japanese Firm: The Sources of Competitive Strength*, ed. Masahiko Aoki and Ronald Dore, pp. 285–309. London and New York: Oxford University Press.

Hrncir, Miroslav. 1994. Reform of the Banking Sector in the Czech Republic. In *The Development and Reform of Financial Systems in Central and Eastern Europe*, ed. John P. Bonin and István P. Székely, pp. 221–56. London: Edward Elgar.

Hutter, Michael, and Günther Teubner: 1993. The Parasitic Role of Hybrids. *Journal of Institutional and Theoretical Economics* 149(4): 706–15.

Hyman, Richard. 1996. Institutional Transfer: Industrial Relations in Eastern Germany. Unpublished manuscript, IRRU, University of Warwick, U.K.

Ickes, Barry W., and Randi Ryterman. 1993. Roadblock to Economic Reform: Inter-Enterprise Debt and the Transition to Markets. *Post-Soviet Affairs* 9(3): 231–52.

1994. From Enterprise to Firm: Notes for a Theory of the Enterprise in Transition. In *The Postcommunist Economic Transformation*, ed. Robert W. Campbell, pp. 83–104. Boulder, CO: Westview Press.

Ickes, Barry W., Randi Ryterman, and Stoyan Tenev. 1995. On Your Marx, Get Set, Go: The Role of Competition in Enterprise Adjustment. Unpublished manuscript, The World Bank.

Jowitt, Ken. 1992. *The New World Disorder: The Leninist Extinction.* Berkeley: University of California Press.

Karl, Terry, and Philippe C. Schmitter. 1991. Modes of Transition and Types of Democracy in Latin America, Southern and Eastern Europe. *International Social Science Journal* 128: 269–84.

1994. The Conceptual Travels of Transitologists and Consolidologists: How Far to the East Should They Attempt to Go? *Slavic Review*, 53(1): 173–85.

1995. From an Iron Curtain of Coercion to a Paper Curtain of Concepts: Grounding Transitologists or Confining Students of Postcommunism? *Slavic Review* 54(4): 965–78.

Katzenstein, Peter J. 1987. *Policy and Politics in West Germany: The Growth of a Semisovereign State.* Philadelphia: Temple University Press.

Keane, John, ed. 1988. *Civil Society and the State.* London: Verso.

Kern, Horst, and Charles Sabel. 1991. Between Pillar and Post: Reflections on the Treuhand's Uncertainty About What to Say Next. Unpublished manuscript, Department of Political Science, MIT.

Kim, Eun Mee. 1991. The Industrial Organization and Growth of the Korean Chaebol: Integrating Development and Organizational Theories. In *Business Networks and Economic Development in East and Southeast Asia*, ed. Gary

Hamilton, pp. 272–99. Hong Kong: Centre of Asian Studies, Occasional Papers and Monographs, no. 99, University of Hong Kong.

1993. Contradictions and Limits of a Developmental State: With Illustrations from the South Korean Case. *Social Problems* 40 (May): 228–49.

Kis, János, Ferenc Köszeg, and Ottila Solt. 1987. *Társadalmi Szerződés (Social Contract). Beszélő*, Special Issue, June.

Kiser, Edgar, and Michael Hechter. 1991. The Role of General Theory in Comparative-Historical Sociology. *American Journal of Sociology* 97: 1–30.

Kitschelt, Herbert. 1995. The Formation of Party Cleavages in Post-Communist Democracies. *Party Politics*, 1(4): 447–72.

1996. Post-Communist Democracies: Do Party Systems Help or Hinder Democratic Consolidation? Paper presented at the Conference on Democracy, Markets, and Civil Societies in Post-1989 East Central Europe, Center for European Studies, Harvard, May 17–19.

Klaus, Václav. 1992. The Adam Smith Address. Delivered to the 34th Meeting of the National Association of Business Economists, Dallas, Texas, September 13.

1993a. Adam Smith's Legacy and Economic Transformation of Czechoslovakia. *Business Economics* 28(1): 7–9.

1993b. The Ten Commandments Revisited. *The International Economy* September–October: 36–9, 70–2.

1994. The Experience with Radical Economic Reforms in the Czech Republic. *The Brown Journal of World Affairs* Spring: 123–7.

Kochanowicz, Jacek. 1993. Transition to Market in a Comparative Perspective: A Historian's Point of View. In *Stabilization and Privatization in Poland: An Economic Evaluation of the Shock Therapy*, ed. Kazimierz Poznanski, pp. 233–50. Boston: Kluwer.

1994. Reforming Weak States and Deficient Bureaucracies. In *Intricate Links: Democratization and Market Reforms in Latin America and Eastern Europe*, ed. Joan M. Nelson, Jacek Kachanowicz, Kálmán Mizsei, and Oscar Munoz, pp. 195–227. New Brunswick, NJ: Transaction Books.

Kogut, Bruce, Weijan Shan, and Gordon Walker. 1993. Knowledge in the Network and the Network as Knowledge: The Structuring of New Industries. In *The Embedded Firm*, ed. Gernot Grabher, pp. 67–94. London: Routledge.

Kogut, Bruce, and Udo Zander. 1992. Knowledge of the Firm, Combinative Capabilities, and the Replication of Technology. *Organization Science* 3(3): 383–97.

Konrád, György, and Ivan Szelenyi. 1979. *The Intellectuals on the Road to Class Power*. New York: Harcourt Brace Jovanovich.

Kornai, János. 1986. *Contradictions and Dilemmas*. Cambridge, MA: MIT Press.

1989. The Hungarian Reform Process: Visions, Hopes and Reality. In *Remaking the Economic Institutions of Socialism: China and Eastern Europe*, ed. Victor Nee and David Stark, pp. 32–94. Stanford, CA: Stanford University Press.

1990. *The Road to a Free Economy*. New York: Norton.

1992. The Post-Socialist Transition and the State: Reflections in the Light of Hungarian Fiscal Problems. *American Economic Review* 82(2): 1–21.

1995. *Highway and Byways: Studies on Reform and Post-Communist Transition*. Cambridge, MA: MIT Press.

Kotrba, Josef. 1993. Privatization in the Czech Republic: An Overview. Prague: Center for Economic Research and Graduate Education (CERGE), Discussion Paper No. 18.

Kovács, János Mátyás. 1990. Reform Economics: The Classification Gap. *Daedalus* 119: 215–48.

Kwon, Jene. 1994. The East Asia Challenge to Neoclassical Orthodoxy. *World Development* 22(4): 635–44.

Lall, Sanjaya. 1994. The East Asian Miracle: Does the Bell Toll for Industrial Strategy? *World Development* 22(4): 645–54.

Lange, Peter. 1984. Unions, Workers and Wage Regulation: The Rational Bases of Consent. In *Order and Conflict in Contemporary Capitalism*, ed. John H. Goldthorpe, pp. 98–123. Oxford: Oxford University Press.

Lehmbruch, Gerhard. 1992. The Institutional Framework of German Regulation. In *The Politics of German Regulation*, ed. Kenneth Dyson, pp. 45–60. Aldershot, U.K.: Dartmouth.

Lewandowski, Janusz, and Jan Szomburg. 1989. Uwlaszczenie jako fundament reformy spoleczno-gospodarczej (Property Change as a Fundamental Aspect of Socio-Economic Reform) In *Propozyce Prtzeksztalcen Polskiej Gospodarki, (Proposals for Transformations of the Polish Economy)*, pp. 63–81. Warsaw.

_____ 1990. The Strategy of Privatization. Paper presented at the Research Centre for Marketization and Property Reform, Gdansk.

Levitas, Anthony. 1992. Rethinking Reform: Lessons from Polish Privatization. In *Changing Political Economies: Privatization in Post-Communist and Reforming Communist States*, ed. Vedat Milor, pp. 99–114. Boulder, CO: Lynne Rienner.

Lijphart, Arend. 1989. Presidentialism and Majoritarian Democracy: Theoretical Observations. In *The Failure of Presidential Democracy*, ed. Juan J. Linz and Arturo Valenzuela, pp. 91–105. Baltimore: Johns Hopkins University Press.

Lincoln, James R., Michael L. Gerlach, and Christina L. Ahmadjian. 1996. Keiretsu Networks and Corporate Performance in Japan. *American Sociological Review* 61(1): 67–88.

Linz, Juan. 1986. Democracy: Presidential or Parliamentary: Does It Make a Difference? In *The Failure of Presidential Democracy*, ed. Juan J. Linz and Arturo Valenzuela, pp. 3–87. Baltimore: Johns Hopkins University Press.

Linz, Juan, and Alfred Stephan. 1996. *Problems of Democratic Transition and Consolidation*. Baltimore and London: Johns Hopkins University Press.

Lipton, David, and Jeffrey Sachs. 1990. Privatization in Eastern Europe: The Case of Poland. *Brookings Papers on Economic Activity* 2: 293–341.

Locke, Richard. 1995. *Remaking the Italian Economy*. Ithaca NY: Cornell University Press.

Lukács, János. 1986. Organizational Flexibility, Internal Labor Market, and Internal Subcontracting, Hungarian Style. In *Economy and Society in Hungary*, ed. Rudolf Andorka and László Bertalan, pp. 15–34. Budapest: MTA Közgazdaságtudományi Intézet.

_____ 1990. Vertical Disaggregation and Privatization in Hungary: Organizational Consequences. Paper presented at the Conference on the Social Economies of Inter-Firm Cooperation, Social Science Center, Berlin.

Mainwaring, Scott, Guillermo O'Donnell, and J. Samuel Valenzuela, eds. 1992. *Issues and Prospects of Democratic Consolidation: The New South American Democracies in Comparative Perspective.* Notre Dame, IN: Notre Dame University Press.

Majoros, Ferenc. 1993. Ungarische Verfassungsgerichtsbarkeit seit 1990. Working paper. Berlin: Berlin Bundesinstitut für Ostwissentschaftliche und Internationale Studien.

March, James G., and Johan P. Olsen. 1995. *Democratic Governance.* New York: Free Press.

McDermott, Gerald A. 1997. Renegotiating the Ties That Bind: The Limits of Privatization in the Czech Republic. In *Restructuring Networks in Postsocialism: Legacies, Linkages, and Localities,* ed. Gernot Grabher and David Stark, pp. 70–106. Oxford and New York: Oxford University Press.

McDermott, Gerald A., and Michal Mejtrik. 1992. The Role of Small Firms in the Industrial Development and Transformation of Czechoslovakia. *Small Business Economics* 4: 51–72.

McFaul, Michael. 1995. State Power, Institutional Change, and the Politics of Privatization in Russia. *World Politics,* 47(2): 210–43.

       1997. Russia's Rough Ride. In *Consolidating the Third Wave Democracies: Regional Challenges,* ed. Larry Diamond, Marc F. Plattner, Yun-han Chu, and Hungmao Tien, pp. 64–94. Baltimore: Johns Hopkins University Press.

McShane, Denis. 1993. IG Metall – Ossis Fight Back. *New Statesman and Society* 6(Issue 252): 10–12.

Meyer, John W., and Brian Rowan. 1991. Institutionalized Organizations: Formal Structure as Myth and Ceremony. In *The New Institutionalism in Organizational Analysis,* ed. Walter W. Powell and Paul DiMaggio, pp. 41–62. Chicago: University of Chicago Press.

Miner, Anne, Terry L. Amburgey, and Timoth M. Stearns. 1990. Interorganizational Linkages and Population Dynamics: Buffering and Transformational Shields. *Administrative Science Quarterly* 35: 689–713.

Mizruchi, Mark S., and Michael Schwartz, eds. 1987. *Intercorporate Relations: The Structural Analysis of Business.* Cambridge: Cambridge University Press.

Montinola, Gabriella, Yingyi Qian, and Barry R. Weingast. 1995. Federalism, Chinese Style: The Political Basis for Economic Success in China. *World Politics* 48(1): 50–81.

Móro, Mária. 1990. Az állami vállalatok álprivatizációja (Pseudo-Privatization of State Enterprises). *Közgazdasági Szemle* 38: 565–84.

Murrell, Peter. 1992. Conservative Political Philosophy and the Strategy of Economic Transition. *East European Politics and Society* 6(1):3–16.

       1995. The Transition According to Cambridge, Mass. *Journal of Economic Literature* 33: 164–78.

Myant, Martin. 1993. *Transforming Socialist Economies: The Case of Poland and Czechoslovakia.* Aldershot, U.K., and Brookfield, VT: Edward Elgar.

       1994. Czech and Slovak Trade Unions. In *Parties, Trade Unions and Society in East-Central Europe,* ed. Michael Waller and Martin Myant, pp. 59–84. Essex, U.K.: Frank Cass.

Neckermann, Peter. 1992. What Went Wrong in Germany After the Unification? *East European Quarterly* 26(4):447–70.

Nee, Victor. 1991. Social Inequalities in Reforming State Socialism: Between Redistribution and Markets in China. *American Sociological Review* 56: 267–82.

Nee, Victor, and Sijin Su. 1996. Institutions, Social Ties, and Credible Commitment: Local Corporatism in China. In *Reforming Asian Economies: The Growth of Market Institutions*, ed. John McMillan and Barry Naughton, pp. 111–34. Ann Arbor: University of Michigan Press.

Nelson, Joan M., ed. 1989. *Fragile Coalitions: The Politics of Economic Adjustment.* Oxford: Transaction Books.

    1991. Organized Labor, Politics and Labor Market Flexibility in Developing Countries. *The World Bank Research Observer* 6(1):39–56.

    1992. Poverty, Equity and the Politics of Adjustment. In *The Politics of Economic Adjustment. International Constraints, Distributive Conflicts, and the State*, ed. Stephan Haggard and Robert R. Kaufman, pp. 221–69. Princeton, NJ: Princeton University Press.

    Ed. 1994. *Precarious Balance: Democracy and Economic Reforms in Latin America.* Washington, DC: Overseas Development Council.

Nelson, Richard, and Sidney Winter. 1982. *An Evolutionary Theory of Economic Change.* Cambridge, MA: Harvard University Press.

Neumann, László. 1991. Labour Conflicts of Privatization in Hungary. Working paper. Budapest: Institute for Labour Studies.

    1996. A Deficiency of the Transition: Lack of Effective Institutionalization of Wage Bargaining and Labor Conflicts in Hungary. Paper presented at the Tenth International Conference of Europeanists, Chicago.

Nohira, Nitin, and Robert G. Eccles, eds. 1992. *Networks and Organizations: Structure, Form, and Action.* Cambridge, MA: Harvard Business School Press.

Numazaki, Ichiro. 1991. The Role of Personal Networks in the Making of Taiwan's *Guanxiqiye* (Related Enterprises). In *Business Networks and Economic Development in East and Southeast Asia*, ed. Gary Hamilton, pp. 77–93. Hong Kong: Centre of Asian Studies, Occasional Papers and Monographs, no. 99, University of Hong Kong.

O'Donnell, Guillermo. 1992. Transition, Continuities, and Paradoxes. In *Issues in Democratic Consolidation*, ed. Scott Mainwaring, Guillermo O'Donnell, and J. Samuel Valenzuela, pp. 17–56. Notre Dame, IN: University of Notre Dame Press.

    1993. On the State, Democratization and Some Conceptual Problems: A Latin American View with Glances at Some Postcommunist Countries. *World Development* 21(8):1355–69.

    1994. Delegative Democracy. *Journal of Democracy* 5(1):55–69.

O'Donnell, Guillermo, Philippe C. Schmitter, and Laurence Whitehead, eds. 1986. *Transitions from Authoritarian Rule: Prospects for Democracy.* Baltimore: Johns Hopkins University Press.

Offe, Claus. 1991. Privatisierung der Ökonomie als demokratisches Projekt? Paradoxen des "Politischen Kapitalismus" in Osteurope. Paper presented at the Zentrum für Sozialpolitik Universität Bremen.

    1994. Das Dilemma der Gleichzeitigkeit–Demokratisierung, Marktwirtschaft und Territorialpolitik in Osteuropa. In *Der Tunnel am Ende des Lichts, Erkundungen der politischen Transformation im neuen Osten*, pp. 57–81. Frankfurt and New York: Campus Verlag.

Olson, David M. 1995 The Sundered State: Federalism and Parliament in Czecho-
    slovakia. Paper presented at the Conference on Comparative Parliamentary
    Development in Eastern Europe and the Former USSR at the Center for
    Soviet, Post-Soviet, and East European Studies, Emory University, April
    9–10.
Orenstein, Mitchell. 1994. The Czech Tripartite Council and Its Contribution to
    Social Peace. Budapest University of Economics Working Paper Series 99.
    1996. Out of the Red: Building Capitalism and Democracy in Post-Communist
    Europe. Ph.D. dissertation, Yale University, Faculty of the Graduate
    School, May.
Orrú, Marco, Nicole Woolsey Biggart, and Gary G. Hamilton. 1991. Organiza-
    tional Isomorphism in East Asia. In *The New Institutionalism in Organiza-
    tional Analysis*, ed. Walter W. Powell and Paul J. DiMaggio, pp. 361–89.
    Chicago: University of Chicago Press.
Ost, David. 1991. Shaping a New Politics in Poland. Paper presented at the Con-
    ference on Transition from State Socialism in East Central Europe, Center
    for European Studies, Harvard University, March 15–17.
Padgett, John F. 1992. Learning from (and about) March. *Contemporary Sociology*
    21(6): 744–9.
Peck, Merten, and Thomas J. Richardson, eds. 1992. *What Is to Be Done?: Proposals
    for the Soviet Transition to the Market*. New Haven, CT: Yale University
    Press.
Pei, Minxin. 1994. *From Reform to Revolution: The Demise of Communism in China and
    the Soviet Union*. Cambridge, MA: Harvard University Press.
    1995. The Puzzle of East Asian Exceptionalism. In *Economic Reform and Democ-
    racy*, ed. Larry Diamond and Marc F. Plattner, pp. 112–25. Baltimore:
    Johns Hopkins University Press.
Piore, Michael, and Charles Sabel. 1984. *The Second Industrial Divide: Possibilities for
    Prosperity*. New York: Basic Books.
Piper, Rosemary Pugh, István Ábel, and Júlia Király. 1994. *Transformation at a
    Crossroads: Financial Sector Reform in Hungary*. Policy Study No. 5, com-
    missioned by the Joint Hungarian-International Blue Ribbon Com-
    mission.
Pitkin, Hanna Fenichel. 1967. *The Concept of Representation*. Berkeley: University of
    California Press.
Pokol, Béla. 1986. A politikai rendszer reformjáról (On the Reform of the Political
    System). *Valóság* no. 12:32–45.
Powell, Walter W. 1990. Neither Market Nor Hierarchy: Network Forms of Or-
    ganization. In *Research in Organizational Behavior*, ed. B. Staw and L. L.
    Cummings, pp. 295–336. Greenwich, CT: JAI Press.
    1996. Inter-Organizational Collaboration in the Biotechnology Industry. *Jour-
    nal of Institutional and Theoretical Economics* 152: 197–225.
Przeworski, Adam. 1988. Democracy as a Contingent Outcome of Conflicts. In
    Constitutionalism and Democracy, ed. Jon Elster and Rune Slagstad, pp. 59–
    80. Cambridge: Cambridge University Press.
    1990a. The Choice of Institutions in the Transition to Democracy: A Game
    Theoretic Approach. Paper presented at the Workshop on the Present and
    Future Party/State Apparatus in Peaceful Transitions, Budapest.

1990b. Transitions and Reforms: East and South. Unpublished manuscript, Department of Political Science, University of Chicago.

1991. *Democracy and the Market*. Cambridge: Cambridge University Press.

Ed. 1992a. Sustainable Democracy. Unpublished manuscript, Department of Political Science, University of Chicago.

1992b. The Games of Transition. In *Issues in Democratic Consolidation*, ed. Scott Mainwaring, Guillermo O'Donnell, and J. Samuel Valenzuela, pp. 105–52. Notre Dame, IN: University of Notre Dame Press.

1993. Economic Reforms, Public Opinion and Political Institutions: Poland in the Eastern European Perspective. In *Economic Reforms in New Democracies: A Social Democratic Approach*, ed. Luiz Carlos Bresser Pereira, Jose Maria Maravall, and Adam Przeworski, pp. 132–98. Cambridge: Cambridge University Press.

Przeworski, Adam, and Fernando Limongi. 1993. Political Regimes and Economic Growth. *Journal of Economic Perspectives* 7(3):51–69.

1994. Democracy and Development. Paper presented at the Nobel Symposium "Democracy's Victory and Crisis," Uppsala University, August 27–30.

Rácz, Barnabás. 1991. Political Pluralization in Hungary: The 1990 Elections. *Soviet Studies* 43(1): 107–36.

Rawls, John. 1971. *A Theory of Justice*. Cambridge, MA: Belknap Press of Harvard University Press.

Remmer, Karen. 1990. Democracy and Economic Crisis: The Latin American Experience. *World Politics* 42:315–35.

1993. The Political Economy of Elections in Latin America, 1989–1991. *American Political Science Review* 12: 393–407.

Roesler, Jörg. 1994. Privatization in Eastern Germany – Experience with the Treuhand. *Europe-Asia Studies* 46(3): 505–17.

Rogers, Daniel. 1993. Transforming the German Party System: The United States and the Origins of Political Moderation. *Journal of Modern History* 65(3): 512–32.

Rutland, Peter. 1993. Thatcherism, Czech-Style: Transition to Capitalism in the Czech Republic. *Telos* 94 (Winter): 103–29.

1994. Workers' Responses to the Market Transition: The Czech Case. Working paper. Washington, DC: National Council for Soviet and East European Research.

Rychard, Andrzej. 1991. Passive Acceptance or Active Participation? The Ambiguous Legacies of Societal Opposition in Poland. *Cornell Working Papers on Transitions from State Socialism* no. 91–3.

Rychetnik, Ludek. 1995. Can the Czech Republic Develop a Negotiated Economy? In *Strategic Choice and Path Dependency in Post-Socialism: Institutional Dynamics in the Transformation Process*, ed. Jerzy Hausner, Bob Jessop, and Klaus Nielsen, pp. 230–58. Aldershot, U.K.: Edward Elgar.

Sabel, Charles. 1979. Ambiguities of Class and the Possibility of Politics. In *The Future of Socialism in Europe*, ed. Andre Liebich, pp. 257–79. Montreal: Interuniversity Centre for European Studies.

1982. *Work and Politics*. New York: Cambridge University Press.

1989. Flexible Specialization and the Reemergence of Regional Economies. In *Reversing Industrial Decline*, ed. Paul Hirst and Jonathan Zeitlin, pp. 17–70. New York: St. Martin's Press.

1990. Möbius-Strip Organizations and Open Labor Markets: Some Consequences of the Reintegration of Conception and Execution in a Volatile Economy. In *Social Theory for a Changing Society*, ed. Pierre Bourdieu and James Coleman, pp. 23–54. Boulder, CO, and New York: Westview Press and Russell Sage Foundation.

1992. Studied Trust: Building New Forms of Cooperation in a Volatile Economy. In *Industrial Districts and Local Economic Regeneration*, ed. Frank Pyke and Werner Sengenberger, pp. 215–49. Geneva: International Labour Organization.

1993. Constitutional Ordering in Historical Perspective. In *Games in Hierarchies and Networks*, ed. Fritz W. Scharpf, pp. 65–123. Boulder, CO: Westview Press.

1994. Learning by Monitoring: The Institutions of Economic Development. In *Handbook of Economic Sociology*, ed. Neil Smelser and Richard Swedberg, pp. 137–65. New York and Princeton, NJ: Russell Sage Foundation and Princeton University Press.

1995a. Design, Deliberation, and Democracy: On the New Pragmaticism of Firms and Public Institutions. Paper presented to the Conference on Liberal Institutions, Economic Constitutional Rights, and the Role of Organizations, European University Institute, Florence, December.

1995b. Intelligible Differences: On Deliberate Strategy and the Exploration of Possibility in Economic Life. Paper presented to the 36th annual meeting of the Societá Italiana degli Economisti, Florence, October.

Sabel, Charles F., and Jane E. Prokop. 1996. Stabilization through Reorganization?: Some Preliminary Implications of Russia's Entry into World Markets in the Age of Discursive Quality Standards. In *Corporate Governance in Central Europe and Russia*, Volume II: *Insiders and the State*, ed. Roman Frydman, Cheryl W. Gray, and Andrzej Rapaczynski, pp. 151–91. Budapest and London: Central European University Press.

Sabel, Charles F., and Jonathan Zeitlin. 1997. Stories, Strategies and Structures: Rethinking Historical Alternatives to Mass Production. In *Worlds of Possibility: Flexibility and Mass Production in Western Industrialization*, ed. Charles Sabel and Jonathan Zeitlin, pp. 1–33. Cambridge: Cambridge University Press.

Sachs, Jeffrey. 1992. Building a Market Economy in Poland. *Scientific American* March: 34–40.

1994. Life in the Economic Emergency Room. In *The Political Economy of Policy Reform*, ed. John Williamson, pp. 501–24. Washington, DC: Institute for International Economics.

Sachs, Jeffrey, and Andrew M. Warner. 1995. Economic Reform and the Process of Global Integration. *Brookings Papers on Economic Activity* 1:1–118.

Sally, Razeen, and Douglas Webber. 1994. The German Solidarity Pact: A Case Study in the Politics of the Unified Germany. *German Politics* 3(1): 18–46.

Saxenian, Anna Lee. 1994. *Regional Advantage: Culture and Competition in Silicon Valley and Route 128*. Cambridge, MA: Harvard University Press.

Schmitter, Philippe C. 1988. Sectors in Modern Capitalism: Modes of Governance and Variations in Performance. Unpublished manuscript, Department of Political Science, Stanford University.

1991. Modes of Transition in Latin America, Southern and Eastern Europe. *International Social Science Journal* 128: 269–84.

Schönfeld, Roland. 1993. Transformation and Privatization in East Germany: Strategies and Experience. In *Transforming Economic Systems in East-Central Europe*, ed. Roland Schönfeld, pp. 159–70. Munich: Südosteuropa-Gesellschaft.

Schöpflin, George, Rudolph Tökés, and Iván Völgyes. 1988. Leadership Change and Crisis in Hungary. *Problems of Communism* September–October: 23–46.

Schumpeter, Joseph A. 1934. *The Theory of Economic Development*. Cambridge, MA: Harvard University Press.

Schwartz, Herman. 1993. The New East European Constitutional Courts. In *Constitution-Making in Eastern Europe*, ed. A. E. Dick Howard, pp. 163–207. Baltimore: Johns Hopkins University Press.

Seibel, Wolfgang. 1992. Necessary Illusions: The Transformation of Governance Structures in the New Germany. *La Revue Tocqueville/The Tocqueville Review* 13:178–97.

1994. Strategische Fehler oder erfolgreiches Scheitern? Zur Entwicklungslogik der Treuhandanstalt. *Politische Vierteljahresschrift* 35: 3–39.

1995. Nicht-intendiert wirtschaftliche Folgen politischen Handelns. Die Transformationspolitik des Bundes in Ostdeutschland seit 1990. In *Regierungssystem und Verwaltungspolitik*, ed. Arthur Benz and Wolfgang Seibel, pp. 214–49. Opladen: Westdeutscher Verlag.

1996. The Organizational Development of the Treuhandanstalt. In *Treuhandanstalt. The Impossible Challenge*, ed. W. Fischer, H. Hax, and H. Schneider, pp. 112–47. Berlin: Akademie Verlag.

1997. Privatization by Means of State Bureaucracy?: The Treuhand Phenomenon in Eastern Germany. In *Restructuring Networks in Postsocialism: Legacies, Linkages, and Localities*, ed. Gernot Grabher and David Stark, pp. 284–304. Oxford and New York: Oxford University Press.

Sewell, William H. Jr., 1992. A Theory of Structure: Duality, Agency, and Transformation. *American Journal of Sociology* 98: 1–29.

1996. Three Temporalities: Toward an Eventful Sociology. In *The Historic Turn in the Human Sciences*, ed. Terence J. McDonald, pp. 245–80. Ann Arbor: University of Michigan Press.

Sklar, Richard L. 1987. Developmental Democracy. *Comparative Studies in Society and History* 29: 686–714.

1996. Towards a Theory of Developmental Democracy. In *Democracy and Development: Theory and Practice*, ed. Adrian Leftwich, pp. 25–44. Cambridge: Polity Press.

Skocpol, Theda. 1979. *States and Social Revolutions*. Cambridge: Cambridge University Press.

Slay, Ben. 1991. Privatization and De-Monopolization in Poland. Unpublished manuscript, Research Institute, Radio Free Europe/Radio Liberty.

Staniszkis, Jadwiga. 1991a. Dilemmata der Demokratie in Osteuropa. In *Demokratischer Umbruch in Osteuropa*, ed. Robert Deppe and Honel Dubiel, pp. 326–47. Frankfurt: Suhrkamp Verlag.

1991b. *Dynamics of the Breakthrough in Eastern Europe: The Polish Case*. Berkeley: University of California Press.

Stark, David. 1986. Rethinking Internal Labor Markets: New Insights from a Comparative Perspective. *American Sociological Review* 51: 492–504.

  1989. Coexisting Organizational Forms in Hungary's Emerging Mixed Economy. In *Remaking the Economic Institutions of Socialism: China and Eastern Europe*, ed. Victor Nee and David Stark, pp. 137–68. Stanford, CA: Stanford University Press.

  1990a. Bending the Bars of the Iron Cage: Bureaucratization and Informalization under Capitalism and Socialism. *Sociological Forum* 4: 637–64.

  1990b. Work, Worth and Justice. Working Papers on Central and Eastern Europe No. 5, Center for European Studies, Harvard University.

  1992. From System Identity to Organizational Diversity: Analyzing Social Change in Eastern Europe. *Contemporary Sociology* 21: 299–304.

  1996a. Networks of Assets, Chains of Debt: Recombinant Property in Hungary. In *Corporate Governance in Central Europe and Russia:* Volume II: *Insiders and the State*, ed. Roman Frydman, Cheryl W. Gray, and Andrzej Rapaczynski, pp. 109–50. Budapest and London: Central European University Press.

  1996b. Recombinant Property in East European Capitalism. *American Journal of Sociology* 101: 993–1027.

Stark, David, and László Bruszt. 1990. Negotiating the Institutions of Democracy: Strategic Interactions and Contingent Choices in the Hungarian and Polish Transitions. *Cornell Working Papers on Transitions from State Socialism* no. 90–8.

Stewart, John, ed. 1951. *A Documentary History of the French Revolution.* New York: Macmillan.

Strang, David, and John W. Meyer. 1993. Institutional Conditions for Diffusion. *Theory and Society* 22: 487–511.

Streeck, Wolfgang. 1992. *Social Institutions and Economic Performance: Studies of Industrial Relations in Advanced Capitalist Economies.* London: Sage.

  1997. Beneficial Constraints: On the Economic Limits of Rational Voluntarism. In *Contemporary Capitalism: The Embeddedness of Institutions*, ed. J. Rogers Hollingsworth and Robert Boyer. New York and Cambridge: Cambridge University Press.

Streeck, Wolfgang, and Philippe C. Schmitter. 1985. Community, Market, State – and Associations? The Prospective Contribution of Interest Governance to Social Order. In *Private Interest Government: Beyond Market and State*, ed. Wolfgang Streeck and Philippe C. Schmitter, pp. 1–29. Beverly Hills, CA: Sage.

Szabó, Máté. 1993. A társadalmi mozgalmak szektora és a tiltakozás kultúrája Magyarországon (Social Movements and the Culture of Social Protest in Hungary). *Politikatudományi Szemle* no. 3: 45–70.

Szalai, Erzsébet. 1989. *Gazdasági mechanizmus, reformtörekvések és nagyvállalati érdekek (Economic Mechanism, Reform Efforts and Corporate Interests).* Budapest: Gazdasági és Jogi Könyvkiadó.

  1990. Integration of Special Interests in the Hungarian Economy. *Journal of Comparative Economics* 15: 284–303.

  1991. A hatalom metamorfózisa? (Metamorphosis of Power?) *Valóság* 6: 1–26.

Szelenyi, Ivan. 1978. Social Inequalities in State Socialist Redistributive Economies. *Theory and Society* 1–2: 63–87.

    1988a. Eastern Europe in an Epoch of Transition: Toward a Socialist Mixed Economy? In *Remaking the Economic Institutions*, ed. Victor Nee and David Stark, pp. 208–32. Stanford, CA: Stanford University Press.

    1988b. *Socialist Entrepreneurs: Embourgeoisement in Rural Hungary*. Madison: University of Wisconsin Press.

    1990. Alternative Futures for Eastern Europe: The Case of Hungary. *East European Politics and Societies* 4: 231–54.

Szelényi, Szonja, Iván Szelényi, and Winifred R. Poster. 1996. Interests and Symbols in Post-Communist Culture: The Case of Hungary. *American Sociological Review* 61(3): 466–77.

Szomburg, Jan. 1991. Poland's Privatization Strategy. Paper presented at the Conference on Transforming Economic Systems in East-Central Europe, Munich.

Tamás, Pál. 1993. Innovációs teljesítmények és vállalati stratégiák (Achievements in Innovation and Company Strategies). Working paper. Budapest: Institute for Social Conflicts.

Tardos, Márton. 1988. A tulajdon (Ownership). *Közgazdasági Szemle* 35 (December): 1405–22.

    1989. Economic Organizations and Ownership. *Acta Oeconomica* 40(1–2): 17–37.

Teubner, Günther. 1991. Beyond Contract and Organization?: The External Liability of Franchising Systems in German Law. In *Franchising and the Law: Theoretical and Comparative Approaches in Europe and the United States*, ed. Christian Joerges, pp. 105–32. Baden-Baden: Nomos Verlagsgesellschaft.

    1993. The Many-Headed Hydra: Networks as Higher-Order Collective Actors. In *Corporate Control and Accountability: Changing Structures and the Dynamics of Regulation*, ed. Joseph McCahery, Sol Picciotto, and Colin Scott, pp. 41–51. Oxford: Clarendon Press.

Tóth, András. 1994. Great Expectations and Fading Hopes, Trade Unions and System Change in Hungary. In *Parties, Trade Unions and Society in East-Central Europe*, ed. M. Waller and M. Myant, Essex, U.K.: Frank Cass, pp. 176–97.

    1995. Workers, Trade Unions and Political Parties: Prisoners of the Past. In *Transition to Democratic Rule and the Role of Organized Labor*, ed. Samuel Valenzuela, pp. 24–34. Notre Dame, IN: University of Notre Dame Press.

Trigilia, Carlo. 1986a. *Grandi partiti e piccole imprese (Big Parties and Small Firms)*. Bologna: Il Mulino.

    1986b. Small Firm Development and Political Subcultures. *European Sociological Review* 2(3): 161–75.

Voszka, Éva. 1990. Ropewalking: Ganz Danubius Ship and Crane Factory Transformed into a Company. *Acta Oeconomica* 43: 285–302.

    1991a. Homályból homályba. A tulajdonosi szerkezet a nagyiparban (From Twilight to Twilight: Property Changes in Big Industry). *Társadalmi Szemle* 5: 3–12.

    1991b. *Tulajdon–reform (Property–Reform)*. Budapest: Pénzügykutató Rt.

1992a. Az ellenkezöje sem igaz: a központosítás és a decentralizáció színevál-
tozásai (The Contrary Is Untrue as Well: Changes of Centralization and
Decentralization). *Külgazdaság* 36(6): 4–16.

1992b. Escaping from the State, Escaping to the State. Paper presented at the
Arne Ryde Symposium on the "Transition Problem," Rungsted, Denmark.

Walder, Andrew. 1995. Local Governments as Industrial Firms: An Organizational
Analysis of China's Transitional Economy. *American Journal of Sociology*
101(1): 263–301.

Weber, Max. 1965. *Politics as a Vocation*. New York: Fortress Press.

Weingast, Barry R. 1995. The Economic Role of Political Institutions: Market-
Preserving Federalism and Economic Growth. *Journal of Law, Economics,
and Organization* 11:1–31.

Wheaton, Bernard, and Zdenek Kavan. 1992. *The Velvet Revolution: Czechoslovakia,
1988–1991*. Boulder, CO: Westview Press.

White, Harrison C. 1992. *Identity and Control*. Princeton, NJ: Princeton University
Press.

1993. Values Come in Styles, Which Mate to Change. In *The Origins of Values*,
ed. Michael Hechter, Lynn Nadel, and Richard E. Michod, pp. 63–91.
New York: Aldine de Gruyter.

Whitley, Richard D. 1991. The Social Construction of Business Systems in East
Asia. *Organization Studies* 12(1): 1–28.

Wilfried, Ettl, and Helmut Wiesentahl. 1994. Tarifautonomie in deindustrialisier-
ten Gelande. Analyse eines Institutionentransfers in Prozess der deutschen
Einheit. *Kölner Zeitschrift für Soziologie und Sozialpsychologie* 40(3): 425–52.

Williamson, John. 1993. Democracy and the "Washington Consensus." *World Development* 21(8): 1329–36.

1994. In Search of a Manual for Technopols. In *The Political Economy of Policy
Reform*, ed. John Williamson, pp. 11–28. Washington, DC: Institute for
International Economics.

Williamson, Oliver. 1985. *The Economic Institutions of Capitalism: Firms, Markets, and
Relational Contracting*. New York: Free Press.

The World Bank. 1992. *Governance and Development*. Washington, DC: The World
Bank.

Zysman, John. 1983. *Government, Markets, and Growth*. Ithaca, NY: Cornell University Press.

1994. How Institutions Create Historically Rooted Trajectories of Growth.
Industrial and Corporate Change 2(1): 243–83.

INDEX